THE HISTORY OF IDEAS

The History of Ideas

An Introduction to Method

Edited by Preston King

CROOM HELM
London & Canberra

BARNES & NOBLE BOOKS
Totowa, New Jersey

Chs 1, 2, 4 and 12 © 1983 P. King; Ch. 3 © 1962 Methuen Ltd; Ch. 5 © 1939
Oxford University Press; Ch. 6 © 1952 *The Review of Metaphysics*; Ch. 7 ©
1936, 1964 by the President and Fellows of Harvard College; Ch. 8 © 1965
Wesleyan University; Ch. 9 © 1949 *Journal of the History of Ideas*; Ch. 10 ©
1978 *American Political Science Review;* Ch. 11 © 1979 *Philosophical
Quarterly*; editorial selection and all other material © 1983 P. King.
Croom Helm Ltd, Provident House, Burrell Row,
Beckenham, Kent BR3 1AT

British Library Cataloguing in Publication Data

The History of ideas. – (Croom Helm international series in social and
    political thought)
    1. Europe – Intellectual life
    I. King, Preston
    190   AZ 605

    ISBN 0-7099-1526-8
    ISBN 0-7099-1527-6 Paperback

First published in the United States of America 1983 by
Barnes and Noble Books,
81 Adams Drive,
Totowa, New Jersey 07512

Library of Congress Cataloging in Publication Data
Main entry under title:

The History of ideas.

    1. History – Philosophy – Addresses, essays, lectures.
    2. Ideas (Philosophy) – Addresses, essays, lectures.
    I. King, Preston., 1936-
    D16.8.H6253   1983   901   83-12278
    ISBN 0-389-20435-8

Printed in Great Britain
by Billing & Son Ltd, Worcester

CONTENTS

TO NAHLA

Clennon Leslie
Una Tamsin
Slater Stern

PART ONE

Suddenly I realized that it's still Monday, like yesterday. Look at the sky, look at the walls, look at the begonias. Today is Monday, too.

Gabriel Garcia Marquez

1 INTRODUCTION*

Preston King

1

A major problem confronted in the history of ideas has to do with whether we can be said to know the past. It might be contended, for example, that all knowledge is exclusively present. The contention can be viewed under two aspects.

First, if the ideas which we *hypothesize* to belong to the past, are now actually being thought in the present, then the hypothesis must appear baseless, since all we have demonstrable evidence for, is present thinking.

Secondly, if the ideas we know ourselves now to be thinking in the present are attributed to the past, then we cannot ever know the attribution to be valid, since we cannot actually think these present ideas in the past. Essentially, what we here confront is a case for all knowledge being present knowledge.

However, a rather different kind of case could be made, namely for the proposition that all knowledge is past knowledge. Any idea which we claim to be present, must be assumed in some fashion to have evolved. Any idea that we formulate on paper or speak aloud, is expressed in language, which is a social convention, and to which may be attributed existence, and therefore duration. Thus, if we take any current doctrine, we are entitled to assume that it, too, as with any word moreover, has a past, and a history. We need not look beyond this very argument where we seek to justify placing a trace on genesis, opening an eye to chains of influence, anchoring what is apparently present in the past. Any idea or doctrine that we at least do not concoct, given that the point at which it was formulated or recorded must precede the point at which we receive and assess it, must be a *past* idea or doctrine. Further, given that very few of our ideas are *our* ideas, and that even the novelties we devise are pieced together from the ready-made components of communal life, it becomes difficult to conclude that there can be a present which is not past.

3

*For citations in Chapters 1, 2, 3 and 12, see Bibliography.

These two positions – that all knowledge is of the present, and alternatively that it is all of the past – take on the appearance of plain contradictories. On the one hand, to understand past ideas, we are enjoined to think them through for ourselves, to bring them to life, perhaps to 'enact' or 're-enact' them. On the other hand, such understanding, we are told, may only be achieved by ceasing to think as we do now, by shedding present outlooks, by removing ourselves to remote times, by appreciating how different *our* thought is from *theirs*, by reconstructing their contexts rather than assume any constancy or continuity between earlier and contemporary ways of thinking.

The object of this anthology is to bring together a small number of the more significant essays which have addressed these questions in the anglophone world over the past four decades and more. It would be foolish to suppose that the issues in dispute can or will be magically resolved. But it will be (or become) apparent enough – on a reading of the pieces published here – that a great deal of the contestation involved in the contemporary debate over the logical status of the history of ideas is in some measure attributable to a failure to provide a clearer and fuller analysis of the interlocking concepts of 'past' and 'present'. The purpose of Chapter 2, which is not intended to be exhaustive, is to provide some minimal assistance in this direction.

2

Michael Oakeshott (1901-), since succeeding H.J. Laski as Professor of Political Science in the London School of Economics (1951-69) has been one of the most influential students of the history of ideas in the English-speaking world. His social philosophy is anchored more in a commitment to historical, rather than to sociological or psychological, method. History, science, ethics, aesthetics are all for Oakeshott so many different ways or 'modes' of seizing experience. These 'arrests' of experience 'modify' it, render it abstract, taking away from the concreteness and totality of experience as such. History Oakeshott perceives to be only one possible, and not a necessary, form of experience. But it none the less remains of prime importance to him. Central to Oakeshott's analysis of history is his view of its character as paradoxical – positing a concern with the past, but a concern which can only be displayed in the present, and by reference to present evidence. Oakeshott's analysis is both sweeping and perceptive. In 1933, in *Experience and Its Modes*, it is expressed in one form. In 1955, in an essay entitled 'The Activity of Being an Historian', it is expressed in a somewhat modified form. 'The Activity of Being an Historian' was reprinted in 1962 in *Rationalism in Politics* and is also reprinted in this volume as the last major statement by Oakeshott presently available on historical method.[1]

A great deal has been written about Oakeshott, but not very much relating to Oakeshott on history. Oakeshott has been variably referred to, in most instances on his own initiative, as conservative, traditionalist, historicist and so on. Much of the secondary literature on him has been critical. For example, Rotenstreich (1976) comments:

> Just as Marx made man a function of his social circumstances, so Oakeshott makes man a function of his historical circumstances as embodied in tradition − and this is a strange affinity. [T]here is as little justification for Marx's . . . historicism as there is for Oakeshott's. (p. 131)

The assessment of Oakeshott which we reprint below, is no less critical, being narrowly set in counterpoint to what it characterizes as Oakeshott's 'historical particularism'. Whatever else this essay may or may not do, it reflects considerable unease regarding the supposed paradox to which Oakeshott draws attention − that which portrays history as to do with a dead past, but a past apprehended in, and only in, the evidence of a living present. In the case of the history of ideas, again, the problem set is: How, in what intelligible sense, can ideas be construed as quite cut off from us, as populating a dead past, and simultaneously prove fully intelligible and accessible by virtue of being incorporated into present experience?

3

R.G. Collingwood (1889-1943) was elected to the Waynflete Chair of Metaphysical Philosophy, at Oxford University in 1935. After early retirement in 1941, Gilbert Ryle was elected to succeed him. In his *Autobiography* (1939), Collingwood characterized his academic objective overall as basically consisting in bringing about 'a *rapprochement* between philosophy and history'. Indeed, in his earliest book (1916), Collingwood went so far as to claim that these disciplines were 'the same thing'. By contrast, in the *Essay on Philosophical Method* (1933), he referred to philosophy as 'a distinct and living form

of thought' and not as 'a part of history'. The *Essay* clearly suggests —
while maintaining a very tight fit between history and philosophy —
that some philosophical systems are truer than others and that the
object of philosophical as distinct from historical enquiry, consists precisely in the assessment of such truth. It is agreed that Collingwood
changed his philosophical views at the latest between 1936 and 1938
(see Knox 1946, p. x and Donagan 1962, p. 12). Knox (1946) in
support of a marked historicist development in Collingwood's thought,
quotes from notes written by the latter early in 1939: 'philosophy as a
separate discipline is liquidated by being converted into history'.
Donagan (1962) agrees that 'Collingwood radically changed his mind'
beween 1926 and 1938 'about the relation of philosophy to history'.
Collingwood, indeed, in the *Autobiography*, in a rather uncompromis-
ing mood, denies 'the permanence of philosophical problems' and
accordingly concludes 'that the alleged distinction between the historical question and the philosophical must be false'. Donagan espies in
Collingwood a marginally greater coherence than does Knox, but the
sense of disarray persists.

The paradox enunciated by Oakeshott is reformulated by Collingwood, but without the same deliberate, intentional and concentrated
effect. To begin, Collingwood held Oakeshott in high regard and believed that the latter had developed 'a brilliant and penetrating account
of the aims of historical thought' (Collingwood 1946, p. 153). In fact,
Collingwood regarded Oakeshott as representing the 'high-water mark
of English thought upon history' (p. 159) — where it is understood
that the period indicated is that prior to the emergence of Collingwood
himself. Anticipatory positions parallel to Oakeshott's were accorded to
Wilhelm Dilthey in Germany and to Benedetto Croce in Italy.

While Collingwood believed that Oakeshott's work represented 'a
new and valuable achievement for English thought' and that it entirely
vindicated 'the autonomy of historical thought' — its independence *qua*
science — he also believed Oakeshott's work to be hobbled by a crucial
failure. This failure, he thought, derived from the fact that Oakeshott
did not or could not show history to be 'a necessary . . . element in
experience as such', and so did not or could not show why there should
be any such discipline 'as history at all'. Collingwood viewed himself as
moving off in a significantly different direction. Oakeshott, on Collingwood's estimate, would have been right to travel with him, but proved
unable to hurdle the view that history was 'either past or present, but
not both'. Collingwood believed that Oakeshott should have, even on
his own analysis, perceived history as 'a living past, a past which, be-

cause it was thought and not mere natural event, can be re-enacted in the present and in that re-enactment known as past'.

There is no doubt but that Oakeshott has a problem. Yet it is not quite the problem which Collingwood took it to be. Collingwood understood Oakeshott to be firmly distinguishing between past and present. This is true enough, unless we place emphasis upon 'firmly'. Because while Oakeshott emphasizes the distinction, he equally intimates the impossibility of ever really making it. History, writes Oakeshott (1933), 'is the continuous assertion of a past which is not past and of a present which is not present' (p. 111). This is much the same as saying that, in history, the past is in the present, and that the present is in the past. Thus, while Oakeshott conceives past and present to be distinct, he also conceives them, somehow, to be simultaneous — and in a manner by no means entirely alien to Collingwood's preferred solution except that Oakeshott warms to the idea of 'a dead past' while Collingwood fancies the idea of 'a living past'.

Collingwood set out then to destroy the distinction between past and present, a distinction attributed to Oakeshott. However, Oakeshott accepts some notion of the simultaneity of past and present but frankly regards the idea as paradoxical and only commits himself to simultaneity (this Collingwood apparently appreciated) as part of his strategy for somehow keeping the past to itself — i.e. in the past. Collingwood (1946), therefore, in his concern to show that the 'fact that [historical experience] is also present does not prevent it from being past', basically presented as a solution what Oakeshott (1933) had styled a 'paradox'. When Collingwood's work is taken as a whole, at least in regard to the question of the logical status of history, what confronts us is a brilliant, a genuinely illuminating, piece of tergiversation. Historical and philosophical thinking are alternately displayed as identical, as distinct and again as identical. Collingwood is not the simple historicist which a selective reading of his work, especially the *Autobiography*, might be assumed to reveal. But he clearly 'oscillates' between the acceptance and rejection of historicism, despite his own resolve to push beyond this impasse. I agree with the conclusion of Rotenstreich (1976) that Collingwood's valuable contribution never achieves any valid synthesis: this, if it is to be achieved, must be built upon a more direct and coherent 'analysis of historical time' (p. 68).

In this volume, we reprint selections from Collingwood's *Autobiography*. According to R.B. McCallum (1943), the book was 'regretted by most of his [Collingwood's] Oxford friends' because of the sudden and unargued change of outlook which it supposedly reflected (p. 467).

All the same, the book's line of argument is on the whole clear and firm. It also represents Collingwood's last major statement on historical method. Further, it develops most fully and interestingly the historicist component in Collingwood's thinking. Finally, these selections are not, to my knowledge, available in any other collection. There is much counterargument available on Collingwood. The criticism reprinted here from Leo Strauss is primarily addressed to Collingwood's *Idea of History*. But Strauss essentially singles out for attack what he regards as Collingwood's historicism. Given Strauss's standing in post-war America, such a critical appreciation will, naturally, be received with interest. In summary, Strauss argues that a sense of history and familiarity with the history of ideas is valuable because it defends against parochialism in an anachronistic guise. But he concludes that what is politically true and right, generally or universally, is to be emphatically distinguished from the separate question regarding how such views have come to be formed.

4

A.O. Lovejoy (1873-1962) has, in one place, been called 'the chief inspirer of the history of ideas'. It is a large claim, which effectively reduces, perhaps, to the fact that he was the most eminent of the founders of the *Journal of the History of Ideas*, which first appeared in January of 1940. In brief, Lovejoy's argument was that we understand ourselves better by understanding the ways in which we have evolved, which largely means to understand the manner in which we have come, over time, to hold the ideas that we do. Lovejoy wrote a great deal, as will be evident from any moderately detailed bibliography, including that supplied at the close of this volume. Four of Lovejoy's essays, however, are of particular relevance. The first is his 'Introduction: the Study of the History of Ideas', which constituted the opening chapter of his book, *The Great Chain of Being* (1936). The second essay is 'The Historiography of Ideas' first published in 1938 and subsequently incorporated into one (1948) of Lovejoy's several volumes of essays. The third is 'Present Standpoints and Past History', originally published in 1939, and reprinted in 1959 in Mayerhoff. Finally, there is Lovejoy's 'Reflections on the History of Ideas' (1940), with which, in effect, the *Journal of the History of Ideas* was launched. These four essays are all marginally distinct from one another; none the less, if we make exception of the third, they cover much the same ground. The argument for reprinting the first (with a few emendations) in preference to any other is basically that it stands more easily on its own, while the analysis it provides is on the whole clearer and more direct.

Lovejoy was much concerned with tracing intellectual influences. In the process, he opposed, not so much the exploration of detail, but rather an excess of specialization. Lovejoy's concern, in his words (1936), was to put 'gates through fences' — these fences being the boundaries of the various academic disciplines. He had reservations about literary and philosophical specialization within the limits, for example, of nation and language — on the grounds that such boundaries too often obscure the actual flow of influences across them. Lovejoy (1938) put his case in the following terms: 'the more you press in towards the heart of a narrowly bounded historical problem, the more likely you are to encounter in the problem itself a pressure which drives you outward beyond those bounds' (p. 6). He adverted to the need to understand some astronomy, and not a little of Aristotle, for example, to be able to provide any adequate exegesis of Milton's meaning in various passages of *Paradise Lost*. Lovejoy warned against any undue concern with major writers, where one seeks to elicit the actual thought of a period, since minor writers, as he wrote (1936), may serve the purpose better, by revealing more that is characteristic of the time. Lovejoy, then, avowed no particular partiality towards writers major or minor, nor more of a commitment to text than context, but essentially committed himself to pursuing historical truth across whatever disciplines and epochs enquiry might dictate. Lovejoy's historical approach was unquestionably interdisciplinary (1928), on the assumption, it would appear, that historical research should be more problem-oriented than period-oriented, as well as on the assumption that the more narrow and detailed one's focus upon a particular subject or period, the less effective one may prove, for that very reason, in achieving any proper understanding of it. Lovejoy placed considerable emphasis upon sweep, upon comprehensiveness, a concern governed by the hope of getting the analysis 'right' — in relation at least to the problem set. Lovejoy (1939) conceived of the past as firmly distinct from the present, as unquestionably objective, but also as equally firmly relevant to the present, and thus as not in any way dead. Lovejoy (1940) believed that historical inquiry should in some degree prove 'instructive', and indeed 'provide material towards possible general conclusions — conclusions which do not relate merely to . . . past and particular events' (p. 8).

In sum, Lovejoy regarded history as vast both in scope and detail, its substance only subject to arrest where the manacles of a specific problem or question are locked round some discrete part of it. He accepted that new problems do arise, but regarded them as rare, and concluded that the best means of coping with the history of ideas consists in (a) breaking down the more encompassing, compound doctrines that emerge (e.g. romanticism, rationalism, primitivism and pragmatism) into analytically smaller units – which he refers to as 'unit-ideas' and (b) in tracing the evolution of those 'unit-ideas' over time. The Lovejoy essay reprinted, in this volume, may be consulted for a more detailed development of this thesis. Lovejoy (1936) was, by his own account, much prejudiced in favour of 'distinguishing and analyzing the major ideas which appear again and again'. It is, of course, a view for which he has been severely criticized in much of the later literature. However openly Lovejoy (1939) accepted the thesis that historical study is a selective undertaking anchored in the present, he energetically rejected the subjectivist implications often attributed to or associated with it.

5

Maurice Mandelbaum, in his critical assessment of Lovejoy's programme, argues that it may (a) disguise or distort the central intent or motive of an author's work and (b) 'minimize the independence of an author's thought' by suggesting connections or influences which are doubtful or non-existent (Mandelbaum 1965, section 1). But Mandelbaum's concern is not to say that these difficulties, following Lovejoy's approach, *must* arise, only that they may do and, by implication, are to be guarded against. Mandelbaum had written earlier (1948) an appreciative notice which argued that Lovejoy's approach represented a 'fruitful conception of history'. He viewed this approach as consistent with a pluralism which excludes any 'single all-pervasive pattern', accommodating not only clearly discernible continuities and limited generalizations, but equally clearly discernible discontinuities, since 'no continuity perseveres unmodified and unbroken' (p. 423).

Mandelbaum (1948) writes of Lovejoy's pluralism as though the views of the latter were essentially identical with those formulated by Mandelbaum himself when a doctoral candidate. In his *Problem of Historical Knowledge* (the doctorate in published form), Mandelbaum (1938) seeks to argue for the objectivity of historical knowledge, to counter the relativism of figures like Benedetto Croce, Wilhelm Dilthey and Karl Mannheim, and to do this in a manner consistent with an 'historical pluralism'. Like so many writers of recent times (e.g. Collingwood, Oakeshott, Popper, Berlin), Mandelbaum argues that there is no one single pattern, purpose, predictable denouement or inevitability about history. No formulation or representation, says Mandelbaum, is 'able to render justice to the pluralist nature of the historical process as a whole' (p. 288). He contends that any 'attempt to decipher the message which is contained in "the historical process as a whole" is futile' (p. 306). Mandelbaum (1971) returns to this theme much later in his attack on 'historicism', although most of what he has to say on this head is formulated more rigorously by Popper and Berlin.

In sum, Mandelbaum perceives a great deal in common between himself and Lovejoy. He reveals a basic sympathy for Lovejoy's aims. Accordingly, he is not unduly ambitious (1956) in his criticism. In his extended essay (1971) on (or 'in') nineteenth-century thought, where he sets himself the task of 'sifting . . . presuppositions which were held in common by a diverse group of thinkers whose antecedents and whose aims often had little in common' (p. ix), Mandelbaum in part exemplifies Lovejoy's approach. He readily employs (what Lovejoy would have called) 'unit-ideas' — like 'historicism', 'development', 'geneticism', 'organicism' and so on — to organize his material. Mandelbaum (1971) explicitly accepts Lovejoy's 'great-chain-of-being' concept as applicable to the work of figures like Lamarck and Darwin (pp. 79 and 396, n. 4).

It remains that Mandelbaum flinches from loose talk about 'an overriding spirit of the age' (a disposition he detects for example in Greene, 1957). He thinks it important to be able to trace influences over time, but that it is vital to avoid any suggestion of a monistic and ineluctable causal flow in the process. He feels it important to be clear about this in a way, perhaps, that Lovejoy was not. Hence his emphasis upon the manifold 'strands' that make up any era or epoch, upon both continuity and discontinuity in temporal sequence, upon the lack of fit between all of these elements, and upon the fact that any historical period is only such in certain respects and not in all (1965, 1977).

While Mandelbaum fleshes out the diversity of types of historical inquiry, he never abandons a basic commitment to some concept of historical unity and coherence. While committed (1938) to some notion of historical particularism, to the view that 'the historian deals with specific events' (p. 3) by contrast with the scientist who, in effect, formulates universal laws (i.e., 'judgments regarding "typical" occurrences'), Mandelbaum accepts all the same that 'the complete separation of the historical method and the method of the physical sciences is impossible', that the two procedures are 'opposed to each other only in ideal cases', and that 'in the practice of the physical sciences they are often blurred' (p. 4). While disposed to define 'the historical enterprise' in terms of 'understanding every event in the light of its actual historical context' (p. 8), Mandelbaum (1938) none the less rejects as unfortunate 'the sharp division which is often made between "research historians" and "great" or "synthetic" historians' (p. 293) — on the grounds that 'historical understanding tolerates no bifurcation between fact-finding and synthesis' (p. 294).

Mandelbaum (1965, part II) is very much concerned to avoid the holistic, and in part historicist, view — as expressed by figures like Comte, Hegel, Marx, Spengler and Toynbee — that to understand any particular historical period, or any aspect of such a period, one must understand the whole of history as such. He is concerned to avoid the notion, especially in the history of philosophy, that each stage somehow leads inexorably and connectedly to the next, so that this supposed movement can be easily read backwards from the present. Although he entertains an overarching view of history, he also is concerned to reveal its variability, and most especially by means of the distinction he establishes between histories that are either 'general' or 'special'.

Mandelbaum means by *special histories* those which 'seek to establish how a particular form of human activity, such as art, or religion, or science, has developed over time, rather than attempting to trace how it has contributed to this or that particular society' (p. 45). Mandelbaum appears to mean by *general histories* those which provide descriptions or accounts of the process of change as this occurs within a specific society or institution (e.g. a nation, army, university or church). He regards general histories as reflecting a broader, more encompassing perspective; by contrast, 'the focus of interest of special histories is narrower' (1965, p. 46); and general histories, he suggests, rely upon special histories to convey 'the social context which governed the life of men at a particular time and place' (p. 45).

For Mandelbaum, general histories, histories of institutions, because of their organized character, which allow them to persist over time, must be continuous. By contrast, special histories, as of philosophy, although they *may* be continuous, are not necessarily so, since influences may leap across historical periods without following any strictly temporal sequence. These special histories then, though not necessarily continuous from an institutional perspective, may be so in other respects. As Mandelbaum (1965) puts it: 'a temporally discontinuous series of events may legitimately be viewed as having a measure of unity and continuity, such that it constitutes a proper subject-matter for historical inquiry' (p. 54). One obvious implication in all this is that one may hold a history of philosophy, for example, to be perfectly legitimate, without necessarily supposing that the pattern of change displayed can be regarded as ineluctable, desirable, progressive or 'developmental'.

Despite Mandelbaum's qualifications, many contemporary critics consider that such an approach to philosophical history, or to the history of ideas — putting it both more broadly and loosely — must none the less fail. To link together different thinkers across different periods may be held to distort their ideas — perhaps because it is really only *our* ideas that we are reviewing, or because we have been unable to reconstruct *their* context (as blurred by undue immersion in our own), or because the limited evidence we select from these thinkers is just unrepresentative of their thought. For example, G.A. Kelly (1975), in his review of Mandelbaum (1971), rounds on our author in precisely these ways. Kelly charges that Mandelbaum's 'linkage of "otherwise divergent thinkers" in "almost identical" contexts' often overlooks their actual purposes, and the variety of these 'and tends to create a pastiche of theory independent of the theorists themselves'. The charge is also frequently levelled that in a philosophical history of this kind we may never be quite clear as to whether the purpose of the writer is genuinely to reconstruct the way in which a set of ideas has actually evolved or merely to employ these ideas as a stalking horse for the author's own philosophy (which he should formulate for himself, it may be thought, both more briefly and more lucidly).

6

Leo Strauss (1899-1973) worked from 1925 for seven years in the Academy of Jewish Research in Berlin. He left Germany for France in 1932, and later removed to England. He finally settled in America in 1938. He joined the university in exile of the New School for Social Research in New York, where he remained for ten years. He moved to the University of Chicago in 1949 and served there for 18 years, the last eight of these (from 1959) as Robert M. Hutchins Distinguished Service Professor of Political Science.

Strauss was one of America's most eminent and productive champions of political philosophy. Strauss's chief academic medium was history, but he attacked historicism and positivism — this last not only in the form of contemporary social science behaviouralism — with notable acerbity. His assumption was that the gap between past and present could and must be bridged, although not in any absurdly literal way. Hence his intense interest in 'pre-modern rationalism, especially Jewish-medieval nationalism and its classical (Aristotelian and Platonic) foundation' (Strauss 1965, p. 31). Strauss's interest was in rationalism, but it was an interest which he usually approached in an approximately revelatory manner, through the almost occult interpretation of texts.

Strauss believed modern rationalism — dating most notably from first, Machiavelli and Hobbes and secondly, Rousseau; and thirdly from Nietzsche — to be engaged in an inevitable process of self-destruction. It reflected a shift from the concern with contemplation and self-understanding (philosophy) to a concern with power and control over nature (science). It also reflected a shift from a condition of moral certainty to that of a certain amorality, principally that of an historicist relativism where a value is held to be valid depending upon the era in which it is uttered. Before Strauss took his leave of England (this was in 1937), Oakeshott, while taking issue with him on important points of interpretation, correctly wrote of Strauss's *Political Philosophy of Hobbes* as 'the most original book on Hobbes which has appeared for many years' (Oakeshott 1975, p. 133).

Strauss *qua* exegete was nothing if not 'original' — in ways which have engendered reactions ranging from fervent adulation to acid rebuke. And all of it is understandable: Strauss was no sceptic or relativist. Although he displayed considerable respect for his texts, conjoined with an uncannily exhaustive, perhaps rabbinical, control of them, his sense of outrage could whip him up to and over the lip of invective and parallel misjudgement. In his analysis of Machiavelli, Strauss moves back and forth across the textual minefield of *The Prince* and *The Discourses* with remarkable ease and adroitness: to Strauss's readers are revealed even the hidden meanings and connections between Machiavelli's chapter numbers. It is all too cabalistic to be true, and is yet convincing. Besides, every decent reader wants somehow to round on Machiavelli: Strauss provides the means. The crude scissors of his morality are brought to bear upon the literary corpus of the quick-witted Florentine with a gratifying finality.

Yet, one can never quite surrender oneself to Strauss's judgement. His coarseness occasions a wariness equal to the delight excited by his mastery of detail. For Strauss (1958), Machiavelli becomes 'a teacher of evil', an 'evil man' (p. 9), 'immoral and irreligious'. Those scholars who 'do not see the evil character of his thought' fail in this respect, following Strauss, 'because they . . . have been corrupted by Machiavelli' (p. 13). The attack is pure *ad hominem*, and it is not an entirely occasional lapse. In one breath, as it were, Strauss would hold the 'indispensable condition of "scientific" analysis' to be 'moral obtuseness' (p. 11); in the next, with no less a display of 'moral obtuseness' (in the manner indeed of an obliging refugee who must praise his protectors) Strauss celebrates 'the foundation of the United States' – by contrast with all the governments of Europe – as an edifice unqualifiedly 'laid in freedom and justice' (p. 13). The breadth of interest, the marvellously heady analysis, the leaden and moralistic misjudgement, the repetitiveness, the excruciatingly partisan commitment – these disparate elements are all wrapped up in one large package. The reader may attend to whichever items he likes: it is excusable, in any reading of Strauss, that one should be fascinated or repelled – or both.

The exegesis provided by Strauss of classical philosophy, specifically Plato, Aristotle and Xenophon, was not that of an antiquarian. The past which he manipulated was not conceived as dead. His justification for these excursions was not to relax as tourist but to train for present or future action: 'the questions raised by the political philosophers of the past are alive in our own society' (Strauss and Cropsey, 1963). The seriousness with which Strauss analysed past thought stemmed from his appreciation of the past as somehow present. And this is basically what Strauss (1949) meant when arguing that 'political philosophy is not a historical discipline'. A sense of history, to be sure, defends one (Strauss maintained) against a certain parochialism, against anachronism, and accordingly proves valuable. But it is not, for all that, 'an integral part' of philosophy itself. A history of philosophy is useful in that it may make one familiar with the way in which characteristic philosophies have come to be formed. But for Strauss there always remained the distinction between how a philosophical view evolves and whether that view proves valid. In effect, Strauss was concerned with the study of the moderns in order to determine how (what he called) 'the crisis of Political Philosophy' came about. He studied the ancients by contrast because he believed theirs represented a perennial philosophy. A 'simple continuation of the tradition of classical political philosophy [was] no longer possible' (Strauss, 1964a). This impossibility was attributable to 'the crisis of our time' in the West, represented at the one extreme by a loss of internal purpose (e.g. liberalism, anarchism, nihilism) and externally by the threat of Soviet communism. ('the most extreme form of Soviet despotism'). The 'return to classical political philosophy', then, though 'necessary', must also prove adaptive or 'experimental'. In Strauss's words: 'Only we living today can possibly find a solution to the problems of today. But an adequate understanding of the principles as elaborated by the classics may be an indispensable starting point' (p. 11).

For Strauss, in fact, the classics *were* the indispensable starting point. And he offered his services as an indispensable guide. He seemed burdened with a superlative reverence for the past. He was not disposed to present himself as harbinger of things new, but rather as the astute sage who would initiate readers and students into the mysteries of a living heritage and help to deploy these mysteries in the defence or construction of a happier present — 'happiness' being understood in the Aristotelian sense of 'virtuous'. Although virtually all of Strauss's work involves an exercise in the history of ideas, it none the less proceeds from the postulate that there are historical problems and philosophical truths which are 'transhistorical', 'perennial', 'enduring', 'fundamental'. His immediate concern was to understand the past, but his ultimate object was simply to attain a genuine philosophical understanding *per se*, independent of historical accident. As Strauss wrote in the 1952 Preface to his book on Hobbes, 'I assumed that political philosophy as quest for the final truth regarding the political fundamentals is possible and necessary.' It is precisely because past thought *is* alive, following Strauss, that one may hope to 'understand the great thinkers of the past as *they understand* themselves' (my italics). Strauss understood the 'enduring questions', those which interpenetrate past and present, to relate to freedom and government, constitutionalism or regime type, tyranny and virtue. In commenting upon Machiavelli, Strauss (1958) observed that many 'contemporaries are of the opinion that there are no permanent problems and hence no permanent alternatives' and that it is precisely Machiavelli, given the supposed novelty of his problem, who best stated their case. Strauss conceded some weight to the argument, but characteristically concludes ('stated baldly') that this 'proves merely that the permanent problems are not as easily accessible as some people believe' (p. 14). Strauss proposed to take the student beyond surface apparances, to seize the true nature of historical problems, to know them, not as dead, but alive, a current irresistibly rippling through the present.

For all its intricacy — and also lack of grace, as one must confess — there can be no mistaking the challenge with which Strauss confronts the relativist outlook in the history of philosophy. Strauss (1953) insists that 'history' has meant 'throughout the ages primarily political history' and accordingly that what is called the "discovery" of history is the work, not of philosophy in general, but of political philosophy' (p. 34). Historicism, accordingly, was regarded by Strauss as more a problem for political and social philosophy than for any other disciplines — although the work of Thomas Kuhn (1970, p. 138) would suggest that Strauss, in this, may have been unduly restrictive. In any event, Strauss's inclination was not numbly to defend his position, but to leap across the trenches to exploit the vulnerability of his enemy. Strauss provides less a direct defence of his approach, than an assault, as he sees it, upon the crucial logical weakness of historicism.

'Historicism', wrote Strauss (1953), 'asserts that all human thoughts or beliefs are historical, and hence deservedly destined to perish; but historicism itself is a human thought; hence historicism can be of only temporary validity, or it [simply] cannot be true'. And Strauss was perfectly entitled, in this, to insist upon consistent self-application as one of the first tests of the coherence of a principle. If a doctrine or method is only true for its time, then to conceive this as a doctrine or method and apply it to itself must yield an incoherence. If a philosophy or method is only true in its own context, then this very contextual observation in turn will only prove true in its own context, which would imply that it cannot always be true. Strauss was inclined to believe that the proponents of historicism always adjudged their doctrine to be true — which must involve the projection of a moral and methodological universal. Hence the difficulty involved in simultaneously embracing the moral and methodological scepticism and relativism which is implicit in notions of epochal uniqueness and historical particularism. In sum, for Strauss, 'this historicist thesis is self-contradictory', since one cannot assert 'the historical character of "all" thought . . . without transcending history, without grasping something transhistorical' (p. 25).

It is in the manner indicated that Strauss (1953) came to draw the following conclusion:

if historicism cannot be taken for granted, the question becomes inevitable whether what was hailed in the nineteenth century as a discovery was not, in fact, an invention, that is, an arbitrary interpretation of phenomena which had always been known and which had been interpreted much more adequately prior to the emergence of the historical consciousness than afterward. We have to raise the question whether what is called the 'discovery' of history is not, in fact, an artificial and makeshift solution to a problem that could arise only on the basis of very questionable premises. (p. 33)

More than any other recent academic thinker, Strauss became identified as the founder of a 'school'. The commitment to the formal need
for a 'transhistorical' ethic and epistemology, however variable its content for any particular spokesman, was emphatic. In the *Festschrift*
published on the occasion of Strauss's retirement (Cropsey, 1964), one
is provided in cameo with some hint of Strauss's influence upon
American letters. Strauss represented a virtually neon-lit target. The
resulting fusillade has been as one might expect. Most of the remaining material reproduced in this volume involves some either direct or
indirect indication of the type and calibre of artillery subsequently
trained upon the Straussian *oeuvre*. The careful and summary article
by J.G. Gunnell, reprinted below, which raises gently the question of
the tenability of Strauss's enterprise, is best interpreted as the marks-
man's anticipatory clearing of the throat.

7

The work of figures like Oakeshott and Collingwood is now the object
of considerable and supportive academic attention. The work of figures
like Lovejoy and Strauss, by contrast, is less well received. The centre
of support for the former two is, naturally enough, located in England
and the Commonwealth. Support for the latter two is concentrated in
the United States. Quentin Skinner, current Professor of Political
Science at Cambridge, betrays considerable hostility to the methodologies espoused by Lovejoy and Strauss. The chains of influence which
they insist upon, he takes to be more nearly mythological, due to the
great difficulty, perhaps impossibility, of actually demonstrating them.
Skinner is concerned, moreover, that to trace a history of ideas must
require that we actually impose these ideas upon history. It is
dangerous, he claims, 'for the historian of ideas to approach his material
with preconceived paradigms'.

Skinner has published a large number of essays, as one may see from
the Bibliography. Most of these may readily be fitted into one of two
categories. The first relates, broadly, to appropriate (and inappropriate)
methods for writing the history of ideas (most importantly Skinner
1966b, 1969a, 1970, 1971, 1972b, 1972c and 1974). The second
relates basically to the historical reconstruction of what Skinner calls
Hobbes's 'ideological' context (most importantly Skinner 1964, 1965a,
1966a, 1966c, 1969b, 1972a and 1972d).

Skinner's essays deal, first, with the general question of valid methodology. They concern, secondly, the application of this methodology to a specific social philosopher of the seventeenth century. Skinner's only book (1978a) provides another, specific test of the general methodology, but in this case as applied to a period rather than to an individual philosopher. A great deal of comment has been generated on Skinner's general programme, as in Parekh and Berki (1973) and Gunnell, 1982 and in an issue of *Political Theory* (August 1974) devoted entirely to Skinner's work. Less has been written about the execution of that programme (although numerous reviews of Skinner, 1978 have appeared, as for example, Shklar, 1979; Holmes, 1979; Kelley, 1979; Mulligan, 1979; Boucher, 1980 and Black, 1980). In Chapter 12 of this volume, an attempt is made to say something both about Skinner's programme and about a specific test of it — but the question here taken to be of prior interest is Skinner's application of his general theory to the work of Thomas Hobbes.

8

There is today, a great deal of literature on the problems associated with writing histories of ideas. It would be desirable, in this connection, for Skinner to bring together his various methodological essays, and to compress and to publish them as a connected statement. It is extremely difficult to consider any one of his essays as genuinely representative of his work as a whole. Also, selections from some more recent writers (there are quite a number of them, for example, Leslie, 1970; Haddock, 1974; Ashcraft, 1975; Kvastad, 1977; Lockyer, 1979 and Femia, 1979) could be usefully brought together to ease the problems of access which hobble readers interested in these matters.

The present collection has inescapably proved selective. We have attempted very broadly to give some impression of the range of argument that has arisen over the past 40 odd years, roughly from the time of the last World War. The key figures are presented as Oakeshott, Collingwood, Lovejoy, Strauss and Skinner. (If there had been more space, it would have been desirable to include a scholar like Pocock or a continental figure like Foucault. But to do all this was simply out of the question.) To these major figures we have sought to oppose other essays in counterpoint — hence the tension in the structure of the book from Part Two onwards.

Note

1. A small book by Oakeshott, *On Historiography*, has appeared since this volume was written.

Source

Specially written for this volume.

2 THINKING PAST A PROBLEM

Preston King

1: History and the Past

When we say of any item or event, including thought, that it exists, we attribute to it duration. We attribute duration, we *assume* it: it is not a matter for proof. It is in order for any existing item, at any point in its existence, to be attributed a past, present and future – none of which three is necessarily to be regarded as unending. A large part of any existence – not necessarily the largest – must be that which we call its 'past'.

'History' means many things. But one of the most conventional of its meanings involves an equation with 'the past'. On this reading, if anything that exists (including any idea) has a past, then every idea, by implication, must have a history. A history of any phenomenon or institution or idea is less to be accounted a *body* of knowledge, than a *way* of (or approach to) embodying knowledge. There is no difficulty in accepting history to be a discipline, as long as we accept it to be such by reference to perspective, and not any distinctive subject-matter.

So what is this historical perspective? It is, as already suggested, duration: to do with persistence, change, growth, evolution, etc. History is not merely to do with change, since everything which endures need not change. History is not merely to do with difference, since identities also endure. History is never beyond the reach of morality, since it cannot be engaged except as an exercise in selection, which is to say choice, as between better and worse, between what fits and what won't. History is not exclusively to do with the unique; were there nothing humdrum in the past, the very concept of uniqueness would collapse for want of opposition, and history (thus defined) with it. History is never subject to total reconstruction, since our evidence is always partial and our formulae about the evidence, again, is selective.

The problem is, that if history is only to do with the past, and we can only comprehend it in the present, indeed only by making it a part of the present, how can we ever really know it as past – as it was (or 'is')? It would seem that, if we genuinely know history in the present, then it can no longer be past; that if we only apprehend it as present thinking, we canot seize it as genuine history; that if we know it only by present excogitation, then perhaps it is not really the past (*wie es eigentlich gewesen*) that we are excogitating at all. Here we have what has been called a paradox, certainly a problem. This is a present problem; it was also a past problem, one which existed before; and our present job, in relation to this past and present difficulty, is to try to think our way past it. In thinking past this problem (if ever we succeed), the trouble is to avoid restating it in a new way. The solution must lie somehow in the interpenetration of past and present. It must lie in some notion of a 'thinking past' or even perhaps a 'living history' — hopefully without blurring the necessary contrast between 'then' and 'now'.

2: Past and Present

Let us take it that whatever we do or think now, is done or thought in *the* present. We may take it too that whatever we do or think at any time, is done or thought in *a* present. Since the idea of the present, or of a present, can in this way seem so all-encompassing, we may be led to believe that there is no past. We may be led to believe at least that we, alive now only in the present, cannot let slip our chains and directly escape into the past. But we may equally conclude — it appears so compelling a conclusion — that there *is* a past, and that the great difficulty is to find our way to it, by escaping the present, slipping past the present, by tacking for what is different, other, not of the here and now. Both conclusions, (1) that the present is all-enveloping, and (2) that to understand history we must escape from the present, are based upon a certain confusion as regards what we may mean by 'present' and, *a fortiori*, 'past'.

If we think of ideas, we can distinguish between them as new and old. A notion like 'tolerance', where we understand 'the inhibition of negative action against a person or item to whom or which we object', represents for our species a relatively new ideal. A notion like 'vengeance', as expressed for example in Mérimée's *Colomba*, represents a much older and far more common aspiration. Such ideas, indeed virtually any ideas, may be attributed 'body' — i.e., a history, a certain temporal depth or extension. An idea which one excogitates or reviews now, is indisputably a present idea. And because one knows it only in a present, one may conclude that it has no past. Yet we reflect that a text first published in 1651 or 1690 or 1748 or 1762 or 1859 or 1867

must indubitably contain past ideas. And the conclusion may somehow prompt us to imagine that, to get a purchase on those ideas, we
must escape the present; that, to understand the past, we must necessarily perceive it as different. Both conclusions − (1) that any thought
presently traipsing through a mind is an exclusively present thought,
and (2) that any genuinely past thought must be different − derive
from a certain confusion about what we mean by 'present' and 'past'.

Past and present are correlative notions. We conceive of the one as
excluding the other. If an item is past, we are tempted to view it as
dead and gone. If it is present, we have a bird in the hand. We often
find it difficult to conceive of a past idea being alive in the present,
since so blessed an event hints that this idea's day is not done − i.e. that
it is really present, not past at all. Anyone in 2051 reading a book originally published in 1651, may release a sigh of agreement; the reader,
astonished to discover such congruence after a lapse of so many centuries, may be tempted to speak of 'universal' or of 'transhistorical'
ideas or values; and yet there remains the suspicion that what is going
on in a given mind today, given that it *is* going on now, cannot quite
be what was occurring then.

To begin to sort out this difficulty, what we must reconsider are
some of the various meanings that are attributed to the 'present' − in
which, as we hypothesize, everything takes place. These different
senses of the 'present' will marry, in a mutually exclusive way, with
correlative senses of the 'past'. What we shall discover of course is that
some senses of the present actually incorporate (perfectly legitimately)
non-correlative senses of the past. For example, if one speaks of the
present as an unfolding event, perhaps a war (in its last stages, but
which could extend backwards for Six Days or Thirty Years), this sense
of the present automatically incorporates some sense of a past − in
this case of all past time traversed by the event up to a time marker
which we may dub the instantaneous 'Now!' In this sort of circumstance, it will be plain that an event, in some sense held to be 'present',
will coherently incorporate a non-correlative sense of the 'past'. In
short, although correlative senses of past and present are mutually
exclusive, it does not follow that non-correlative senses are so.

It will now be in order to inspect more closely some of the senses of
the 'present'. What we discover is that in every case but one, history is
never understood as necessarily excluding the present. Nor is the past,
in any general and encompassing sense, understood as being divorced
from the present. Nor do all languages consecrate the past-present-
future distinction as ours does. Swahili, for example, distinguishes

between past-present-future via the tense prefixes *li-na-ta*. But there are two other such prefixes, at par with these, which precisely signal continuity and duration — i.e. the *a* tense and the *me* tense— as for example in *ndege waruka* (birds fly), as opposed to *ndege wanaruka* (birds *are* flying) or as in *amefika* (he is coming and is now here) as opposed to *anafika* (he is arriving) — to use textbook examples.

3: Chronology: the Instantaneous Present

In general, our notions of time have two distinct aspects. On the one hand, we consider time as pure temporal sequence, as 'passing time', rather than in terms of what may occur within whatever sequence we demarcate. We may call this *chronological time*.

We may also consider time as an event-full sequence, as an occurrence or phenomenon which takes place, which fills up the time, and which governs chronology — rather than an abstract chronology which governs the event. We may call this *substantive time*.

Present time, then, has its chronological and substantive aspects. We shall begin with two types of chronological present. We shall then proceed to consider two types of substantive present. The first of the two types of chronological present may be called the *instantaneous* present.

The commonest — and most stringent — means of distinguishing between past and present is achieved as follows. First, we stipulate time to be represented by a three-point sequence of past, present and future; secondly, we represent the present as the middle point in this sequence; and finally, we represent this middle point as instantaneous, as what occurs . . . now. If we locate the present as that which we read or hear or say (etc.) . . . *now*, then whatever transpired or was recounted earlier in this paragraph, in this essay, in this day (and so on), is already past, is already final, is already history, including the 'now' last cited, together with the 'present' allusion to it (as soon at least as we move to consider the present parenthetical clause).

One may write a history, at least some part of a history, *in* the instantaneous present, but it is impossible simultaneously to write a history *of* it. Theoretically, the history of an instant might be written. In practice, the thing has never been done. But not even theoretically can we conceive that we may instantly record the history of the same instant through which we now live. As soon as we put pen to paper, the subject of our concern has vanished, is past.

If we write about the present, it cannot be the instantaneous present that we write about. It is none the less the case that, in the instantaneous present, we continue to write, to act, to reflect. There is then no bar to our 'doing' history in such a present. But as this history cannot, within the instant, be of itself, it must entertain as an object something other — i.e. a past.

If we wish to write a history of the present, then this sort of history we cannot write where we mean the 'present' to be instantaneous. This present is such that whatever is written or recorded within it is necessarily historical. At least this is so where we intend 'history' to signal the study of the past. In the instantaneous present, *every* object of study is 'historical'. One has no choice. The historian may well entertain an interest in past events for their own sake. He may well feel disposed to loosen the tie between past and present. But it really cannot matter. In the instantaneous present, logically speaking, nothing remains open to reflection and reconstruction except the past.

If any subject that we would write about, at the point of our writing, is necessarily already past, and thus a part of history, then no event, which it is open to us to write about, can possibly be denied to us as a subject, on the ground that to write about it will prove unhistorical. If we construe all events, at the point that we reflect on them, as historical, then we are left with no basis on which to designate some accounts as historical and others as 'unhistorical'. To enjoin writers of history to seek to be historical can only prove redundant, at least where we take the present to be instantaneous, on which reading no possible event about which we might write could prove to be other than 'past'.

If we start from the distinction between past and present which renders the latter 'instantaneous', we see that the conclusion which follows is that it is only possible ever to write about 'the past'. Accordingly, to suggest in any way that the historian *should* write about it, is superfluous.

It may of course be argued that the present, however instantaneous, remains the time-point we occupy when inspecting what we choose to call 'the past'. This would imply that the ideas we form of the past, since they only exist for us in the present, are not (properly speaking) past. But this conclusion is based upon a confusion. The ideas we *now* have of the past only exist for us in *the* present. But we have had ideas before, which existed in *a* present, a present which no longer is, and which therefore now forms a part of the past. In other words, the ideas we now have are present ideas, but in as far as they existed or were expressed before, they are properly to be called past ideas.

The reason why we are not, in this, confronted either with paradox or contradiction, is that we entertain not just one framework concept of the present, but at least two, neither of which we have so far mentioned. The first of these notions encompasses all actual consciousness, awareness, reflection, whether new or old, repeated or not, as long as it remains *actual*. This, indeed, is the most encompassing framework sense of the present we employ and it will be useful to call it 'P'. By contrast, the second of these framework concepts, simultaneously the more common and the less encompassing, is that which assumes a three-point sequence of past-present-future, in which, whatever its duration, the 'present' occupies the middle point. It will be convenient to call this less encompassing framework concept of the present, 'p'. Accordingly, if we speak of the 'present', but meaning P, and not p, then it will be clear that P deliberately ignores distinctions between past-present-future. It is precisely in this sense that we speak, without qualification, of 'eternity'. But if we speak of the 'present', now meaning p, and not P, then of course we shall confuse matters in suggesting that p also incorporates the 'past'.

If we say, 'whatever happens, happens in the present', then presumably we intend by 'present', P, if, that is, we seek to be consistent. Our trouble starts with the temporal ambiguity associated with an expression like 'whatever happens', since it may imply the specific time-marker 'now', but may equally imply an infinitive function indifferent to tense. A world leader, in his situation room, who says (just having assumed office): 'what happens here decides the fate of the world', may be talking as much about what has been the case as about what he expects to occur in future. This framework sense of the present, of a tenseless present, to be represented as P, is perfectly coherent. But it must become paradoxical where we understand it as p.

When we spoke earlier of 'present time' (p. |24), what was intended was p, not P. The instantaneous present, therefore, constitutes one sub-variety of p, i.e. p_1 The other sub-varieties of p shall accordingly be labelled p_2, p_3, p_4, and p_n.

4: Chronology: the Extended Present

That view of the present which locates it as the middle point on a time-scale, which begins with 'past' and ends with 'future' is p. On that view of the present, already discussed, where p is construed as p_1, the present is regarded as an instantaneous middle point, such that it becomes impossible for present experience, so understood, instantly and simultaneously to be written about. On the instantaneous view, what is written about always occurs *earlier* in time than the business of writing about it; thus one only writes *in* the present, but necessarily and always *about* the past.

This view of the present as instantaneous, however, is only one view. Beside it we may set another, which is perhaps quite as persuasive, and in any event a very widely held notion. This is a view which we may hold of the present as extended. The instantaneous present is the merest fraction of time and no sooner are we aware of it than it has quite slipped past us, beyond any possibility of our seizing it — save in retrospect, as something that has already happened. By contrast, the *extended* present is a concept of the present as an episode which, if not 'enduring', at least persists; it is a process in which we may be engaged, at the same time as we reflect upon and even produce accounts of it. The instantaneous present appears to defy the prospect of duration or persistence; the extended present does not. The extended present has 'body'. There is something about it we can hold onto and account for. This indeed becomes its defining characteristic: a display of body sufficient to enable one to 'seize' it, to provide an account simultaneous with one's experience of it. The longer the present, so conceived, is permitted to 'endure', the more there is to reflect upon and to write about, the more of an account can be provided. Conversely, the shorter the duration, the less there is to seize and to account for. This extended present we shall summarily label p_2.

Where we conceive ourselves to be at work within the extended present, we may posit as present virtually any period of time whatever — as long as we do not slip from the constraints of p (which keep us boxed in between some past and future) into the eternity of P (which by contrast makes us entirely tense-free). We may conceive ourselves to be locked within an extended present by reference to a great variety of chronological criteria, such as a daily or weekly or monthly or yearly or millennial, etc., cycle.

Any p_2 is coextensive with the daily or weekly or other unit of duration stipulated for it. The New Year, which has as its correlative the old year, may serve as one such unit. The old year is conceived as 'present' even if one is down to its last hour. The New Year is conceived as 'present' even if one is only into its first hour. The old year, even into its last hour, remains present — as a p_2 extending mostly backwards. The New Year, even in its first second, becomes present — as a p_2 extending mostly forward — in this case for in excess of 364 days. The extended present, then, is just a fixed period of time; within that period, all earlier and later times, whether spent or prospective, become 'present' simply by virtue of remaining within the period stipulated. Thus, when one rings in the New Year, or rings out the old, one does so by grace and favour, in this case of p_2. This extended present allows us to say 'now' to more than a moment and for longer than an instant, as when we speak of 'the present year', or of 'the present century' and sometimes of groups, reduced to a temporal measure, such as 'our generation'. The crucial consideration about p_2 is that we are able to contemplate and recount it at the same time as remaining within it.

The concept of 'the present' has, as we see, significantly different senses. It is because of these differences that we are entitled, without paradox, to say for example that 'most of the *present* year, alas, is *past*' or that 'the *present* century has only just begun and our future success [within it] is already assured'. Strictly speaking, of course, the *'present* year', taken as a case of p_2, cannot also be *'past'*. Except that the speaker here does not intend the *year* as 'past', but rather that part of the year which antedates the present conceived as instantaneous. Thus p_1 and p_2 are here being employed at the same time, without setting up (in this sort of case) the faintest ripple of confusion. But the potential for confusion is evident enough.

The present as p_2 both includes the 'past' and excludes 'it'. But it is not the same past that is both included and excluded. Where p_2 is read as 'the New Year', then the correlative past of p_2 is 'the old year': p_2 (the New Year) can never include its own correlative past, p_2 (the old year). What p_2 presumably may include is a non-correlative past, such as that which correlates with p_1. In p_1, the instantaneous present, the correlative past is all or any previous time up to the present instant. Although the meaning of p_1 cannot include this past (because it is correlative to p_1), p_2 can be said to include it (precisely because it is non-correlative to p_2). Thus only is one able intelligibly to say things such as that 'most of the *present* year, alas, is *past*'.

The instantaneous present does not *contain* any past. We know that it cannot have itself as its object. And this leads us to think that its *object* can only be the past. But the inescapable evanescence of p_1 makes it difficult to say anything further about its content at all.

The extended present, however, does contain a past. It is not merely that it takes some past as an object of attention, but also that it contains some past as a part of its present (p_2) content or meaning. It is then in this sense, for a start, that the past, certainly *a* past, can be said to exist in the 'present'. One only has to be clear about the type of present one envisages, and also that the correlative past to this particular sense of the present is excluded.

The upper and lower limits which we may fix for this extended present are almost entirely arbitrary. A p_2 can be understood as one year or less or as a thousand years or more. There are no purely chronological reasons which argue for making it one or the other.

If, however, one makes p_2 too long, one risks conflating it with P. If one makes it too short, one risks conflating it with p_1. One difficulty with any instant is, of course, its shallowness of depth: its eerie evanescence is too elusive to come to grips with. And this is one of the problems with the instantaneous present: as instant, it can have no object but the past; but by the same token, it can constitute no object of itself.

The extended present, despite its apparently arbitrary limits, can at least be the object of its own study. And that is the utility of the concept. In attempting to understand any present, we must presumably give it 'body' — which is some degree of temporal depth. When we speak of 'the' present, or of 'this' present, what we refer to, if it is to be understood, cannot simply evaporate as soon as cited. Where we slap the label, 'present', upon a length of time, it must have something to stick to. The present, understood as p, where it is to be understood at all, must be extended — hence p_2.

The problem (reverting to the extended present) is to determine by how much the present must minimally be made to stretch beyond an instant in order to become comprehensible. Despite the difficulties we confront in attempting to seize it, even an instant has duration, i.e. upper and lower temporal limits. The extended present cannot have entirely arbitrary limits, since if it did there would be nothing to stop it merging with the instantaneous present. This is the question we must now address — even as we pass over (safely enough, I think) the question how far back in time the extended present may reach, at least as long as we do not confound p_2 with eternity.

To curtail discussion of the appropriate cut-off point for the nearer limit of p_2 — this could in principle be reduced to a year, a quarter, a month, a week, a day, an hour, a minute, *seriatim*, until we approach an instant — I propose that we simply apply the simultaneity criterion. The thrust of this criterion is that p_2 must at least extend sufficiently far over time to enable any observer, whether historian, experimenter, or other, to provide an account of p_2 (e.g. the old year) while remaining within it. On this criterion, the dimensions of p_2 will necessarily vary. The only thing to be avoided is a time-unit which is insufficiently extended (taking account of available and relevant recording techniques and equipment, such as shorthand and cameras) to accommodate both an experience and an intelligible record of it. Any other conclusion that one draws, on the practical level, will prove falsely tidy. I think it worthwhile none the less to risk the falseness in the tidy by plumping for a commonsensical circadian cycle, consistent with the keeping of diaries, to represent for most purposes the lower limit of p_2.

We may say, correctly enough, that we commonly attribute to our concept of a present some body or duration, and thus conventionally allow ourselves to dilate upon this 'present' as 'history'. But having said as much, it must be clearly understood that the 'simultaneity' involved is of a kind which still in no way excludes *sequence*: the record, fashioned at a later time, has always as its object some activity located earlier in time.

When we advance to project a concept of the present as extended, it in no way implies that we have overcome the notion of temporal sequence. We can and do extend the present beyond the form it assumes as an instant; so extended we are perfectly well able to experience and to record it — 'simultaneously'. We do not in this deny that the record, in the process of being recorded, always follows, in time, that which it is its object to record. It does not follow that, in p_2, the 'simultaneity' of the present (as experience) and of history (as a record of experience) is to be regarded as unreal. In the extended present, 'simultaneity' must be defined in terms of the time-unit (the day or month or year) constituting the p_2. In p_2, accordingly, we are less to do with experience and the recording of experience being enacted *at the same instant*, than with experience and the recording of experience occurring within *the same time-span*.

The heart of the matter turns round what time-span is designated as 'present' for any given purpose. If it is an hour that we take to be 'present', then we may be later in the hour or earlier in the hour. But as it is 'the hour' which constitutes the content of the present, then whatever happens within it, happens *in* the same time, and, in this sense, *at* the same time.

Time present, taken as p, may be a day, it may be a second. We are aware that, within the day, each hour succeeds the next: here is sequence. But each fraction of a second also succeeds the next: here too is sequence. It all depends upon the fineness of our measure. The 'instant', chronologically speaking, cannot represent an absolute. Time, taken as a whole, must in principle be infinitely divisible. Time present (p) may be represented as a fraction of time $(\frac{p}{t})$, of which p_2, no less than p_1, is equally fractional and infinitely divisible. It does not therefore matter that the day is longer than the second. If it is only the *day* (as a whole) that we are talking about, as when it is only the second (as a whole) that we are talking about, then (from this perspective) everything that happens in the day or in the second happens *at the same time*.

The extended present, although it enables us, for example, to write 'current affairs' or 'contemporary history', does not for all that enable us to dispense with temporal sequence. It merely designates the duration of the units which are taken to enter into, or to constitute, any such sequence. If we take 'today' to be 'the present', and then set about counting off the passing hours, we have merely shifted from the day as the unit of succession, to the hour as that unit. And in this case it is the hour that becomes the 'present'.

Any record or reflection can always be perceived as involving activity, at a later time, adverting to activity (of some sort) at an earlier time. This is so, at least, if the unit of time chosen is small enough. For much activity, which can be so construed, i.e. as later/earlier, can also be seen, as in the case of p_2, as simultaneous. If we take a piece of writing or reflection, for example, to occur at time t, we shall conclude that the subject (the writing or reflection) cannot take itself as its own object at t. But this is only so if $t = p_1$. For a piece of writing or reflection, occurring at t, may well take itself as its own object at that time — if $t = p_2$. In short, p_2 allows for simultaneity of reflection and experience; p_1 does not. But one can always reduce a given time-span from a large p_2 to a smaller, and from this to a p_1, either of which steps may eliminate simultaneity for the unit chosen and readmit sequence.

If we are dealing with an instantaneous present, it is superfluous to recommend that historians not write about it. A present that is instantaneous can be written *in* but not *about*. In p_2, the present can be written about while lived in. Sequence in time depends upon movement across the present from past to future. If the unit of present time is a second, then the transition is instantly made. If it is a full year, then the simultaneity that was at first impossible suddenly becomes manageable. Of course, when writing about this year, what is being written about always precedes in time the process of writing about it. But we can only say this where we have ceased to focus upon the year as the governing unit of present time, contracting it to some far smaller measure, such as a minute or second.

It remains, however, when writing about the present, conceived as extended, and despite the simultaneity criterion, that it is never possible to write about it *fully* while still caught up in it. One may well write about some of the events of 1983, for example, while still alive in 1983. But to cover the *entire* time-span represented by 1983, it will be necessary to enter a time-span designated 1984 or later. Accordingly, one cannot fully write about 1983 while still alive in 1983. It is not intended by 'fully' anything impossible, but only to traverse the entire temporal range of the unit designated as 'present', which in this case is '1983'. Thus, even with the extended present, an account of any p_2 which is to cover it fully can only be completed where the agent providing it stands wholly outside the time-unit designated as present — where, in short, the present, for the historian recording it, has been turned into the past.

The point at which present becomes past is, of course, determined by the extent of the duration assigned to the former. The extended present, taking account of its duration, is necessarily confined within variable limits. Thus, if it is recommended that the historian not dilate upon the present, and this is understood as the extended present, it must remain unclear as to the precise period about which he is enjoined not to pronounce. The extended present, constituting an arbitrarily (and so variably) stipulated duration, is characterized by a peculiar problem where it is sought in some general way that historians should not write about it.

When we are told that the historian *does* not write, or *should* not write, about the (extended) present, this might mean that he does or ought not to provide an account of any of the developments of the last quarter or year or decade or century or millennium or whatever. As a general description of what historians actually do or omit, it is confused and does not help us. As a general recommendation, it is neither good nor bad, merely inapplicable. Not knowing the duration intended to be covered by such a recommendation, we could never be clear, precisely, as to the relevant point at which to bring it into force. On the face of it, there is no more reason why the present should be restricted to a year than to a decade, or to a decade instead of a century. If, after establishing a vague circadian minimum, we can only *arbitrarily* stipulate the duration of the extended present, then any recommendation that the historian should not write about it must prove equally arbitrary. Although our concept of p_2 is more helpful than that of p_1, it still does not carry us nearly as far as we require to go, and largely because of its purely chronological character. A more substantive concept is needed.

5: Substance: the Unfolding Present

We now approach a third concept of the present, p_3. This I shall refer to as the *unfolding* present. It should be clear, once attention is drawn to it, that we do not necessarily, nor perhaps usually, delineate the limits of the present purely chronologically. We are not compelled to simply dream up time-sequences, such as a week or fortnight or quarter or triennium or quinquennium, and accordingly to conceive of the duration of this 'present' as restricted in the implied degree. Where we do, the sort of present with which we are concerned is either an 'instantaneous' or an 'extended' present. But time, including present time, may be fixed by reference to criteria which are not themselves temporal.

In order to determine the duration of the 'present' or 'past', we may establish criteria which exclude the priority of time, or any fixed unit of time, and substitute for this some pre-selected set of circumstances conceived as unfolding over time. Take, for example, a footrace. It might be devised in at least two distinct ways. First, a winner might be declared to be that competitor who is ahead after the lapse of a specified period. What would control such a race as this is the notion of the expiry of an agreed temporal sequence. Alternatively, the race (as normally happens) may be devised such that the winner is he who first covers a circuit or reaches a specified terminus. What basically controls this second (and customary) sort of race is the notion of describing or completing a spatial trajectory in front of competitors, not (as in our hypothetical first race) being ahead after a specific lapse of time. Where the concern is with being first to reach the finish, however long this takes, then the governing criterion involved cannot in any significant way be temporal. This race – which is present, in being, in process, taking place – must take place *over* time, but is at no point itself directly governed *by* time.

The non-temporal criteria governing the unfolding present are highly variable. We have taken note of a species of race in which the chief governing criterion is the traverse of a determinate spatial field. But one could as readily have instanced an embrace, a quarrel, a discussion, trial, concert, tennis match; perhaps a protracted set of negotiations, a lifelong rivalry, a great depression, a world war, an attempt to control world population growth, or to develop energy resources alternative to fossil fuels. Any one of these cases presents us with an example of the unfolding present. Each one implies different (but always non-temporal) criteria for the determination of the duration of this present.

The present may be considered to evolve for so long as the embrace, match, negotiations, depression, war or whatever lasts. Since each of these cases must be governed by distinct criteria, it is neither useful nor even possible to touch upon them individually. We only require to note what it is that they have in common. What they all reflect is an attitude towards the present which characterizes or delimits it by reference to some specific event or activity which is evolving or developing or unfolding. While we conceive the event as unfolding (match, depression, war), we demarcate the time as present. But when we conceive the evolution of the event as completed, we consign the spent time which enfolds it (no matter how recent) to the past. It is in this sense that we speak of an activity or arrangement, when ended, as being 'over and done with'; and it is only in this sense that we may properly speak of the past as 'dead'. The content of the unfolding present is only transmogrified into a past when the evolutionary sequence attributed to (or assumed for) it is regarded as having reached its term. Thus, for the evolving present, the past is 'dead', but only in the sense that some action or process is seen to be completed. (But it is always essential to retain that any one process, even if completed, must always be assumed to contain others, which are not.)

When we think of the present, which we frequently do, as an evolving or unfolding present, time itself (chronology alone) is expressly excluded as the criterion by reference to which we demarcate its boundaries — which are boundaries of contemporaneity. It is with reference to the event only, and not some otherwise arbitrarily determined quantum of time, that we say in this case what is 'present'. When we fix the present in this way, we presuppose for it a beginning, middle and end. This concept of the unfolding present presupposes that we can fairly clearly demarcate a specific time as a beginning. But nothing more need be assumed, to determine the beginning of the unfolding present, than an understanding and recognition of those characteristics which mark the event itself. The determination of the completion of the occurrence (together with its initiation) is derived only from the agreed characteristics of the occurrence — not from any abstractly postulated temporal sequence. In this way, one may conceive of the present as congruent, perhaps, with one's lifetime, or with the triumph of republicanism in France, or with the global proliferation of nuclear technology, or with the continuing desiccation of the Sahara or even with the projected burning out of the sun. In none of these cases is the present conceived as an instant, nor as an extended (and already agreed) chronological sequence. The unfolding present is of course subject to chronological measurement, but its duration is determined only by the time it takes some specific event (which is its essence) to unfold.

Any given case of chronological time or substantive time may naturally coincide with the other. We may instance a second, minute, hour, day, week, fortnight, month, year, decade, century, etc. as purely temporal or chronological sequences. But whereas seconds, minutes, weeks, fortnights, decades, centuries etc. have not much to be said for them, except as perfectly abstract chronological markers, the same is not quite true for the day, the month and the year − the day roughly correlating with the turning of the earth upon its axis, the month with the waxing of the moon, and the year with the earth's circuit round the sun. In such cases as these (the day, the month, the year) we have examples of 'time' which may be intended merely chronologically ('After a year, we shall take legal measures') or by contrast substantively ('If Winter comes, can Spring be far behind?'). Though we may merge these senses of time, it is only important to retain that they are always in principle separable − the one recording the abstract passage of time, and the other being riveted upon an unfolding drama.

Like p_2, and unlike p_1, p_3 contains a past within itself. Obviously, the past which p_3 contains cannot be that which is correlative to its present. The past correlative to p_3, is the same specific event designated for p_3 where p_3 is conceived as terminated. It is also any *other* event which can be conceived as terminated by an agent located within p_3. The specific event designated as the content of p_3 cannot at the same time be terminated, although termination may be projected for it as a future possibility: this 'projected past' cannot be an *actual* past for p_3. Any other event than that specifically designated as constituting p_3, and conceived as terminated, cannot with certainty be supposed to have *no* continuing effect; it remains, after all, located within p_3. In other words, an unfolding situation, upon which a variety of apparently alien ideas or models may impinge, cannot with certainty ever be said entirely to escape the influence of such ideas and models (which is not the same as saying that all are equally 'relevant'). With p_3, accordingly, although in principle it must be held to exclude its correlative past, it is difficult to locate any *actual* 'past' that is entirely excluded. An unfolding event cannot itself be past. And any other correlative 'past', however remote, as long as it can be conceived in p_3, cannot be reliably excluded as entirely devoid of effect upon p_3, nor therefore, in this sense, as 'past' or 'dead'.

Any event, which we specify as the specific content of p_3 on a given occasion (call it ap_3), must be attributed a beginning. But, under pressure, this position will yield one more moderate, agreeing the possibility of an unlimited trace on influences: these can be chased as far back as the evidence will allow. The event ap_3 (call it the Falklands War) must also be attributed an end. Under pressure, however, this position, too, will yield somewhat, here to the consideration that no element in any event can ever be said entirely and definitively to have run its course. A beginning and end are implicit in the very idea of an event. But we may trace the causes of the 1982 Falklands War between Britain and Argentina as far back at least as 1833; and presumably its consequences — in bitterness, estrangement, destruction, and unrecuperated minefields — will reach indefinitely far into the future. These causes and consequences precede and follow the specific event, ap_3, but also form some part of it. In p_3, then, a past, in this perfectly coherent sense, always penetrates the present.

The correlative past of the unfolding present cannot speak to us and we have no access to it. The correlative past of this p_3 is strictly dead and is thus a past about which we can know absolutely nothing. It is a past which, in p_3, cannot even be formulated. In p_3, one may posit antecedents and consequents, not the simple and unquestioned 'death' of any factor of which we remain aware. In p_3 one may posit earlier or later, and also much or little relevance, but not the complete irrelevance of one to the other. Although the correlative past of p_3 is not available in p_3, other pasts are. The correlative pasts of p_1 and p_2 *are* available; they are alive and form a necessary part of the meaning of an unfolding present. An event or phenomenon, like learning from one's mistakes (and successes) only emerges as a possibility because of the interpenetration of the present and its non-correlative pasts. For p_3, only a non-correlative past is dead, not any other, and not the past as such. In p_3, the past, in several of its senses, relates to, connects with and influences the present. Tennis players and military strategists are constantly engaged in the study of earlier games or wars, with a view to learning what went wrong, or right. What they study may be earlier, even 'over' — but not past *tout court*. Past laboratory experiments may be 'over', but they would be regarded as pointless were it concluded that nothing was presently to be learned from them. How indeed is it to be imagined that there should ever be any improvement in the arts or sciences, or even survival for the species as a whole, were the past as such (here we address particularly the non-correlative pasts of p_3) really closed to us, and in this stripped of any instructive effect?

There must in principle remain many more senses than four of 'the' present. Enough has been said, all the same, to suggest something of the complexity of our ideas about present time, whether as P or p. Virtually any statement about the present must carry certain implications about the past and about the complex way in which we conceive the past. Certainly every statement about the past must presuppose 'the' present – first in the sense that a 'past' assumes *opposition* to some present, secondly, in the sense that it assumes incorporation into some other, non-correlative present, and third, in the sense that, generally, 'knowledge' of the past (we ordinarily call such knowledge 'history') is only a present knowing, grounded in presently available evidence, reasoning and conjecture. In this analysis there lies some suggestion, even demonstration, of the necessary and non-paradoxical ways in which the past penetrates, and coheres with, the present. Given that the past is, in so many ways, a necessary part of 'the' present, perhaps (in fully recognizing this) we shall be less tempted than heretofore to expect or demand that these two should in any indiscriminate sense be kept apart. Analytical or political or social or economic theory is assumed to have its past; it certainly has its history; from the point that a past is assumed, histories are sure to follow. Familiarity with history helps, in turn, to keep the *analysis* relevant. It is precisely when we cease to perceive the past as in many senses present, when we conceive it as comprehensible only in its differentia, when we cease altogether to conceive it as enduring, as germane, as a source of enrichment, that we are likely to render analysis sterile.

6: Substance: the Neoteric Present

So far we have discussed three concepts of the 'present' (p): as instantaneous (p_1) as extended (p_2), and as unfolding (p_3). Among further senses of p that might be disengaged, there is only one (p_4) of which, I believe, we require to take account. Incurring some apparent pleonastic risk, we may call p_4 the *neoteric present*.

When we say, perhaps of a fashion, that it is contemporary, we may mean not only that it is something which may be observed *in* the present, but also that it is distinctively characteristic *of* the present. On one view, whatever happens in the present *is* present. But often, as in the case of fashion, we wish to distinguish what merely *happens* in the present – which in various ways may be 'ancient', 'hackneyed', 'conventional' 'traditional' etc. – from that which is 'novel', 'innovative' and 'modern'. This contrast is constantly at work within the present. A play now being staged may be modern or ancient. A form of speech may be up-to-date, or obsolescent. A constitutional procedure may be traditional in the sense of having 'withstood the test of time'; alternatively it may be markedly innovative, having withstood little more than the experimental twists and turns of a few legal minds.

The neoteric present, then, assumes a distinction within the substantive, behavioural content of the present, as between what is new and what is recurrent (often as between present forms of behaviour alternately labelled 'modern' and 'primitive'). The notion of a 'neoteric' present fastens upon the present not (first and foremost) as a unit of time, whether as instantaneous or extended chronological sequence, or as the unfolding of some specified event.

In all concepts of the 'present' as p, p's assumed intermediacy between past and future is held constant. Beyond that, there is considerable variation between the different sub-varieties of p. The neoteric present, as suggested, is not an instant: it represents an extended period of time. Unlike p_1 or p_2, its limits (or duration) are determined by non-chronological criteria. Unlike p_3, the criterion of 'presentness' in p_4 is not just an event,but some more complex and recurrent pattern of behaviour. An event may be human (war) or natural (flood); a pattern of behaviour, by contrast, if not exclusively human, is at least only animal. An event is fairly easily singled out for attention, with its obvious and predetermined rules, traits, features; a pattern of behaviour is a more involuted way of doing things, which may be revealed repeatedly over a great number and range of specific happenings.

The neoteric present registers a concern less with any specific event, than with a complex and recurrent pattern of behaviour. It is this notion which is reflected in the inclination to perceive the present in terms of specific behaviours, fashions, outlooks, commitments, orientations; or characteristic institutions, technologies and so on. Periodization — dividing history into periods — is of course characteristic of the extended present (and of its correlative or counterpart past) where the concern is to divide time by reference to quite arbitrary temporal criteria: whence the 'quinquennium', 'decade', 'century', 'millennium' and so on. But periodization is even more characteristic of the neoteric present, where the determining criteria are less arbitrary, and are intricately behavioural. The neoteric present (and its counterpart past) is constituted of a characterization of a particular temporal sequence by reference to the recurrent, but historically distinctive, behaviours which are (or appear to be) displayed within it. Where we speak of a 'stone' or 'iron' age, of the 'middle' ages, of a 'steam' age, 'nuclear' age, a revolutionary age; of a 'time of troubles', of the *Mfecane*, of the age of the '*renaissance*', of the 'reformation'; of an age of slavery or tyranny or independence or democracy or whatever — what we are in each case referring to is a set of behaviours or practices taken (sometimes mistakenly) to be distinctively characteristic of a given temporal sequence. And this is as readily done for the chronological present as for the chronological past.

If the present is but an instant, then it is never possible to write about anything other than the past. If the present is protracted, then we can write about it while remaining within it — but only in so far as we recognize that when we write, we are always writing (later) about something which has already occurred (earlier). Also, where the present is attributed duration, there is no one, compelling, non-arbitrary criterion we may impose for determining the degree of its duration. Accordingly the limits of the present may be fixed by perfectly arbitrary chronological criteria (the 'extended' present), or by developmental criteria (the 'unfolding' present), or by behavioural criteria (the 'neoteric'present). In the two cases last cited, we are confronted with substantive, non-chronological (or non-temporal) criteria for demarcating the present. Where we demarcate the present by reference to an unfolding event, or by reference to a set of recurrent behaviours (which are regarded as distinctively contemporaneous), we are not so much measuring activity by time, but time by activity. We are not imposing a chronological sequence upon activity, and taking chronology as master of the measure; we are imposing activity upon chronology, and taking activity as arbiter of duration (and, in this case, of the duration of present time).

Where we invoke a non-chronological criterion of the present (as in the 'unfolding' or 'neoteric' present), the whole concept is built upon some assumption of the persistence of action through an infinitely divisible series of temporal loci. Earlier and later points in time are assimilated to one another by reference to some selected activity, which is assumed to persist across these points. If we take a *specific event* — such as a tennis match, a test match, a baseball 'world series', a depression, a war — what we are dealing with is activity spread out over time. The time involved (its duration) may stretch from a day to a week to a decade and more. If we take *recurrent* (but contemporaneously distinctive) *behaviours*, we are again confronted with activity spread out over time, and probably (on average) over greater periods of time. (It is to be assumed that alterations of outlook, institutions, technologies and the like normally persist for rather longer than do determinate events.) But whether we take specific events, or the persistence of recurrent behaviour, as the measure of present time, it is clear that such notions of the present refer to activities which occur or unfold across an infinitely divisible sequence of points in time.

Where we are dealing with concepts of the present which establish its duration by reference to an unfolding event or a recurrent pattern of behaviour, what we are automatically assuming is that distinct points in time, or indeed periods of history, are not (and cannot be) significantly unique simply by virtue of representing such distinct points or periods. The distinctions between these points in time, or periods in history, follow only — as in the neoteric present — from the positing of a unity of action or behaviour across distinct temporal loci. A neoteric or unfolding present is posited only where the persistence of coherent behaviour across time is assumed; and it is only this assumed persistence which generates the delimitation of distinct points in time, or temporal sequences, or periodization.

Of course it is normally assumed that every 'period' is distinct from every other, perhaps 'unique' *par rapport* with every other. It is a claim, moreover, which we must sympathetically consider. But what is often ignored is the criteria we are permitted to entertain for establishing the bounds of a 'period'. Certainly, if the criterion is substantive or non-chronological, as in the neoteric present, the omission is monumental. For if the duration of the period — present or other — is determined by reference, for example, to the persistence of a pattern of behaviour, then such a period, if 'unique', is from the start unique only on the basis of a comparison between behaviours spread out over a vast number of (different) points in time. The uniqueness of a distinct period, in short — following non-chronological concepts of 'present' and 'past' — does not spring from the fact that it is located at some distinct point in *time* (for it is in fact spread over an *infinity* of points in time) but from the fact that it betrays distinct and divergent *activities* or *behaviours* (which, incidentally as it were, are restricted to some roughly determinate duration). Any periodization, thus come by, represents a duration far more substantial than an instant; the determinant of the duration is the activity, not any abstract notion of time itself. And such periodization necessarily presupposes comparison — and thus continuity — across a lengthy sequence of distinct temporal points.

The prejudice which supports the notion of historical uniqueness is, it would appear, basically that: *prejudice*. But the prejudice is understandable, in so far as the skeleton of supportive argument can be detected. That is to say, it seems plainly true that what happens at an earlier point in time cannot be quite the same as what happens at a later point in time — for these two points in time are themselves (and necessarily) different. If a part of the character of an event is the time at which it occurs, then the conclusion for uniqueness is dramatically demonstrated.

This then is valid enough: What happens at time t_1 can never be exactly the same as what transpires at t_2 — for the simple reason that t_1 and t_2 are different. It is only important to see, however, that the force of this argument is purely temporal or chronological. Any event which occurs at an earlier time *will* necessarily differ from any which supervenes later — but the only necessary difference is chronology itself, nothing else. It cannot be maintained that a difference in temporal location *necessarily* matters in other respects. We cannot maintain that any given difference in time creates an exactly proportionate difference in activity or behaviour. There is no such correlation. It is perfectly meaningful to say, for example, that fishing techniques for a given people are exactly the same at t_1 as at t_2. (The interval covered by those points may be one year or one hundred years.) If we select for such techniques, and engage in periodization on the basis of these, we shall not necessarily discover that changes in behaviour strictly coincide with some fixed chronological progression.

It is said of a subsistence people of the Andaman Islands, the Onges, that they have no tomorrow, nor any means of measuring time. Probably this is not quite so. All peoples measure time minimally by the rising and setting of the sun, or by the waning or waxing of the moon, or by the changing of seasons, a phenomenon apparent under every latitude. It is none the less so that no individual is ever involved in the business of counting time always; there are times when everyone 'marks' time; and this is only to say that on occasion (at least) one takes no notice of it. There are at least two ways of ignoring time. The first is when one is lost in reverie. The other is when one 'measures' time only by reference to what happens within it. (This covers both the unfolding present and the neoteric present.) But to measure time only by reference to the activity that fills it is none the less to have a concept of time — one which ignores mere chronology. Suppose us to encounter a people who have little or no sense of *pure* chronological progression; who are not governed by clocks; who characterize past and present essentially (which is in no way historically uncommon) by reference to the distinct occurrences or behaviours which are regarded as differentiating them; but who, moreover, do not imagine earlier times to have been very different from their own; and who, earlier in time, did not in fact instance activity or behaviour very different from their contemporary activity and behaviour. In these circumstances, there will be no marked contrast entertained by such a people between past and present. The reason will be that, measured by substantive behavioural criteria, the contrast is not in fact very great.

One might speak of such a people as entertaining an enveloping view of the present. If so, they reflect a no less enveloping view of the past: the persistence of standard behaviours and practices makes it difficult, on any substantive criteria, to establish a marked difference. It is misleading to speak of such a people as devoid of 'a sense of history'. Less theatrically and more precisely, their chronological history is marked less by substantive change than by continuity. Whether substantive continuity is to be viewed as good or bad is subject to endless dispute. But if one chooses to think it bad, one cannot hold by way of explanation to the misplaced notion that no 'sense of history' is as yet in place. All that matters is that one avoid reducing the notion of 'little or no substantive change over a given chronological trajectory' to the notion either of 'having no history' or of 'having no *sense* of history'.

The past, then, may be — and often is — distinguished from the present not by reference to chronology ('the passage of time') but by reference to significant and substantive changes in behaviour and activity. Where there is great substantive change, the duration of the chronological 'present' may be severely circumscribed. Where there is little substantive change, the 'present' may assume more encompassing chronological dimensions. What is clear is that the assertion of persistent, substantive, behavioural identity over distinct temporal zones is perfectly intelligible. At least it is so in principle. It cannot follow that any particular assertion of persistence will necessarily be correct. But it is equally apparent that it will not necessarily be incorrect. To recognize that different historical periods are only necessarily different in time, does not convert the 'uniqueness' principle into a mistake. It only highlights its triviality. The notion of the uniqueness of the past is most impressive where it suggests that the substantive *behaviour* of the past (by virtue of being chronologically past) is consequently and necessarily unique. But such a conclusion, as indicated, is false. A progression in time necessarily means that any later event is later *in time*. But it cannot mean that it is necessarily different *in substance*. In expressing approval of a performance, audiences today, as hundreds of years ago in many places, may still clap loudly with their hands. The passage of time does not of itself necessarily alter the behavioral content of the act. One's manner of hunting, fishing, speaking, rearing and so on may remain much the same, whether over a year or a thousand years. Substantive procedures or norms may persist in a very similar fashion over considerable stretches of time. On the other hand, they may change radically and swiftly. (And this latter condition, as A.N. Whitehead observed at Harvard in 1925, is peculiarly characteristic of the West in the post-nineteenth-century period.)

We cannot merely assume that every period *is* (non-trivially) different from every other, most especially where we are dealing with a neoteric present (with its counterpart past). Periods necessarily differ in temporal location, but not necessarily in activity or behaviour. Where there is little change (as we are disposed to say) 'time stands still'. Of course, if we circumscribe a period by reference to the activity or behaviour which is thought to differentiate it from earlier periods, it automatically follows that one period will (necessarily) differ from another. But in such a case, the criterion for periodic differentiation is activity or behaviour, not time. Thus the determination of the duration of a 'period' often or usually follows on from the determination of the persistence or lapse of some specified activity or behaviour. The 'period' is automatically assumed to cover a vast number of points in time. In making of these a temporally coherent unit, i.e. a 'period', we assert either a continuation or similarity of activity or behaviour or outlook or style or ideas for the duration stipulated.

7: The Past: Identity and Comparison

It is not possible to maintain that 'history is a world from which identity has been excluded' nor that 'the institution of comparisons and the elaboration of analogies are activities which the historian must avoid if he is to remain an historian' (Oakeshott, 1933, pp. 167-8). Suppose we take a view of the present as 'unfolding' or as 'neoteric', together with counterpart (or corresponding) views of the past. A view of the past as 'unfolding' must clock certain developments (a match, a blockade, a war) up to the point where they end. A counterpart view of the 'neoteric' present — call it the 'démodé past' — must recount certain behaviours (e.g. a leadership style or battle formation) perhaps up to the point where (from a present perspective) they become obsolete or inoperative. On either of these views of the past, it has duration. The duration which it has is circumscribed (and so determined) not by the mere passage of time, not by mere chronological 'pastness', but by the sum of points in time required for a particular process to draw to a close or to be superseded by some other. The condition for being an historian in such a case as this must necessarily consist in being able to compare activities or behaviours over distinct temporal periods. If the past is held to be characterized by behaviours that are no longer present, this can only meaningfully be maintained on the basis of some explicit or implicit comparison with behaviours which are present. If the comparison disengages a difference, then we have in this a substantive distinction between past and present. But just to be able to compare always assumes, at some more fundamental level, a continuity, and even – if one likes – an 'identity'. Where the chief criteria for distinguishing between past and present – as when we employ concepts of an unfolding or neoteric present, together with their counterpart pasts – become, not the dreary ticking of a clock, not the bare succession of second upon second, but, rather, altered activity, behaviour, institutions, then the entire exercise, the establishment of this great divide between periods, can be seen to consist in an irremediably comparative exercise, the upshot of which is a mutual and unavoidable hingeing of past upon present. We may well insist upon the past as entirely alien, but then this is a past that we can never know nor comment upon in any way whatever. The past that we do know, which is aptly styled 'history', is only conceivable on the basis of comparison and interpenetration with the present: no bounds could be set to it without such comparison.

We may well insist upon the unique, the distinctive, the incomparable character of the past. But the 'past', while always suggesting a point in time anterior to some 'present', is distinguished from the present according to different (and inconsistent) criteria. If the present is 'instantaneous', then its counterpart past is all antecedent time. On this view, we are always forced back upon the past, and can never talk about the present, in such a way as to compare it to the past. The consequence must be that it is pointless and inconsequential for us to view this past as 'unique', 'incomparable' or whatever. If the past that absorbs us is the counterpart to the instantaneous present, it is effectively all in all: far too encompassing to be captured by such feeble phrases.

If, by contrast, the present is 'extended', and is assigned duration by reference to purely arbitrary chronological criteria – as for a week, fortnight, quarter, semester, triennium, decade, century and so on – then there will be an illimitable profusion of past times (such as the 'sixteenth' century or the 'seventeenth'). A history of nineteenth-century philosophy covers a period that endures *chronologically* for a time equal and thus identical and thus comparable to any similar operation performed on 'the twentieth century'. On this most elementary of levels there is comparability. Every specific concept imposes a framework and creates a basis for comparison. Any given assumption of continuity may of course be misplaced. We may find equally misplaced assumptions of periodic uniqueness. Simply because periods are chronologically differentiated, it does not follow (as already indicated) that they are substantively or behaviourally different, or that such differences accord with the chronological units designated.

If the present is evolving, then the counterpart past has 'evolved'. If the present is 'in process', then the past is a process that is spent. On this view, the present is present by reference to some activity that is unfolding, and the past is past by reference to some activity that is terminated. But on this view of the 'present', one will almost unavoidably — and simultaneously — occupy more 'presents' than one. Suppose the unfolding present is identified with reference both to a depression and a war, but where the depression is 'bottoming out' and the martial indulgence is just beginning to 'hot up'. The end of one case of an unfolding present would, in this circumstance, overlap with the beginning of another. These two constitutive elements of the unfolding present (there will, simultaneously, be very many more) overlap and are not congruent. This must mean that the unfolding present, if defined simultaneously in terms of more than one evolutionary process (which is what we would expect), can have no single pair of temporal bounds, but a plurality of these. And if this is so for the unfolding present, it must equally apply to its counterpart past. In these circumstances, the overall criterion for demarcating past from present will never be entirely clear. Suppose Stalin, perhaps, simultaneously to have identified the unfolding present with the invention of writing and with the triumph of communism. The one criterion would take the present back by as much as 6,000 years, the other only 60.

The present, to be understood at all, must have body. The corollary to this notion is (broadly put) that any 'past', if it is to be seized, must enter the present — in at least one of its different senses. What occurred in the past is trivially, i.e. temporally, non-identical with what is occurring now. But if the past is conceived as *wholly* different from the present, then we are left with no means of presently making sense of it. If the 'war', 'famine', 'pestilence', 'depression', 'civil war', 'inflation', and so on of a past cannot be captured by concepts presently intelligible, then this 'past' is quite closed to us — it must, beyond doubt, remain beyond understanding. The condition for there being a past to which we can attest consists in the latter (a) being, in principle, assimilable – not strictly speaking to *the* present – but to *a* present, and (b) in this past being non-correlative to the present through which it surfaces.

8: History as Past and Present

History, where conceived as some particular species of reflection, some given set of ideas, is always present reflection, always some present set of ideas. Thus the historian, where we take him to be reflecting upon the past, is naturally and always reflecting in the present – or at least in a time zone which is 'present' for him. History, or what we know to be history, is always part of some present. History, of course, always adverts to the 'past', but this in turn can only constitute a particular ordering of present ideas. The history that we know is not and cannot be past experience itself. Such experience is by definition 'past' – out of reach. It can, equally naturally, be said that we *do* know past experience, but only in the sense that this part of what we presently know we choose, for reasons however good or bad, to call 'past'.

To say that historical study or writing, at the time it transpires, is a present activity, is to talk – unless we are talking about Eternity – in such a way as automatically to presuppose a chronological dimension, the category of time. The reflection involved in historical study or writing may well be present, but to say as much straightaway implies a distinction between this 'present', on the one hand, and a 'past' and 'future', on the other. This tripartite distinction corresponds well enough to what we know, or to what we think we know, based upon our experience of such phenomena as night and day, the succession of the seasons, and diurnal traffic jams. The only difficulty, if indeed it is a difficulty, is that we never actually occupy a past or future; we only occupy different varieties of present time: and so, however much we move about within and agitate it, whether as toddlers or nonagenarians, we do not escape the present.

It is in the above sense that history, taken as something we do or think about, is always a present activity. But it does not follow, given the chronological presuppositions from which we cannot escape, that that is all that history is about. It is always present in so far as we are thinking about it, or writing it (now). But this very activity, overwhelmingly present as it is, necessarily posits something else as the object of its concern. What historical reflection presupposes, as present activity, is past activity both similar to and different from itself. History is always present, then. but only in the sense that historical reflection is always reflection *in* the (or a) present. What does not follow is that the supposed *object* of this reflection is also present. It is of course present in the elementary sense that evidence for it is now, at the point of being reflected upon, *available*. But this is not to say that presently available evidence for a past event is the same thing as the past event itself. Of course we are never able to seize a past event 'itself', or a past thought 'itself'. We may offer opinions, press arguments, present evidence. But such activity is at best approximative, hypothetical. We may well believe that A murdered B, and have good reason for it. But the 'reason' is always that — and is never to be construed as amounting to more than a present reading of available evidence. History is not *simply* the present. If it were, we should not call it history. History is seized, grasped, intuited, understood *in* the present. But it is present reflection whose object is to portray and explain the past — a past which by definition cannot be re-entered. The past as such we have no evidence for; we never seize nor know the 'past' itself as such. The past, strictly speaking, is never seen, but only assumed, and such evidence as we have in the present may be set out in accordance with this assumption.

Reading and writing about history are — as they take place — 'present' events. History itself, despite the fact that it projects the past as its object, is a present event. 'History' can never be equated with the actual 'past'; it is only a 'record' or 'evidence' of, or an hypothesis about, the past. History is certainly written in and by the present; thus there must inescapably be some reflection of the present, if only a perspective, in what is written about the past. But the claim that the past *is* the present will not quite do. No more than will the claim that what *is* true is what we *think* to be true.

The sort of problem with which one has to cope in all this is, none the less, understandable enough. No problem comparable to time displacement arises, for example, in spatial displacement. We may live in Atlanta and doubt the existence of Vladivostok. Yet it is at least possible (in principle) to make our way from the one to the other, and *à vue d'oeil* (so to speak), surrender our doubts to that heaven to which troubled thoughts ascend. But however much we move from Atlanta to Vladivostok, we are never conceived to move out of the present, whether into a past or future. However sure I may be that I travelled to the other city; however much evidence I may tender in the form of tickets, stickers and stories; however numerous may be those witnesses who will vouch for my departure, exposure and return — there remains one thing that I cannot do, which is directly to journey back to the event, or bring it forward into the present. The indifferent observer cannot attend me while I rerun the experience and thus does he find it impossible – in the most direct of senses – to *see* that what I say is true. There is, in short, no way of directly salvaging what we experience as the past, whether to bring it forward to us, or project ourselves backwards into it.

Danto (1965, pp. 81-2, 84) seems to imply that scepticism about the existence of the past (or duration) is exactly parallel to that about space (or extension). By the example I provide, it will be clear that I take a different view. Certainly existence implies both duration and extension. Of course the tenability of duration and/or extension can be challenged – but not convincingly. None the less, it does not appear that the problem of defending against scepticism in the one case provides an exact parallel to the problem which obtains in the other. When one says one did something at an earlier point in time, it may well be possible to establish that what one says is true, although never by literally reconstructing and – as it were – re-entering the event itself. But when one declares that one building or one city is at some given remove from another, one's interlocutor does not in principle require either testimony or witnesses to decide whether what one says is true. He need only pace off or otherwise measure the distance for himself.

When we talk or read or think about the past, we take the concept of a past – and the implied notion of duration – for granted. We have no choice. It is never a particular account of the past that we must take on trust, but the concept of a pact *per se.* Any particular account will be subject to the rules of evidence which must apply in distinguishing between true and false assertions about the past. Such accounts, within these evidential limits, are ever subject to dispute. And the historian has no specially privileged access; he is neither oracle nor deity; he is no better able, in the strict sense, to re-enter the past than his readers. His advantage, in principle, lies only in a greater command of the evidence (not of the *past* as such) and perhaps greater skill (or fuller briefing) in arguing his case. The vital point is that the positing of a past, where this involves some notion of duration, and irrespective of whether we assume change or constancy, is not to be avoided. We cannot posit a past without assuming a present. We cannot assume past or present, change or constancy, without assuming duration. And indeed, without some assumption of duration, we cannot posit any species of existence. Existence implies duration, as does any form whatever of causal explanation. Thus although we only have evidence *for* a past (being one thing or another), and can never directly test assertions about it (as we can in principle with assertions about spatial extension), it is not possible for us to speak sensibly and intelligently about existence or causality without positing some such notion. In this sense, historical knowledge is a crucial component of any knowledge. But given that it projects a non-recuperable temporal dimension, it is proved doubly conjectural.

The past is only to be understood through the present; but, *in* the present, we can have no *direct* experience of the past. We shall have *memories* of what we take it to have been and *evidence* for what we suppose it was, but nothing more. Memory and evidence exist in the present. But memory becomes unintelligible if taken severely as memory of itself; present evidence becomes absurd where exclusively construed as evidence *for* the present. Memory is to be conceived as memory of a past; present evidence is consistent with the supposition of a past. Memory serves as an equivalence, not for what *is* taking place, but as a present account of what may have occurred. We must recognize historical reflection always to be present — at the point engaged in. We must recognize too that in retrojecting the object of such reflection into the past, we simultaneously accept that we are forever denied direct access to it. This is not the same as to say that we have no idea about it as past. For if we had *no* idea, there could, equally, be no problem. We have memories, we have documents, we have various evidences. But evidence for an event is not itself the event. And so there must always abide a discrepancy between the past that we assume, and the evidence — as presently available — which we display in support of it.

In as far as we have any knowledge of the past, the past must be rendered present. This rendering is what we call 'history', and because it supplies only a part of the past, and because the past as such cannot in any event be directly re-entered, historical knowledge is always perforce conjectural. History — taken as record, chronicle, conjecture — is always present.

The present, accordingly, must not be conceived as barring access to the past. On the contrary: without the present we are necessarily denied access of any kind — even of the conjectural variety presently available, conjecture which we are too often emboldened to equate with certifiable knowledge of the past *per se*. No 'reconstruction' of the past, after all, is ever literally that; it is an essay in the formulation of a truth. The impediment to be removed is not a present perspective, which is literally inescapable, but a false or inappropriate perspective, whether assignable to the past or present.

9: Chronology and Substance

Every writer, even when immersed in fiction, is also something of an historian. Every being who entertains any notion of personal or corporate identity incorporates into that identity an historical dimension — a concept of duration. Since we must face the *general* inescapability of history, we must recognize, too, that it cannot, in any *general* sense, prove irrelevant. This is especially true in regard to that view of history which conceives it to do with the counterpart past to the instantaneous present. Any actual event which we may recount, allude to or reflect upon, is already, at the point that we do these things, an historical phenomenon. The central consideration is that recounting or alluding or reflecting, at the point it actually takes place, is present, not past. An agent must decide at that point how it will be done, indulged, pursued. And, for the agent, decision and orientation and commitment cannot be recycled and revivified as something which they are not, namely, as the past or an action completed or a thing *done* — as opposed to a potential presenting itself as something *that has to be done*. Past and present are continuous, as are fact and value, history and philosophy, but in each case the one is not to be reduced to, or explained by, the other.

If every actual event we write about is necessarily past (as in the instantaneous present, and its counterpart, call it the 'enveloping' past) then the concern to keep the present out of the past, or to have historians *qua* historians isolate themselves from the present, is necessarily misplaced. The recommendation is not one that can be acted upon. In so far as the historian writes about actual events, he *can only* write about events that have already occurred, that are instantly located within the past. He may, on this view, write *in* the present, but not *of* it; for when he turns his hand to this, the present about which he would write is already past. If we distinguish between past and present as, respectively, instantaneous and enveloping, then we shall see that it cannot be that there was ever a history of actual events written which could possibly have failed to be *historical*.

We have indicated that some contemporary writers are much concerned that historical writing should remain historical, intending that it is improper for the present to impinge upon the past. But we have also suggested, invoking one set of matching notions of present and past, that the sort of miscegenation feared cannot occur anyway.

If the past does not begin . . . *now*, marching backwards, unendingly, then where does it begin? We might say, as do governments in respect to delimiting access to archival materials, that the past does not begin from *now*, but from 100 or 50 or 20 or 5 years ago – or begins indeed at whatever point in time that takes the fancy (or suits the interests) of those who decide these matters. And depending upon the decision taken at a given time, or in a given country, historians will be presented with deeds of title to appropriate stretches of the 'past'. This concept of the past we might call 'extended', by contrast with the first, which we called 'enveloping'. Both are purely chronological. We use different concepts of the past of course on different occasions and to serve different purposes. The enveloping past is one both recent and distant. The extended past is one that may be either recent or distant, as when we refer to the 1970s on the one hand or the fifth century BC on the other. The past where defined as recent or distant can only be so defined according to the tastes of those involved, which is to say by reference to their canons of relevance.

The past, like the present, has both chronological and substantive dimensions. The purely *chronological* perspective mechanically locates some events closer to us *in time* than others – as when we say that Christ was born about 2,000 years ago or that Magna Carta was devised approximately 800 years ago. The *substantive* perspective, by contrast, operates in terms of persistence, duration, influence, causality, recurrence and even injunction – as when it is claimed that the Divinity (of 2000 years ago) should be worshipped (now) or that political rights (of some kind – retrojected to an origin 800 years back) should be defended or extended (now). We may see that what is reckoned to be chronologically distant may prove substantively proximate. A present awareness of historical events, or the contemporary operationalization of hoary maxims and practices, without taking these matters out of the chronological past, does insert them into the substantive present. And the implication of this must be that the substantive past does not positively correlate with the chronological past. Thus an event which we adjudge to have transpired some time ago is not necessarily to be accorded less substantive relevance or contemporaneity than last year's drought in Australia or the outcome of yesterday's footrace in Athens, Ohio. What happened a chronological century ago will not necessarily, today, belong exclusively to 'another age'. Difficulties constantly arise regarding how deeply buried the 'past' really is – or (alternatively) how inextricably embedded it is in the present. What is certain is that the substantive and chronological pasts do not coincide and are not to be conceived as correspondingly distant from the present.

We have suggested, on the one hand, that there is nothing easier to do than disentangle past from present, since a precise criterion is ever available to serve this purpose. But we have also suggested that the influence of the past is suffused throughout the present, pointing to the contrary conclusion that distinguishing between them cannot really be so easily accomplished. Both positions are correct. And this can only mean that they are not really 'contrary'. The past is chronologically everything which accumulates backwards from the now. But the influence of the past, the substantive past, necessarily survives into the present. This substantive past is not uniform as between all societies, nor between the different components of the same society. The past is not present.But no present is entirely divorced from or uninfluenced by the past. The past is not *chronologically* present. But there is no escaping the fact that much of it is *substantively* so. It is only from the substantive perspective that one may remark that the past remains alive in the present. There are vast stretches of the chronological past which remain dead for us (whether forever or not is a different matter) simply because we have no consciousness of them. But the saint, politico, executive or writer (at work in the present) is nothing without a memory, even if only a memory of linguistic conventions, and memory is but a record of past activity or reflection or conclusions. It is therefore the substantive, not the chronological, past which is necessarily suffused throughout the present.

From the perspective of the instantaneous present, there is no actual event we can recollect or write about which is not historical (in the chronological past). From the same perspective, there is no historical event which we can recollect or write about other than in the present. The condition for writing about any aspect of the past is that we survive into the present. The present, 'the now', may as easily be filled by reflecting upon the Book of Genesis, by bathing in the waters of the Pacific, or by landing on the Moon. 'Now' is logically and necessarily distinct from 'then' in chronology only. 'Now' is only accidentally distinct from 'then' in content or substance. In the chronological present we may fill our minds with different concerns. What we fill our minds with will depend upon an interplay between personality and opportunity (perhaps an opportunity represented by fields filled with rattlesnakes, or libraries lined with books). The doing of anything requires perspective, while serious and sustained 'thinking' is in this respect perhaps the most demanding of all 'doings'. The historian certainly requires perspective, but it is important to see that he is only one species of thinker, while no thinker, serious or otherwise, can do what he does if cut off from the substantive past. It is only by being mired in the chronological present that one can revel in the substantive past. And the substantive past is almost everything one might think about or puzzle over or work upon in the present. Indeed, it is and has to be present. We can only put it down as 'past' by counting off its chronological distance from the present, or by assessing its degree of irrelevance (*qua* style, tradition, behaviour, etc.) *vis-à-vis* contemporary concerns, interests, or commitments.

There can be no perception of the past as past other than in and from time present. The content or substance of the 'past' is nothing more than the content or substance of the present, but (1) rearranged in terms of a time chart or (2) ordered by reference to some imputed degree of irrelevance or insignificance – and usually both. The *conditio sine qua non* of an awareness of the past as past is the existence of the present. The present is not only a condition for the perception of the past, but an eternal opportunity, too, for seizing and appraising it in novel ways. The chronological past can never be reproduced. But with the substantive past, there is never anything else one can do. Whether or not new factual components surface, new ways of assembling these components are enduringly on offer. And the historian, along with the rest of us, cannot refuse. The present will continually disgorge new ways of viewing the past, further factual components to be incorporated into it, and new techniques (like carbon-dating and computerization) to aid and abet those whose professional purpose it is to 'recapture' the infinity of past time (in its substantive aspect). The present can never be denied the potential for harbouring additional evidence or new methods of investigation or simply new perspectives on both evidence and methods.

There can be no complete or finished or definitive history. Such history as is written can only be partial, incomplete, even tentative. No study even of a limited period can actually exhaust that period. The writer, consciously or otherwise, is always governed by his inadequacy (and usually, too, of course by a *sense* of his inadequacy). The historian does not attempt to study 'the past' as such. He only concerns himself with those stretches of it – and from such perspectives – that interest him. He may have consciously formulable reasons for his interest (as because he thinks the period really important or merely because it is a manageable subject for which research funds happen to be available). It is equally possible that he may be quite unable to formulate any reasons for his interest at all. But in the degree that no coherent perspective is imposed upon historical data, we may suppose it will prove incoherent in proportionate degree. In short, historical writing is always selective. Were it not, it would merely prove unintelligible. The past then neither is nor can be presented 'pure'. It is not only mediated through present perspectives but it is also embodied in them.

The past is never exclusively past, and the historian cannot in part avoid the 'anachronism' of assimilating past to present. One must of course concede the obvious: which is that the chronological past cannot but be past, that the actual sequence of events is unalterable, that time is non-reversible. But we must also concede what may be less obvious: which is that the past cannot be inspected at all except through some lens (there are many) of the present, that present perspectives are not optional in historical writing, and that they impose upon the past something (an orientation) which is not actually *in* the past. A writer, for example, who wishes to show that John Locke was governed by hidden assumptions wholly alien to contemporary exegetes, in this rivets upon the historical figure in question a characteristically contemporary orientation. That is to say, he draws attention to those facets of Locke's work which render the latter least relevant to certain contemporary concerns, from which approach is abstracted the more general principle that such a procedure is the most fruitful to be applied in the history of ideas.

It is perfectly in order that we should deplore so narrow, parochial and even (at times) self-righteous an orientation. But it would never be right to deplore it on the grounds that it is 'anachronistic' or 'unhistorical'. No writer who aims to speak to the future, which is to say (almost literally) beyond the grave, can logically expect to be judged by standards peculiar only to his own time.

10: The History of Ideas

We may assume that history is somehow to do with the 'past'. And when we speak of history alternatively as governed by laws or by accident, as instancing universals or particulars, as consisting of unique or recurrent events, as being like or unlike science, as being displayed in encompassing narrative or brittle factuality (and so on) it is always understood that we are somehow making assertions about the 'past'.

We may, of course, have histories of anything — including history itself. Not least important, we may have histories of ideas. Just as we may have histories of politics, so may we have histories of ideas about politics. If questions may be raised about the appropriate method or methods to be adopted in the writing of political, economic, military, scientific and other forms of institutional history, it will be clear that such questions may be raised with equal or greater force in relation to the history of philosophy. And any history of ideas, in its most significant dimensions, is effectively reducible to a history of some branch or aspect of the history of philosophy. As regards the history of philosophy, observers may urge us to direct attention essentially to the great texts, or alternatively to reconstruct the intricate contexts out of which these texts emerge. We may be advised to be faithful only to the past, or alternatively to seek after those contemporary lessons which the past may teach. Perhaps we shall be urged to make sense of the way in which we have come to think as we now do – even to pursue solutions to contemporary difficulties. Such approaches as these may be combined in a virtually illimitable number of ways.

Much of what is said about the writing of history, and particularly the history of ideas, assumes a concept – the 'past' – which requires closer inspection. Otherwise, any recommended method for writing about 'it' will not only begin, but also end, in confusion. One might begin by inspecting directly different concepts of the past. This task I am content to leave to others. For present purposes it must suffice basically to draw attention, as has been done, to different varieties of 'present' time. In any event, all concepts of 'the past' are drawn in opposition to some one or more concepts of present time while equally being conceived as integral to non-correlative senses of the present. (Thus an unfolding war – a case of $\dot{p}_3$ – has depth, or duration, and, accordingly, earlier and later phases. Any earlier phase is 'past', and yet remains a part of this unfolding present, but only because the sense in which it is past is non-correlative to the concept of present time (p_3) here being instanced.)

The problem of reconstructing past arguments is an enduring one. We have already observed that the substantive past cannot be entirely divorced from the present, and thus that a methodology which would recommend this must be misconceived. At the same time, the perception of what happened in one mind, or time, may be distorted by confounding it with what happened in some other mind, or at another time. It is only important to see that eliminating this sort of distortion in no way depends upon erecting a massive logical breakwater between the substantive past and the present. The basic problems involved in historical distortion, are not to do with confounding past and present, are not to do with chronological reversals ('reading history backwards'), but merely to do with an inadequate grasp of a particular occasion, and its corollary, which is the confusion of distinct occasions.

In seizing a particular event, or a particular proposition, one may easily misapprehend it in a variety of ways. One may mistranslate and misinterpret, as has been observed. When we attempt to assess a philosophical argument, the fact that it has already been argued automatically renders it an historical phenomenon. Conceived as a philosophical phenomenon, the proposition may be assessed in terms of logical cogency. Conceived as an historical phenomenon, it may be assessed in terms of the circumstances in which, and the reasons for which, it was enunciated. If we seek to reconstruct the event or the proposition in terms of its meaning, then 'meaning' is potentially ambiguous since it may be construed to refer either to the matter of cogency or to the matter of circumstantial reasons for uttering it – or to both. It is true that a proposition (by itself) is open to variable interpretation and that to understand it, as an historical event, is in part to reconstruct the concrete social presuppositions upon which it rests. But it is also true that such reconstruction, taken *au pied de la lettre*, cannot fail to sink into an infinitely regressive pursuit.

There can be nothing wrong, of course, with attempting to secure a better purchase on a writer's meaning by exploring his circumstances, psychology and the like. In mining any vein, it is difficult to know when one will strike it rich, so to say. But there can equally be nothing wrong with attempting to recapture this meaning by exploring the logic of the author's formulae. I suspect that it is the latter orientation which should take priority. There is always the risk, in exploring an author's reasoning,that we may simply confound his with our own. But there is no reason to be unduly fearful of such an outcome. For it is clear, in view of the impossibility of our ever placing a limit on the regressive inspection of context and circumstance, that we are never able to put ourselves in a position where we can claim, without cavil, that we really have, completely and entirely reliably, recovered the given author's actual 'historical' meaning.

It is reasonable enough to suppose that thinkers address themselves to audiences. It is doubtful as to how much can be learned by insisting that these audiences are of some specific and limited kind, unless this is somehow (and plainly) revealed by the thinker himself. Social thinkers are almost always concerned to recommend that some specific action be undertaken. Where they become major figures in the history of ideas, however, they are normally far more concerned to *explain* the logic of concepts and the character of social activity. Where the thinker makes a singular and specific recommendation, such as to overthrow or preserve a particular government, much is presupposed about a local situation which the exegete of a successor generation must lay bare. But where the thinker is concerned, by contrast, with the logic of a concept or with understanding social activity or some aspect of it, the need is usually less pressing. The problem is that too many observers appear disposed to think that social thought, such as political theory, is merely to do with recommending behaviour. Some of it always has to do with this. But it may be that such recommendations are of least interest to later students precisely because they are so time-bound. The methodological recommendation that we exhaust ourselves reconstructing the context, conceived somehow to lie outside the simple text, is probably inspired by the thought that we should only inspect a theory from the perspective of the (usually limited) discrete recommendations that may be unobtrusively embedded within it, rather than from the perspective of methodology, logical analysis, and powers of descriptive generalization (which normally comprise its most important historical elements).

It has been observed that (some) words, over time, change their meanings, and thus that one had best be careful not to suppose that they always mean the same thing. This is true enough. But we may equally observe that (some) words, over time, also preserve their meanings, and thus that one had best be careful not to imagine that there is not or cannot be continuity. Words may change their meaning over time, but they may equally change their meaning over space. The word 'entrée' in France means 'main course', but,in Australia, it means 'first course'. And just as the meaning of words may change over time and space, so they may *persist* over the same continua. The reference to geography is only intended to emphasize a small but significant point: that change of meaning is not exclusively or even most importantly a function of chronological time.

Without any reference to time at all, we may safely state that words are often used differently (*tout court*). This is no more exclusively a problem for historical than for any other species of analysis. When the Anglican minister (from the pulpit) urges that we 'love' our neighbour, it is obvious that he means something different from what is intended when, on honeymoon, in the bridal chamber, lights extinguished, he solicits the 'love' of his spouse. Words *are* used in different ways. But that is a general problem, not an exclusively historical problem, and context is the crutch of understanding which any text, however limitedly, will itself hold out to us.

A connected argument in part creates its own context; or better, it in part constitutes its own context. No serious historical argument takes place *sui generis*. The fact that it is serious suggests that it refers to other events, assumptions, or points of view which are, all the same, not actually and fully and directly, stated in the text itself. Nor does any serious analysis of such a text presuppose that it is *sui generis*, entirely detached from its environment, such that it is possible that one can, let alone should, simply focus on the text itself. To focus on the text itself is in any event and necessarily to focus upon all that to which it adverts and relates. To focus first and foremost upon a text, where it is primarily the text which is to be understood, cannot possibly therefore involve the error of ignoring the 'context'. The text is not enough. But the very fact that it can in some degree be understood implies reference to a common fund of understanding which is in the text but which also points beyond (or beneath) it. We do not begin to grasp the meaning of an argument by first looking over our shoulders at other considerations, which at best are only other arguments anyway. If a text expresses an argument, and it is this we seek to understand, then we seek first to capture the meaning of the argument within its own textual confines. The fact that an individual can write an essay or a book must mean that he is dealing with a social system, a set of practices, of which his book-writing only constitutes a more connected element. The fact that such a text points beyond itself is not merely commonplace but universal. This can in no way imply that the text may be ignored, or relegated to some secondary level of importance. In so far as the intention is to understand *it*, it is important to focus upon it. Only when the text appears anomalous, inconsistent, incomprehensible or laughably false, have we genuine cause to look frankly beyond to see whether other, external evidence may not better help to establish its sense.

There may be distortion where the historian of ideas supposes that his subject of study has something to say about each topic normally treated in the discipline. It of course is one thing to suppose that every great thinker has something to say about every significant topic, and another to satisfy a curiosity as to whether he actually does, and|if so, what it is. There is nothing any more misconceived about tracing the origins of an idea (this is a research programme) than about trying to demonstrate that some particular thinker was advancing a moral or a message relevant only to his own epoch (yet another research programme). In the one case the writer rightly assumes that beliefs and practices established today have evolved (and will continue to evolve) over time, and that there must be some *connection*, possibly up to and including identity, between the substantive content of past and present.

In the other case, the writer rightly assumes that practices established today, having evolved, *are not totally identical* with those of any earlier time, and thus may choose to spy out these differences. In the case of either programme, the execution may be admirable or poor. But it is difficult to suppose that there are convincing arguments that either researcher might advance to demonstrate that the other's programme was wholly absurd.

There may be distortion where the historian of ideas presupposes that his subject of study has enunciated a doctrine that is more coherent than it is, the danger being that he may read into the original text arguments that are not actually there. There is indeed always such a risk. But it would appear that there is a notable difference between, on the one hand, assessing the degree of coherence in a philosophical position (which presupposes that coherence of some kind was actually sought) and, on the other, falsely interpolating arguments, with the result that a spurious coherence is imposed. The fact that past thinkers, who are substantively present as subjects of study, may be less coherent than many exegetes have supposed, cannot of course be taken as an argument either against summarizing their work (how else could we discuss anything?) or for providing textbooks in the history of ideas. A textbook does summarize, it does select, but these exercises do not necessarily convey distortion. No more than a road-map, through compression, misleads. The only error is for the naïve or the over-educated to misread a decent and self-confessed summary as constituting something more than it would ever likely pretend to be. Imagine a motorist travelling through highland Kenya and complaining the while that the splendour which envelops him is not properly recorded on the mean little Shell map obtained at a Nairobi petrol station.

Some students have objected that it is conceptually impossible to write the history of an 'idea'. The basic reason for this objection appears to stem from the consideration that the words which give expression to an idea change their meaning, that words are used (even in the same time-space continua) in different and conflicting ways, from which it appears to be concluded that a single history cannot be written of all these divergent meanings. All of this is sound. And who would wish to write a history of an indiscriminate heap of topics, even should this prove possible? It still does not follow, from the words being accorded different meanings, that one cannot focus, even concentrate, on them. The fact that words mean different things is a commonplace. But it does not and cannot bring meaningful and fruitful trading in them to a halt. Even so simple and indispensable a word as 'the' has a wide range of distinct meanings and usages (as in 'the wife' where it means *my* or as in 'the lion' where it refers to a particular species of animal). We can live comfortably with the fact that different words will mean different things – that is, as long as we have a reasonable idea of what the particular meaning is on any particular occasion. Without such knowledge there is confusion. But it is never variability of usage as such which creates the confusion. Where we are confronted with a piece of writing, the ideas it expresses are perforce expressed in words. Assuming that we can seize in particular sentences the particular meanings of these words, and assuming that the sentences together convey some coherent meaning (much that is written *is* confused, *is* jibberish) then we are in a position to seize the sense of an idea through the words that express it. Were we not able to do this, then the bulk of human communication, as known to persons reading these lines, would simply collapse. In so far as it is possible to convey ideas through words, so is it possible to reconstruct a history of ideas through the study of words. Ideas may of course be expressed otherwise than in words. There is always art and architecture and dance and mime. But the bulk of the ideas which those who read this will have imbibed are the gift of words. Without these, it is difficult to imagine our ideas being other than confused or elementary, and if both, then possibly moronic. Words can convey an idea. They can do so over time. It would seem plain, accordingly, that an idea – in this sense – may have a genealogy, a history. And it must in principle be possible to write a history of an idea if the latter has a past.

It should be obvious that words, certainly, have a history. Otherwise it would be difficult to suppose that etymology could constitute a possible subject of study. It is perhaps less obvious that ideas have a history. A word, although only a mere sign or symbol, is none the less some sort of thing. As 'things' have a certain materiality about them, they endure over time, and through that endurance reflect an historical dimension. Ideas, by contrast, although expressed through words, cannot be exhausted by some one fixed form of words. There are many different words and combinations of words which will express the same idea, whether in one language, or as in translations between different languages. Whereas words normally correspond exclusively to fixed symbols, ideas never correspond exclusively to particular words or arrangements of words. Further, ideas often correspond to nothing that actually exists at all. (Take the famous case of *phlogiston*.) As ideas cannot be expressed exclusively through some one form of words, and as they often correspond to nothing real anyway, one can readily understand the inclination of many to conceive of them as immaterial (in more than one sense) and following on that to conclude that they do not have a history or (at the least) that no history of them can be written.

The problem is, that if it is impossible to write a history of ideas, it is impossible to write a history of anything at all. For it is inevitably the case that any history is also a history of ideas. The subject of any history is always in some degree arbitrarily designated. Suppose it to be said that we can write a history (a biography) of a person, like Napoleon or Attila or Chaka. It is plain that none of these figures at 40 years of age was the same as at four. If we take the simple matter of physical continuity in relation to cell regeneration, it will be clear that there will not be a single cell which will have endured or survived in its original form over such a period of time. So that in the most physical of senses there will be no one Napoleon or Attila or Chaka to write about. What holds for them will hold for any other figure at all. Similarly with the thinking of individuals. The intellectual difference between Einstein at six and Einstein at 60 is so great as to enable one to say, in respect of such differences, that the two minds are not the same. Yet neither the fact of total physical change, nor of a spectacular and comprehensive intellectual development would warrant the conclusion that to write a biography of such a figure must prove an absurd or impossible undertaking. Biographies are written. But in order to do so, we must work from the assumption, the *idea*, of personal identity as borne by distinct individuals. If we assert a personal and continuing identity for Marx, despite the possibility of a radical divide between the younger and the older Marx, then we shall not be persuaded that we cannot, or that there is something illegitimate about, providing an account of Marx's intellectual life as a whole.

Suppose it to be said that we can write a history of a state (like the United Kingdom or France) or of some institution within the state (like Parliament). Whatever may be remarked of a history of 'ideas', it is not normally suggested that histories of this (supposedly more concrete) type are impossible or illegitimate. And yet similar problems arise. The United Kingdom covers so many different ideas that it would appear impossible to write a single history of the whole. There is much of art, music, drama, culture, style, politics, technology and so on. The 'idea' of the United Kingdom is in itself entirely geographical. But the geographical 'logic' of the unit adverted to is in no way self-evident. This unit consists of one large island, the northern tip of another, and a miscellany of tiny islands nearby, together with a variety of colonial possessions, in the Caribbean, South Atlantic, South Pacific and Indian Oceans. It could be argued that the geographical 'idea' of the United Kingdom is so incoherent that it could not repay study. But one may be thankful that few historians would allow themselves to be distracted by such fatuous declamations. Of course, one way in which a geographical unit like the United Kingdom might be conceived and studied more coherently is by battening upon its *political* rationale. But that too is largely arbitrary. The emphasis upon political unity may be more than offset by class, cultural, ethnic and other disunities. In any event, the political unit is grossly unstable. At one time it included perhaps half of Africa, plus India, Pakistan and Sri Lanka, Australia, New Zealand and North America, etc. At an earlier time it included no part of Ireland; earlier still it included no part of Scotland; and we may well argue that, yet earlier, it equally excluded all of Wales and much even of what we now call England. (The Normans of course are identified as the initiators of the present political system which, interestingly, is commonly styled 'English'.) If we wished to argue in this way we could conclude that it is not 'possible' even to write a political history of the United Kingdom. But those engaged to write such histories will no doubt reply to such arguments with the silence they deserve.

If we look at an institution like Parliament we are presumably not thinking of a particular building or timepiece that may adorn it. We are presumably thinking of a set of practices. These practices could be described in different words, in different combinations of words, and naturally in different languages. But let us say that the object of our concern was the notion of 'representative government', which may fairly be thought to have something to do with 'democracy', 'liberty', 'rights', 'habeas corpus', but also with 'power' and 'authority' and other notions besides. It would appear, at the least, unavailing to urge that a history of 'representative' or 'parliamentary' government in the Island(s) could not be written: certainly it is known to have been done. But to write such a book is most assuredly to write the history of an 'idea'. Histories may be well or badly written. And so with histories of 'ideas'. But the major problem will stem from assuming that ideas are necessarily distinct from practices. We have already remarked that an idea may very well refer or correspond to nothing that really exists. But even here a history may be written. (It is perfectly possible, for example, to provide a history of theories of spontaneous generation, astrology, demonology and so on). We cannot study a practice, a behaviour, a phenomenon or whatever without conceptually divorcing it from its environment. Thus to study something in particular, whether historical or otherwise, is to impose upon it, or to make of it, an idea. It is only with such an idea that we select for relevance. And without that idea, being unable to select, we can write no history whatever. Thus to suggest that a history can ever be written such that it in no way contains or reflects a 'history of ideas' is a serious (but dull) mistake. History may not be reducible to mere ideas. But there can be no history without them, nor any history which is not also 'of ideas'.

There are of course different levels of abstraction, and some ideas, like 'representative government', are arguably less abstract than others, like 'justice'. On the other hand, it may be that the problem with what we more restrictively call histories of 'ideas', may have less to do, strictly speaking, with their being 'abstract', than with the possibility of their being executed in some manageable way. One of the first criteria of manageability is that the idea being investigated should somehow correspond to a determinate practice. If we wish to write a history of 'equality' where this is intended to mean 'treating everybody in every way precisely and exactly the same', then presumably there is no actual practice of which one can provide an account. We would do better perhaps to analyse the logic of the concept or possibly subject it to various forms of ethical investigation. But if, by contrast, 'equality' is taken to mean 'all adults are entitled to vote', then the evolution of the idea *qua* practice can certainly constitute a subject of historical inquiry. And so with 'liberty', 'toleration', 'justice' and related notions. Abstraction is not a bar; unmanageability is. And the two are not the same.

It is pointless to advise either historians or philosophers not to concentrate exclusively upon a particular idea or a particular text 'in itself'. That is all that may interest them or all they may have time for. It is impossible to show that there is some one best way of seizing the meanings of ideas or texts. Approaches differ and doubtless always will do. In any event, to the extent that texts have meanings, the meanings refer to events which extend beyond the texts themselves. Thus no one who studies a text, to the extent that the text makes any sense, is studying that alone. For the text implicates a reality which lies beyond itself. Similarly with ideas. Ideas are not texts, but may be expressed through them. To the extent that they are focused upon, and the focus betrays a meaning, and the meaning is other than circular, then the idea is not a 'mere' idea, but something which extends beyond itself into the so-called 'real' world. By focusing upon an 'idea', one is not focusing upon 'nothing'. And any suggestion that there is some one best way of comprehending an idea as 'something' can scarcely fail to prove spurious.

It no more follows that to understand an idea requires that we understand all of the different ways in which it has been formulated, than that understanding a country (like the United Kingdom) requires a knowledge of every conceivable thing about it. To argue otherwise is all very well. But such an argument can only, at best, constitute a counsel of perfection. To say that understanding an idea literally involves understanding '*all* the occasions and activities in which a given agent might have used the *relevant* form of words' is only to say that one can never possibly understand any idea whatever. The occasions on which one *might* use (or have used) a particular form of words surely cannot be numbered. And indeed we can never be sure that we have ever tabulated all *possible* usages, if for no other reason than that these possible usages must be regarded as infinite.

11: Conclusion

It is appropriate now to draw the discussion to a close. To write any history, one might have an 'idea', and select for it. Although one may distinguish between institutional and philosophical history, between the history of a system and that, more broadly, of a practice, the engagement remains selective and is no more fatuous in the one case than in the other. It is not so much that the writing of history requires that its object should have endured, as that the substantive matter dilated upon be arranged in such a way as to assume duration. In writing history, the idea that we select for, such as 'the state', must be attributed some degree of duration. The substantive criteria that we entertain for such a notion may be plucked from a time that is chronologically very distant. But whatever these ideas, whatever their origins, to the extent that they take on some coherent meaning in our minds in the present, then it can be said that they are alive in this present. They are, at the least, alive for us. This does not *prove* that they are 'transhistorical', 'timeless', or 'eternal'. It is not possible, in the nature of tings, to prove matters of this kind. But what is clear is that if these ideas, whether as institutions or practices or philosophies, ever existed in the past, we shall only know them as ideas present in our minds. If we hold the past to be 'dead' then we also hold that we have no access to it. If we claim, as we do, that we 'know' the past, then we only know it as a part of the present. We must understand this tyranny, in order to reconcile to it our 'knowledge' of the past. The past we know, or that we claim to know, is known only because it is somehow in and of the present. Once we inspect more closely the different notions that we entertain of the present, we are well positioned to begin to discern the different notions we entertain of the past. As this work of understanding proceeds, particularly as regards the interpenetration of non-correlative senses of past and present, we may expect to discover that this interpenetration, if complex, is not in the least paradoxical.

Source

Specially written for this volume.

PART TWO

OAKESHOTT

3 THE ACTIVITY OF BEING AN HISTORIAN

Michael Oakeshott

I

Activities emerge naïvely, like games that children invent for themselves. Each appears, first, not in response to a premeditated achievement, but as a direction of attention pursued without premonition of what it will lead to. How should our artless ancestor have known what (as it has turned out) it is to be an astronomer, an accountant, or an historian? And yet it was he who, in play, set our feet on the paths that have led to these now narrowly specified activities.[1] For, a direction of attention, as it is pursued, may hollow out a character for itself and become specified in a 'practice'; and a participant in the activity comes to be recognized not by the results he achieves but by his disposition to observe the manners of the 'practice'. Moreover, when an activity has acquired a certain firmness of character, it may present itself as a puzzle, and thus provoke reflection; for, there may come a point at which we not only wish to acquire and exercise the skill which constitutes the activity, but may wish also to discern the logic of the relation of this activity (as it has come to be specified) to others and to ascertain its place on the map of human activity.

What we now understand as the activity of being an historian was generated in this manner. Beginning in a direction of attention naïvely pursued, it has achieved the condition of a specific activity whose participants are known by their faithfulness to the 'practice' that has emerged. And during the last 200 years or so this activity has been much reflected upon.

Reflection has taken two directions. First, what has been sought is a satisfactory general description of the activity of being an historian as it has come to establish itself. The assumption here is that the activity is itself an historical emergence and that the degree of specification it has now achieved is sufficient to identify it as a coherent manner of thinking about the world. And the fruits of such an inquiry would be the disclosure of the kind of intelligibility that historical thinking, in its present condition, imparts to the world, and the manner in which this activity can be distinguished from others which (in the process of emergence) it has succeeded in separating itself from. This, no doubt, is a difficult inquiry; but it is one that seems capable of yielding some conclusions.

The second direction of inquiry may be said to spring (but not necessarily) from the first. Assuming a satisfactory description of the current condition of the activity of being an historian has been achieved, the questions asked are: Does this condition intimate (or, must we not on general grounds assume) the possibility of further specification which would not merely modify in detail the present specification of the activity but would generate its definitive character? And if so, what is this character? And since I propose to concern myself very little with this line of inquiry, I should, perhaps, say a word about it before putting it on one side. Briefly, the notion appears to be this: the activity of being an historian is that of understanding the past, but, since the current manner of doing this leaves the past incompletely intelligible, there must (in principle) be another manner of understanding the past which, because it is free from this defect, may be regarded as the consummation to which 'history' in its present condition points. And, although there may be others yet unproposed, the most favoured candidate has, for some time, been an inquiry designed to make past events intelligible by revealing them as examples of general laws. I do not myself understand how this line of thought could lead to profitable conclusions; but at least it is clear that it rests upon far from self-evidently true presuppositions, and whether or not it may turn out to be profitable will depend upon our satisfying ourselves that they are warranted. Moreover, it should be observed that what is being sought here is not merely a demonstration that historical thinking in its present condition must, in principle, leave the past incompletely intelligible, but a manner of thinking about the past which is at once superior to 'history' in its present condition and is capable of taking its place.

2

I propose, then, to consider the manner and achievements of current reflection about the present condition of the activity of being an historian; the reflection, that is, which seeks a general description of the activity as it has come to establish itself, and to determine the kind of intelligibility it imparts to the world.

The historian is understood, in the first place, to be distinguished on account of the direction of his attention; he is concerned with the past. He is interested in the world around him considered as evidence for a world that is no longer present; and we recognize his activity as one of inquiring into 'the past' and making statements about it. Nevertheless, we recognize, also, that to inquire into the past and to make statements about it is an exceedingly commonplace activity and one that we engage in every day of our lives: it is represented, for example, in the activity of remembering, and in so simple an inquiry as, 'Where did you get that hat?' Consequently, if we are interested, we cast around in order to discern some special characteristics which will serve to distinguish the activity of an historian from that of others who share with him an interest in 'the past'. And many who have reflected upon this subject have reached a conclusion something like this:

Whoever pays attention to the past and asks questions or makes statements about it must be understood to be participating in some measure in the activity which is the pre-eminent concern of an historian. All statements about the past are, in some sense, 'historical' statements. But an historian is distinguished by reason of the care he takes to verify his statements. 'History' emerges as a specific activity out of a general and unspecified interest in the past whenever there is a genuine concern for 'truth'; and an 'historical' event is any happening which we are warranted in believing (in virtue of its being a conclusion to a certain method of inquiry) took place in the manner described.[2] Thus, the activity of inquiring into and making statements about the past appears as a hierarchy of attitudes towards the past. At the head of this scale of attitudes stands 'the historian', specified by his care for 'truth', his technical skill in eliciting 'truth', and perhaps also by a propensity to regard some observations about the past, and some events, as more significant than others. In this manner his activity is differentiated, not only from the informal inquiries about the past which every man from time to time, in the course of business or pleasure, engages in, but also from the activity (for example) of an annalist or a chronicler, whose utterances spring from inquiries recognized to be less extended and less critical than those of an historian.

This general account of the matter has much to commend it. At least, it recognizes 'the historian' (in virtue of a 'practice') to be engaged in a specific activity. No doubt it is an incomplete account; and no doubt, also, it is philosophically naïve. But it has the virtue of not forbidding further investigation: indeed, it may be observed to point to two directions of further inquiry. For its incompleteness and philosophical naïvety lie, not in the formulation of the problem as one of ascertaining the *differentia* of 'historical' research, but only in the conclusions reached.

It urges us, first, to be more exact in our understanding of the details of the 'practice' of 'the historian'. And in response to this suggestion, attempts have been made to elicit a heuristic of historical investigation and to reduce the 'practice' of 'the historian' to a set of rules. But, as reflection might have warned us would be the case, this has not turned out a very profitable enterprise. And I do not propose to pursue it here.

There is, however, another direction of inquiry which this formulation of the problem suggests: it provokes us to consider whether the activity of being an historian may be more exactly specified in terms of the *kind* of question he asks and the *kind* of statement he makes about the past. And since in this direction of inquiry there remains a yet unfulfilled promise of profit, I propose to consider where it has led us and what further conclusions it is capable of yielding.

Investigators who have followed this path have already reached certain conclusions. They have observed, for example, that inquiry into the past may take the form of asking what *must* have happened, or what *might* have happened, or what *did* happen; and, for the most part, they have concluded that an *historian* is distinguished by an exclusive concern with what *did* happen. Or, again, a distinction has been drawn between the 'natural' world and the 'human' world; and it has been concluded that the events with which an historian is concerned are those which may be imputed to human actions and those which (though they belong to the 'natural' world, like earthquakes and climatic changes) we are warranted in believing to have conditioned or determined specific human conduct. And, as a refinement of this, Collingwood considered that the *res gestae* of 'history' are not *any* human actions, but only 'reflective' actions; that is, actions which spring from a purpose pursued. Further, it has been suggested that an attitude towards the past which provokes an inquiry into the 'origins' of some feature of the present world is an attitude foreign to an historian. In the same manner, the very recent past has been considered inappropriate for 'historical' investigation. And (a last example) some inquirers into the activity of the 'historian' have concluded that he is not concerned with the moral rightness and wrongness of human actions and that statements of moral approval or disapproval, of praise or condemnation, are out of place in his writings.

Now, all these suggestions may be recognized as attempts to determine more exactly the *kind* of questions it is appropriate for 'the historian', to ask, and the *kind* of statements it is appropriate for him to make about the past. They are attempts to distinguish a specifically 'historical' attitude towards 'the past' from other current or possible attitudes and thus to specify more precisely the activity of being an historian. Each suggestion is supported by some show of reasoning. The questions excluded from the concern of 'the historian' are identified either as questions inherently impossible to answer, or as questions which his evidence or his technique does not equip 'the historian' to answer; or they are excluded for some other reason. And, so far, there is much to be said for this manner of gradually elucidating the activity of 'the historian'; it has the virtues of moderation and empiricism.

Nevertheless, there remains something unsatisfactory about this procedure of piecemeal exclusion. Even if the reasoning which supports each exclusion were more cogent than it often is, the absence of attachment to a comprehensive view of the situation gives to each the indelible appearance of arbitrariness. Each remains a separate exclusion (or prohibition), supported by *ad hoc* reasoning which is apt to be either misconceived or inadequate because it is unrelated to any conspectus of the *kind* of inquiry and the *kind* of utterance appropriate to an 'historical' investigation of the past. In short, the current manner of exploring the activity of 'the historian' sets us a task to discern the logic of these piecemeal attempts to delineate the field of historical inquiry.

The imperfectly considered assumptions of the current view appear to be something like this. It is believed that among the different kinds of statement that may be made about the past, it is possible to detect and to specify certain kinds, or even a certain kind which it is the peculiar province of 'the historian' to make. It is believed that there are many statements we, quite properly, make about the past which (even though they cannot be denied to be in some sense 'true') are, nevertheless, not 'historical' statements. It is believed that an 'historical' event is not any happening which we have warrant for thinking took place, but a happening of a peculiar sort which reveals itself in answer to a certain kind of question. Our task is to elucidate these assumptions so that the view of the activity of 'the historian' which they entail may be more fully disclosed and perhaps more firmly based.

3

It is proper to begin with our attitudes towards the world around us, because inquiring into 'the past' is the exhibition of a certain attitude towards the components of this world. Every happening that we see taking place before our eyes, if we attend to it at all, arouses a response. And every happening is capable of arousing a variety of responses. For example, I may observe the demolition of an old building, and my reponse may be merely a movement of self-preservation — to get out of the way of the débris. It may, however, be a more complicated response. I may recognize what is happening as an act of vandalism, and suffer anger or depression; or I may understand it as evidence of progress, and be elated on that account; or indeed, the whole scene may be contemplated without *arrière pensée*, as a picture, an image whose design is a delight to the eyes. In short, to attend to what is happening before us is always to make something of it for ourselves. Seeing is recognizing what we see as *this* or *that*. And if I have a companion I may make a statement about what I am seeing whose idiom reveals the manner in which I am attending to it and understanding it.

Everything that goes on before our eyes is, then, eligible for a vast variety of interpretations. But, in general, it seems that our responses to the world are of two kinds. Either we may regard the world in a manner which does not allow us to consider anything but what is immediately before our eyes and does not provoke us to any conclusions; or we may look upon what is going on before us as evidence for what does not itself appear, considering, for example, its causes or its effects. The first of these reponses is simple and unvarying; and I shall call it the response of *contemplation*. It is pre-eminently the reponse of the artist and the poet, for whom the world is composed, not of events recognized as signs or portents, but of causeless 'images' of delight which provoke neither approval nor disapproval, and to which the categories 'real' and 'fictitious' are alike inapplicable. The second response, however, is capable of internal variety; and in it two main idioms may be distinguished, which I shall call, respectively, the *practical* and the *scientific* response.

First, we may recognize what is happening in respect of its relation to ourselves, our fortunes, desires and activities. This is the commonest kind of response; we absolve ourselves from it with difficulty, and relapse into it easily. I call it a *practical* response, and its partner is the perception of a *practical* event.

From birth we are active; not to be active is not to be alive. And

what concerns us first about the world is its habitableness, its friend-
liness or hostility to our desires and enterprises. We want to be at home
in the world, and (in part) this consists in being able to detect how happenings will affect ourselves and in having some control over their
effects.

This service is performed, in the first place, by our senses. In 'seeing',
'hearing', 'tasting', touching', we become acquainted with what is happening: and, at the same time, we place a certain interval between ourselves and what is happening, giving ourselves an opportunity to act in
what we judge to be an appropriate manner. 'Seeing' places the greatest
space-time interval between ourselves and events; 'hearing', a smaller,
but still useful interval; in 'tasting' the interval is further contracted;
and in 'touching' it is reduced to almost nothing at all.

But in order to understand the world in relation to ourselves we
make use of certain conceptual distinctions. We recognize events as
friendly or hostile, things as edible or poisonous, useful or useless,
cheap or expensive, and so on. And most, if not all, of these distinctions
are examples of the recognition, in practical life, of what may be called
'cause' and 'effect'. For, in practical life, to recognize an event as a
'cause' is to understand it as a sign or signal that other events are likely
to follow: to understand an event as friendly is to expect it to be followed by other events of a certain kind; to recognize a commodity as
'cheap' is to recognize it as a signal of other events to come. And the
ability to recognize events as, in this sense, 'causes' at once gives us a
greatly enhanced mastery over the world; it enables us to anticipate
events that have not yet taken place and thus gives us an added opportunity of controlling their impact upon ourselves.

Moreover, it is to this practical attitude towards the world that our
judgements of approval and disapproval and our moral appraisals and
imputations belong. The categories of 'right' and 'wrong', 'good' and
'bad', 'justice' and 'injustice' etc. relate to the organization and understanding of the world in respect of its relationship to ourselves, in
respect (that is) of its habitableness. 'Hero' and 'villain' may be crude
categories, but their place is in the world of practical activity. And in
condemning 'vice' and applauding 'virtue' we express our beliefs about
what is desirable and what is undesirable in human conduct and character.

The practical attitude, then, admits us to a world of discourse, but
it is not the only world of discourse available to us. It has a partner and
an alternative in what I have called the *scientific* attitude. In this, we
are concerned, not with happenings in their relation to ourselves and to

the habitableness of the world, but in respect of their independence of ourselves. In short, the attitude here is what we vulgarly call an 'objective' attitude; and this 'objectivity' is reflected in the idiom of the statements we make about the happenings we observe. While the hunter recognizes animals as dangerous or friendly (denoting some as specifically 'man-eating'), while the house-wife distinguishes commodities in respect of their price, while the cook knows things in respect of their taste, and while the moralist expresses himself in statements of approval or disapproval, the categories of the scientist arrange things in a different manner — not at all as they affect him or his fortunes, but as they are in their independence of himself.

The general character of the scientist's concern with the world appears in his notion of 'cause' and 'effect'. When the practical man recognizes an event as a 'cause' he recognizes it as a *sign* that some other event may be expected to follow; and the ground of his recognition is his experience of the world in relation to himself. For the scientist, on the other hand, 'cause' is a much more precise and more restricted notion; and 'cause' in his sense is so difficult to determine that it lacks practical usefulness. It is the necessary and sufficient conditions of a hypothetical situation. 'Cause' and 'effect', that is, denote general and necessary relations and not merely a relation which has proved practically useful to observe.

The contrast between the practical and the scientific responses to the world may be illustrated as follows: When we are concerned with things in their relation to ourselves and to the habitableness of the world, it is appropriate to say that 'seeing' puts things at a greater distance from ourselves than 'hearing'. And consequently we recognize that it is a greater handicap to be blind that to be deaf. But when we are concerned with things in respect of their independence of ourselves, we say, instead, that the speed of light is greater than the speed of sound. 'Light' and 'sound' are, so to speak, the 'scientific' equivalents of the practical activities of 'seeing' and 'hearing'.

Or again, if I say: 'I am hot,' I shall be recognized to be speaking in the idiom of practice. I am making a statement about the world in relation to myself, and the manner in which it is made will certainly convey either satisfaction or dissatisfaction. If I say: 'It is a hot day', I am still making a statement about the world in relation to myself. Its reference is more extended, but the remark is unmistakably in the practical idiom. If I say: 'The thermometer on the roof of the Air Ministry stood at 90°F. at 12 noon GMT' I may not have emancipated myself completely from the practical attitude, but at least I am capable of being suspected of making a statement, not about the world in relation to myself but about the world in respect of its independence of myself. And when, finally, I say: 'The boiling point of water is 100° Centigrade', I am making a statement which may be recognized to have achieved the idiom of 'science'. The situation described is hypothetical, and the observation is not about the world in relation to myself.

In both the practical and the scientific responses, then, the world appears as a world of 'facts'; 'truth' and 'error' are relevant categories, though in the one case it is 'practical' truth and in the other 'scientific'. And in both these attitudes we are provoked to look for what is not present: events are the 'effects' of 'causes' and the portents of events to come. On the other hand, the attitude of contemplation discloses to us a world of mere 'images' which provoke neither inquiry nor speculation about the occasion and conditions of their appearance, but only delight in their having appeared.

4

We have been considering events as they take place before our eyes and we have concluded that these are capable of a variety of interpretation, and what we see is relative to how we look. And, further, we have agreed that the historian is concerned with 'the past'. What we must now observe is that 'the past' is a construction we make for ourselves out of the events which take place before our eyes. Just as the 'future' appears when we understand the present events as evidence for what is about to happen, so what we call 'the past' appears when we understand current happenings as evidence for what has already happened. In short (to confine ourselves to our immediate concern) 'the past' is a consequence of understanding the present world in a particular manner.

Consider: what we have before us is a building, a piece of furniture, a coin, a picture, a passage in a book, a legal document, an inscription on stone, a current manner of behaviour or a memory. Each of these is a present event. And one response (though not of course the only possible response) to these events is to understand them as evidence for events that have already taken place. There is, indeed, nothing in the present world which is incapable of being regarded in this manner; but also there is nothing which can be regarded *only* in this manner.

'The past', then, is a certain way of reading 'the present'. But in addition to its being a reading of the world in which present events are understood as evidence for events that have already taken place, it is a reading which may denote a variety of attitudes towards these past events. And (if we are to be guided by the utterance of those who have spoken and written about past events) the three most important attitudes available to us may be called the *practical*, the *scientific* and the *contemplative*. And there is a manner of speaking about past events which is appropriate to each of these attitudes.

First, if we understand a past event merely in relation to ourselves and our own current activities our attitude may be said to be a 'practical' attitudes.

This, for example, is the attitude of a practising lawyer to a past event which he concludes to have taken place by understanding a present event (a legal document before him) as evidence for something that has already happened. He considers the past event solely in relation to its present consequences and he says to his client: 'under this will you may expect to inherit £1,000'; or, 'we must take Counsel's opinion on the validity of this contract'. And further, of course, he is interested only in past events which *have* present practical consequences.

Now, just as our commonest attitude towards what we see taking place before us is a practical attitude, so our commonest attitude to what we conclude (on the evidence of a present experience) to have already taken place is a practical attitude. Usually, we interpret these past happenings in relation to ourselves and to our current activities. We read the past backwards from the present or from the more recent past, we look in it for the 'origins' of what we perceive around us, we make moral judgements about past conduct, we call upon the past to speak to us in utterance related to the present; and what appears is a practical past. And the questions we ask, and the statements we make about the past, are those that are appropriate to our practical attitude. They are statements such as these:

> You are looking very well: where did you go for your holiday?
> The summer of 1920 was the finest in my experience.
> He died too soon.
> King John was a bad King.
> The death of William the Conquerer was accidental.
> It would have been better if the French Revolution had never taken place.
> He dissipated his resources in a series of useless wars.
> The Pope's intervention changed the course of events.
> The evolution of Parliament.
> The development of industrial society in Great Britain.

The Factory Acts of the early nineteenth century culminated in the Welfare State of the twentieth century.

The loss of markets for British goods on the continent was the most serious consequence of the Napoleonic Wars.

The effect of the Boer War was to make clear the necessity for radical reform in the British Army.

The next day the Liberator addressed a large meeting in Dublin.

Here, in each of these statements, the idiom is that of practice.

Secondly, our attitude to what we conclude to have happened in the past may be, generally speaking, what I have called a 'scientific' attitude. Here, we are concerned, not with past events in relation to ourselves and to the habitableness of the world, but in respect of their independence of ourselves. The practical response is the response of a partisan, of one sort or another; in the scientific response what appears is the past unassimilated to ourselves, the past for its own sake.

But while the word 'scientific' may properly be used, in a general way, to denote an interest in past events in respect of their independence of ourselves, it is necessary to make two qualifications. First, the concern of 'the scientist' with necessary and sufficient conditions will be reflected in the idiom in which he speaks about the past. And a model of the kind of statement he will be disposed to make is to be found in this sentence from Valery: 'all the revolutions of the nineteenth century had as their necessary and sufficient conditions the centralized constitutions of power, thanks to which . . . a minimum strength and duration of effort can deliver an entire nation at a single stroke to whoever undertakes the adventure'. In short, if we give a stricter meaning to the word 'science', what appears is not merely statements in which the past remains unassimilated to the present, but also statements in which events are understood to exemplify general laws. And secondly, if we speak still more strictly, there can in fact be no 'scientific' attitude towards the past, for the world as it appears in scientific theory is a timeless world, a world, not of actual events, but of hypothetical situations.

Lastly, our attitude — and consequently the manner in which we recognize past happenings and the utterances we make about them — may be what I have called a 'contemplative' attitude. This is illustrated in the work of a so-called 'historical' novelist, for whom the past is neither practical nor scientific 'fact', but a storehouse of mere images. For example, in Tolstoy's *War and Peace* Napoleon is an image about whom it is as irrelevant to ask: Where was he born? Was he really like that? Did he in fact do this, or say that? Where was he in the intervals when he was not on stage? as it would be to ask similar questions about Shakespeare's Orsino, Duke of Illyria in *Twelfth Night*. But here a qualification is necessary. Since 'the past', as such, cannot appear in 'contemplation' (this attitude being one in which we do not look for what does not immediately appear), to 'contemplate' past events is, properly speaking, a dependent activity in which what is contemplated are not past events but present events which (on account of some *other* attitude towards the present) have been concluded to have taken place. To remember, and to contemplate a memory, are two different experiences; in the one past and present are distinguished, in the other no such distinction is made. In short, just as when an object of use (a ship or a spade) is 'contemplated' its usefulness is neglected, so when what in another attitude would be recognized as a past event is 'contemplated', its pastness is ignored.

What we call 'past events' are, then, the product of understanding (or having understood) present occurences as evidence for happenings that have already taken place. The past, in whatever manner it appears, is a certain sort of reading of the present. Whatever attitudes present events are capable of provoking in us may also be provoked by events which appear when we regard present events as evidence for other events – that is, by what we call 'past' events. In short, there is not one past because there is not one present: there is a 'practical' past, a 'scientific' past and a (specious) 'contemplative' past, each a universe of discourse logically different from either of the others.

5

Now, among those who regard present events as evidence for events that have already taken place, 'the historian' is taken to be supreme. And properly so. For, although the practical man often finds it useful to take this attitude towards the present, and although both the scientist (in a general way) and the poet are each capable of doing so (or of making use of the results of others having done so), 'the historian' never does anything else. The activity of the historian is pre-eminently that of understanding present events – the things that are before him – as evidence for past happenings. His attitude towards the present is one in which the past *always* appears. But in order to understand his activity fully, the question we must ask ourselves is: Can we discern in the attitude of 'historians' towards the past and in the kind of statements they are accustomed to make about it, any characteristics that warrant us to conclude that, besides a 'practical' past, a 'scientific' past and a (specious) 'contemplative' past, there is a specifically 'historical' past?

There is one difficulty which seems to stand in the way of our inquiry, but which may be disposed of at once; it is, in fact, a fictitious difficulty. The practical manner of understanding the past is as old as the human race. To understand everything (including what we believe to have happened in the past) in relation to ourselves is the simplest and least sophisticated manner of understanding the world. And the contemplative attitude towards what are otherwise recognized as past events is, also, generally speaking, primordial and universal. Circumstances may hinder it; and even in people accustomed to it, it may get over-laid and pushed aside in favour of some other attitude. But the great poetic sagas of European and Eastern peoples show that from very early times what in other idioms of observation are known as past events have been recognized not as 'facts' but as 'images' of contemplation. The questions that are appropriate and those that are inappropriate to be asked about Jude the Obscure are the same as those that are respectively appropriate and inappropriate to be asked about Homer's Ulysses or Roland and Oliver. In short, when we consider the kind of statements men have been accustomed to make about the past, there is no doubt that the vast bulk of them is in the practical or the artistic idiom. Consequently, if we go to writers who have been labelled 'historians' (because they have displayed a sustained interest in past events) and ask, what kind of statement are they accustomed to make about the past, we shall find a great preponderance of practical and contemplative statements. And this observation seems to take the wind out of the sails of our inquiry. For where, it will be asked, are we to go to find out what it is to be an historian but to the practice of those who have displayed a sustained interest in the past? And if we go there, the answer ready for us seems to be: History is a miscellany of utterances about the past in which the practical and the contemplative idiom is predominant. And unless we are prepared to erect an imaginary character called, for no good reason, 'the historian', there remains nothing more to be said.

However, this difficulty need not disconcert us. There are, indeed, two considerations which enable us to avert this collapse of our inquiry. First, it must be remembered that in considering 'history' we are considering an activity which (like many others) has emerged gradually and has only recently begun to acquire a specific character. We easily recognize that the activity of being an astronomer, and the statements we expect from those whom we understand to be engaged in astronomy, are in many respects different from what they were when the activity was less exactly specified than it now is. We do not regard all the different kinds of statement (or even all the different kinds of 'true' statement) that have been made about the stars as proper to be made by the man whom we recognize to be 'an astronomer'; indeed, we exclude many of these statements as clearly foreign to what we now recognize as the activity of being an astronomer. And although we have been more hesitant in applying the same reasoning to the activity of being an historian, the two activities are, in this respect, similar to one another. Moreover, inquiry has disclosed in considerable detail the process in which the activity of being an historian has become specified. It is a process (similar to that in which the 'natural scientist' as we now understand him emerged) in which new techniques for the critical treatment of sources of information have been developed, and in which general organizing concepts have been generated, criticized, experimented with and rejected or reformulated.[3] And in neither of these respects has there been unbroken progress; valuable achievements have often been forgotten or allowed to lapse, only to be recovered again when a turn in the fortunes of historiography has recalled them. And again, the activity of being an historian has been dispersed over a variety of circumstantially separated fields of study, and often a closer specification of the activity has been achieved in some fields before it has appeared (often by a process of diffusion) in others. Thus, it is generally true to say that the pioneers of specification have been biblical and ecclesiastical historians, and advances made in these fields have gradually spread to others. And, for example, the rapid and remarkable achievements of historians of the Middle Ages during the last 80 years were often made possible only by the application of the earlier technical achievements of the historians of the ancient world. In short, although we may hope to discern in it some special characteristics, we are not looking for the necessary and sufficient conditions of the activity of being an historian. The activity is what it has become and our present analysis begins and ends with what has been achieved.

And secondly, if we study the utterances of those who have displayed a sustained interest in the past, especially those of recent writers, we shall find, in addition to practical and contemplative statements, statements in what appears to be another idiom. And since this other kind of statement is, generally speaking, found *only* in the writings of those whom we are now accustomed to recognize as 'historians' we may think it profitable to consider whether they do not provide a hint of an attitude towards the past which, being neither specifically practical, nor scientific, nor contemplative, may properly be called 'historical'.

6

Now, with these considerations in mind we are perhaps in a better position to tackle the question, what is the activity of being an historian? with greater expectation of reaching a reasoned conclusion.

We have observed, first, that 'the historian' is one who understands the events of the world before him as evidence for events that have already taken place. Other sorts of inquiries do this also; 'the historian' is unique in never doing anything else. But, what sort of statements does he make about the past thus revealed? What is the character of these statements about the past which 'historians' (but not other kinds of writer about the past) sometimes (but not always) make?

Their first characteristic is that they are *not* designed to assimilate the past to a present, either of fact or desire: the attitude towards the past is *not* what I have called a practical attitude.

The practical man reads the past backwards. He is interested in and recognizes only those past events which he can relate to present activities. He looks to the past in order to explain his present world, to justify it, or to make it a more habitable and a less mysterious place. The past consists of happenings recognized to be contributory or non-contributory to a subsequent condition of things, or to be friendly or hostile to a desired condition of things. Like the gardener, the practical man distinguishes, in past happenings, between weeds and permissible growths; like the lawyer, he distinguishes between legitimate and illegitimate children. If he is a politician, he approves whatever in the past appears to support his political predilections and denounces whatever is hostile to them. If he is a moralist he imposes upon the past a moral structure, distinguishing virtue and vice in human character, right and wrong in human action, approving the one and condemning the other. If his point of observation gives him a wide view, he perceives in the more profound movements of events those that are malign and those that are beneficent. If he is governed by a favourite project, the past appears as a conflict of events and actions relative to that project. In short, he treats the past as he treats the present, and the statements he is disposed to make about past actions and persons are of the same kind as those he is disposed to make about a contemporary situation in which he is involved.

But in the specifically 'historical' attitude (as represented in the kind of statements about the past I have in mind as peculiar to historical writers), the past is *not* viewed in relation to the present, and is *not* treated as if it were the present. Everything that the evidence reveals or points to is recognized to have its place; nothing is excluded, nothing is regarded as 'non-contributory'. The place of an event is not determined by its relation to subsequent events.[4] What is being sought here is neither a justification, nor a criticism nor an explanation of a subsequent or present condition of things. In 'history' no man dies too soon or by 'accident'; there are no successes and no failures and no illegitimate children. Nothing is approved, there being no desired condition of things in relation to which approval can operate; and nothing is denounced. This past is without the moral, the political or the social structure which the practical man transfers from *his* present to *his* past. The Pope's intervention did not change the course of events, it *was* the course of events, and consequently his action was not an 'intervention'. X did not die 'too soon'; he died when he did. Y did not dissipate his resources in a series of useless wars: the wars belong to the actual course of events, not some imaginary illegitimate course of events. It was not 'the Liberator' who addressed the meeting in Dublin; it was Daniel O'Connell. In short, there is to be found an attitude towards the past which is discernibly different from the 'practical' attitude; and since this attitude is characteristic (though, of course, with some qualifications) of those whom we are accustomed to call 'historians' because of their sustained and exclusive interest in the past, its counterpart may be called the specifically 'historical' past. And further, on this reading of the situation, statements in the practical idiom about the past must be recognized, not as 'untrue' statements (because there is nothing to exclude them from being true within their own universe of discourse: if anyone died 'accidentally', William the Conqueror certainly did; and, so far as Charles V's policy was concerned, the Pope *did* intervene), but merely as 'non-historical' statements about the past.

This distinction between the 'practical' and the 'historical' past may be re-enforced by a further observation. The attention of the practical man is directed to the past by the miscellany of present happenings which, on account of his current interests, ambitions and directions of activity, are important to him, or by the present happenings which chance puts in his way or in which the vicissitudes of his life happen to involve him. That is to say, the materials of which he may ask the question, What evidence does it supply about the past? come to him either by chance or in an uncriticized choice. In short, his evidence, what he begins with, is something he merely accepts from the happenings around him; he neither looks for it, nor rejects anything that is offered. But with the historian this is not so. His inquiry into the past is not determined by chance encounters with current happenings. He collects for himself a world of present experiences (documents, etc.), which is determined by considerations of appropriateness and completeness. It is from *this* world of present experiences that the 'historical' past springs.

In this reading of it, then, the activity of 'the historian' may be said (in virtue of its emancipation from a practical interest in the past) to represent an interest in past events for their own sake or in respect of their independence of subsequent or present events. In short, it may be recognized as what I have called, in a general sense, a 'scientific' attitude towards the past. And on this account we are not surprised to observe that what, generally speaking, may be called a 'scientific' attitude towards the world, and an 'historical' attitude towards the past, have emerged together, and with some interdependence, in modern Europe. For, the specification of the activity of being a 'scientist' and the specification of the activity of being an 'historian' were both achieved in a process of emancipation from the primordial and once almost exclusive practical attitude of mankind. Nor, again, is it surprising that, for example, an inquiry into the stars emancipated from a practical interest and partnered by statements about them in the 'scientific' idiom and not the practical idiom,[5] should have appeared somewhat in advance of a similar emancipation in respect of inquiry into the past. The past choices and actions of mankind are so supremely eligible to be regarded and spoken about as if they were present, and the past is so important a component in practical activity, that to free oneself from this attitude must be recognized as an immensely difficult achievement — far more difficult than the parallel achievements of not *always* understanding the world before us only in relation to our current desires and enterprises.

Nevertheless, the observation of this general affinity between a 'scientific' attitude towards the world and and an 'historical' attitude towards the past has been an occasion of stumbling. It provoked a disposition to think it proper that wherever the activity of being a scientist led (as that activity became more narrowly specified), the activity of being an historian should follow. And, in particular, the concern of the scientist with general causes and with necessary and sufficient conditions was taken as a model which 'the historian' should follow as best he could. What was forgotten was that the condition of these concerns of the 'scientist' was their application to hypothetical situations, a condition which should at once have been recognized as separating his activity from any that could be properly attributed to an 'historian'. However, the intoxication of the historian with the more specific (as distinct from the general) concerns of the scientist, was short lived; it lasted little more than 100 years. And, paradoxically, it must be regarded as a belated intrusion of a practical attitude into an activity which was already in process of specifying itself by means of an emancipation from this interest. For the enterprise of distinguishing general causes in respect of past events is now to be recognzed as an attempt to assimilate once more (but in a new and apparently more profitable manner) the past to the present and the future, an attempt to make the past speak to the present, and consequently as a relapse in the direction of practice.

In the 'historian's' understanding of events, just as none is 'accidental', so none is 'necessary' or 'inevitable'. What we can observe him doing in his characteristic inquiries and utterances is, not extricating general causes or necessary and sufficient conditions, but setting before us the events (in so far as they can be ascertained) which mediate one circumstance to another. A scientist may detect a set of conditions which compose the necessary and sufficient conditions of a hypothetical situation denoted by the expression 'combustion' or 'oxidation'; when these are present, and nothing else is present to hinder their operation, combustion takes place. But 'the historian', although he sometimes writes of the outbreak of war as a 'conflagration', nevertheless leaves us in no doubt that he knows of no set of conditions which may properly be called the necessary and sufficient conditions of war. He knows only a set of happenings which, when fully set out, make the outbreak of *this* war seem neither an 'accident', nor a 'miracle', nor a necessary event, but merely an intelligible occurrence. This, for example, is what de Tocqueville does in *L'Ancien Régime*: the French Revolution is come upon, and its character is exhibited, not as the necessary and inevitable consequence of preceding events, but as an intelligible convergence of human choices and actions.

Or, consider this passage from Maitland:

The theory that land in the last resort is held of the King becomes the theory of our law at the Norman Conquest. It is assumed in Doomsday Book . . . quietly assumed as the basis of the survey. On the other hand we can say with certainty that before the Conquest this was not the theory of English law. Towards such a theory English law had been tending for a long while past, very possibly the time was fast approaching when the logic of the facts would have generated this idea; the facts, the actual legal relationships, were such that the wide principle 'all land held in the last resort of the King' would not greatly disturb them. Still this principle had not been evolved. It came to us from abroad; but it came in the guise of a quiet assumption; no law forced it upon the conquered country; no law was necessary; in Normandy lands were held of the Duke, the Duke again held of the King; of course it was the same in England; no other system was conceivable. The process of confiscation gave the Conqueror abundant opportunity for making the theory true in fact; the followers whom he rewarded with forfeited lands would of course hold of him; the great English landowners, whose lands were restored to them, would of course hold of him. As to the smaller people, when looked at from a point of view natural to a Norman, they were already tenants of the great people, and when the great people forfeited their rights, there was but a change of lords. This assumption was sometimes true enough, perhaps in other cases quite false; in many cases it would seem but the introduction of a new and simpler terminology; he who formerly was a landowner personally bound to a lord, became a land tenant holding land of a lord. There was no legislation, and I believe no chronicler refers to the introduction of this new theory. As to the later lawyers, Glanvil and Bracton, they never put it into words. They never state as a noteworthy fact that all land is held of the King: *of course* it is.

Here what is being disclosed is a process of change. Maitland is not concerned with general causes or with necessary and sufficient conditions. He shows us a happening (in this case, a manner of thinking about land); and in order to make it intelligible he shows us how events converged to provoke this happening.

Briefly, then, and without supposing it to be the last word on this difficult subject, it seems that there is an attitude towards the past, which has emerged gradually and in the face of many hindrances, in which past events are understood as 'facts' and not mere 'images', are understood in respect of their independence of subsequent events or present circumstances or desires, and are understood as having no necessary and sufficient conditions. That is, there is an attitude towards the past, which provokes a specific kind of inquiry and utterance, but is neither a practical, nor a scientific, nor a contemplative attitude. There

may be few inquirers into the past who persevere in this attitude without any relapse into other attitudes; but when we find this attitude
adhered to consistently we recognize it as a noteworthy achievement.
And the propriety of denoting it as a specifically 'historical' attitude
rests upon two observations. First, although this attitude is not *always*
exhibited in the inquiries and utterances of writers we are accustomed
to call 'historians', it is exhibited *only* by such writers. And secondly,
the activity of being an historian is not a gift bestowed suddenly upon
the human race, but an achievement. It has emerged gradually from a
miscellany of activities in which present events are understood as
evidence for past happenings; and what seems to have been thrown up
in this process of specification is an attitude of the kind I have described.

Nevertheless, it must be acknowledged that it imparts to the past,
and so to the world, a peculiarly tentative and intermediate kind of
intelligibility, and we may find ourselves provoked to look beyond it. It
exhibits an elementary 'scientific' character, and thus often seems to
point to a more comprehensively 'scientific' understanding of the world
in which past events are recognized as examples of general laws. But
while the pursuit of this more strictly 'scientific' understanding is
enticing, and might (for a while) divert attention from what we now
recognize as the enterprise in 'historical' understanding, the difficulties
it would encounter (both in making its conceptual structure coherent
and in the acquisition of appropriate information) would be great; and it
is not easy to see how (even if it achieved conclusions of some sort) the
one could ever be shown to supersede the other.

7

My contention has been that, in current reflection, the enterprise of
specifying more exactly the character of 'history' has taken the course
of excluding 'the historian' from certain kinds of inquiry and certain
kinds of utterance, but that, in default of a concerted understanding of
what at present it is to be an historian, we are unable to judge the
cogency of these exclusions or the appropriateness of the reasoning
with which each is supported. And, whatever the defects of the view of
the activity of an historian I have put before you, it at least has the
merit of allowing us to do what we were not able to do before. (Whether
it enables us to do it correctly is, of course, another matter.) For it
now appears that most, if not all, the exclusions which current reflec-

tion has suggested are designed to insulate the activity of 'the historian' more conclusively from what I have called a 'practical' attitude towards past events; indeed, this has been the effect of nearly all the technical achievements of historiography during the last 200 years. And because, in the piecemeal method of determining the character of 'historical' inquiry, this has been lost sight of (or has never properly appeared), the exclusions have often been imperfectly specified and have often been supported by irrelevant reasoning.

For example, the suspicion we have of the notion of historical inquiry as an inquiry into 'origins' turns out to be a proper suspicion, but not for the reasons usually given. 'The historian' is disposed to decline the search for 'origins', not because the expression 'origin' is ambiguous (opening the door to a confusion between a 'cause' and a 'beginning'), or because 'origins' are beyond the reach of discovery, or because they are of insignificant interest, but because to inquire into 'origins' is to read the past backwards and thus assimilate it to subsequent or present events. It is an inquiry which looks to the past to supply information about the 'cause' or the 'beginning' of an already specified situation. And governed by this restricted purpose, it recognizes the past only in so far as it is represented in this situation, and imposes upon past events an arbitrary teleological structure. It is, for example, the practising lawyer, and not Maitland, who is disposed to regard inquiry into the past as a search for 'origins'. In short, such expressions as 'the origins of the French Revolution', 'the origins of Christianity', or 'the origins of the Tory Party' denote a backward reading of the past and the incursion of a practical attitude into what purports to be an 'historical' inquiry. Instead of provoking the inquirer to discover the manner in which one concrete situation is mediated into another, it provokes him merely to an abstract view of the past, the counterpart of the abstraction he has chosen to investigate.

Further, we have been warned to be sceptical about the possibility of genuine historical inquiry into the events of the recent past; and we have been warned of the qualified 'historical' character that we should expect of 'official' inquiries into the past. Here also, the view of 'history' I have suggested reinforces these warnings; indeed it extends their scope. But at the same time it transforms, rather than merely confirms, the reasoning with which they are usually supported. A variety of reasons is given for believing that inquiring into the recent past, and 'official' inquiry into the past, cannot be expected to achieve the status of 'historical' investigation. It is said that recent events are particularly difficult to get into focus, that the survival of prejudice hinders detachment and that the evidence to be mastered is at once vast in bulk and at the same time often frustratingly incomplete. And it is said that 'official' inquiring into the past is liable to be qualified by the presence of interests other than that of the discovery of the 'truth'. And all this is well observed. But the real ground of our scepticism is the observation that the past always comes to us, in the first place, in the idiom of practice and has to be translated into the idiom of 'history', and that it is specially difficult for 'the historian' to perform his task of translation when change of circumstances, the passage of time, or the intrusion of indifference has done little or nothing to assist him. Just as it is easier to 'contemplate' an object which uselessness and irrelevance to current enteprises insulates and puts a frame round, and just as it is easier to see the joke when it is not against oneself, so it will be easier (other things being equal) to make 'history' out of a past which does not positively provoke a non-historical attitude.

Moreover, this reading of the situation not only puts our scepticism upon firmer ground; it also enlarges its scope in two directions. First, it becomes clear that a wide sympathy for all the persons and interests engaged in a situation (that is to say, mere absence of bias) can never, by itself, turn a 'practical' account of the situation into an 'historical' account: we are dealing here with two discrete universes of discourse. And secondly, it appears that it is not only the recent past that it is difficult to see 'historically'; it is any period or situation that circumstantially provokes a practical interest. Not so long ago what are called 'the middle ages' of Europe were pre-eminent in provoking a practical attitude; it was exceedingly difficult not to assimilate the events of those times, in one way or another, to later times and to the present. Indeed, the expression 'middle ages' (like the expressions 'ancient', 'modern', 'renaissance', 'enlightened', 'gothic', etc.) began life as 'practical' not 'historical' expressions, and have only recently begun to acquire a limited 'historical' usefulness.[6] The study of the middle ages began under the shadow of the political destruction of the institutions of feudal society, and it was a long time before it escaped from this shadow. And there is much to be said for the belief that the seventeenth century past of England, and perhaps the Norman past of Ireland, are, at the present time, less easy for us to insulate from a practical (political or religious) attitude, and more difficult for us to view 'historically', than almost any other period of our past. An 'historical' attitude towards the Duke of Alva is, even now, difficult to achieve in Belgium; and it is still not easy for Spanish writers to translate the Iberian civilization of the Moors into the idiom of 'history';

that is to say, not to write about it as if it were an intrusion, illegitimate and regrettable. In short, when the true ground of the difficulty of writing near-contemporary 'history' is made to appear, it reveals itself as the ground of a much wider field of difficulties in the 'historical' investigation of the past.[7]

But the recommendation to the historian to exclude moral judgment (not, of course, the description of conduct in, generally speaking, moral terms) from his utterance affords the best example both of the usefulness and the defects of our current manner of specifying the activity of 'the historian'. On the view of the activity I have suggested, the exclusion of expressions of moral approval and condemnation and of expressions which purport to determine the moral value of conduct in the past, is confirmed; but the reasoning with which this exclusion is usually supported is seen to be, for the most part, misconceived or irrelevant. Various reasons are given. We are told that the moral assessment of past conduct involves the application either of absolute moral standards (about which nevertheless there is no agreement), or of the standards current when and where the actions were performed (and in this case the inquirer is merely concerned to elicit what a moralist of the time *would* have said; whereas he would be much better employed in eliciting what was in fact said, and thus make his inquiry a 'history' of moral opinions), or of the standards of some other place and time, the present time, for example (and 'historically' there seems no more reason to choose one time and place as our point of reference rather than another, and the whole activity is revealed as arbitrary and redundant). And we are told, further, that since the moral goodness and badness of conduct relates to the motives of actions and since motives are always hidden in the recesses of the soul, evidence will always be lacking to pronounce moral judgements of this sort about either past or present conduct. But this argument would only exclude moral imputations, not moral appraisals, from the writings of 'the historian'; whereas the intention was to exclude both. The truth is, however, that the ground for excluding moral judgement from 'historical' inquiry and utterance is not the difficulty of agreeing upon a standard to apply, nor the alleged absence of evidence, but the observation that to pronounce upon the moral value of conduct, and the imposition of a moral structure upon the past, represents the incursion of a practical interest into the investigation of the past. And, as we have seen, when this interest intrudes there is room for no other. The investigator of the past who appears as an advocate in the cause of good behaviour succeeds only in setting before us a practical past. When we judge the *moral* value of past conduct, just as when we judge the value or usefulness of past conduct from any other point of view ('useless' wars, for example), we are treating it as if it were present; and no other reason than this need be given for the exclusion of moral judgement from the activity of 'the historian'. In short, to inquire into the moral value of past conduct is to relapse into a practical attitude towards the past, and if relapse were allowed at this point, it could not properly be disallowed at any other.

It seems, then, that our current manner of specifying the activity of 'the historian' has resulted in a number of observations which, taken together, have gone some way towards delineating the activity. But when the logic of these separate observations is considered, it not only provides a means of confirming or rejecting them, but it also suggests modifications and extensions which put our specification on firmer ground.

8

There are many conclusions which seem to follow from this reading of the activity of being an historian. It would appear that the task of 'the historian' cannot properly be described as that of recalling, or of re-enacting the past; that, in an important sense, an 'historical' event is something that never happened and an 'historical' action something never performed; that an 'historical' character is one that never lived. The idiom of happening is always that of practice and the record of happening is usually in the idiom of practice; and 'practice' and 'history' are two logically distinct universes of discourse. The task of 'the historian' is, thus, to create by a process of translation; to understand past conduct and happening in a manner in which they were never understood at the time; to translate action and event from their practical idiom into an historical idiom. But, instead of pursuing any of these conclusions of detail, I wish to end with a more general observation on the present difficulty of being an historian.

We have come to believe that (in the same manner as other activities) the activity of being an historian has now achieved some measure of specification; and perhaps this is so. But while we have learnt to recognize some of the enemies of the 'historical' attitude towards the past, we have still far to go in defeating them. If I interpret correctly current reflection on this subject, we consider ourselves (in an intellectual effort spread over nearly 100 years) to have struggled out of the *cul de sac* into which historical inquiry wandered under the guidance of 'science'; and we have come to recognize what I have called the 'practical' attitude to the past as the chief undefeated enemy of 'history' (although there is still both hesitation and confusion about this). But we recognize, also, that it is a very difficult enemy to defeat. In this engagement, one of our difficulties springs from our perception that a practical attitude towards the past, and the use of a practical idiom in speaking about the past, certainly cannot be dismissed as merely illegitimate. Who are we to forbid it? On what grounds should the primordial activity of making ourselves at home in the world by assimilating *our* past to *our* present be proscribed? This, perhaps, is no great difficulty; it is surmountred when we recognize that the practical past (including moral judgements about past conduct) is not the enemy of mankind, but only the enemy of 'the historian'. But we are left with the more serious difficulty that springs from the fact that the practical idiom has imposed itself for so long upon *all* inquiry into the past that its hold cannot readily be loosened, and the fact that we live in an intellectual world which, because of its addiction to 'practice', is notably hostile to 'history'.

Nor should we encourage ourselves with false hopes; with the belief that an 'historical' attitude towards the past is now more common than it used to be, the belief (as it is said) that this is in some relevant sense a peculiarly historically-minded age. This, I think, is an illusion. Certainly the disposition of our time is to regard the events that take place before our eyes as evidence for past events, to understand them as 'effects' and to turn to the past to discover their 'causes'; but this disposition is joined with another no less strong, the propensity to assimilate the past to the present. Our predominant interest is not in 'history' but only in retrospective politics. And the past is now more than ever a field in which we exercise our moral and political opinions, like whippets in a meadow on Sunday afternoon. And even our theorists (from whom something better might have been expected) are bent rather upon elucidating the tie between past and present than upon pointing out that what matters is the *kind* of 'present', and that it is precisely the task of 'the historian' to loosen the tie between the past and the 'practical' present.

The 'historian' adores the past; but the world today has perhaps less place for those who love the past than ever before. Indeed, it is determined not to allow events to remove themselves securely into the past; it is determined to keep them alive by a process of artificial respiration or (if need be) to recall them from the dead so that they may deliver their messages. For it wishes only to learn from the past and it constructs a 'living past' which repeats with spurious authority the utterances put into its mouth. But to the 'historian' this is a piece of obscene necromancy: the past he adores is dead. The world has neither love nor respect for what is dead, wishing only to recall it to life again. It deals with the past as with a man, expecting it to talk sense and have something to say apposite to its plebeian 'causes' and engagements. But for the 'historian', for whom the past is dead and irreproachable, the past is feminine. He loves it as a mistress of whom he never tires and whom he never expects to talk sense. Once it was religion which stood in the way of the appearance of the 'historical' past; now it is politics; but always it is this practical disposition.

'History', then, is the product of a severe and sophisticated manner of thinking about the world which has recently emerged from the naive interest in what surrounds us on account of its intimations of what is no longer present. It represents neither an aesthetic enjoyment, nor a 'scientific' recognition, nor a practical understanding. Like these, it is a dream; but it is a dream of another sort. There is a past, that of legend and saga, which is a drama from which all that is casual, secondary and unresolved has been excluded; it has a clear outline, a unity of feeling and in it everything is exact except place and time. There is a past in which contingencies have been resolved by being recognized as products of necessary and sufficient conditions and as examples of the operation of general laws. And there is a past in which every component is known and is intelligible in respect of its relation to a favoured present. But the 'historical' past is of another sort than these. It is a complicated world, without unity of feeling or clear outline: in it events have no overall pattern or purpose, lead nowhere, point to no favoured condition of the world and support no practical conclusions. It is a world composed wholly of contingencies and in which contingencies are intelligible, not because they have been resolved, but on account of the circumstantial relations which have been established between them: the historian's concern is not with causes but with occasions. It is a picture drawn on many different scales, and each genuine piece of historical writing has a scale of its own and is to be recognized as an independent example of historical thinking. The activity of being an historian is not that of contributing to the elucidation of a single ideal coherence of events which may be called 'true' to the exclusion of all others; it is an activity in which a writer, concerned with the past for its own sake and working to a chosen scale, elicits a coherence in a group of contingencies of similar magnitudes. And if in so new and so delicate an enterprise he finds himself tempted into making concessions to the idiom of legend, that perhaps is less damaging than other divergencies.

Notes

1. Cf. Plato, *Laws*, 672B.

2. Thus, Cicero distinguished the 'historical' from the 'imagined' past, the one being concerned with 'truth' and the other with 'pleasure'.

3. In one of his notebooks (Add. 5436, 62), quoted in H. Butterfield, *Man on His Past* (p. 98), Acton observes: 'Expressions like: the growth of language, physiology of the State, national psychology, the mind of the Church, the development of Platonism, the continuity of law – questions which occupy half the mental activity of our age – were unintelligible to the eighteenth century – to Hume, Johnson, Smith, Diderot.' But it is not less true to say that the last 80 years have seen the rejection of most, if not all, of these concepts; they have again become unintelligible.

4. Compare Maitland's attitude to a legal document with that of the practising lawyer.

5. By a 'scientific' inquiry into the stars I do not, of course, mean either an inquiry unprovoked by a desire for useful information (in connection with navigation, for example), or an inquiry by its character excluded from providing such information; I mean an inquiry in which the stars are not regarded (as they once were) as interesting on account of their power to determine or reveal human destiny. Indeed, an attitude towards the stars in which they are understood in respect of their independence of ourselves is a condition of any inquiry which could produce useful information (e.g. in navgiation).

6. It is worth recalling Huisinga's observation that these and similar expressions (e.g. 'Carolingian', 'feudal', 'christian', 'humanist') in historical writing are not to be regarded as hypotheses to be proved or foundations upon which large structures may be built, but as terms to be used lightly for whatever particle of intelligibility or illumination they may contain.

7. 'The fact that the political struggles, so to call them, of modern history being part of the same in which we are ourselves engaged, affects the value of the history both ways. It increases our concern, while at the same time it blinds and distorts our view. To what an extent it is likely to do this latter may be concluded from the fact that, even as regards ancient history and times long past, if there is any resemblance between the politics then and now, we seem scarcely able to look fairly at them. A certain degree of remoteness, then, in the objects of history is desirable, though not always effective against prejudice similar to our prejudice now, and quite necessary against the actual mixture of our present prejudiced views of things with the history: we want it for every reason to stand well off from us.' John Grote, in *Cambridge Essays*, 1856, p. 111.

Source

Michael Oakeshott, 'The Activity of Being an Historian' in *Rationalism in Politics and Other Essays* (London, Methuen, 1962), pp. 137-67.

4 MICHAEL OAKESHOTT AND HISTORICAL PARTICULARISM*

Preston King

1

History occupies a central position in the political theory of Michael Oakeshott. In 1934, reviewing *Experience and Its Modes*, R.G. Collingwood (CM, 1970) described 'the chapter on history' as 'the real nucleus' of the book, and characterized the account overall as 'the most penetrating analysis of historical thought that has ever been written'. There is the risk, of course, when drawing near to such evidence as this, that those in whom we repose our trust, may themselves be snared in a circle of mutual admiration. I have in mind Oakeshott's later reception (1938) of Collingwood's *Principles of Art*. In his review, Oakeshott wrote (CM, 1970): 'I can do no better than state at once that it is the most profound and stimulating discussion I have ever read of the question.' But no matter. To chasten those disposed to regard Collingwood's testimony as suspect, we may recall E.H. Carr's verdict. Carr (1964) declared Collingwood to be 'the only British thinker in the present century who has made a serious contribution to the philosophy of history', despite the fact that Carr had severe strictures to lay both upon Collingwood and Oakeshott.

The view that history is central to Oakeshott's *œuvre* is in fact widely accepted. J.L. Auspitz, contributing to the most elaborate recent symposium on Oakeshott's work, and discussing Oakeshott's *On Human Conduct* (1975), addresses this point. Auspitz, occupying somewhat neutral ground, writes (PT, August 1976): 'History is the understanding of events as contingently related, and Oakeshott sketches the outline of a case, to be elaborated elsewhere, for the irreducibility of contingent relations to the causal or probabilistic relations which are paradigmatic in the social sciences.' (That case may well have been elaborated elsewhere, as Auspitz augurs, but not yet in published form.) Kenneth Minogue, who is close to Oakeshott, and in this sense occupies the government front bench, also understands Oakeshott to perceive

*For citations refer to Bibliography.

96

'human conduct' as 'essentially contingent' and therefore as incapable of being 'understood in terms of systems and processes'. Minogue's conclusion: 'The fundamental "logic" of human explanation is that of history' (Q, October 1975).

As for the loyal opposition, the perception of the centrality of history in Oakeshott persists. A.H. Birch (1969) for example, in arguing with Oakeshott, none the less identifies the latter's view of history as the chief question to be disputed. Birch contends that political scientists are given to understand by Oakeshott 'first, that the nature of political activity makes historical explanation the only appropriate mode, and second, that the nature of historical explanation prevents them from seeking answers to many of the questions which are normally regarded as central to their subject' (p. 222). Birch perceives Oakeshott's retreat into a particularly restrictive concept of history unrealistically to exclude the prospect of identifying 'regularities, tendencies, types and typical sequences' (p. 225) — all such, for Birch, constituting 'sociological explanation'. Birch, while effectively arguing against what one might call Oakeshott's 'particularist' concept of history, and while arguing for what Birch himself calls 'sociological explanation', none the less hints that the latter need only be viewed as an addition to Oakeshott's other modes of experience. The important consideration, in all this, is the proper emphasis that must be placed upon Oakeshott's commitment to historical explanation as that most appropriate to the understanding of human conduct. Oakeshott is little disposed to say clearly that which is susceptible to more ambiguous formulation. This comment will not be thought unfair. What Minogue more boldly asserts, Oakeshott (HC) formulates less robustly: 'The theoretical understanding of a substantive action or utterance is, then, in principle, a "historical" understanding' (p. 107). Where we turn directly to the subject of our concern, we may not expect that he shall ever quite tear the veil from the face of this argument.

2

It will be clear as to the centrality of history for Oakeshott. But history may be conceived in different ways. The most extreme contrast is that in which it is regarded, on the one side, as governed by laws and thus predictable, and, on the other, as governed by no laws and so as unpredictable. It is most uncomfortable to be made to divide a large cake in two, and then to choose which of the two it were better to eat. This would prove an uncomfortable challenge, but not one, all the same, from which every brave man will withdraw. Oakeshott, certainly, is less timorous than most. As a part of this, naturally, one cannot but applaud his 'deep respect for the individual action', his 'eye for shades of difference between plausible likenesses', indeed his 'ear for echoes and the imagination' (HC, p. 106). But one fears that the emphasis upon history as non-recurrence, difference, individuality, context, contingency, circumstance, uniqueness and the like, must often ultimately collapse into self-enclosure and the unintelligibility associated with a great profusion of private worlds. It does not matter that the concept of history as physics, as determinism or materialism or predictability should sin in some rather different way.

Oakeshott's assertions about the nature of history may be construed as constituting a defence of historical 'particularism'. In the face of this construction, we may encounter the rebuttal that Oakeshott is as much concerned with generality as with particularity. There are indeed statements which may be extracted from Oakeshott's most recent work which are consistent with this rebuttal. For example: 'A specific engagement to understand begins in a "going-on" abstracted from all that may be going on and understood in terms of an ideal character specified as a composition of characteristics, a unity of particularity and genericity' (HC, p. 12). Or again: 'there can be no relationship save between identities, and all identities are unities of particularity and genericity' (HC, p. 102). And most forcefully: 'particularity is neither intelligible nor capable of inviting investigation' (HC, p. 12).

Despite these quotations, it remains that Oakeshott suggests an identity between 'particularity' and 'uniqueness'. This is done in *On Human Conduct* (p. 102). There are similar suggestions in *Experience and Its Modes*. And were we to say that Oakeshott's arguments constitute a defence of historical 'uniqueness', there could not subsist any possible grounds for complaint. The point is not that, in Oakeshott, 'history is made up of details'. Everything is. There is no more a need to defend Oakeshott than Gangesa or Democritus against so tepid a charge. The point rather is that, for Oakeshott, history is experience perceived as 'unique events'. It will be true of course that particular events, as with particular facts, cannot be seized other than in relation to other events and facts — and on the basis of an infinite range of assumptions. But a distinction is to be made between a particular as merely a unit in a series (e.g. one copy of *Leviathan* among tens of thousands) and a particular more singularly as the only one of a kind (such as the last Tasmanian tiger or Mauritian dodo — should either chance to be out and about somewhere). It is this second type of particularity which Oakeshott projects upon history, and characterizes as unique. What Oakeshott is arguing against, albeit in an almost exclusively definitional manner, is the idea of history as science, of 'unique events' being governed by 'universal laws', of 'practice' (the wink) being explained in terms of 'process' (the blink).

3

The doctrine of historical particularism — the notion that historical events are unique — is in no way peculiar to Oakeshott. It is a view for which we are all disposed to evince some degree of sympathy. Nor is it necessarily a conservative view. It could in part be anarchistic (as with Kropotkin) or Marxist or Darwinian or Popperian. Nor is it patently absurd, for the reason that every unit in a set or integer in a series or member of a group is, in some stipulable sense, 'unique'. Peter, like John, was one of twelve disciples, and thus not singular; but to the extent that it was him and no other who was denominated father of the church, his position was unique. Any event, historical or other, may be regarded, depending entirely upon one's perspective, as either particular or general, as either unique or commonplace (and therefore as both). All that matters is to say, and with good reason in any given case, whether and in what respects the event or phenomenon inspected is either one or the other. To call history, as such, unique is to commit a category mistake; it is to confound what is common and recurrent with what is not. But we shall return to critical considerations of this sort later.

The categorization of history by Oakeshott as a plenum of unique events is intended to exclude the notion of there being universal or inexorable laws at work within it. If one took a static or cyclical view of history (as with the Book of Ecclesiastes in the one case or Vico in the other) one would in either case assume a form of determinism which would somehow imply the existence of such laws. The odd thing about the nineteenth-century 'discovery' — or rediscovery — of history as something other than theological or scientific determinism, is that it posited epochal and periodic differentiation or uniqueness married to an overarching and rational dynamic. Hegel assumed that the free individual was the agent of history and that through him there laboured 'the cunning of reason', so that what was 'accidental' or 'incidental' was controlled by a higher (or deeper) rationale or purpose which the individual himself could not know. Hegel was struck by the way in which the obvious and fundamental truths of one era become the equally obvious absurdities of another. Marx, of course, like Hegel, sought to retain the appreciation of historical particularity while insisting none the less upon an underlying rationale, in this case of 'historical materialism' or, as Plekhanov later put it, of 'dialectical materialism'. Darwin, though he assumed every species was unique, managed to unlearn the notion that each species represented a special, single, instantaneous act of creation, and instead of this perceived indeed a 'process', of what he called 'natural selection'. In all of these cases, there is joined some notion of historical periodicity, individuality or uniqueness, with historical rationality, causality and sometimes predictability.

Oakeshott is certainly reacting against Hegel and Marx while none the less being much subject to the influence of the former. The chief difference for our purposes is that Oakeshott's historical particularism attempts to break away most decisively from the notion of causality in history as accepted by his nineteenth-century predecessors. But even in this respect, Oakeshott does not stand alone. Even Karl Popper, in *The Poverty of Historicism* (1960), takes a position which is in some respects similar. Popper, however, is much more careful, and his judgement more rounded. He distinguishes, for example, between 'trends' and 'laws', arguing that history at least displays the former if not the latter. Furthermore, Popper does not maintain that *all* historical hypotheses are singular statements about one or more individual events (PH, p. 107), but only that they are so 'as a rule', which is to say in some (possibly even most) but not in all cases. Finally, Popper insists that one of the major tasks of history must remain 'the disentanglement of causal threads' and does not merely or exclusively involve 'the description of the "accidental" manner in which these threads are interwoven' (PH, p. 147). Popper, then, asserts with Oakeshott that history involves 'the appreciation of the unique'. But, unlike Oakeshott, he does not repudiate what he calls 'causal explanation' in history.

Overall, Oakeshott perceives history as a sequence of unique events, events which have no purpose or end, events which are dead, beyond hope of modification, beyond the applause or catcalls of moral praise or blame, events none the less which are inferred from present evidence, and present evidence only. This is an odd, interesting, bewildering, in part contradictory, and no doubt 'unique' set of ideas. And they, again in part, have set up their resonances. One might even say that they have, if not started, then accentuated — in Popper's sense — a 'trend'.

The trend is against making moral judgements in historical analysis, against treating the ideas of the past as though they were present (even though paradoxically, they are), against confusing one period with another, and towards differentiating every period (however impossible the task) from every other, towards placing the emphasis upon discontinuity rather than continuity, and upon the uniqueness and irrelevance of the past despite its inevitable apperception in and only in the present.

Oakeshott believes that human conduct is to be understood 'in terms of contingent relations' and that such understanding 'is contextual' (HC, p. 105). If historical events are unique, then each, for Oakeshott, must be assimilated on its own terms, for its own sake, and as a whole. This differentiation between diverse historical moments is nothing other than periodization, with its commitment to contextual analysis in the history of ideas. The discussion has by now been pushed much beyond Oakeshott. But Oakeshott's self-enclosed definitionalism, with its recommendatory import, has encouraged many scholars to further differentiate themselves, and to place a stress upon what is limited and local, on the comfortable assumption that it could not, in any event, ever legitimately prove much more than this. On the other hand, one suspects that it would prove out of place to blame such a writer as Oakeshott for an orientation which may merely prove symptomatic of the brittleness of an age.

One of the most celebrated proponents of contextual analysis in our own time is of course Quentin Skinner. Skinner (1969a) does not argue, with respect to the history of ideas, that the context determines what a given writer says, but only that it places a negative limit upon what he could have meant. It is clear that, to grasp the meaning of any communication, we must in some degree be familiar with the conventions which qualify what is conveyed as a communication. It remains that, at any point we think that we have grasped what was intended, we may be mistaken. But we only think our grasp is secure where we think we understand the conventions. And a convention, like a tradition, as Oakeshott has observed, is a tricky thing to get to know. And how, one may ask, is it ever possible to be sure? Skinner suggests that we may undertake 'the study of all the facts about the social context of a given text'. Oakeshott, in parallel, characterizes the historian as totally immersed in the past, suffering no lacuna, in search of the whole.

The obvious question is whether any programme which enjoins the study of *all* the facts is in any way feasible. The answer will be obvious. Now we never know in itself when something has been communicated.

From the point that we think we know even that much, quite apart from the substance of any communication, it is already to be presumed that we have some familiarity with the conventions involved. The problem is to determine how much of a contextual understanding we require in order to be able to grasp what an author has to say. One may easily sink into an infinite regress of putting thoughts in context — without any clear criterion to stipulate what would constitute an adequate level of such attainment. In sinking beneath the waves of such 'contextual' analysis, the original author's 'intentions' may directly escape recovery. This, for the reason that psychological *intentions* are never entirely to be divorced from the logic of one's formulae and their associated *implications*. In this way, too, a philosopher who takes the logic of his own argument seriously, may easily be led to embrace implications which are demonstrated by another to follow from his premises, even where those logical implications are inconsistent with some psychological or moral intentions which the author may originally and explicitly have embraced. In as far as a past thinker displays a logic, he also proffers it as a handle, one by which his meaning may be relevantly gripped in future, and in relation to the concerns of that future.

John Dunn (1969) for example is one of those who sinks into a bog of 'contextual' analysis in a rather turgid attempt to recapture 'Locke's *own* meaning'. In his 'excavation', Dunn eschews the notion that he should provide 'a critique of [Locke's] argument'. Dunn will not argue with Locke apparently on the assumption that the one in the present and the other in the past cannot possibly share any relevant common ground. 'I simply cannot conceive of constructing an analysis of any issue in contemporary political theory around the affirmation or negation of anything which Locke says about political matters' (p. 2). Dunn then commits himself to historical periodization, to an unequivocal divorce between past and present, and to the idea that no moral should be abstracted from the one and applied to the other. Only Dunn's sort of account of Locke is characterized as 'historical' — i.e. as valid — not such accounts as those provided by Alan Ryan or C.B. Macpherson or Leo Strauss or Richard Cox or Raymond Polin.

Dunn, given the commitment to a radical divorce between past and present, appears disposed to want to deny us the possibility of fitting Locke into a tradition (that of 'English empiricism'). The danger for the particularist is clear. If we stipulate the nature of the tradition, that stipulation is a contemporary exercise, and its consequence must be to shape the way in which we see past events building up to and influencing the present. And if the past, in this way, does influence the present, then of course it is also somehow a part of the present, and in this sense requires to be contended with, even argued with. Of course it will be true that it could not have been Locke's 'own ambition', in the seventeenth century, to espouse Marxist and liberal views which only became current from the nineteenth century. But it has never been the case that contributing to an outcome necessarily requires a psychological intention or commitment to do so. There can be no question that the Newtonian theory of gravity contributed to the Einsteinian theory of relativity. But to say that Newton had this influence does not require us to add that he knew Einstein's theory or intended to contribute to it. It is always probable that a great thinker will somehow spark or inspire the emergence of new ideas with which he could not possibly be familiar in their evolved form. And this is because the logic of a position, although it may correlate with a writer's meaning, is never reducible to the 'psychology' of his mind.

In attempting to explain Locke's ideas, Dunn feels compelled to fall back upon his 'psychology', his 'biography'. Dunn identifies in Locke two incompatible concepts of 'substantive morality'. He conceives of Locke as torn between the disposition to concoct an ethic built upon obedience to God and one built upon an increasing individual pursuit of power. In Dunn's own words, 'one of these [Lockeian commitments] is purely secular', the terrestrial utilitarian object being 'to maximize the influence and power of the individual'. The other commitment is religious and is ' concerned with individual salvation'. Dunn's conclusion is that Locke joins these two moralities, but (contra Macpherson) makes the power motive subsidiary to the religious object of achieving salvation (pp. 257-8). The 'highly conjectural explanation which [is] implicit throughout [Dunn's] account' (p. 256) is that Locke never surrendered himself to pleasure, never became 'a gay and careless libertine' (p. 258), never threw off the restraints imposed by his religious morality — because . . . Locke 'was brought up in a Calvinist family' (p. 259); lacked 'assurance' and 'confidence'; 'suffered too much anxiety'; was 'distinctly ill physically'; was 'too anxious', 'very neurotic', and characterized by 'personal weakness'. All of this is intended to explain the priority system attributed by Dunn to Locke's ethics — to explain why Locke *thought* as he did. We must concur with Dunn in the view that the account is 'crude' and even 'vulgar' — but not on the grounds that to admit an offence is necessarily exculpatory. In this example one may detect something of the difficulty associated with attempting to comprehend some aspect of the past, in this case systems of thought, by reference to contextual readings — which so often reduce to vulgar biography. Dunn, in his 'historical account' of Locke's politics, attempts to cut himself off from the present to secure a firmer grip on the past. His success consists merely in using some Lockeian part of the past to support one of the sides in a contemporary debate over the possibility or impossibility of neutralizing history *vis-à-vis* present concerns and commitments. To the extent that he succeeds, to that extent does he demonstrate a larger failure.

Dunn is surely correct in saying that Locke, given his seventeenth-century English context, most probably could not even imagine the possibility of an egalitarian social revolution — and that it might prove inappropriate to judge him morally in relation to such a (for Locke non-existent) possibility. 'A Locke confronted by the possibility of achieved social revolution is no longer the Locke on whose attitudes we have the evidence to pronounce' (p. 240). What is important to recognize is that this stricture cuts two ways. Dunn and those of like views are only concerned with one of these ways. The principle the particularist stipulates is this: do not transfer a writer from an earlier period to a later and assume that one can say anything whatever about what such a writer, in altered circumstances, would have thought. The principle the particularist overlooks, however, is that one must be equally obliged, logically, not to transfer a later period to an earlier and to make a pronouncement on behalf of an earlier writer located there regarding what he would *not* have thought. In this respect, the complaints levelled against Macpherson by Dunn can equally well be levelled against Dunn himself — as where the latter confidently assures us that Locke's 'deepest social and moral assumptions . . . would probably have placed him among the defenders of the Ancien Régime' a century later. How could one possibly say, psychologically, *what* Locke would, even probably, have done? Of course, one can make the *type* of statement made by Macpherson or Dunn — about what a past writer, in a future at some remove from him, would or would not have done — on the assumption of a continuity between past and present, and of the relevance of one to the other. What one cannot do is to deny the continuity and relevance and then proceed to hypothesize about what past figures would not (even probably) have thought at some later time.

But the object here is not again to enter directly into a discussion of the status of historical contexts and of traditions of ideas. It is merely to say that what Oakeshott offers us is associated with an important stream of contemporary thought to do with historiography and the study of society. In doing this, it is not necessary to exaggerate the substantive achievement, as with Kenneth Minogue, where the latter declares Oakeshott's *On Human Conduct* to be 'worthy to stand beside . . . *Leviathan*' (Q, 1975).

4

The similarity or congruence of (1) Oakeshott's argument and (2) much present practice is such as to suggest the utility of reviewing the tenability of the second by reference to the more elaborate arguments of the first. Certainly Oakeshott's argument can be reasonably construed as constituting a defence — perhaps the defence — of an approach which we may label historical particularism. But we are not required to insist that all of those who appear ideologically addicted to historical particularism have necessarily read Oakeshott.

The most important statements in Oakeshott's philosophy of history are contained in *Experience and Its Modes* (1933) and in the essay entitled 'The Activity of Being an Historian' (1955).[1] The latter amplifies the former in certain important respects, although W.H. Greenleaf (1966) has recorded the view that 'The Activity of Being an Historian' succeeded in adding 'little to the earlier analysis'. In my judgement, *On Human Conduct* (1975) adds nothing of significance to the discussion. For Oakeshott, experience may be construed in four different ways: contemplatively (or poetically), practically, scientifically and historically. In the first case,[2] we 'regard the world in a manner which does not allow us to consider anything but what is immediately before our eyes and does not provoke us to any conclusions'. (This *contemplative* perspective is that 'of the artist and the poet'.) In the second case, we recognize the play of cause and effect in events, but our concern is only with the effect upon ourselves, only with the (good or evil) consequences which these events have for us. (This practical response 'is the response of a partisan'.) In the third case, we still consider events in terms of their causal relationships, but independently of any impact upon ourselves. (This theoretical response is the achievement of the scientist.)

The world through which we move is, for Oakeshott, a single and unitary world of experience. All of the events which populate it, to be perceived at all, must be *present* to the mind (as must be any study of the *past*). The difference between the historical response — or perspective — and all the others, is that these never relinquish experience as present, while history only perceives experience as past. The historical perspective, in short, is one which envisages no use or application of the past; it is one which accepts the past as it is, and 'for its own sake'. Oakeshott states that 'what the historian is interested in is a dead past; a past unlike the present'.

We shall not, for the moment, concern ourselves with the question of how or in what way Oakeshott differentiates between history and the other modes of experience which he identifies. We need only emphasize here the fact that Oakeshott establishes a rigid distinction between these various modes. This is not the same as saying that Oakeshott intends that there can be no other modes than those he identifies ('the choice . . . must, to some extent, be arbitrary'). It is only to say that he affirms that each of the modes which he identifies is 'wholly and absolutely independent of any other' (EiM, p. 75). Oakeshott insists upon this separation: 'No one of these modes of experience is, in any sense whatever, based upon or dependent upon any other; no one is derived from any other, and none directly related to any other' (p. 76). These modes, he says, these worlds of experience, 'are wholly irrelevant to one another' (p. 327).

Of course, we shall confront a problem if Oakeshott's modes of experience are held to be 'wholly and absolutely independent' of one another and if, at the same time, they are held to represent distinctions which are admittedly arbitrary. Oakeshott makes both claims. If these modes are admittedly arbitrary, but still legitimate, then presumably their experiential content must be equally legitimately divisible in other ways. If that is so, then it becomes difficult to understand how the 'attempt to pass in argument from one world [mode] of ideas to another' should constitute, following Oakeshott, a 'case of irrelevance', of 'error', of 'confusion'. In this argument, we confront a preliminary difficulty. Granted, the notion of 'passing' is imprecise. But it is not clear, for example, how one could be or why one should be categorically denied the possibility of writing 'history' while making scientific or 'practical' (i.e. moral) judgements in the course of doing so. Political history would appear to necessitate 'practical' judgements. It may be an important part of the explanation of Zulu imperialism that Chaka was ruthless or of European imperialism that figures like Francis Drake (as Captain of *The Golden Hind*) or Cecil Rhodes (as head of the British South Africa Company) were driven by greed: the ethic of unlimited material accumulation. Attributions of motives and characteristics such as 'ruthlessness', 'greed', 'fairness' do after all serve an explanatory purpose, while constituting nonetheless substantive moral ('practical') judgements. To begin to be able to deny the possibility of such a connection as this between historical and practical modes must at least require that the distinction between them prove more than merely arbitrary.

5

Oakeshott wishes to distinguish between events in terms of perspectives on them which are contemplative or scientific or practical or historical. He assumes that all experience is present experience. He assumes that we can enjoy no direct experience of anything that is past, due to the fact that it is *past*. We can only perceive what is present. As we live only in the present, we cannot simultaneously live in (what we may take to be) the past. We have only present evidence for the past — whether in the form of documents, letters, monuments or whatever. It is such evidence as this which permits us to infer that a past did exist, without permitting us directly to enter into and to inhabit it. Thus an *historical* perspective, for Oakeshott, is still by implication a *present* perspective. (As Oakeshott puts it, 'the past . . . is a certain sort of reading of the present'.)

Since, for Oakeshott, all experience is present experience, the crucial consideration is the distinction between historical and other responses to experience, and the tenability of this distinction. As a part of this, it is necessary to provide some connotative stipulation about the content of history. It is inescapable that Oakeshott should oblige us in this matter. But we shall discover that Oakeshott imparts to history and to the historian an equivocal character. But let us begin with the first aspect of the historian's identity — where he is recommended to us as 'one who understands the events of the world before him as evidence for events that have already taken place'.

This statement — although only one of two (the second is taken up in section 7) which Oakeshott offers us — is sufficient to permit us to consider directly the tenability of history conceived as a distinct mode of experience. The basic question must be whether all other modes of experience contain within them any historical dimension, actual or potential. If, of course, the three other 'modes of experience' either explicitly or implicitly understand present events as 'evidence for events that have already taken place', then there can be no clear distinction between 'history' (so understood) and these other non-historical modes.

Oakeshott observes that the attitude of the poet, as distinct from that of the historian, is one of wonder. And yet, we may rightly inter-ject, the poet may wonder at something which he takes to be *past*. For

Oakeshott, the attitude of the practical man is that of a partisan. But we may insist that, even as a partisan makes the past serve a present purpose — he may be a patriot or a zealot — this very orientation presupposes that this 'practical man' *qua* 'practical man' has some distinct sense of a *past*. The attitude of Oakeshott's scientist reveals a sense of timelessness. But it will be clear to us that the assumption of a causal process assumes sequence, and thus there is also implicit in 'science' some sense of a *past*. The historian, it must follow from all this, cannot be alone in regarding 'present events as evidence for events that have already taken place' (RiP, p. 150). In this understanding of present events as evidence for events that have already taken place, we have, accordingly, no clear criterion for distinguishing between the historian, on the one hand, and the practical man, poet, or scientist, on the other.

It is possible for the universe to be tidily packed into four or more small self-contained boxes, such as those Oakeshott passes round. The merely taxonomic business of dividing the intelligible world into so many distinct realms of discourse is perfectly acceptable at least in as far as (1) the classification is intended to be exhaustive, (2) the same material cannot be organized more satisfactorily in other ways, and (3) the purpose of and criteria for the classification are clear and coherent. Oakeshott is placed in a difficult position straightaway where he accepts that his categories or modes are not exhaustive (i.e. the three or four are not the only ones) and yet holds that the differences between them are 'absolute'. If his categories or modes are not exhaustive, so as to cover all experience relevant to them, then there can be no guarantee that some different experience — whether genuinely new or merely overlooked — will fit into the established categories or modes, will not overlap them and require them to be restructured. A classificatory scheme which is not exhaustive can never claim that its component parts are in any way mutually exclusive, or absolute. It is indeed for this reason that Birch (1969) is perfectly entitled to support his claims for 'the possibility of sociological explanation' by quoting against Oakeshott the latter's own formula (EiM) that 'there can be no limit to the number of possible modifications in experience'. A vital part of the difficulty for Oakeshott's own argument lies in the non-exhaustive character of his modes.

In any event, the only new category or 'mode' for which Oakeshott makes a case is 'history'. The others — roughly, 'poetry' for aesthetics, 'practice' for 'ethics' and 'science' for itself — are conventional, although again not exhaustive. But history, as has been hinted, is not a category (as Oakeshott first defines it) which we can separate out from any experience whatever. If we say our experience is present, and that it can be read or reconstructed in such a way as to yield some sense of a past, then this will be true for all experience. This is no more than to say that we have some concept of duration, or of temporal 'extension'. In as far as we have a sense of the present — and Oakeshott insists (wrongly) that all experience is present — it is clear that such a concept is logically meshed with some notion of a past. If we mean by *history*, 'understanding the past' (as Oakeshott sometimes does) it will be clear that every present understanding contains within itself some past dimension. If all experience is present (never mind if it is not) and if we can have no sense of a present divorced from some assumption of a past and if (as Oakeshott suggests) history merely consists in inferring or intuiting or reconstructing a past from the present, then no experience is non-historical. If no experience is non-historical, then 'history' cannot be said to constitute an absolutely or otherwise distinct mode of experience.

In fact, there is no subject of study — whether philosophy or physics, whist or history itself — which hasn't a history. We may well say that history is somehow distinct. But we may as readily maintain that it is indistinct. For if history — taken as duration — may project as its object all of experience, or any subsidary study or aspect of experience, then it is always married to such studies and aspects, and in such a way as to make any notion of a categorical divorce between it and them logically unacceptable. In this sense, history is less a subject of study than a way to study a subject. History most certainly is not — again taken as duration — a specific method or methodology, since there are many different methods compatible with it. But as we shall see later, Oakeshott is disposed to confound his preferred historical methodology with 'history' *per se*.

In sum, Oakeshott wishes to distinguish between history and other parallel activities; but he leaves us, in the end, with at least two different notions of what 'history' is. The first of these, as we have seen, characterizes history as a past which we infer from present evidence. Given this general criterion, however, it must follow that anyone — whether a poet, moralist, politician or scientist — who makes such an inference, is *pro tanto* enveloped in history. It is difficult to imagine, moreover, that any agent could avoid making such an inference. Were Oakeshott to accept, however, that the other modes — poetry, practice and science — also assume an 'historical' character, then his original attempt to distinguish between them (certainly in any categorical sense) must fail.

6

Although Oakeshott has occasion to insist that the modes he stipulates are 'wholly irrelevant to one another', 'wholly and absolutely independent' etc., he eventually equivocates over the tenability of this absolute independence and mutual irrelevance. Oakeshott proceeds to change the rules. The first rule he advances requires us to regard history and the other modes stipulated as wholly distinct. But a second rule quickly permits us to enjoy 'pasts' which are contemplative, practical, scientific, *and* historical.

Oakeshott's concept of history, taken as a wholly distinct category or mode of experience, fails to maintain a distinction between itself and the other modes. What is revoked is less Oakeshott's direct *characterization* of history than his stipulation regarding its *independence* as a mode. This retrenchment is explicit in *Experience and its Modes*, but its implications are never directly addressed by the author. Oakeshott comes to write that '[h]istory is certainly a form of experience in which what is experienced is, in some sense, past'. He continues, 'But the past in history is not the only past, and a clear view of the character of the past in history involves the distinction of this past from that in other forms of experience' (EiM, p. 102). What this implies is that 'other forms of experience' also and self-consciously enjoy a past (inferred from present experience). Hence the author's reference to the contemplative past ('poetry'), the practical past, the scientific past and the 'historical' past.

The nature of the reversal which Oakeshott hereby achieves is of interest and warrants fuller attention (as under 1, 2 and 3 below). But the most salient feature of the analysis is that it quite contradicts the position earlier stipulated. What he says, in as far as the concern is to maintain that (the study of) science, poetry, ethics and history . . . all have a history, or that they all have a past, is perfectly sound. But we encounter problems to the extent that the concern is to maintain that the 'pasts' attributed to these subject areas have no genuinely 'historical' dimension. This unfortunately is the road which Oakeshott seeks to have us travel. All four modes, he suggests, reveal a 'past', only one of which he thinks historical. Poetry yields a 'contemplative past' (the reality) but is not genuinely historical, is 'specious'. Practice yields a practical past (the reality) but it is history front to back, is 'unhistorical'. Science yields a scientific past (the reality) but the timelessness of its propositions undermines their historicity.

(1) Oakeshott says little directly about contemplation as a perspec-

tive on history. The important thing about it, however, is that it does not locate history in the past, which is the only place where history is 'history'. The contemplative response is no more concerned to moralize about the past than it is concerned to unearth the causes or consequences of historical events. The attitude it strikes is one of wonder. But, for Oakeshott, such an attitude has nothing to do with 'history'. For any object of contemplation, in the course of being contemplated, is automatically ensnared by, and assimilated to, the present. Indeed, although Oakeshott refers to contemplation as a 'response' to 'the past', his object is to deny it any genuinely 'historical' status at all. Thus Oakeshott qualifies contemplative history as 'specious'. He suggests that the historical novel, for example, is fiction, not history. The contemplative past is present imagination flooding the broken plains of past record. Thus overwhelmed, the past loses its distinctiveness as past; it and the present are merged together in a uniform offering which, for Oakeshott, is simply 'unhistorical'.

(2) Oakeshott has far more to say about the 'practical' past. But the central observation is the same − namely that it is 'unhistorical'. The 'practical' man is accused of 'reading the past backwards', only recognizing those past events which can be related to present activity. In the 'practical' past, Oakeshott suggests, history is only assimilated in terms of its present or future effects, whether desirable or abhorrent. Such sounds and signals which touch neither of these poles remain unperceived and inexistent in the 'practical' past; here there is no equipment available to receive such affectively weak emissions. In such circumstances, the past, for Oakeshott, cannot exist on its own or for itself; it only exists as a part of the present and indeed in order to serve present purposes. The 'practical' perspective, then, suffers from the fact that it obliterates from view a 'past' that is distinctly past; it makes it impossible to come to grips with the past as such. The practical response 'is the response of a partisan', convering 'past' into 'present', and so altering its character as history. Like the 'contemplative' past, therefore, Oakeshott denies the 'practical' past a distinctly 'historical' status.

(3) Oakeshott thinks of the scientific past as providing a more 'objective' perspective, which assimilates events in terms of cause and effect, without reference to whether they harm or hurt us, or serve any practical purpose. The scientific perspective thus perceives the past, if not on its own terms, at least 'for its own sake'. For Oakeshott, however, this is still insufficient. For a scientific view of (or response to) an historical event may convert the actual event into an hypothetical situation. The result of this can only be that such an event, although

detached from the present, is also wrenched out of the past. It becomes conjectural and merely serves as an instance of a general law, which has no specifically historical character at all. The conclusion must be that the scientific response to the past, being 'timeless', for that very reason cannot possibly be 'historical'.

To put the matter summarily, Oakeshott makes history, poetry, science and practice absolutely distinct. Next, he gives each of these an 'historical' dimension, thus apparently destroying the absolute distinction at first established. He then appears to halt in this train of reflection before the consideration that to have a 'past' and to have an 'historical past' are not quite the same. (Thus, for example, Oakeshott does not attempt to show that the sense of a 'past' involved in 'practice' is not a sense of a 'past' — but that it is somehow not an 'historical' past that is involved. The patriot and the zealot have a sense of a past, it is implied, but not an 'historical' sense, in so far as they seek to employ 'past' evidence for present purposes.) Oakeshott, in short, admits that each of his modes is penetrated by some sense of a past. Rather than accept the implication that would follow from such an admission — that science, practice and poetry all have an historical dimension — Oakeshott assumes a new but unargued distinction between having a sense of past, on the one hand, and having an historical sense, on the other.

This raises for us the question of the connection between the notions 'past' and 'historical'. We must note, to begin, that 'past' is a noun and 'historical' an adjective. The 'past' will refer to any former moment of time or to all such moments. 'History', as the parallel noun, will generally refer to the more momentous of such moments. Oakeshott employs 'past' in the first sense, but not 'history' in the second sense. He asserts that history is distinguished by the activity of 'reading present evidence as evidence for events that have already taken place'. We may take it that this is much the same as 'understanding the past'. In any event, unqualified reference to history as what has 'already taken place' must imply that 'its object is an all-encompassing past', not some more restricted past to do merely, say, with great men and great deeds. In these circumstances, Oakeshott provides no distinction, clear or otherwise, between 'the past' and 'history'.

Oakeshott tells us that we may infer the past from the present, which is to say that we cannot attest to the existence of a past in itself. He also tells us that history consists in such inferences. But if the past does not exist in itself, and if history provides us with (or consists in) such inferences, then the past (for us) can only be understood as history. If this is so, it will not appear to matter greatly whether we speak of a contemplative, practical, scientific and 'historical' *history*, or of a contemplative, practical, scientific and 'historical' *past*. And it will not appear to matter greatly whether this last is called an historical history, a past past, a past history or 'the historical past'.

Where 'the past', as conventionally, is taken to signify any or all former time, and 'history' to signify important aspects of this, the two notions overlap without being identical, in the sense that 'the past' need not imply 'history', while 'history' does assume 'the past'. There is no evidence to suggest that Oakeshott contemplates such a distinction. If this had been the intention, he would perhaps have been more disposed to speak of an 'historic past' than of an 'historical past'.

Of course 'the past', as above, may be taken to cover prior moments of time, while 'history', not as above, may allude to the selective *study* of some of these. In this case, too, the two notions overlap, in that 'history', so understood, assumes 'the past', but not vice versa. Indeed, such a distinction — like the first — assumes that 'the past' may stand outside 'history'. What is important here is that Oakeshott's analysis formally excludes such a possibility. For him, there is no past which is not an object of study, which in any way stands outside evidence present to the mind of an ever-contemporaneous beholder. The 'past' is merely a contemporary construct through which we order experience, and cannot intelligibly be said to 'exist' beyond our perception of it in present evidence. Nor can it impliedly be known apart from some form of study of it. Here we are not concerned with a failure (in the form of an omission) to distinguish between 'the past' and 'history', but rather with a *decision* to conflate them. In so far as this is so, there is, for Oakeshott, no past to which we can humanly attest which is not history, as well as no history which is not to do with the past.

Of course, it may be said that what Oakeshott intends in referring to an 'historical past' is 'an historical perspective on the past'. It is clear that the poet-author of *The Waste Land* or the political writer of *Mein Kampf* or the geneticist discoverer of the double helix is not primarily concerned to offer lessons in history. The question is whether one can say anything very much more precise than this. Is it true that the scientist is concerned with 'timelessness'? His concern may be to elaborate a theory of evolution. Is it the case that the patriot is 'unhistorical'? His report on the past may of course be mistaken or biased or distorted; he may even have deliberately 'cooked the books'; but in none of these respects can he be absolutely and categorically distinguished from the common and garden variety of historian, nor even from the most exceptional of these, for we shall find none above mistakes, bias, the occasional distortion and sometimes worse. Is it so that the poet's sense of wonder, that his desire to experience and to communicate delight, renders his sense of the past 'specious'? The delight he wears about him may be the savory jacket of a tale or of a theory. Witness Swift:

> So, naturalists observe a flea
> Hath smaller fleas that on him prey;
> And these have smaller fleas to bite 'em
> And so proceed *ad infinitum*.

It may even be that Oakeshott seeks to distinguish between historians and the rest by reference to an attitude — as in the form of a commitment to the past. But such an attitude could never be established on any other basis than that of degree. We all in part share the commitment to the past. Indeed, without it we could have no present. We shall make the sort of distinctions Oakeshott advances between history and science and so on and there will be no harm in this — as long as the necessary elasticity of these terms is not destroyed. In the end, it cannot greatly matter how we distinguish between say, history and science. (We might say, for example, that statements of the first sort are usually singular and that scientific statements are generally universal — but neither characterization could itself be universalized.) The important question, in the end, should be whether statements of either sort are correct, or at least testable. The trouble is that we may manipulate definitions such that an individual, normally (and loosely) regarded as a 'scientist', is denied the title where he makes the sort of statement or conducts the sort of investigation normally regarded as the province of one whom we loosely characterize as an 'historian' — and vice versa. We may do the same with political scientists and political philosophers and moral philosophers and so on. But we shall not thereby make the concrete statements they advance one whit the more intelligible or unintelligible or the more true or false. These labels for human performances, where transmuted into rigid barriers, whether between intellectual 'fields' or experiential 'modes', do little to advance our understanding.

The past is implicit in all intellectual and other endeavour. We have located no way of studying it which we can agree upon as categorically better than every other. It is not unusual to encounter distinctions between the 'past' and 'history'. Some of these may prove helpful, but none in any notable degree. One aspect of Oakeshott's argument denies the distinction — since 'history/the past' is taken to be no more than a reading of present data as evidence for events that have already taken place, and because all experience, even at the point where it has expressly become practical or scientific, may be so read. Another aspect of Oakeshott's argument affirms the distinction — which is instanced where he speaks of the 'historical past', in this qualifying 'history' as a particular type of 'past'. But he nowhere demonstrates what sort of distinctive past history could be, other than in terms, perhaps, of an attitude — the historian's commitment to or immersion in his craft. In any event, one cannot implicitly deny and then expressly affirm the distinction. The point is not that the distinction cannot be made. E.H. Carr (1964), for example, writes: 'excellent books can be written about the past which are not history' (p. 48). The distinction is of a trivial kind, but Carr is at least explicit about his purpose — which is to reserve the word 'history' to cover *man's* past.

7

We now turn to Oakeshott's second formulation (for the first, see section 5) where he stipulates that the historian does not merely read the present as evidence for the past — as originally argued — but, instead, that he 'never does anything else'. As Oakeshott puts it, the historian's 'attitude to the present is one in which the past *always* appears'. And Oakeshott, at various points, remarks that it is this which makes the historian 'different' or 'supreme' or 'unique' and so on. What is to be remarked about this second formulation is that it involves a divergence from the first. In the first, the difference is not quantified, and in this sense represents a difference of *kind*. In the second, it is quantified and in this sense represents a difference of *degree*. The historian, on this second stipulation, is not an historian by virtue of his present and *categorical* concern with the past, but by virtue of the fact that he is aggregatively more concerned with the past than is the poet or practical man or scientist. There is not a great deal in such a formula. Oakeshott, perhaps made uncomfortable by the prospect, and wishing to avoid the difficulty, reveals an inclination towards escalation. Hence the desire to say, not that the historian is merely *more* concerned, but that he is *only* and *exclusively* concerned, with the past.

The assertion that the historian is *only* concerned with the past proves trivial on one understading of 'past'. That is to say, if we make a distinction between past, present, and future, and insist upon the present as a severe and instantaneous line of demarcation between past and future, then the historian has little option in the business of concentrating his entire attention upon the past. For the future, after all, since it is not yet at hand, must remain forever inaccessible; and the present, as soon as one seeks to write about it, is of course (conceived as an instant) already past.

There is a second problem. This relates more directly to the distinction between the historical and other modes of experience. On the above view — of the present constituting an instantaneous line of demarcation between past and future — not only is the historian always forced back upon his past, but so are the poet, practical man and scientist. The poet may dream his dreams — as do we all moreover — but at the point where he wishes to communicate these to us, he must make of them some sort of record; and in the course of doing this he must recall his thoughts, and remember, too — perhaps in ways almost too subtle to record — the sort of understanding which we have been educated to give to the various signs and symbols that will be paraded before us as language. The position of the practical man and scientist will not prove notably different. The practising lawyer in search of a precedent, the ethologist reviewing data (recorded an hour, day, month or year before) are directly at work *upon* a past, if not *within* a past, and a past moreover that is conceived as such. For them, there can be no magical access to a future, and the present may be too evanescent to warrant considering. It is redundant now to say, but perhaps necessary to emphasize, that for the 'scientist' of our dreams, one concerned with universals, and enveloped (as we may think) in the 'timelessness' of these, there is equally no escape. The universal can never be known as such, although it may be hypothesized. It can never be known for the reason that the *total* accumulation of such data as might prove it remains a prisoner of the future, and is thus again inaccessible. Accordingly, where we argue that the historian is *only* concerned with the past, it should be clear that a similar case can be made for the 'practical' or 'scientific' man. This is only so, of course, on that reading of the 'past' to which we have drawn attention. The object is merely to suggest that, on one significant rendering of 'past', there is no reflectve experience which can possibly focus upon anything else.

There is finally a third problem, of which Oakeshott is aware. It is tied to the second. As we have already seen, if it is possible to conceive of the historian being *wholly* wedded to the past, then an equally convincing case can be made for the poet or practical man or scientist as being wholly committed to the past. But one may put a slightly different question: How would it be possible for any contempoary or *present* activity to be concerned *exclusively* with the *past?* The question applies to historical, as well as to any other, activity. And the answer, presumably, is that such exclusive commitment to the past — in the present — is not a feasible programme. If we make a distinction between past and present, and make this distinction as narrowly severe now as before, and identify the historian as operating in the present, and identify his commitment to the past as a *present* commitment, then his commitment to (or immersion or involvement in) the past cannot be *exclusively* (if at all) to the past. His 'exclusive' commitment to the past is not properly speaking exclusive. It is a commitment to a certain type of engagement in the present. And since one can *only* now be engaged in the present, the historian's can be seen to be a present engagement, and indeed as a certain type of commitment *to* the present. (Even if the commitment is only to the effect that the present should emulate or celebrate the past.)

Just as it may be difficult to imagine any poet or practical man or scientist being concerned with the past only, and exclusively for its own sake, so with the historian. The disinterested observer, therefore, may well be provoked to enquire — and to doubt — whether it is possible that any historian could ever actually be concerned with the past only and exclusively 'for its own sake'. There is obviously a serious logical difficulty associated with the prospect of achieving such detachment. More modestly, one might be moved to ask whether any actual historian ever was motivated to do so. The answer to this is probably affirmative. But motivation and execution remain two quite distinct spheres of concern. And we return to the problem of the non-existence of any concrete historian whose work could accurately be said to be (or to have been) concerned exclusively with the past.

If the historian is an historian, in the end, by reference to his degree of immersion — which for Oakeshott is *total* immersion — in the past, we must ask where we shall find such an historian. Oakeshott, for example, has much praise for Tocqueville and Maitlaid as historians. But they certainly cannot qualify on the grounds which Oakeshott stipulates. Take Tocqueville: in the study of America he was much absorbed by what France might likely become; while in the study of the *Ancien Régime* he was clearly motivated by a desire to determine how France had come to be what she was — particularly by reference to the centralizing tendencies which he detected and feared in his own time. Tocqueville and Maitland and Ranke and Carr and Toynbee and Trevor-Roper are, of course only examples. But *à travers* these and similar examples, one remains unaware of any historians who, as historians, are or were wholly and exclusively immersed in the past — other perhaps than in some quite trivial sense (such as that every event on which one might reflect is past, with the consequence that any form of sustained reflection may imply 'total' immersion in the past).

One anonymous critic goes further, to maintain that studying the past within its own intellectual horizons is not to study it at all. It is observed, for example, that the contemporaries of Socrates had no perception of him as the great figure we see in him. To attempt to comprehend him merely from their perspective is automatically to overlook his genuine importance — which cannot certifiably exist in itself. The moral is that, without perspective (another sense of the present providing access to the past) there can be no just appreciation of the value of the past. And this is valid enough. But the central logical consideration is what matters. And this is that, in as far as one can only gain access to the past through the present, there can be no understanding of the past which is not also an understanding of the present; nor can there be any commitment to the past which is not also a commitment in the present, and therefore a (variant) present commitment.

We must assume that the historian — the student of history, whether he writes or not — is influenced by the past. In as far as this is so, then we have an example of the past influencing the present. The example is ever present and inescapable. For this reason, it does not matter that the historian does, or does not, wish to influence the present. He is part of the present. And he is influenced by the past of which he has become aware. He may imagine that there is nothing to be learned, or by contrast that he serves as an oracle in transmitting the truth which has been vouchsafed to him. But in the degree that he speaks to his contemporaries, he seeks — and selectively by necessity — to pass on what he thinks he has learned, whether it is of little moment or great. All that is ruled out is the idea of the past existing in and for itself. For if it did, we could not know it to exist at all.

8

In the end, Oakeshott is not so much concerned to tell us what history is. For all experience, not just history, projects and presupposes some sense of a past. Nor is he obsessed with the historian where conceived as an agent wholly immersed in the past. For no contemporary agent, including the historian, can be wholly immersed in the past. If indeed we insist on reading Oakeshott merely descriptively, or merely analytically, which is the way he consciously seeks to be read, then we collide straightaway with an impossibility. For Oakeshott is really less concerned to advise us as to what history *is* or as to what historians *do* than to tell us what the methods of history *ought* to be and how historians *ought* to proceed. In other words, Oakeshott is providing us, in a highly disguised fashion, with an historical methodology for the humanities and social sciences.

Some elaboration on this is in order. The first point to stress is that, somewhat contrary to Greenleaf, Oakeshott's views on the identity or character of the 'historian' evolved and changed between 1933 and 1955. In his 1955 essay, Oakeshott attempts to correct some of the ineptness of the earlier analysis. In 1933, Oakeshott quite confidently wrote of *the historian*, as much as to suggest that he knew him well, and how he performed. In *Experience and Its Modes*, he revealed little interest in what some one or random group of historians might *think*. He was concerned rather with what he took them to be *doing*. 'Our business', he declared, ' . . . is to discuss all that the historian merely assumes, to consider what he merely postulates'. He remarked that his view of history 'may differ considerably' from that of the practising historian; he was not concerned to say how history had been or should be written; he was only concerned 'with history itself' (p. 88) — whatever (as he puts it) 'the historian may think' (p. 91). Oakeshott had occasion to refer to the historian who may take a different view as 'the unreflective historian'. 'The historian's business', he declared, 'is not to discover, to recapture, or even to interpet; it is to create . . . ' (p. 93). In the early work, in short, Oakeshott was not really concerned with what any actual historian might *think* he was doing. Oakeshott was only concerned with what he, Oakeshott, took the historian actually to be doing, whatever else the historian might mistakenly imagine himself to be about. There is of course just a touch of arrogance — perhaps misplaced — in this procedure. But what is clear is that, after 22 years, most of it disappears.

By 1955, Oakeshott is compelled to drop the categorical statements of 1933 relating to what the historian, consciously or otherwise, actually does. No longer do we attest to these firm and dogmatic references to *the historian*, but only to the 'historian' (tidily packaged in inverted commas). No longer are we advised so uncompromisingly of the *business* of the historian. Our attention is drawn, more diffidently, to 'the *activity* of being an historian'. Oakeshott is no longer discussing 'history' (as it is) or historians (as they are) but an 'activity' which may somehow differ from both. Thus in 1955 Oakeshott believed that he could concede what in 1933 he could not conceive: 'if we go to writers who have been labelled "historians" . . . and ask, what kind of statement are they accustomed to make about the past, we shall find a great preponderance of practical and contemplative statements' (RiP, p. 151). In other words, and more explicitly than heretofore, Oakeshott comes to the conclusion that history is not just what historians do. Thus we open the door to the question as to whether it is not something they *ought* to do.

In 1933, Oakeshott had maintained that the historian was one who never did anything else but reflect on the past. In 1955, this position is entirely abandoned —since it is admitted that the 'preponderance' of statements made by practising historians are of an 'unhistorical' kind. In 1933, Oakeshott insists that the historian is an 'historian' by virtue of the fact that, professionally, he always and only reads the present as evidence for the past. In 1955, he — like we — can identify no *actual* historian who performs in this way.

Oakeshott then divorces 'the activity of being an historian'·from (what he earlier took to be) the actual historian. Oakeshott no longer believes, as it would appear, in the 'historian', but he does believe that one may glean from the latter, corrupt as his art may be, intimations (we may say) of truly historical writing. His revised view appears to run to the effect that most of those whom one might earlier have called 'historians', do not consistently reveal an 'historical' attitude, but that where this attitude is (intermittently) found, it 'is, generally speaking, found *only* in the writings of those whom we are now accustomed to recognize as "historians" ' (RiP, p. 153). Accordingly, for the later Oakeshott, someone whom we are accustomed to call an historian, may be devoid of an attitude which would qualify him as being engaged in the activity of being an 'historian'. By implication, one may no longer start from an individual or body of these as concerned with history. One may only start with some prior criterion of historicity by which to measure the degree of historical commitment of any such person or body. Oakeshott, as it happens, strains to avoid this explicit methodological denouement. He does not wish to be caught telling the historian in any way what to do. But Oakeshott's failure to oblige in this respect only generates an unavailing circularity.

Let us then review the itinerary of this Oakeshottian Odyssey. Oakeshott came to settle upon a characteristic which would distinguish the historian from other specialists. This characteristic, in effect, was that of total immersion in the past for its own sake. To apply this Oakeshottian criterion, however, of an absolute or exclusive commitment to the past for its own sake, creates the immediate and striking difficulty of eliminating any actual historian, alive or dead, as an 'historian' — since it becomes plain that no practising historian is ever (and perhaps in principle never can be) immersed in or committed to the past in the degree Oakeshott requires. Oakeshott, in short, finding it impossible to locate an actual historian who conforms to his criterion of an 'historian', is inclined to withdraw his somewhat awkward concept of the historian conceived as an *agent* and to substitute for it a more accommodating view of history conceived as an *activity* in which the historian may be said to be engaged. To do this makes it easier for him to advance an abstract assertion about what the historian *qua* historian 'does', without being so readily committed to the notion that any concrete historian actually and necessarily does these things. Although this change of emphasis makes it easier for Oakeshott to dispose of the practising historian as irrelevant, it equally makes it easier to see how fundamentally definitional Oakeshott's basic approach is. For if it is not the historian to whom we look to disengage the character of historical writing, then there must be some prior criterion which we must posit by which to judge the degree of the historian's historicity. But the chief abstract criteria advanced by Oakeshott relate, in effect, to immersion in the past — whether in some unquantified degree or totally. Since everyone is in *some* degeee immersed in the past, and since no historian is *totally* immersed in the past, Oakeshott leaves us with no means of determining precisely and distinctly what 'the activity of being an historian' can be.

Oakeshott accordingly entertains us with a digression about the progress of historical writing. He begins by suggesting that the attitude of total immersion in the past, which is what properly characterizes the activity of being an historian, is 'an activity which (like many others) has emerged gradually'. His argument, as best as I can reconstruct it, continues roughly as follows. Historians, in the past, were not as professionally accomplished as some historians of today. There have been significant technical improvements in the writing of history. Thus a real difference exists as between some contemporary and all earlier historical writing. The latter was not genuinely historical, nor is the former entirely so. But one may observe the evolution from a less to a more 'historical' mode of writing, even if no particular historian embodies that mode perfectly (RiP, pp. 151-3).

Oakeshott, of course, has a heuristic. But he is notable for the lengths to which he will go to obscure this. Even in 1955, he presents his view of history as an evolutionary fact, not as a preferred way of writing history. But this is all that it is. As description, what he has to say about what historians actually do is obviously untenable. The fairest option must be to restructure his description of historical activity as a methodology for the writing of history. In *Experience and its Modes*, accordingly, we should not interpret Oakeshott as portraying what historians do. Where he tells us what history *is* or what the historian *does* we do better to interpret him to mean that this is what it *ought* to be and what he *should* do. As here:

> History is the past for the sake of the past. What the historian is interested in is a dead past; a past unlike the present. The *differentia* of the historical past lies in its very disparity from what is contemporary. The historian does not set out to discover a past where the same beliefs, the same actions, the same intentions obtain as those which occupy his own world. His business is to elucidate a past independent of the present, and he is never (as an historian) tempted to subsume past events under general rules. He is concerned with a particular past . . . with the detailed dissimilarity of past and present . . . with the past as past . . . with each moment . . . in so far as it is unlike any other . . . (p. 106)

Again, what Oakeshott says, in the above, cannot begin to work as a reliable statement about what historians actually *do*. We need not even suppose that he intends it so; certainly not all historians yield their assent. E.H. Carr (1964), for example, writing as an historian, sketches a sharply opposed view of what historians do: 'We can view the past, and achieve our understanding of the past, only through the eyes of the present.' He continues: 'the historian is of his own age . . . The very words he uses . . . have current connotations from which he cannot divorce them.' Thus: 'The historian belongs not to the past but to the present.' And he concludes: 'the function of the historian is . . . to master [the past] as the key to the understanding of the present' (pp. 24-6).

What Oakeshott and Carr and so many others are saying in this sort of way is not first and foremost related to what the historian is doing but to what they think he ought to be doing and how he ought to look upon his role. The one may emphasize detachment from, the other commitment to, the present. But the emphasis is, all the same, a methodological recommendation. This is not to say, abstractly, that any statement about what historians do can be translated into a matching statement about what they ought to do. The point, rather, is that in these and similar cases the argument will often only make sense when restructured as a recommended procedural formula.

Oakeshott's attempted distinctions between 'history' and other 'modes of experience' as well as between four different types of past are of no great moment. What is plainly communicated is less these distinctions than the writer's opposition to certain ways of writing about the past — most especially ways (1) which involve the continual interjection of moral judgements and quite other ways (2) which would portray historical sequence as an instance of some one or several iron laws of change. Of course there are many other writers who have advanced quite direct and straightforward arguments against the vice of moralizing in history, as well as against the pernicious tendency to regard everything that happens in history as inevitable (as an instance of a scientific law). Significant attention has been directed by Isaiah Berlin and Karl Popper, for example, to the latter position. Popper's argument is particularly helpful, especially that part directed against historical prediction. Of course, to the extent that he argues that science is not really predictive either, we have less a case for non-predictive history, than for the non-predictive character of knowledge in general. What matters, however, is that such arguments should be directly and unambiguously addressed to the specific methodologies that are proposed for the writing of history. Oakeshott has enjoyed some influence among historians of ideas, and yet he displays virtually no direct argument whatever of the sort alluded to. His case against the 'practical' or 'scientific' past is less an argument than a simple statement of distinctions (within the 'past') which, in a merely definitional manner, is intended to 'persuade' us of the sole legitimacy of the 'historical past'.

9

Oakeshott's distinction between a sense of the past in general and an *historical* sense of the past in fact serves to draw a line between such writing (about the past) as he favours (which supposedly betrays no moral commitments and serves no broader purpose) and that to which he is antipathetic. When Oakeshott argues against, say, the concept of a practical past or of a scientific past as history, he is leaning upon a logical distinction between a commitment to contemporary purposes (the scientist or patriot, for example, may *use* the past but does not really *believe* in it) and a commitment to the past *per se*. (Even on Oakeshott's own understanding of the matter, however, there cannot be a commitment to the past − *per se* or otherwise − which is not *a fortiori* a *present* commitment.)

Oakeshott never satisfactorily resolves the question of the relationship between 'past' and 'present' − where the study of the past is simultaneously projected as a *present* world of experience and an experience which is none the less *past*. 'The historical past', he observes, ' . . . because it cannot be mere past, is present; but it is not merely present' (EiM, p. 110). 'The historical past is always present; and yet historical experience is always in the form of the past' (p. 111). 'History . . . is present . . . ; but . . . it is the continuous assertion of a past which is not past and of a present which is not present' (p. 111). 'It is not merely that the past must survive into the present . . . ; the past must *be* the present . . . ' (p. 109). In none of this is there any clear indication as to how history can be both past and present − at the same time. In fact, Oakeshott regards this relationship as paradoxical (i.e. as a genuine contradiction which cannot be logically resolved): 'we *appear*', he writes, 'to be faced with a paradox' (my italics, p. 109). The appearance becomes certainty a few pages on, where we are advised − with reference to historical experience being simultaneously past and present − that 'this contradiction must remain unresolved so long as we remain in the world of historical ideas' (p. 111). Oakeshott clearly appreciates that to characterize the historical mode as simultaneously 'past' and 'present' is awkward. But he cannot help us to move beyond this elementary recognition. He appears even to imagine that he does not have to. But this difficulty, left unresolved, undermines his analysis. Oakeshott leaps deftly into the adjoining argument just as the timbers of the first can be heard to creak. In fact, a remark which he applies to Weldon's *Vocabulary of Politics* applies with particular force to parts of *Experience and its Modes*. 'Reading this book', Oakeshott wrote, 'is rather like listening to somebody who talks very fast; speed of utterance sometimes carries us over awkward points.'

Oakeshott's paradox is not, in fact, a paradox. If we say that 'all experience is present', this must imply that the past is something we infer from present evidence. This need not imply either that there is no past or that we cannot have access to it. Where we infer past from present, this must suggest both that it existed and that we are not denied knowledge of it. Otherwise, we could not infer it. Where we identify an experience as past, present or future, we fix it from the perspective of time, or duration. In as far as we have no sight, sound, smell, taste or touch of time, neither have we any direct *experience* of time – where 'experience' is projected as 'sensation'. Thus our direct experience is of experience. It is not of past, present or future time. Time, together with its three non-sentient tenses, is not so much a part of experience, as a means by which we may structure experience. This will bring us back to the beginning, now to deny that *'all* experience is present'. For some experience *was* present. Experience is *in* the present. But assuming that the past is as real as the present, there must also have been past experience – experience *in* the past. Thus there *was* experience in the past. Just as there *is* experience in the present. But since experience is assigned both to past and present, it cannot *all* be in the present.

The point is that there can no more be direct experience of the present (as abstract time) than of the past (as abstract time). There is merely experience which we order by reference to time. By our canons of time, there can be no present study of past events which does not unfold in present time. Not even the scientist knows timelessness. Nor can the historian ever cut himself adrift in times unqualifiedly past. The past is studied in our present – just as it was in our past. Such present study involves, not so much a commitment in the past as a commitment (in the present) *to* the past. But any commitment in the present is also a present commitment. It most certainly is not a past commitment. Thus a present study of the past is not even a present commitment to the past – but a present commitment to the present *study* of the past. Any present commitment, supposedly 'to the past', is normally only intended to refer to a present emulation or adoration of some past event, style or process. But present emulation unfolds in present time. Hence the elimination of the 'paradox': there can be no commitment in the present *to the past* but only *to its present study* or emulation. And that commitment can only serve a present or future – it cannot now serve a past – purpose. Obviously, it does not follow that a present purpose – such as serving the truth– must prove to be partisan because it is not past.

10

Oakeshott's argument, as it bears upon the distinctiveness of history, fails. The argument for a distinctly 'historical past' also fails. The relation between 'past' and 'present' is not well-conceived. The methodological premises of the engagement are disguised. If Oakeshott's view of history were frankly marshalled as a methodology, then it could be directly argued for − and against − in these terms. But he strenuously resists such a move by enveloping his prescriptivism in an evolutionary version of the *Zeitgeist*. He invites us to view history, and the manner of writing it, as conveniently evolving to meet some criteria which he has rather more hinted at than stated. Consequently, Oakeshott never directly seeks to persuade us that the criteria which he *prefers* are actually preferable.

Consider Oakeshott's promotion of detail. In writing history, he maintains, one supplies detail, fully, completely, without lacunae, avoiding generalization, always explaining more by detailing more:

> the only explanation of change relevant or possible in history is simply a complete account of change. History accounts *for* change by means of a full account *of* change. The relation *between* events is always other events . . . The conception of cause is thus replaced by the exhibition of a world of events intrinsically related to one another in which no *lacuna* is tolerated . . . History, then, . . . is the narration of a course of events which . . . explains itself . . . And the method of the historian is never to explain by means of generalization but always by means of greater and more complete detail. (EiM, p. 143)

This can be taken as a statement about what historians do or ought to do or both. It will not quite convey what they do: there are always lacunae, events never explain themselves. One does not explain the Great Depression by merely piling on more and more detail to do with the characters feasting on (or conjured up within) Steinbeck's *Grapes of Wrath*. Time is short and history, perforce, is selective and is thus compelled to seek out those facts which are somehow regarded as significant. But neither is Oakeshott's programme sufficiently elaborate to be able to persuade us that this is something that historians should do − were doing it genuinely possible. Facts are infinite; life is not; all gaps can never be filled.

In summary, the salient features of Oakeshott's philosophy of history are as follows. There is first and foremost the notion of history being *entirely* committed to the past (even if this is a commitment in and of − and implicitly to − some present activity). There is conjoined with this some notion of such commitment being ethically neutral (even if it is never clearly explained how the notion of complete commitment to a present pursuit can entirely escape some moral colour or evaluative overtone). There is, too, the suggestion that any understanding of the past can only be achieved through the pursuit of the unique, not the typical; that we must place our emphasis upon differences, not similarities.

One may conveniently label Oakeshott an historical particularist where this is meant to suggest that he 'paradoxically' insists upon a commitment to the past rather than the present, assumes that comparison between 'different' periods is vicious or impossible, seeks to exclude generalization from past to present and vice versa, assumes that avoiding contemporary issues is much the same as being objective, and demands (more or less in the manner of traditional empiricists) the accumulation of sheer detail as a means of reaching up to the heaven of historical truth. All of this is permeated by the assumption that to understand an historical event is to penetrate its context, to see it as distinct, to regard it as unique.

We may now return to a criticism adumbrated at the start. To say of any event, '*This* is what happened', cannot automatically presuppose that that event is unique. For having remarked upon its occurrence, evolving circumstances may entitle or require that one note a recurrence: 'It is happening *again*.' We are only entitled to remark of an historical event that it is unique where we seek to contrast it with other events which are not so singular. Where we render every historical moment, era or circumstance unique, it may be presumed that, in this, we advert to the principle of time, and to the logical consideration that each moment is its own and no other and is always formally distinguishable from the rest. As that is likely so, it will not prove inappropriate to note that precisely the same observation may be made of space, or extension.Indeed, every square inch of matter (whether of wool or gelignite or pig iron) is uniquely itself and no other — its spatial locus alone guarantees as much. It remains, all the same, that the atoms of this or that mass of iron or the 'events' of this or that stretch of time will prove much the same as those of some like mass or time. It is important that we do not speak of history as such as a repository of unique events, since in doing this we remove all hope of contrasting the exceptional with the unexceptional.

It has been said often enough that it is right to regard history as a field of action, replete with unique events, where nothing repeats itself and where no event is to be regarded as subject to general laws — as perhaps in science. And it is true that so complex a notion is not on the face of it absurd. None the less, if history is so understood, it must be the case either that (a) each historical event (every moment of the past) is unique or that (b) only some are. Let us take it that (b) at least is true. One of the things we mean when holding an event to be unique is that it is exceptional, one of a kind, somehow unusual, even extra-ordinary. There is always room for such observations. And one reason why we shall feel compelled to exclude consideration of (a) is because it commits us in advance to excluding (b) — as well as because the evidence suggests the idea to be nonsensical.

When characterizing an event as unique, besides intending that it is unusual, we may mean further that it is beyond explaining — much as Hobbes suggests that in describing an event as magical we merely signify that we find it incomprehensible. If that is so, then again we shall accept that only some historical events are in this sense unique, not that all are. Further, if historical events are described as unique, in the sense of being incomprehensible, it cannot be consistent to suggest that the historian enjoys any form of privileged access to the understanding of these events. A great deal may be made of the difference between science and history by reference to the fact that the historical event to be explained cannot be recaptured, by contrast with the laboratory experiment, which one is able (in principle) to repeat. The object of the observation may be to suggest both that the historical event is some-how ineffable and that the determination of it is permitted only to the few. But too much may be made of the distinction. Let us indeed accept that history is not events-in-themselves, out there, beyond our grasp, but that it is a reconstruction of a past on the basis of evidence presently available. The event does not repeat itself, of course. But neither does the evidence simply disappear. The event-in-itself, if we are allowed to conceive it thus, may not be re-enacted, but the evidence, apart from parts of it being added or subtracted, can still be rerun. And that is what happens every time the student of history assesses it.

In the sense indicated, historical assertions are in principle as test-able (by reference to the surviving record) as are scientific assertions (by reference to repeatable experiments). What one seeks to establish in either case is the grounds, and the soundness of these, for drawing some given conclusion. If the scientist does this on the basis of an experiment, it is vital that the experiment be replicable. If the his-torian does this on the basis of the surviving record, it is only necessary that his evidence should remain intact. A successful experiment does not guarantee the truth of a scientific conclusion, but it may check the subversion of the conclusion. A proper immersion in the historical record does not guarantee the validity of an historical reconstruction, but it will prove essential even if the reconstruction is only to prove plausible. If then it is accepted that the writing of history depends — as it does — on a great range of causal generalizations, it only remains to establish the nature of the distinction that obtains between the nature of historical and scientific explanation.

I suspect that most observers would be content to follow Popper where he records that 'history is characterized by its interest in actual, singular, or specific events, rather than in laws or generalizations' (PH, 30). Popper is assuming a distinction between singular, general and universal statements, and that most scholars denominated 'historians' are primarily concerned with the first, while those denominated 'scientists' are primarily concerned with the second and third. Popper's position is only satisfactory, however, if we treat it as being itself a descriptive, historical *generalization*. It is typical of so very many generalizations that can and have been made about the past. It can be tested against the record of the past, and be tucked into our expectations for the future. What is clear is that Popper's is not a merely singular statement, that it does not contradict the fact that many historians (like Arnold Toynbee) and myriad social scientists perceive history as a sociological or generalizing 'science' or 'subject', and that one can only exclude the concept of history as a 'generalizing' venture by definitional fiat.

I shall conclude by suggesting that it is of no use whatever to seek to characterize historical events as unique. If it is merely intended that only some of them are unique, then the conclusion is so obvious as scarcely to require saying. If it is intended that all historical events are unique, then we confront an absurdity in the attendant implication that none is commonplace. Where historical events are viewed as unique, then none, each being one of a kind, can be related or compared to any other (there is no understanding without comparing). Each unique event must prove as inaccessible as every other. If history is unique, it is beyond understanding. If it is beyond understanding, to call it unique will not improve our understanding. Because we do not perceive history to be governed by universal laws, it does not follow that we can demonstrate that there are no such laws. If Moses or Vico or Hegel or Marx or Toynbee insists upon these laws, it will behove us to check their proposals for concrete historical flaws, rather than seek to prove, quite beyond our possibilities, that such thinkers are mistaken 'by definition'.

Oakeshott is by no means the only contemporary figure to adopt a particularist position, with its emphasis upon periodization, the distinctiveness of each intellectual identity in the past, and the uniqueness of both period and identity. It is a view advocated, albeit in marginally different ways, by many, if not most, practising historians. G.R. Elton (1969), for example declares that 'the unique event is a freak' but insists that historical events 'must be . . . particular' (p. 23). History, he declares, 'is "idiographic", that is, it particularizes, and not "nomothetic", that is, designed to establish general laws'. (p. 41) He defines history as consisting of all human developments of which we have some record: 'it deals with them from the point of view of happening, change, and the particular' (p. 24).

Historians of course are frequently disposed to think that any of their number who paints on too broad a canvas is not an 'historian' (e.g. Spengler, Toynbee, Sorokin). Just as philosophers are disposed to think that any one of them who writes too extensively is a 'journalist' (e.g. Bertrand Russell or Jean-Paul Sartre). Although Elton does not insist upon a strict historical uniqueness, it is clear that his emphasis is very much upon the particular. Indeed, there is no good reason why it should not be. He clearly prefers to work to a smaller scale, and that is as well. But his mistake consists in generalizing from this particular preference so as to turn it into a universal: 'unfortunately', he advises us (and it is a delightful turn of phrase), 'bird's-eye views are strictly for the birds' (p. 94). But of course the conclusion is false. Were it true, then we should all be transmogrified into birds. We all have overviews, and can discover no way of working without them; the more we look at our subject in detail, the more extensively modified will our overview become; but to modify an overview is not to eliminate it; this is no less evident in Elton's own excellent work on the Reformation.

The late Pieter Geyl (1962), in raining blows upon the limp *oeuvre* of the late Arnold Toynbee, reveals a disposition akin to that of Elton's: 'Every historical fact', he comments, 'is unqiue and therefore incomparable with other historical facts'. It is clearly impossible for so sensible and attractive a writer as Geyl to adhere rigidly to such a view, but he will emphasize that, 'in a certain sense, no historical fact is detachable from its circumstances, and in the elimination of the latter violence is done to history' (p. 123). It is a point he frequently makes in different places: parallels in history may well be indispensable and even instructive but generally they 'are never wholly satisfactory' — because 'each phenomenon' is distinct, 'never to be repeated' (p. 150). Comparisons are permissible, 'but there are peculiar dangers attached to them' (p. 157). 'The circumstances may be similar; they will never be the same.' Factors 'may belong to one . .. class', but each 'will always have . . . something exclusively its own' (p. 184).

There is no valid reason for us to complain too loudly about such an orientation. The eternal struggle engaged as between the General and the Particular is enacted here, as it were, before our eyes, in the arena of history. Geyl stresses the particular. But there is instanced here, too, the inclination to go further, and to extend the particular preference into some species of universal injunction. It is a bit like the tired idea — real as it may be — of every comedian aspiring to be tragedian. We may imagine the particularist, working away, and very well too, in his sacred and sacrosanct abode; we need him, we cannot work without him; but this genial and modest being, at some point finds his ambition suddenly transformed; his hopes rocket into the heavens; and the message of his ascent is that *he* is the message, there is no other.

Geyl, like Elton, is not simply concerned to act out his particularism; he must profess it; he must convert it — inconsistently — into a universalism. 'The historian', for Geyl, is basically the particularist. And anyone who does not fit the description cannot, impliedly, be an historian. The historian, he tells us (in coming down rigorously against Sorokin) is one who 'has his attention primed for the endless variety of reality, for the particularity or singularity of each country, of each age, and, more than that, of each incident or phenomenon within these larger frameworks' (p. 158). Well, yes. That is *one* type of historian. But we are surely not compelled to say that such is the character of *the* historian. Geyl has a firmly fixed notion of what the historian is, and once he begins to compare or to generalize (however necessary these activities may prove) he ceases to be an historian. For Geyl, writers like Toynbee are not historians, they are prophets. And historians, he declares, 'feel that the best traditions of their profession are insulted when the prophet poses as a historian' (p. 203).

Elton (1969) proceeds in much the same way. He pours cauldrons of molten contempt upon the heads of 'the great system-makers, such as A.J. Toynbee'. These 'system-makers' are characterized by the fact that they select their facts following 'some principle of choice implicit in the question' asked. (I am not clear that it is possible — if that is implied — to select one's facts *without* following a principle somehow implied in the question one asks.) Elton, too, has a firmly fixed idea of what an historian is. And where he asks some such question as who it is that will slip through the eye of the needle, and into the historical promised land of genuine historical writing, it is clear that scholars with prophetic humps on their backs, will (by Geyl) be attributed unpleasant lumps of nonsense in their heads — and they will not get through.

Oakeshott, then, expresses a view not uncommonly held among historians themselves. But he is certainly one of the earliest and most accomplished philosophical advocates of such an orientation. To insist upon the limitations of Oakeshott's philosophy of history is not to say that he has nothing to teach us. Oakeshott's 'conservatism' (his own expression), like Burke's, is one of the very few examples of such an outlook which one has cause to enjoy and admire. Oakeshott expresses his aversions, whether to 'ideology' or 'rationalism' or 'liberalism', in a manner that is more than impressive and one that always bears the stamp of a thinker who is very much his own man. Thus does one maverick pay homage to another. This judgement may not prove salutary, but neither is it solitary (see for example, Himmelfarb, 1975). It remains that Oakeshott's philosophy of history is denied the coherence that might be wished for it. It does not follow that other likeminded advocates cannot sustain a case. But one may infer that the closer their position(s) approximates to Oakeshott's, the more likely are they to encounter the range of problems to which I have sought to draw attention.

Notes

1. Reprinted in *Rationalism in Politics* (1962). (RiP)
2. This 'mode', which is aesthetic, is not considered in *Experience and Its Modes*. It is taken up in the *Voice of Poetry in the Conversation of Mankind* (1959), which is reprinted in RiP (1962).

Source

This chapter appeared in an earlier form under the same title in *Politics*, vol. 16, no. 1 (1981).

PART THREE

COLLINGWOOD

5 THE HISTORICAL LOGIC OF QUESTION AND ANSWER

R.G. Collingwood

1

My work in archaeology . . . impressed upon me the importance of the 'questioning activity' in knowledge: and this made it impossible for me to rest contented with the intuitionist theory of knowledge favoured by the 'realists'. The effect of this on my logic was to bring about in my mind a revolt against the current logical theories of the time, a good deal like that revolt against the scholastic logic which was produced in the minds of Bacon and Descartes by reflection on the experience of scientific research, as that was taking new shape in the late sixteenth and early seventeenth centuries. The *Novum Organum* and the *Discours de la Méthode* began to have a new significance for me. They were the classical expressions of a principle in logic which I found it necessary to restate: the principle that a body of knowledge consists not of 'propositions', 'statements', 'judgements', or whatever name logicians use in order to designate assertive acts of thought (or what in those acts is asserted: for 'knowledge' means both the activity of knowing and what is known), but of these together with the questions they are meant to answer; and that a logic in which the answers are attended to and the questions neglected is a false logic.

I will try to indicate, briefly as the nature of this book requires (for it is an autobiography, not a work on logic), the way in which this notion developed in my mind as I reflected day by day upon the Albert Memorial. I know that what I am going to say is very controversial, and that almost any reader who is already something of a logician will violently disagree with it. But I shall make no attempt to forestall his criticisms. So far as he belongs to any logical school now existing, I think I know already what they will be, and it is because I am not convinced by them that I am writing this chapter. I shall not use the word 'judgement', like the so-called 'idealistic' logicians, or Cook Wilson's word 'statement': the thing denoted by these words I shall call a 'proposition': so that this word will always in this chapter denote a logical, not a linguistic, entity.

I began by observing that you cannot find out what a man means by simply studying his spoken or written statements, even though he has spoken or written with perfect command of language and perfectly truthful intention. In order to find out his meaning you must also know what the question was (a question in his own mind, and presumed by him to be in yours) to which the thing he has said or written was meant as an answer.

It must be understood that question and answer, as I conceived them, were strictly correlative. A proposition was not an answer, or at any rate could not be the right answer, to any question which might have been answered otherwise. A highly detailed and particularized proposition must be the answer, not to a vague and generalized question, but to a question as detailed and particularized as itself. For example, if my car will not go, I may spend an hour searching for the cause of its failure. If, during this hour, I take out number one plug, lay it on the engine, turn the starting-handle, and watch for a spark, my observation 'number one plug is all right' is an answer not to the question, 'Why won't my car go?' but to the question, 'Is it because number one plug is not sparking that my car won't go?' Any one of the various experiments I make during the hour will be the finding of an answer to some such detailed and particularized question. The question, 'Why won't my car go?' is only a kind of summary of all these taken together. It is not a separate question asked at a separate time, nor is it a sustained question which I continue to ask for the whole hour together. Consequently, when I say 'Number one plug is all right', this observation does not record one more failure to answer the hour-long question, 'What is wrong with my car?' It records a success in answering the three-minutes-long question, 'Is the stoppage due to failure in number one plug?'

In passing, I will note (what I shall return to later on) that this principle of correlativity between question and answer disposes of a good deal of clap-trap. People will speak of a savage as 'confronted by the eternal problem of obtaining food'. But what really confronts him is the problem, quite transitory like all things human, of spearing this fish, or digging up this root, or finding blackberries in this wood.

My next step was to apply this principle to the idea of contradiction. The current logic maintained that two propositions might, simply as propositions, contradict one another, and that by examining them simply as propositions you could find out whether they did so or not. This I denied. If you cannot tell what a proposition means unless you know what question it is meant to answer, you will mistake its meaning if you make a mistake about that question. One symptom of mistaking the meaning of a proposition is thinking that it contradicts another proposition which in fact it does not contradict. No two propositions, I saw, can contradict one another unless they are answers to the same question. It is therefore impossible to say of a man, 'I do not know what the question is which he is trying to answer, but I can see that he is contradicting himself'.

The same principle applied to the idea of truth. If the meaning of a proposition is relative to the question it answers, its truth must be relative to the same thing. Meaning, agreement and contradiction, truth and falsehood, none of these belonged to propositions in their own right, propositions by themselves; they belonged only to propositions as the answers to questions: each proposition answering a question strictly correlative to itself.

Here I parted company with what I called propositional logic, and its offspring the generally recognized theories of truth. According to propositional logic (under which denomination I include the so-called 'traditional' logic, the 'idealistic' logic of the eighteenth and nineteenth centuries, and the 'symbolic' logic of the nineteenth and twentieth), truth or falsehood, which are what logic is chiefly concerned with, belongs to propositions as such. This doctrine was often expressed by calling the proposition the 'unit of thought', meaning that if you divide it up into parts such as subject, copula, predicate, any of these parts taken singly is not a complete thought, that is, not capable of being true or false.

It seemed to me that this doctrine was a mistake due to the early partnership between logic and grammar. The logician's proposition seemed to me a kind of ghostly double of the grammarian's sentence, just as in primitive speculation about the mind people imagine minds as ghostly doubles of bodies. Grammar recognizes a form of discourse called the sentence, and among sentences, as well as other kinds which serve as the verbal expressions of questions, commands, etc., one kind which express statements. In grammatical phraseology, these are indicative sentences; and logicians have almost always tried to conceive the 'unit of thought', or that which is either true or false, as a kind of logical 'soul' whose linguistic 'body' is the indicative sentence.

This attempt to correlate the logical proposition with the grammatical indicative sentence has never been altogether satisfactory. There have always been people who saw that the true 'unit of thought' was not the proposition but something more complex in which the proposition served as answer to a question. Not only Bacon and Descartes, but Plato and Kant, come to mind as examples. When Plato described thinking as a 'dialogue of the soul with itself', he meant (as we know from his own dialogues) that it was a process of question and answer, and that of these two elements the primacy belongs to the questioning activity, the Socrates within us. When Kant said that it takes a wise man to know what questions he can reasonably ask, he was in effect repudiating a merely propositional logic and demanding a logic of question and answer.

Even apart from this, however, logic has never been able to assert a *de facto* one-one relation between propositions and indicative sentences. It has always maintained that the words actually used by a man on a given occasion in order to express his thought may be 'elliptical' or 'pleonastic' or in some other way not quite in accordance with the rule that one sentence should express one proposition. It is generally held, again, that indicative sentences in a work of fiction, professing to be that and nothing more, do not express propositions. But when these and other qualifications have been made, this can be described as the central doctrine of propositional logic: that there is, or ought to be, or in a well-constructed and well-used language would be,[1] a one-one correspondence between propositions and indicative sentences, every indicative sentence expressing a proposition, and a proposition being defined as the unit of thought, or that which is true or false.

This is the doctrine which is presupposed by all the various well-known theories of truth. One school of thought holds that a proposition is either true or false simply in itself, trueness or falseness being qualities of propositions. Another school holds that to call it true or false is to assert a relation of 'correspondence' or 'non-correspondence' between it and something not a proposition, some 'state of things' or 'fact'. A third holds that to call it true or false is to assert a relation between it and other propositions with which it 'coheres' or fails to 'cohere'. And, since in those days there were pragmatists, a fourth school should be mentioned, holding (at least according to some of their pronouncements) that to call a proposition true or false is to assert the utility or inutility of believing it.

All these theories of truth I denied. This was not very original of me; any one could see, after reading Joachim's *Nature of Truth*, that they were all open to fatal objections. My reason for denying them, however, was not that they were severally open to objections, but that they all presupposed what I have called the principle of propositional logic; and this principle I denied altogether.

For a logic of propositions I wanted to substitute what I called a logic of question and answer. It seemed to me that truth, if that meant the kind of thing which I was accustomed to pursue in my ordinary work as a philosopher or historian — truth in the sense in which a philosophical theory or an historical narrative is called true, which seemed to me the proper sense of the word — was something that belonged not to any single proposition, nor even, as the coherence-theorists maintained, to a complex of propositions taken together; but to a complex consisting of questions and answers. The structure of this complex had, of course, never been studied by propositional logic; but with help from Bacon, Descartes, and others I could hazard a few statements about it. Each question and each answer in a given complex had to be relevant or appropriate, had to 'belong' both to the whole and to the place it occupied in the whole. Each question had to 'arise'; there must be that about it whose absence we condemn when we refuse to answer a question on the ground that it 'doesn't arise'. Each answer must be 'the right' answer to the question it professes to answer.

By 'right' I do not mean 'true'. The 'right' answer to a question is the answer which enables us to get ahead with the process of questioning and answering. Cases are quite common in which the 'right' answer to a question is 'false'; for example, cases in which a thinker is following a false scent, either inadvertently or in order to construct a *reductio ad absurdum*. Thus, when Socrates asks (Plato, *Republic*, 333B) whether as your partner in a game of draughts you would prefer to have a just man or a man who knows how to play draughts, the answer which Polemarchus gives — 'a man who knows how to play draughts' — is the right answer. It is 'false', because it presupposes that justice and ability to play draughts are comparable, each of them being a 'craft', or specialized form of skill. But it is 'right', because it constitutes a link, and a sound one, in the chain of questions and answers by which the falseness of that presupposition is made manifest.

What is ordinarily meant when a proposition is called 'true', I thought, was this: (*a*) the proposition belongs to a question-and-answer complex which as a whole is 'true' in the proper sense of the word; (*b*) within this complex it is an answer to a certain question; (*c*) the question is what we ordinarily call a sensible or intelligent question, not a silly one, or in my terminology it 'arises'; (*d*) the proposition is the 'right' answer to that question.

If this is what is meant by calling a proposition 'true', it follows not only that you cannot tell whether a proposition is 'true' or 'false' until you know what question it was intended to answer, but also that a proposition which in fact is 'true' can always be thought 'false' by any one who takes the trouble to excogitate a question to which it would have been the wrong answer, and convinces himself that this was the question it was meant to answer. And a proposition which in fact is significant can always be thought meaningless by any one who convinces himself that it was intended as an answer to a question which, if it had really been intended to answer it, it would not have answered at all, either rightly or wrongly. Whether a given proposition is true or false, significant or meaningless, depends on what question it was meant to answer; and anyone who wishes to know whether a given proposition is true or false, significant or meaningless, must find out what question it was meant to answer.

Now, the question 'To what question did So-and-so intend this proposition for an answer?' is an historical question, and therefore cannot be settled except by historical methods. When So-and-so wrote in a distant past, it is generally a very difficult one, because writers (at any rate good writers) always write for their contemporaries, and in particular for those who are 'likely to be interested', which means those who are already asking the question to which an answer is being offered; and consequently a writer very seldom explains what the question is that he is trying to answer. Later on, when he has become a 'classic' and his contemporaries are all long dead, the question has been forgotten; especially if the answer he gave was generally acknowledged to be the right answer; for in that case people stopped asking the question, and began asking the question that next arose. So the question asked by the original writer can only be reconstructed historically, often not without the exercise of considerable historical skill.

"Sblood!' says Hamlet, 'do you think I am easier to be played on than a pipe?' Those eminent philosophers, Rosencrantz and Guildenstern, think *tout bonnement* that they can discover what the *Parmenides* is about by merely reading it; but if you took them to the south gate of Housesteads and said, 'Please distinguish the various periods of construction here, and explain what purpose the builders of each period had in mind', they would protest 'Believe me, I cannot'. Do they think the *Parmenides* is easier to understand than a rotten little Roman fort? 'Sblood!

It follows, too, and this is what especially struck me at the time, that whereas no two propositions can be in themselves mutually contradictory, there are many cases in which one and the same pair of propositions are capable of being thought either that or the opposite, according as the questions they were meant to answer are reconstructed in one way or in another. For example, metaphysicians have been heard to say 'the world is both one and many'; and critics have not been wanting who were stupid enough to accuse them of contradicting themselves, on the abstractly logical ground that 'the world is one' and 'the world is many' are mutually contradictory propositions. A great deal of the popular dislike of metaphysics is based on grounds of this sort, and is ultimately due to critics who, as we say, did not know what the men they criticized were talking about; that is, did not know what questions their talk was intended to answer; but, with the ordinary malevolence of the idle against the industrious, the ignorant against the learned, the fool against the wise man, wished to have it believed that they were talking nonsense.

Suppose, instead of talking about the world, the metaphysician were talking about the contents of a small mahogany box with a sliding top; and suppose he said, 'The contents of this box are both one thing and many things'. A stupid critic may think that he is offering two incompatible answers to a single question, 'Are the contents of this box one x or many x's?' But the critic has reconstructed the question wrong. There were two questions: (a) Are the contents of this box one set of chessmen or many sets? (b) Are the contents of this box one chessman or many chessmen?

There is no contradiction between saying that something, whether that something be the world or the contents of a box, is one, and saying that it is many. Contradiction would set in only if that something were said to be both one x and many x's. But in the original statement, whether about the world or about the chessmen, there was nothing about one x and many x's. That was foisted upon it by the critic. The contradiction of which the critic complains never existed in his victim's philosophy at all, until the critic planted it upon him, as he might have planted treasonable correspondence in his coat pockets; and with an equally laudable intention, to obtain a reward for denouncing him.

Thus, if a given doctrine D is criticized as self-contradictory because it is divisible into two parts E and F, where E contradicts F, the criticism is valid only if the critic has correctly reconstructed the questions to which E and F were given as answers. A critic who is aware of this condition will of course 'show his working' by stating to his readers the evidence on which he has concluded that the author criticized really did formulate his questions in such a way that E and F in his mouth were mutually contradictory. Failing that, a reader disinclined to work the problem out for himself will naturally assume the criticism to be sound or unsound according as he has found the critic to be, in a general way, a good historian or a bad one.

2

The Oxford tradition insisted upon a fine training in philosophical scholarship, the knowledge of some at least among the classical works of philosophical literature and the ability to interpret them. Under the reign of 'realism' this tradition certainly survived, and was in fact the most valuable part of an Oxford philosophical training; but it weakened almost year by year. Successive boards of examiners in 'Greats' used to complain that the standard of work on Greek philosophy was declining. When I myself examined in the mid-1920s, I found that very few candidates showed any first-hand knowledge of any authors about whom they wrote. What they knew was their notes of the lectures they had attended upon these authors, and the lecturers' criticisms of their philosophies. This decline of interest in philosophical history was openly encouraged by the 'realists'; it was one of their most respected leaders who, expressly on the ground that the 'history' of philosophy was a subject without philosophical interest, procured the abolition of the paper so entitled in the school of Philosophy, Politics, and Economics.

During the War, in the course of my meditations on the Albert Memorial, I set myself to reconsider this 'realist' attitude towards the history of philosophy. Was it really true, I asked myself, that the problems of philosophy were, even in the loosest sense of that word, eternal? Was it really true that different philosophies were different attempts to answer the same questions? I soon discovered that it was not true; it was merely a vulgar error, consequent on a kind of historical myopia which, deceived by superficial resemblances, failed to detect profound differences.

The first point at which I saw a perfectly clear gleam of daylight was in political theory. Take Plato's *Republic* and Hobbes's *Leviathan*, so far as they are concerned with politics. Obviously the political theories they set forth are not the same. But do they represent two different theories of the same thing? Can you say that the *Republic* gives one account of 'the nature of the State' and the *Leviathan* another? No; because Plato's 'State' is the Greek πόλις, and Hobbes's is the absolutist State of the seventeenth century. The 'realist' answer is easy: certainly Plato's State is different from Hobbes's, but they are both States; so the theories are theories of the State. Indeed, what did you mean by calling them both political, if not that they were theories of the same thing?

It was obvious to me that this was only a piece of logical bluff, and that if instead of logic-chopping you got down to brass tacks and called for definitions of the 'State' as Plato conceived it and as Hobbes conceived it, you would find that the differences between them were not superficial but went down to essentials. You can call the two things the same if you insist; but if you do, you must admit that the thing has got *diablement changé en route*, so that the 'nature of the State' in Plato's time was genuinely different from the 'nature of the State' in Hobbes's. I do not mean the empirical nature of the State; I mean the ideal nature of the State. What even the best and wisest of those who are engaged in politics are trying to do has altered. Plato's *Republic* is an attempt at a theory of one thing; Hobbes's *Leviathan* an attempt at a theory of something else.

There is, of course, a connection between these two things; but it is not the kind of connection that the 'realists' thought it was. Anybody would admit that Plato's *Republic* and Hobbes's *Leviathan* are about two things which are in one way the same thing and in another way different. That is not in dispute. What is in dispute is the kind of sameness and the kind of difference. The 'realists' thought that the sameness was the sameness of a 'universal', and the difference the difference between two instances of that universal. But this is not so. The sameness is the sameness of an historical process, and the difference is the difference between one thing which in the course of that process has turned into something else, and the other thing into which it has turned. Plato's πόλις and Hobbes's absolutist State are related by a traceable historical process, whereby one has turned into the other; any one who ignores that process, denies the difference between them, and argues that where Plato's political theory contradicts Hobbes's one of them must be wrong, is saying the thing that is not.

Pursuing this line of inquiry, I soon realized that the history of political theory is not the history of different answers given to one and the same question, but the history of a problem more or less constantly changing, whose solution was changing with it. The 'form of the πόλις' is not, as Plato seems to have thought, the one and only ideal of human society possible to intelligent men. It is not something eternally laid up in heaven and eternally envisaged, as the goal of their efforts, by all good statesmen of whatever age and country. It was the ideal of human society as that ideal was conceived by the Greeks of Plato's own time. By the time of Hobbes, people had changed their minds not only about what was possible in the way of social organization, but about what was desirable. Their ideals were different. And consequently the political philosophers whose business it was to give a reasoned statement of these ideals had a different task before them; one which, if it was to be rightly discharged, must be discharged differently.

The clue, once found, was easily applied elsewhere. It was not difficult to see that, just as the Greek πόλις could not be legitimately translated by the modern word 'State', except with a warning that the two things are in various essential ways different, and a statement of what these differences are; so, in ethics, a Greek word like δεῖ cannot be legitimately translated by using the word 'ought', if that word carries with it the notion of what is sometimes called 'moral obligation'. Was there any Greek word or phrase to express that notion? The 'realists' said there was; but they stultified themselves by adding that the 'theories of moral obligation' expounded by Greek writers differed from modern theories such as Kant's about the same thing. How did they know that the Greek and the Kantian theories were about the same thing? Oh, because δεῖ (or whatever word it was) is the Greek for 'ought'.

It was like having a nightmare about a man who had got it into his head that τριήρης was the Greek for 'steamer', and when it was pointed out to him that descriptions of triremes in Greek writers were at any rate not very good descriptions of steamers, replied triumphantly, 'That is just what I say. These Greek philosophers' (or, 'these modern philosophers', according to which side he was on in the good old controversy between the Ancients and the Moderns) 'were terribly muddle-headed, and their theory of steamers is all wrong'. If you tried to explain that τριήρης does not mean steamer at all but something different, he would reply, 'Then what does it mean?' and in ten minutes he would show you that you didn't know; you couldn't draw a trireme, or make a model of one, or even describe exactly how it worked. And having annihilated you, he would go on for the rest of his life translating τριήρης 'steamer'.

If he had not been quite so clever, he might have known that by a careful sifting and interpretation of the evidence you can arrive at some conclusions, though certainly incomplete ones, about what a trireme was like. And by similar treatment of the evidence you can arrive at some conclusions about the meaning of words like δεῖ But in both cases you have to approach the matter from an historical point of view, not from that of a minute philosopher; and in the conviction that whatever the Greek word in question means it will not necessarily (indeed, not probably) mean anything that can be rendered by one word, if indeed by any words, in English.

Ideals of personal conduct are just as impermanent as ideals of social organization. Not only that, but what is meant by calling them ideals is subject to the same change. The 'realists' knew that different peoples, and the same peoples at different times, held different views, and were quite entitled to hold different views, about how a man ought to behave; but they thought that the phrase 'ought to behave' had a meaning which was one, unchanging, and eternal. They were wrong. The literature of European moral philosophy, from the Greeks onwards, was in their hands and on their shelves to tell them so; but they evaded the lesson by systematically mistranslating the passages from which they might have learnt it.

In metaphysics the corresponding analysis was easy to one who had been addicted from childhood to the history of science. I could not but see, for example, when Einstein set philosophers talking about relativity, that philosophers' convictions about the eternity of problems or conceptions were as baseless as a young girl's conviction that this year's hats are the only ones that could ever have been worn by a sane woman. One heard them maintaining the 'axiomatic' or 'self-evident' character of doctrines about matter, motion, and so forth which had first been propounded by very adventurous thinkers, at risk of their own liberty and life, three or four hundred years ago, and had become part of every educated European's beliefs only after long and fanatical propaganda in the eighteenth century.

It became clear to me that metaphysics (as its very name might show, though people still use the word as if it had been 'paraphysics') is no futile attempt at knowing what lies beyond the limits of experience, but is primarily at any given time an attempt to discover what the people of that time believe about the world's general nature; such beliefs being the presuppositions of all their 'physics', that is, their inquiries into its detail. Secondarily, it is the attempt to discover the corresponding presuppositions of other peoples and other times, and to follow the historical process by which one set of presuppositions has turned into another.

The question what presuppositions underlie the 'physics' or natural science of a certain people at a certain time is as purely historical a question as what kind of clothes they wear. And this is the question that metaphysicians have to answer. It is not their business to raise the further question whether, among the various beliefs on this subject that various peoples hold and have held, this one or that one is true. This question, when raised, would always be found, as it always has been found, unanswerable; and if there is anything in my 'logic of question and answer' that is not to be wondered at, for the beliefs whose history the metaphysician has to study are not answers to questions but only presuppositions of questions, and therefore the distinction between what is true and what is false does not apply to them, but only the distinction between what is presupposed and what is not presupposed. A presupposition of one question may be the answer to another question. The beliefs which a metaphysician tries to study and codify are presuppositions of the questions asked by natural scientists, but are not answers to any questions at all. This might be expressed by calling them 'absolute' presuppositions.

But the statements which any competent metaphysician tries to make or refute, substantiate or undermine, are themselves certainly true or false; for they are answers to questions about the history of these presuppositions. This was my answer to the rather threadbare question 'how can metaphysics become a science?' If science means a naturalistic science, the answer is that it had better not try. If science means an organized body of knowledge, the answer is: by becoming what it always has been; that is, frankly claiming its proper status as an historical inquiry in which, on the one hand, the beliefs of a given set of people at a given time concerning the nature of the world are exhibited as a single complex of contemporaneous fact, like, say, the British constitution as it stands to-day; and, on the other hand, the origin of these beliefs is inquired into, and it is found that during a certain space of time they have come into existence by certain changes out of certain others.

By degrees I found that there was no recognized branch of philosophy to which the principle did not apply, that its problems, as well as the solutions proposed for them, had their own history. The conception of 'eternal problems' disappeared entirely, except so far as any historical fact could be called eternal because it had happened once for all, and accordingly any problem could be called eternal because it had arisen once for all and once for all been solved.[2] I found (and it required a good deal of hard detailed work in the history of thought) that most of the conceptions round which revolve the controversies of modern philosophy, conceptions designated by words like 'state', 'ought', 'matter', 'cause', had appeared on the horizon of human thought at ascertainable times in the past, often not very distant times, and that the philosophical controversies of other ages had revolved round other conceptions, not indeed unrelated to ours, but not, except by a person quite blind to historical truth, indistinguishable from them.

Having thus with regard to the supposed permanence of philosophical problems found the 'realist' conception of philosophical history false at every point where I could think of testing it, I turned to another aspect of the same conception: namely the 'realists'' distinction between the 'historical' question 'what was So-and-so's theory on such and such a matter?' and the 'philosophical' question 'was he right?'

This distinction was soon condemned as fallacious. I will not here explain, since the reader can easily see it for himself, how it broke down in the light of the question 'how is the so-called philosophical issue to be settled?' and the answer that it could only be settled by what I was simultaneously discovering to be the sophistical methods of 'realist' criticism. I will rather point out that the alleged distinction between the historical question and the philosophical must be false, because it presupposes the permanence of philosophical problems. If there were a permanent problem P, we could ask 'what did Kant, or Leibniz, or Berkeley, think about P?' and if that question could be answered, we could then go on to ask 'was Kant, or Leibniz, or Berkeley, right in what he thought about P?' But what is thought to be a permanent problem P is really a number of transitory problems p_1 p_2 p_3 . . . whose individual peculiarities are blurred by the historical myopia of the person who lumps them together under the one name P. It follows that we cannot fish the problem P out of the hyperuranian lucky-bag, hold it up, and say 'what did So-and-so think about this?' We have to begin, as poor devils of historians begin, from the other end. We have to study documents and interpret them. We have to say 'here is a passage of Leibniz; what is it about? what is the problem with which it deals?' Perhaps we label that problem p_{14}. Then comes the question 'Does Leibniz here deal with p_{14} rightly or wrong?' The answer to this is not quite so simple as the 'realists' think. If Leibniz when he wrote this passage was so confused in his mind as to make a complete mess of the job of solving his problem, he was bound at the same time to mix up his own tracks so completely that no reader could see quite clearly what his problem had been. For one and the same passage states his solution and serves as evidence of what the problem was. The fact that we can identify his problem is proof that he has solved it; for we only know what the problem was by arguing back from the solution.

If anybody chooses to deny this, I will not try to convince him. Everybody who has learnt to think historically knows it already; and no amount of argument could teach it to a person who had not learnt to think historically. How can we discover what the tactical problem was that Nelson set himself at Trafalgar? Only by studying the tactics he pursued in the battle. We argue back from the solution to the problem. What else could we do? Even if we had the original typescript of the coded orders issued by wireless to his captains a few hours before the battle began, this would not tell us that he had not changed his mind at the last moment, extemporized a new plan on seeing some new factor in the situation, and trusted his captains to understand what he was doing and to back him up. Naval historians think it worth while to argue about Nelson's tactical plan at Trafalgar because he won the battle. It is not worth while arguing about Villeneuve's plan. He did not succeed in carrying it out, and therefore no one will ever know what it was. We can only guess. And guessing is not history.

A teacher who puts into his pupils' hands a philosophical text, and invites them to attend to a certain passage, may therefore say to them, 'This is a confused passage; we can see that the author was thinking about some problem or other, and we may reasonably conjecture that it was a problem somewhat like that discussed in such and such a passage by So-and-so. But he is muddled about the business, and no one can ever tell exactly what it was that worried the poor man.' He may say this; but if he does, his pupils will not greatly cherish his memory in after life. He had no business to waste their time on a passage of that sort.

Or, pointing them to a different passage, he may say, 'here our author, being neither illiterate nor idiotic (which is why I am asking you to study his works), has expressed in such a way that we can understand it a thought that was worth expressing. At first sight you cannot tell what he is trying to say. But if you will think carefully about the passage you will see that he is answering a question which he has taken the trouble to formulate in his mind with great precision. What you are reading is his answer. Now tell me what the question was.'

But he cannot have it both ways. He cannot say 'our author is here trying to answer the following question . . . That is a question which all philosophers ask themselves sooner or later; the right answer to it, as given by Plato or Kant or Wittgenstein, is . . . Our author is giving one of the wrong answers. The refutation of his erroneous view is as follows.' His claim to know what question the author is asking is a fraud which any one could expose by asking for his evidence. As a matter of fact, he is not basing his assertion on evidence; he is only trotting out some philosophical question of which the passage vaguely reminds him.

For me, then, there were not two separate sets of questions to be asked, one historical and one philosophical, about a given passage in a given philosophical author. There was one set only, historical.

3

According to the very ancient Oxford tradition — a tradition far older than Oxford itself — philosophy is taught by reading, expounding, and commenting on philosophical texts. Because the tradition is a living one, these texts are not those of ancient authors alone. The repertory of texts, which is nowhere printed and has no statutory sanction, is constantly changing; though it does not change very fast, and rightly, since no book is ripe for use in this peculiar way until it has become a classic. Yesterday's work of genius may have revolutionized its subject; but, even so, the best way of teaching undergraduates exactly how the subject has been revolutionzed is by lecturing on the old classics and showing in your commentary how their doctrine has been modified.

Here was a field of activity which exactly suited me. My inclinations have always led me rather towards detail than towards generalization; a general principle never comes to life in my mind except by exhibiting itself in its various special forms and in crowds of instances for each form.

The historian is a person whose questions are about the past. He is generally supposed to be a person whose questions are exclusively about the past; about a past, namely, that is dead and gone, and in no sense at all living on into the present. I had not gone very far in my study of historical thought before I realized that this was a delusion. The historian cannot answer questions about the past unless he has evidence about it. His evidence, if he 'has' it, must be something existing here and now in his present world. If there were a past event which had left no trace of any kind in the present world, it woud be a past event for which now there was no evidence, and nobody — no historian; I say nothing of other, perhaps more highly gifted, persons — could know anything about it.

4

So long as the past and present are outside one another, knowledge of the past is not of much use in the problems of the present. But suppose the past lives on in the present; suppose, though incapsulated in it, and at first sight hidden beneath the present's contradictory and more prominent features, it is still alive and active; then the historian may very well be related to the non-historian as the trained woodsman is to the ignorant traveller. 'Nothing here but trees and grass', thinks the traveller, and marches on. 'Look,' says the woodsman, 'there is a tiger in that grass'. The historian's business is to reveal the less obvious features hidden from a careless eye in the present situation.

5

If ready-made rules for dealing with situations of specific types are what you want, natural science is the kind of thing which can provide them. The reason why the civilization of 1600-1900, based upon natural science, found bankruptcy staring it in the face was because, in its passion for ready-made rules, it had neglected to develop that kind of insight which alone could tell it what rules to apply, not in a situation of a specific type, but in the situation in which it actually found itself. It was precisely because history offered us something altogether different from rules, namely insight, that it could afford us the help we needed in diagnosing our moral and political problems.

In a great part of our actions we act according to rules, and that is what makes our action successful. This is because we are moving among situations of certain standard types, and trying to manipulate them so as to obtain certain standard results. Action according to rule is a very important kind of action, and the first question which any intelligent man asks, when he finds himself in a situation of any kind, is 'What are the rules for acting in this kind of situation?'

But although action according to rules is a very important kind of action, it is not the only kind. There [is] a kind of action which is not determined according to rule, and where the process is directly from knowledge of the situation to an action appropriate to that situation, without passing through the stage of formulating a rule appropriate to the situation. And it must be very common, for a vast deal of it must go to the formulation of even the most trivial rule of conduct.

(1) The first kind of occasion on which it is necessary to act without rules is when you find yourself in a situation that you do not recognize as belonging to any of your known types. No rule can tell you how to act. But you cannot refrain from acting. No one is ever free to act or not to act, at his own discretion. *Il faut parier*, as Pascal said. You must do something. Here are you, up against this situation: you must improvise as best you can a method of handling it.

(2) The second kind of occasion on which you must act without rules is when you can refer the situation to a known type, but are not

content to do so. You know a rule for dealing with situations of this kind, but you are not content with applying it, because you know that action according to rules always involves a certain misfit between yourself and your situation. If you act according to rules, you are not dealing with the situation in which you stand, you are only dealing with a certain type of situation under which you class it. The type is, admittedly, a useful handle with which to grasp the situation; but all the same, it comes between you and the situation it enables you to grasp. Often enough, that does not matter; but sometimes it matters very much.

Thus everybody has certain rules according to which he acts in dealing with his tailor. These rules are, we will grant, soundly based on genuine experience; and by acting on them a man will deal fairly with his tailor and helps his tailor to deal fairly by him. But so far as he acts according to these rules he is dealing with his tailor only in his capacity as a tailor, not as John Robinson, aged 60, with a weak heart and a consumptive daughter, a passion for gardening and an overdraft at the bank. The rules for dealing with tailors no doubt enable you to cope with the tailor in John Robinson, but they prevent you from getting to grips with whatever else there may be in him. Of course, if you know that he has a weak heart, you will manage your dealings with him by modifying the rules for tailor-situations in the light of the rules for situations involving people with weak hearts. But at this rate the modifications soon become so complicated that the rules are no longer of any practical use to you. You have got beyond the stage at which rules can guide action, and you go back to improvising, as best you can, a method of handling the situation in which you find yourself.

From this point of view I could see that any one who asked for rules, in order to obtain from them instruction how to act, was clinging to the low-grade morality of custom and precept. He was trying to see only those elements in the situation which he already knew how to deal with, and was shutting his eyes to anything which might convince him that his ready-made rules were not an adequate guide to the conduct of life.

Rules of conduct kept action at a low potential, because they involved a certain blindness to the realities of the situation. If action was to be raised to a higher potential, the agent must open his eyes wider and see more clearly the situation in which he was acting. If the function of history was to inform people about the past, where the past was understood as a dead past, it could do very little towards helping them to act; but if its function was to inform them about the present, in so far as the past, its ostensible subject-matter, was incapsulated in the present and constituted a part of it not at once obvious to the untrained eye, then history stood in the closest possible relation to practical life.

Notes

1. Hence that numerous and frightful offspring of propositional logic out of illiteracy, the various attempts at a 'logical language', beginning with the pedantry of the text-books about 'reducing a proposition to logical form', and ending, for the present, in the typographical jargon of *Principia Mathematica*.

2. If 'eternal' is used in its vulgar and inaccurate sense, as equivalent to 'lasting for a considerable time', the phrase 'eternal problem' may be used to designate collectively a series of problems connected by a process of historical change, such that their continuity is discernible even by the presumably rather unintelligent eye of the person who thus misuses the word, but the differences between them not so discernible.

Source

Excerpts from R.G. Collingwood, 'The Historical Logic of Question and Answer' in *An Autobiography* (Oxford, Oxford University Press, 1939).

ON COLLINGWOOD'S PHILOSOPHY OF HISTORY

Leo Strauss

1

R.G. Collingwood's *The Idea of History* (Clarendon Press, 1946) 'is an essay in the philosophy of history'. Philosophy of history, as Collingwood understood it, is of very recent origin. It emerged as a sequel to the rise of 'scientific history' which took place in the latter part of the nineteenth century (254). If one assumes that 'scientific history' is the highest or final form of man's concern with his past, the understanding of what the 'scientific historian' does, or epistemology of history, may become of philosophic interest. And if the older or traditional branches of philosophy cannot make intelligible the 'new historical technique' or solve the problems 'created by the existence of organized and systematized historical research'; if, in other words, 'the traditional philosophies carry with them the implication that historical knowledge is impossible' (5-6), epistemology of history becomes of necessity a philosophic concern or a philosophic discipline. But philosophy of history must be more than epistemology of history. In the first place, epistemology of history is likely to be of vital concern only to certain technicians, and not to men as men. Above all, thought about historical thought must be thought about the object of historical thought as well. Hence philosophy of history must be both epistemology of history and metaphysics of history (3, 184). Philosophy of history comes then first to sight as an addition to the traditional branches of philosophy. But philosophy hardly permits of mere additions. Certainly philosophy of history cannot be a mere addition: philosophy of history necessarily entails 'a complete philosophy conceived from an historical point of view' (7, 147). For the discovery on which philosophy of history is based concerns the character of all human thought; it leads therefore to an entirely new understanding of philosophy. In other words, it was always admitted that the central theme of philosophy is the question of what man is, and that history is the knowledge of what men have done; but now it has been realized that man is what he can do, and 'the only clue to what man can do' is what he has done (10); therefore, 'the so-called science of human nature or of the human mind resolves itself into history' (220, 209). Philosophy of history is identical with philosophy as such, which has become radically historical: 'philosophy as a separate discipline is liquidated by being converted into history'(x).

Collingwood was prevented by his death from elaborating his philosophy of history in the full sense of the term. He believed that he could do no more than to attempt 'a philosophic inquiry into the nature of history regarded as a special type or form of knowledge with a special type of object' (7). Since philosophy of history in the narrower sense admittedly points to philosophy of history in the comprehensive sense, it might seem that Collingwood unjustifiably postponed the discussion of the fundamental issue. But it is perhaps fairer to say that philosophy of history in the comprehensive sense presupposes philosophy of history in the narrower sense, or that the fusion of philosophy and history presupposes the soundness or adequacy of 'scientific history': if the historical understanding of the last four or five generations is not decisively superior to the historical understanding that was possible in the past, the conversion of philosophy into history loses its most convincing, or at least its most persuasive, justification.

Scientific history, being 'now a thing within the compass of everyone' (320), is the co-operative effort of a very large number of contemporaries which is directed toward the acquisition of such knowledge as 'ideally' forms part of 'a universal history' or of knowledge of 'the human past in its entirety' (27, 209). It is a theoretical pursuit; it is 'actuated by a sheer desire for truth' and by no other concern (60-1). The attitude of the scientific historian, however, is not that of a spectator. Knowledge of what men have done is knowledge of what men have thought: 'All history is the history of thought' (215, 304). Scientific history is thought about thought. Past thought cannot be known as such except by being re-thought, or re-enacted, or re-lived, or reproduced (97, 115, 218). For the scientific historian, the past is not something foreign, or dead, or outside his mind: the human past is living in his mind, though living as past. This does not mean that the entire past can be re-enacted by every scientific historian; there must be a kind of sympathy between the historian's thought and his object; and in order to be truly alive, 'the historian's thought must spring from the organic unity of his total experience, and be a function of his entire personality with its practical as well as its theoretical interests' (305). Since 'all thinking is critical thinking' and not a mere surrender to the object of thought, re-thinking of earlier thought is identical with criticism of earlier thought (215-16, 300-1). The point of view from which the scientific historian criticizes the past is that of the present of his civilization. Scientific history is then the effort to see the human past in its entirety as it appears from the standpoint of the present of the historian's civilization (60, 108, 215). Yet history will not be self-knowledge if the historian sees the past in the light of the present of his civilization without making that present his primary theme. The scientific historian's task is therefore to show how the present of his civilization, or the mind of the present-day, or that 'determinate human nature' which is his civilization, has come into existence (104, 169, 175, 181, 226). Since scientific history is a peculiarity of modern Western thought, it may be described as the effort of present-day Western man to understand his peculiar humanity and thus to preserve it or enrich it.

Since genuine knowledge of the past is necessarily criticism and evaluation of the past from the point of view of the present, it is necessarily 'relative' to the present, that is, to the present of a given country or civilization. The point of view of a given historian is 'valid only for him and people situated like him' (60, 108). 'Every new generation must rewrite history in its own way' (248). Objectivity in the sense of universal validity would then seem to be impossible. Collingwood was not disturbed by this danger to 'scientific' history (cf. 265). There were two reasons for his confidence. In the first place, the belief in progress, and hence in the superiority of the present to the past, still lingered on in his thought. He could therefore believe that if historical knowledge is relative to the present, it is relative to the highest standpoint which has ever existed. To see that the belief in progress survived in Collingwood's thought, it almost suffices to look at the Table of Contents of his book: he devoted more space to Croce, to say nothing of other present-day thinkers, than to Herodotus and Thucydides. He took it for granted that the historian can and must distinguish 'between retrograde and progressive elements' in the phenomena which he is studying (135). More than half of his book is devoted to a comparison of the modern scientific conception of history with 'the medieval conception of history with all its errors' (56) and the classical conception with its grave 'defects' (41-2). The second reason why Collingwood was not disturbed by the 'relativity' of all historical knowledge was his belief in the equality of all ages. 'The present is always perfect in the sense that it always succeeds in being what it is trying to be,' or the present has no standard higher than itself (109). There are no ages of decline or of decay (164). Augustine looked at Roman history from the point of view of an early Christian, and Gibbon did so from that of an enlightened eighteenth-century Englishman: 'there is no point in asking which was the right point of view. Each was the only possible for the man who adopted it' (xii). The historian who sees the past from the point of view of a present must not be worried by the prospect of a future progress of historical knowledge: 'the historian's problem is a present problem, not a future one: it is to interpret the material now available, not to anticipate future discoveries' (180). Being thus protected against the surprises which the future may have in store, the scientific historian can be satisfied that the historical knowledge which is relative to the present, and is based on the material accessible at present, fulfils all the requirements of certainty or science. The fact that all historical knowledge is relative to the present means that it is relative to the only standpoint which is possible now, to a standpoint which is in no way inferior to any standpoint which was possible in the past or which will be possible in the future. Regardless of whether or not Collingwood found a way for reconciling the two different reasons indicated, each of them, if sound, would justify him in assuming that understanding of the past from the point of view of the present is unobjectionable, and in fact inevitable.

The procedure which we have just outlined is characteristic of *The Idea of History*. Collingwood moved consciously and with enthusiasm toward a goal which most of his contemporaries were approaching more or less unconsciously and haltingly, that goal being the fusion of philosophy and history. But he was not very much concerned with examining the means by which he tried to reach his goal. He vacillated between two different views of history, the rationalistic view of Hegel, and a non-rationalistic view. He never clearly realized that these two views are mutually incompatible. The historical reason for this failure was his lack of acquaintance with Nietzsche's epoch-making critique of 'scientific history.'

There is a tension between the idea of universal history and the view that in history 'the mind of the present day apprehends the process by which this mind itself has come into existence through the mental development of the past' (169). If the modern Western historian studies Greek civilization, he may be said to re-enact the genesis of his own civilization, which has formed itself 'by reconstructing within its own mind the mind of the Hellenic world' and thus to enter upon the possession of his inheritance (163, 226-7); he may be said to attempt to understand himself as modern Western man, or to mind his own business. But the case of the modern Western historian who studies Chinese or Inca civilization is obviously different. Collingwood did not reflect on this difference. He justly rejected Spengler's view that 'there is no possible relation whatever between one culture and another.' But he failed to consider the fact that there are cultures which have no actual relations with one another, and the implications of this fact: he dogmatically denied the possibility of 'separate, discrete' cultures because it would destroy the dogmatically assumed 'continuity of history' as universal history (161-4, 183).

According to one view held by Collingwood, the idea of scientific history, 'the idea of an imaginary picture of the past [is], in Kantian language, *a priori* . . . it is an idea which every man possesses as part of the furniture of his mind, and discovers himself to possess in so far as he becomes conscious of what it is to have a mind' (248); scientific history is therefore the actualization of a potentiality of human nature. According to another view also held by Collingwood, one cannot speak of the furniture of the human mind, and not even of *the* human mind, which as such would be subject to 'permanent and unchanging laws'; the idea of scientific history is not, in principle, coeval with the human mind but is itself 'historical'; it has been acquired by Western man on the basis of his unique experience (of the Christian experience in particular); it is rooted in modern Western thought and its needs; it is meaningful only for modern Western thought (xii, 12, 48-9, 82, 224, 226, 255). Collingwood regarded history as a theoretical pursuit, but he also said that the historian's thought must be 'a function of his entire personality with its practical as well as its theoretical interests.' All history, Collingwood repeatedly said, is the history of thought or of rational activity or of freedom (215, 304, 315, 318) one cannot abandon 'Hegel's belief that history is rational' without abandoning history itself (122); by speaking of 'the contingency of history', the historian 'expresses [the] final collapse of his thought' (151). Accordingly, Collingwood held that understanding of the thought of the past is not only compatible with criticism of thought of the past from the point of view of the present, but inseparable from it. On the other hand, however, he tended to believe that the ultimate facts of history are free choices which are not justifiable by rational activity; or that the ultimate facts of history are mere beliefs, and hence that history is not rational or that it is radically contingent or that it is, so to speak, a sequel of different original sins. Accordingly, he tended to hold that the historian cannot criticize the thought of the past but must remain satisfied with understanding it (cf. 316-18).

Collingwood's failure to clarify his position sufficiently can be explained in part by the need which he felt 'to engage in a running fight' with positivism or naturalism (i.e., 'the confusion between historical process and natural process') (228,181-2). His main preoccupation was with vindicating 'the autonomy of history' against the claims of modern natural science. The view that historical knowledge is partly dependent on modern natural science was based on the fact that man's historical life is dependent on nature; and man's knowledge of nature is not identical with modern natural science. Collingwood was therefore driven to assert 'the autonomy of history' without any qualification: 'the historian is master in his own house; he owes nothing to the scientist or to anyone else,' for 'ordinary history,' rightly understood, 'contains philosophy inside itself' (155, 201). History does not depend upon authority nor on memory (236-8). ' . . . in history, just as there are properly speaking no authorities, so there are properly speaking no data' (243). 'Freed from its dependence on fixed points supplied from without, the historian's picture of the past is thus in every detail an imaginary picture, and its necessity is at every point the necessity of the *a priori* imagination. Whatever goes into it, goes into it not because his imagination passively accepts it, but because it actively demands it' (245). It is because of its 'autonomy' that history must be universal history (246): truth is totality. Collingwood should not have hesitated to call this view 'idealistic' (cf.159). It is indeed not a solipsistic view: historical thought is both autonomous and objective; the historian's house 'is inhabited by all historians' (155). More precisely, it is inhabited by all present day historians. It is a house without windows: the mind of the present day is autonomous or master in its own house because it cannot understand the thought of the past without criticizing it, that is, without transforming it into a modification of present day thought, or because it is not disturbed by problems which it cannot solve ('To ask questions you see no prospect of answering is the fundamental sin in science', 281) or because it is not disturbed by the possibilities of the future ('the only clue to what man can do is what man has done', 10, 180). A particularly noteworthy consequence of Collingwood's idealism is the banishment of biography from history: the limits of biography are 'biological events, the birth and death of a human organism: its framework is thus a framework not of thought but of natural process' (304). This decision had the additional advantage of keeping the subjectivity of scientific history within limits which, for Collingwood, were reasonable. If the 'biographical' is sub-historical, it will as little go into the making of the subject which acquires or possesses historical knowlege, as it will become an element of the object of historical knowledge. Historical knowledge will not become relative to the individual historian. It will retain its objectivity by being relative to 'the mind of the present day'. A difficulty is created by the circumstance that 'the historian's thought must spring from the organic unity of his total experience', which experience, being total, could be thought to include his 'immediate experience with its flow of sensations and feelings' and those 'human emotions [which] are bound up with the spectacle of [his] bodily life' (304): 'total experience' would seem to include the most 'personal' experiences.

To do justice to Collingwood's idea of history, one must examine his practice as a historian. The largest part of his book is devoted to a history of historical knowledge. That history is on the whole conventional. In studying earlier thinkers, Collingwood never considered the possibility that the point of view from which the present day reader approaches them, or the questions which he addresses to them, might be in need of a fundamental change. He set out to praise or blame the earlier thinkers according to whether they helped or hindered the emergence of scientific history. He did not attempt to look at scientific history, for once, from the point of view of the earlier thinkers. What is not quite conventional in Collingwood's history, are some of his judgements: he had the courage to wonder whether Thucydides and Tacitus deserve the title of historians (29, 38-9). Furthermore, his history of historical knowledge is somewhat obscured by an ambiguity which he did not consistently avoid. His discussion of 'Human nature and human history' culminated in the assertion that historical knowledge is coeval with the historical process, because the historical process is a process in which man inherits the achievements of the past, and historical knowledge is the way in which man enters upon the possession of that inheritance (226-7; cf. 333-4). In this crucial context Collingwood thus identified historical knowledge with accepting a tradition or living in a tradition. As a rule, however, he assumed that historical knowledge is not coeval with historical life but is an 'invention' made at a certain time in Greece (19) and developed later on by the heirs of the Greeks.

The most revealing section of Collingwood's history of historical knowledge is his statement about the Greek conception of history. The Greeks created scientific history. This fact is paradoxical, for Greek thought was based 'on a rigorously anti-historical metaphysics' (18-20). The 'chief category' of that metaphysics 'is the category of substance', and 'a substantialist metaphysics implies a theory of knowledge according to which only what is unchanging is knowable' (42). 'Therefore history ought to be impossible', i.e., impossible as a science; history must be relegated to the realm of 'opinion'. Yet the very view that what is truly, or what is truly knowable, is the permanent, implied a fundamental distinction between the permanent and the changeable, and hence the insight that change is necessary: the Greeks' pursuit of the eternal presupposed 'an unusually vivid sense of the temporal'. In addition, they lived in a period of rapid and violent change: hence their 'peculiar sensitiveness to history'. For this reason however 'their historical consciousness' was of a peculiar kind: it was 'not a consciousness of age-long tradition molding the life of one generation after another into a uniform pattern; it was a consciousness of violent περιπέτειαι, catastrophic changes from one state of things to its opposite . . . ' (22; cf. 26, 34). But since they believed that only the permanent is knowable or intelligible, they regarded 'these catastrophic changes in the condition of human life' as unintelligible. They did not deny 'that in the general pattern of these changes certain antecedents normally led to certain consequents', and that these sequences can be established by observation; but they could not tell why 'certain antecedents normally led to certain consequents': 'There is here no theory of causation.' 'This conception of history was the very opposite of deterministic': the sequences of antecedents and consequents are not necessary; they can be modified by the men who know of them; 'thus the Greeks had a lively and indeed a naïve sense of the power of man to control his own destiny'. Since the Greeks were compelled to consider history 'as, at bottom, not a science, but a mere aggregate of perceptions', they had to identify 'historical evidence with the reports of facts given by eye witnesses of these facts'. They did not uncritically accept those reports. But their criticism could not go beyond making quite certain whether the eye witness really told what he had seen, and reaching a decision as to which of various conflicting reports deserved to be accepted. This conception of historical evidence limited history to the study of 'events which have happened within living memory to people with whom [the historian] can have personal contact'; it made impossible scientific history of the remote past: the historian cannot be more than 'the autobiographer of his generation' (22-7).

Some critical remarks seem to be necessary. When asserting that thinking historically and thinking in terms of substance are incompatible, Collingwood presupposed that 'it is metaphysically axiomatic that an agent, being a substance, can never come into being and can never undergo any change of nature' (43). Did the Greeks then not know that human beings, for example, come into being? Or is it necessary to refer to Aristotle's statement that coming into being simply is said only of substances? Why then should the Greeks have been unable to observe and to describe the coming into being of substances and their changes? Collingwood asserted that in 'substantialist' classical historiography 'all the agencies that appear on the stage of history have to be assumed ready-made before history begins' (45) and that the classics therefore regarded nations and cities as substances, 'changeless and eternal' (44). He did not even attempt to prove that the classics conceived of cities and nations as substances. But even if they did, their almost daily experience would have convinced them that cities at any rate are not 'changeless and eternal' substances, that they are founded and grow and decay and perish, to say nothing of other changes which they undergo. Why then should the Greeks have been unable to observe and describe the coming into being and the changes of cities? To say nothing of the fact that it is safe to infer what men could do from what they did. ' . . . the Greeks could not even contemplate the possibility of raising the problem which we should call the problem of the origin of the Hellenic people' (34). But, to take the most obvious case, were there no Greek thinkers who taught that the human race had come into being, that in the beginning men roamed in forests, without social bonds of any kind and in particular without language, and hence without the Greek language? Certainly these thinkers did not merely contemplate the possibility of raising the problem of the origin of the Hellenic people, but they did raise it and, according to their lights, solved it. Collingwood did not see that the reflections of the Greek philosophers on the nature and origin of language are equivalent to reflections on the nature and origin of nations. If they did not attempt to give historical accounts of the genesis of this or that nation, or of any nation, they had reasons like these: They did not have at their disposal historical evidence of events of this kind; they regarded the city as a higher form of society than the nation; and they thought that societies in their full vigour and maturity were more instructive regarding the highest possibilities of man than are societies newly coming into being. There may be a connection between these views and 'substantialism'. It suffices to note that Collingwood did not even try to reveal that connection. Prudence would have dictated to Collingwood to refrain from speaking of 'substantialism' and to limit himself to saying that the classics were, for whatever reason, more concerned with the permanent and hence with the recurrent than with what is merely temporal and local, or that they believed that the unique can ultimately be understood only in the light of the permanent or recurrent. From this he could legitimately have concluded that from the point of view of the classics, history is inferior in dignity to philosophy or science. To prove his thesis, it would have been necessary for him to show, in addition, that the primacy of the concern with the permanent or recurrent precludes or endangers serious concern with what happens here and now or what happened there and then. He did not show this. To say nothing of other considerations, one may be chiefly concerned with the permanent or recurrent and yet hold that a given unique event (the Peloponnesian War, for example) supplies the only available basis for reliable observation which would enable one to form a correct judgement about certain recurrences of utmost importance. A man who held this view would of course study that unique event with utmost care, and, assuming that he was a superior man, he might have surpassed as a historian, that is, as a man who understands actions of men, all the scientific historians of the nineteenth and twentieth centuries.

Collingwood held that the Greeks had a 'historical consciousness' of a particular kind: it was 'not a consciousness of age-long tradition moulding the life of one generation after another into a uniform pattern', but a consciousness of 'catastrophic changes' (22). This statement is, to say the least, very misleading. 'The Greeks' were perfectly conscious of the existence of 'age-long traditions moulding the life of one generation after another into a uniform pattern'. But they believed, or at any rate Plato believed or suggested, that Greek life — in contradistinction especially to Egyptian life — was not dominated by such traditions: 'you Greeks are always children . . . you are, all of you, young in soul; for you do not possess in your souls a single ancient opinion transmitted by old tradition nor a single piece of learning that is hoary with age'. The Greeks were less dominated by age-long traditions than were other nations because there lived in their midst men who had the habit of questioning such traditions, i.e. philosophers. In other words, there was a greater awareness in Greece than elsewhere of the essential difference between the ancestral and the good. On the basis of this insight there existed in classical Greece 'a historical consciousness', not merely of 'catastrophic changes' but also of changes for the better, of progress, and this consciousness was a consciousness not merely of progress achieved but also of the possibility of future progress. Collingwood did not even allude to this element of 'the Greek conception of history'. He apparently never tried to understand 'the historical consciousness' which expresses itself in the first book of Aristotle's *Metaphysics*, for example. Consideration of this book alone would have sufficed to make him hesitate to write that 'the Greek historian was only the autobiographer of his generation ' (27).

But let us concede that a man like Thucydides was primarily concerned with 'catastrophic change' rather than with long periods in which practically no change, or only slow changes for the better, took place; and let us assume that Collingwood has given an account, based on Thucydides' work, of this preference, although Collingwood did not even attempt to do this. Was he entitled to say that the Greeks were forced to regard catastrophic changes as unintelligible, i.e. as in no way traceable to determinate causes? The mere fact that he could not help censoring Thucydides for being 'the father of psychological history' which is 'natural science of a special kind' (29) would seem to prove that there was at least one Greek who regarded catastrophic change as intelligible. According to Collingwood, the Greeks regarded the change from a state of extreme wealth or power to a state of extreme poverty or weakness, as a mysterious rhythm; 'the universal judgment that very rich men, as such, fall . . . is, in Aristotle's view, only a partially scientific judgment, for no one can say why rich men should fall' (24). If Collingwood had considered the analysis of the characters of the rich and the powerful in the second book of the *Rhetoric*, or the analysis of tyranny and dynastic oligarchy in the *Politics*, he could have told us that Aristotle had a good explanation for the fall of rich and powerful men if they are not virtuous or lucky. Collingwood mistook for no theory of causation what is in effect a theory of causation that includes chance as a cause of historical events.

Only because Collingwood disregarded, among other things, what the classics have to say about the power of chance, could he confidently assert that 'the Greeks had a lively and indeed a naïve sense of the power of man to control his own destiny' (24) or that for Hellenic thought 'self-consciousness [was] a power to conquer the world' (36) or that classical thought implied 'that whatever happens in history happens as a direct result of the human will' (41). It taxes the imagination to understand how the same man could have written these sentences a few pages after he had written 'that these catastrophic changes in the condition of human life which were to the Greeks the proper theme of history, were unintelligible' (22).

As for Collingwood's remark that, for the Greeks, history was 'at bottom . . . a mere aggregate of perceptions' (24), it suffices to say that one page later he noted that men like Herodotus and Thucydides succeeded in calling up a fairly 'coherent' 'historical picture' of the events which they studied. In his discussion of the Greek conception of historical evidence, he was silent about the basic distinction between seeing with one's own eyes and hearsay, and the use which the classical historians made of that distinction for evaluating traditions or reports.

In particular, he did not consider that seeing with one's own eyes includes understanding of the nature of man and of the nature of political things, an understanding which fulfils in Greek history approximately the same function which 'historical imagination' fulfils in Collingwood's 'scientific history'.

Collingwood's account of the classical conception of history, which had to be 'in every detail an imaginary picture' in order to conform with his standards of historical truth (cf. 245), indirectly reveals more about 'the idea of history' than do all the subsequent sections of his book. The idea of history is more than the view that knowledge of what men have done or thought is possible or necessary. It is the view that such knowledge properly understood is identical with philosophy or must take the place of philosophy. The idea of history thus understood is indeed alien to classical thought. According to Collingwood, it could not emerge before classical 'substantialism' was abandoned and classical 'humanism' was profoundly modified. If history is the account, or the study, of what men have done, and philosophy is the study of something which is presupposed by all human doings, the idea of history requires in the first place that the apparent presuppositions of all human doings be resolved into products of human doings: this is what Collingwood meant by the need for abandoning 'substantialism'. The apparent presuppositions of all human doings are objects of human knowledge, as distinguished from the products or results of human action. The first step in the direction of the idea of history was therefore that the distinction between knowledge and action or between theory and practice be questioned. Knowledge had to be conceived as a kind of making or production. Collingwood referred in the usual manner to Vico's *verum et factum convertuntur* (64). But he failed to go back to Vico's source, i.e., to Hobbes, and hence he could rest satisfied with the conventional way of describing the genesis of the idea of history. Now, if the thinker or maker is man as man, or every individual regardless of time and place, philosophy remains 'unhistorical'. If there is to be an essential connection between thought, or the content of thought, and time and place, what we know or think must be such a making as is essentially dependent on the making of earlier men, or rather of earlier men who lived 'here', and yet it must be different from earlier thought. It cannot be different from earlier thought if it could have been anticipated, i.e., thought, by earlier, men: it must be the unforeseen and unforeseeable outcome of earlier thought. It is this requirement which Collingwood had in mind when he demanded the abandonment or radical modification of Greek 'humanism' which attributed 'far too little to the force of a blind activity embarking on a course of action without foreseeing its end and being led to that end only through the necessary development of that course itself' (42), i.e., without being led to that end by the plan of a god or of nature (55, 57, 58, 81, 104). He described the requirement in question somewhat more accurately when he contrasted Greek thought with the determinism of seventeenth century natural science which laid the foundation for conceiving of thought as such, and of every 'stage' of thought, as the necessary and unintended 'product of a process' (23, 57, 58, 81, 87). For the reason indicated, he failed, however, to raise the question regarding the connection between the conception of thinking as making and the peculiar 'determinism' of modern natural science. He thus failed to see that the basic stratum of 'the idea of history' is a combination of the view that thinking is making, or 'creative', with the need, engendered by that view, of giving a 'deterministic' account of thinking, or such a 'genetic' account as presupposes at no point anything except 'motion' or 'process'. Collingwood's 'idealism' prevented him from looking beyond the antagonism of 'idealism' and 'naturalism' or from seeing that 'history' and 'scientific materialism' are inseparable from each other. (Compare, however, the remark on p. 269 about the kinship between scientific history and Baconian natural science.)

2

Collingwood did not prove 'by deed' the superiority of scientific history to the common-sense type of history which prevailed, on the most different levels, in the past. His most important statements are errors which competent men in earlier times would not have committed simply because they were more careful readers than we have become. Scientific history is based on the assumption that present day historical thought is the right kind of historical thought. When it is confronted with the fact that earlier historical thought is different from present day historical thought, it naturally concludes that earlier historical thought is defective. And no one can be blamed if he does not study very carefully such doctrines or procedures as he knows in advance to be defective in the decisive respect. Collingwood wrote the history of history in almost the same way in which the eighteenth-century historians, whom he censored so severely, are said to have written history in general. The latter condemned the thought of the past as deficient in full reasonableness: Collingwood condemned it as deficient in the true sense for history.

This is not to deny that Collingwood also believed in the equality of all ages and that he therefore tended to regard the historical thought of any one period as equally sound as that of any other period. One might think that to the extent to which he held that belief, he would have tried to understand the historical thought of each period of the past on its own terms, without measuring it by the standard of scientific history. Yet the belief in the equality of all ages leads to the consequence that our interpretation of the thought of the past, while not superior to the way in which the thought of the past interpreted itself, is as legitimate as the past's self-interpretation and, in addition, is the only way in which we today can interpret the thought of the past. Accordingly, there arises no necessity to take seriously the way in which the thought of the past understood itself. In other words, the belief in the equality of all ages is only a more subtle form of the belief in progress. The alleged insight into the equality of all ages which is said to make possible passionate interest in the thought of the different ages, necessarily conceives of itself as a progress beyond all earlier thought: every earlier age erroneously 'absolutized' the standpoint from which it looked at things and therefore was incapable of taking very seriously the thought of other ages; hence earlier ages were incapable of scientific history.

The two beliefs which contended for supremacy in Collingwood's thought implied that earlier thought is necessarily relative to earlier times.

> The *Republic* of Plato is an acount, not of the unchanging ideal of political life, but of the Greek ideal as Plato received it and reinterpreted it. The *Ethics* of Aristotle describes not an eternal morality but the morality of the Greek gentleman. Hobbes' *Leviathan* expounds the political ideas of seventeenth century absolutism in their English form. Kant's ethical theory expresses the moral convictions of German pietism . . . ' (229)

Collingwood understood then the thought of a time in the light of its time. He did not then re-enact that thought. For to re-enact the thought which expresses itself in Plato's *Republic*, for example, means to understand Plato's description of the simply good social order as a description of the true model of society with reference to which all societies of all ages and countries must be judged. Collingwood's attitude towards the thought of the past was in fact that of a spectator who sees from the outside the relation of an earlier thought to its time.

The deficiencies of Collingwood's historiography can be traced to a fundamental dilemma. The same belief which forced him to attempt to become a historian of thought, prevented him from becoming a historian of thought. He was forced to attempt to become a historian of thought because he believed that to know the human mind is to know its history, or that self-knowledge is historical understanding. But this belief contradicts the tacit premise of all earlier thought, that premise being the view that to know the human mind is something fundamentally different from knowing the history of the human mind. Collingwood therefore rejected the thought of the past as untrue in the decisive respect. Hence he could not take that thought seriously, for to take a thought seriously means to regard it as possible that the thought in question is true. He therefore lacked the incentive for re-enacting the thought of the past: he did not re-enact the thought of the past. We draw the conclusion that in order to understand the thought of the past, one must doubt the view which is at the bottom of scientific history. One must doubt the principle which is characteristic of 'the mind of the present day'. One must abandon the attempt to understand the past from the point of view of the present. One must take seriously the thought of the past, or one must be prepared to regard it as possible that the thought of the past is superior to the thought of the present day in the decisive respect. One must regard it as possible that we live in an age which is inferior to the past in the decisive respect, or that we live in an age of decline or decay. One must be swayed by a sincere longing for the past.

Collingwood had to face this necessity when he had to speak of Romanticism. According to him, Romanticism is in danger of developing into 'a futile nostalgia for the past', but 'that development was checked by the presence in Romanticism of . . . the conception of history as a progress' (87). This remark lacks precision. Its deficiency is partly due to Collingwood's insufficient familiarity with the German intellectual movement around the year 1800. For instance in his statement on Friedrich Schiller (104-5), he limited himself to a survey of Schiller's lecture on the value of universal history without taking any notice of Schiller's essay on naïve and sentimental poetry. Similarly he asserted that 'Hegel wrote the first sketch of his philosophy of history in the Heidelberg *Encyclopaedia*' (111). The romantic soul, we prefer to say, is characterized by longing, by 'futile' longing, by a longing which is felt to be superior to any fulfilment that is possible 'now,' i.e., in post-revolutionary Europe. A perfect expression of Romanticism is *Madame Bovary*: the dead Emma, who, in spite of, or because of, the fact that she had an *esprit positif*, had spent her life in a longing that led to nothing but failure and degradation, is more alive than the contemporary representatives of the ancient faith and the modern faith who, with the corpse of Emma between them, engage in a noisy disputation, that is, share between themselves the rule over the nineteenth century. True Romanticism regards the highest possibility of the nineteenth or twentieth century, 'futile' longing, as the highest possibility of man, in so far as it assumes that the noble fulfilments of the past were based on delusions which are now irrevocably dispelled. True Romanticism believes that while the past was superior to the present as regards 'life' or 'culture' or 'art'or 'religion' or the nearness of God or gods, the present is superior to the past as regards the understanding of 'life' or 'culture', etc. It believes therefore that the present is superior to the past in regard to knowledge of the decisive truth, i.e., in the decisive respect. It therefore never submits its notions of 'life'or 'culture' or 'art' or 'religion' to a criticism which is enlightened by what the assumed models of 'life' or 'culture', etc., explicitly thought about these themes. Hence Romanticism perpetuates the belief in the superiority of modern thought to earlier thought, and Romantic history of thought is fundamentally as inadequate, or as 'un-historical', as non-romantic, progressivist history of thought.

Collingwood believed that 'in history as it actually happens there are no mere phenomena of decay: every decline is also a rise' (164). This sanguine statement cannot be reconciled with his remark that if we abandoned scientific history, 'we should be exemplifying and hastening that downfall of civilization which some historians are, perhaps prematurely, proclaiming' (56). Here Collingwood admitted that a decline which is not 'also a rise' is possible. Yet this momentary insight did not bear fruit in his understanding of earlier thought. He blamed Tacitus for representing history 'as essentially a clash of characters, exaggeratedly good and exaggeratedly bad', and he blamed the philosophies of Tacitus' age as 'defeatist philosophies which, starting from the assumption that the good man cannot conquer or control the wicked world, taught him how to preserve himself unspotted from its wickedness' (39-40). Since Collingwood dogmatically excluded the possibility of unqualified decay, he could not imagine that there might be ages in which virtuous political action is impossible, and 'defeatist' withdrawal is the only sane course of action; he could not consider the possibility that such ages may allow of an excess in wickedness in tyrannical rulers, and of a heroic virtue in their victims, for which there are no parallels in happier epochs. His 'historical consciousness' or historical imagination did not leave room for the possibility which Tacitus assumes to have been a fact. His historical consciousness could not be broadened by a study of Tacitus because scientific history recognizes no authority, but is master in its own house: it is not guided by a presumption in favour of the judgements which the wise men of old passed on their own times.

Collingwood was forced to admit the possibility of decline when he discussed the conditions under which progress is possible. For to admit that progress is possible and not necessary means to admit the possibility of decline. But it is precisely his discussion of the conditions of progress which shows how largely he remained under the spell of the belief in necessary progress or how far he was from understanding the function of historical knowledge. Progress, he said, 'happens only in one way: by the retention in the mind, at one phase, of what was achieved in the preceding phase' (333). The retention of earlier achievements is 'historical knowledge' (326). It is therefore 'only through historical knowledge that [progress] comes about at all' (333). Collingwood assumed that 'what was achieved in the preceding phase' has merely to be retained; he did not consider the possibiilty that it may have to be recovered because it had been forgotten. Accordingly, he identified historical knowledge, not with the recovery of earlier achievements, but with their retention: he uses Aristotle's knowledge of Plato's philosophy, and Einstein's knowledge of Newtonian physics, as examples of historical knowledge (333-4). He further assumed that progress requires the integration of earlier achievements into a framework supplied by the later achievement. He did not consider the possibility that progress may consist in separating recent achivements from their present framework and integrating them into an earlier framework which must be recovered by historical knowledge proper. But whatever might be true of progress, certainly the awareness of progress requires that the thought of the past be known as it actually was, that is, as it was actually thought by past thinkers. For, if to understand the thought of the past necessarily means to understand it differently from the way the thinkers of the past understood it, one will never be able to compare the thought of the present with the thought of the past: one would merely compare one's own thought with the reflection of one's own thought in ancient materials or with a hybrid begotten by the intercourse of one's own thought with earlier thought. What we might be inclined to regard as decisive insights alien to the thought of the past may in fact be delusions produced by the oblivion of things known to the thinkers of the past. Awareness of progress presupposes the possibility of understanding the thought of the past 'as it really has been'. It presupposes the possibility of historical objectivity.

Collingwood implicitly denied the possibility of historical objectivity by asserting that criticism of the thought of the past from the point of view of the present is an integral element of understanding the thought of the past (215). The historian is forced to raise 'such questions as: Was this or that policy a wise one? Was this or that economic system sound? Was this or that movement in science or art or religion an advance, and if so, why?' (132). Such questions cannot be answered except from the standpoint of the historian's time (60, 108). This conclusion depends in the first place on the premise that there are no unchangeable standards for judging human actions or thoughts. But it depends also on the further premise that the historian's primary task is to pass judgement on the past. Yet before one can pass judgement on the wisdom of, for example, a given policy, one must establish the character of that policy. 'For example, to reconstruct the history of a political struggle like that between the Roman emperors of the first century and the senatorial opposition, what the historian has to do is to see how the two parties conceived the political situation as it stood, and how they proposed to develop that situation: he must grasp their political ideas both concerning their actual present and concerning their possible future' (115). The primary task of the political historian would then seem to consist in understanding a given situation and given ends as they were understood by those who acted in the situation. The contemporaries of a struggle that is similar to the contest between the Roman emperors and the senatorial opposition have an easier access to that historical phenomenon than have people who lack experience of this particular kind of politics. But this does not make the understanding of the phenomenon in question relative to different situations: the difference in regard to the length and the difficulty of the way towards the goal does not affect the goal itself. In addition, 'historical imagination' liberates the historian from the limitations caused by the experiences peculiar to his time.

It may be objected that the very selection of the theme implies the inescapable subjective element: the reason for the historian's interest in a given situation is different from the reason for the actors' interest in it. The reason for the historian's interest in a historical phenomenon expresses itself in the questions which he addresses to the phenomenon concerned and hence to his sources, and this question is in principle alien to his sources.

> The scientific historian no doubt spends a great deal of time reading . . . Herodotus, Thucydides, Livy, Tacitus, and so forth . . . but he reads them . . . with a question in his mind, having taken the initiative by deciding for himself what he wants to find out from them . . . the scientific historian puts them to the torture, twisting a passage ostensibly about something quite different into an answer to the question he has decided to ask. (269-70)

There is no doubt that one may use the classical historians as a quarry or as ruins, to supply oneself with materials for erecting the edifice called the economic history of classical antiquity, for example. In doing this one makes the assumption that economic history is a worthwhile enterprise, and this assumption is indeed apparently relative to the preoccupations of the nineteenth and twentieth centuries, and alien to the classical historians. An intelligent or conscientious use of the classical historians for a purpose alien to them requires, however, a clear recognition of the fact that that purpose is alien to them and of the reason for that being so. It therefore requires that the classical historians first be understood on their own terms, that is, as answering their own questions, and not the questions with which the modern historian tortures them. Collingwood admitted this necessity in his way: 'The question [the scientific historian] asks himself is: "What does this statement mean?" And this is not equivalent to the question "What did the person who made it mean by it?" although that is doubtless a question that the historian must ask, and must be able to answer' (275). But this admission is much too weak. The answer to the question 'What did the person who made the statement mean by it?' must precede the answer to the question 'What does this statement mean within the context of my question?' For 'the statement' is the statement as meant by the author. Before one can use or criticize a statement, one must understand the statement, i.e., one must understand it as its author consciously meant it. Different historians may become interested in the same statement for different reasons: that statement does not alter its authentic meaning on account of those differences.

Collingwood severely criticized 'the scissors-and-paste historian' who reads the classical historians 'in a purely receptive spirit, to find out what they said' and 'on the understanding that what they did not tell him in so many words he would never find out from them at all' (269). But he did not realize that both 'the scissors-and-paste historian' and the scientific historian make the same mistake: they use the classical historians for a purpose alien to the latter before having done justice to the purpose of the classical historians. And both make this identical mistake for the same reason: they take 'history' for granted. Whatever may be the standpoint or the direction of interest or the guiding question of the present day historian, he cannot use his sources properly if he does not, to begin with, rigorously subordinate his question to the question which the author of his sources meant to answer, or if he does not, to begin with, identify his question with the question consciously raised by the author whose work he intends to use. The guiding question of the historian who wants to use Herodotus, for example, must become, for some considerable time, the question as to what question was uppermost in Herodotus' mind, that is, the question of what was the conscious intention of Herodotus, or the question regarding the perspective in which Herodotus looked at things. And the question regarding Herodotus' guiding intention, as well as the answer to it, is in no way affected by the diversity of questions with which modern historians approach Herodotus. In attempting to answer the question regarding Herodotus' intention, one must not even assume that Herodotus was a 'historian.' For in making this assumption one is likely to imply that he was not a 'philosopher' and thus to exclude without examination the possibility that Herodotus' intention cannot be understood without a complete revision of our 'categories'. Collingwood did not merely fail duly to appreciate the fact that the historian must provisionally subordinate his own question to the questions which the authors of his sources meant to answer. He likewise failed to consider the possibility that the historian may eventually have to retract his own question in favour of the questions raised by the authors of his sources.

Yet while the critical function of the historian may not become noticeable most of the time, or ever, the historian is, nevertheless, necessarily a critic. He selects a theme which he believes to be worthwhile: the critical judgement that the theme is worthwhile precedes the interpretation. He provisionally subordinates his question to the question guiding his author: eventually the historian's own question reasserts itself. Nor is the interpretation proper — the activity which follows the reasoned selection of the theme and which is coextensive with the subordination of the historian's question to the question guiding his author — separable from criticism. As Collingwood put it, it is a 'self-contradictory task of discovering (for example) "What Plato thought" without inquiring "Whether it is true"'(300). One cannot understand a chain of reasoning without 're-enacting' it, and this means without examining whether or not it is valid. One cannot understand premises without understanding them as premises, i.e., without raising the question whether they are evident or intrinsically necessary. For if they are not evident, one must look for the supporting reasoning. The supporting reasoning, a crucial part of the teaching of the author as the author understood it, might easily pass unnoticed if one failed to look for it, and one is not likely to look for it unless one is prompted to do so by a realization of the inevident character of the premises concerned. Therefore the establishment of the fact (if it is a fact) that an author makes a dogmatic assumption may be said to be inseparable from the interpretation of the author in question.

But the fact that the historian is necessarily a critic does not mean, of course, that his criticism necessarily culminates in partial or total rejection; it may very well culminate in total acceptance of the criticized view. Still less does it mean that the historian necessarily criticizes the thought of the past from the point of view of present day thought. By the very fact that he seriously attempts to understand the thought of the past, he leaves the present. He embarks on a journey whose end is hidden from him. He is not likely to return to the shores of his time as exactly the same man who departed from them. His criticism may very well amount to a criticism of present day thought from the point of view of the thought of the past.

The fact that interpretation and criticism are in one sense inseparable does not mean that they are identical. The meaning of the question 'What did Plato think' is different from the meaning of the question 'Whether that thought is true'. The former question must ultimately be answered by a reference to texts. The latter question cannot possibly be settled by reference to texts. Every criticism of a Platonic contention implies a distinction between the Platonic contention, which must be understood as such, and the criticism of that contention. But interpretation and criticism are not only distinguishable from each other. To a certain extent they are even separable from each other. Plato's thought claims to be an imitation of the whole; as such it is itself a whole which is distinguished from the whole simply. It is impossible to understand the imitation without looking at the original. But it is possible to look at the original in compliance, or without compliance, with the directives supplied by the imitation. To look at the original in compliance with the directives supplied by the imitation means to try to understand the whole as Plato understood it. To understand the whole, as Plato understood it is the goal of the interpretation of Plato's work. This goal is the standard which we presuppose, and to which we ultimately refer, whenever we find someone's interpretation of Platonic doctrine defective: we cannot find an interpretation defective without having 'seen' that goal. The attempt to understand Plato's thought as Plato understood it is inseparable from criticism, but that criticism is in the service of the striven-for understanding of Plato's thought. History as history, as quest for the understanding of the past, necessarily presupposes that our understanding of the past is incomplete. The criticism which is inseparable from interpretation is fundamentally different from the criticism which would coincide with the completed understanding. If we call 'interpretation' that understanding or criticism which remains within the limits of Plato's own directives, and if we call 'criticism' that understanding or criticism which disregards Plato's directives, we may say that interpretation necessarily precedes criticism because the quest for understanding necessarily precedes completed understanding and therewith the judgement which coincides with the completed understanding. The historian who has no illusions about the difference of rank between himself and Plato will be very sceptical in regard to the possibility of his ever reaching adequate understanding of Plato's thought. But what is impossible for most men is not therefore intrinsically impossible. If one denies the legitimacy of the goal which we called adequate understanding of Plato's thought, i.e., if one denies the possibility of historical objectivity, one merely substitutes a spurious right of subjectivity and of arbitrary assertions for the honest confession that we are ignorant of the most important facts of the human past.

It is then indeed a 'self-contradictory task of discovering "What Plato thought" without inquiring "Whether it is true".' It is indeed impossible to understand a line of Plato if one is not concerned with what Plato was concerned with, that is, the truth about the highest things, and hence if one does not inquire whether what Plato thought about them is true. It is indeed impossible to understand what Plato thought without thinking, i.e., without articulating the subjects about which Plato thought. Thinking about Plato's subjects cannot be limited by what Plato said or thought. It must take into consideration everything relevant, regardless of whether Plato seems to have considered it or not. That is to say, trying to understand Plato requires remaining loyal to Plato's guiding intention; and remaining loyal to Plato's intention means to forget about Plato and to be concerned exclusively with the highest things. But Collingwood assumed that we must not forget about Plato in spite, or rather because, of the fact that we must aim at no other end than the truth regarding the highest things. This assumption is legitimate and is not defeated by its consequences, if it means that we may have to learn something from Plato about the highest things which we are not likely to learn without his guidance, that is, that we must regard Plato as a possible authority. But to regard Plato as a possible authority means to regard him for the time being as an actual authority. We must, indeed, ourselves articulate the subjects about which Plato thought, but in doing this we must follow Plato's indications as to the manner in which these subjects should be articulated. If Plato took something for granted which we are in the habit of doubting or even of denying, or if he did not push the analysis of a given subject beyond a certain point, we must regard it as possible that he had good reasons for stopping where he stopped. If it is necessary to understand Plato's thought it is necessary to understand it as Plato himself understood it, and therefore it is necessary to stop where he stopped and to look around: perhaps we shall gradually understand his reasons for stopping. As long as we have not understood Plato's thought, we are in no position to say 'Whether it is true'. The 'historian of philosophy' is a man who knows that he has not yet understood Plato's thought and who is seriously concerned with understanding Plato's thought because he suspects that he may have to learn from Plato something of utmost importance. It is for this reason that Plato's thought cannot become an object, or a spectacle, for the historian. It is to be feared that Collingwood underestimated the difficulty of finding out 'What Plato meant by his statements' or 'Whether what he thought is true'.

History, that is, concern with the thought of the past as thought of the past, takes on philosophic significance if there are good reasons for believing that we can learn something of utmost importance from the thought of the past which we cannot learn from our contemporaries. History takes on philosophic significance for men living in an age of intellectual decline. Studying the thinkers of the past becomes essential for men living in an age of intellectual decline because it is the only practicable way in which they can recover a proper understanding of the fundamental problems. Given such conditions, history has the further task of explaining why the proper understanding of the fundamental probems has become lost in such a manner that the loss presents itself at the outset as a progress. If it is true that loss of understanding of the fundamental problems culminates in the historicization of philosophy or in historicism, the second function of history consists in

making intelligible the modern notion of 'History' through the understanding of its genesis. Historicism sanctions the loss, or the oblivion,
of the natural horizon of human thought by denying the permanence of
the fundamental problems. It is the existence of that natural horizon
which makes possible 'objectivity' and therefore in particular 'historical objectivity'.

Source

Leo Strauss 'On Collingwood's Philosophy of History', *The Review of Metaphysics*, vol. 5, no. 4 (June 1952), pp. 559-86.

PART FOUR

LOVEJOY

7 THE STUDY OF THE HISTORY OF IDEAS

A.O. Lovejoy

These lectures are primarily an attempt to offer a contribution to the history of ideas; and since the term is often used in a vaguer sense than that which I have in mind, it seems necessary, before proceeding to the main business in hand, to give some brief account of the province, purpose, and method of the general sort of inquiry for which I should wish to reserve that designation. By the history of ideas I mean something at once more specific and less restricted than the history of philosophy. It is differentiated primarily by the character of the units with which it concerns itself. Though it deals in great part with the same material as the other branches of the history of thought and depends greatly upon their prior labours, it divides that material in a special way, brings the parts of it into new groupings and relations, views it from the standpoint of a distinctive purpose. Its initial procedure may be said — though the parallel has its dangers — to be somewhat analogous to that of analytic chemistry. In dealing with the history of philosophical doctrines, for example, it cuts into the hard-and-fast individual systems and, for its own purposes, breaks them up into their component elements, into what may be called their unit-ideas. The total body of doctrine of any philosopher or school is almost always a complex and heterogeneous aggregate — and often in ways which the philosopher himself does not suspect. It is not only a compound but an unstable compound, though, age after age, each new philosopher usually forgets this melancholy truth. One of the results of the quest of the unit-ideas in such a compound is, I think, bound to be a livelier sense of the fact that most philosophic systems are original or distinctive rather in their patterns than in their components. When the student reviews the vast sequence of arguments and opinions which fill our historical textbooks, he is likely to feel bewildered by the multiplicity and seeming diversity of the matters presented. Even if the array of material is simplified somewhat by the aid of conventional — and largely misleading — classifications of philosophers by schools or -isms, it still appears extremely various and complicated; each age seems to evolve new species of reasonings and conclusions, even though upon the same old problems. But the truth is that the number of essentially distinct philo-

179

sophical ideas or dialectical motives is — as the number of really distinct jokes is said to be — decidedly limited, though, no doubt, the primary ideas are considerably more numerous than the primary jokes. The seeming novelty of many a system is due solely to the novelty of the application or arrangement of the old elements which enter into it. When this is realized, the history as a whole should look a much more manageable thing. I do not, of course, mean to maintain that essentially novel conceptions, new problems and new modes of reasoning about them, do not from time to time emerge in the history of thought. But such increments of absolute novelty seem to me a good deal rarer than is sometimes supposed. It is true that, just as chemical compounds differ in their sensible qualities from the elements composing them, so the elements of philosophical doctrines, in differing logical combinations, are not always readily recognizable; and, prior to analysis, even the same complex may appear to be not the same in its differing expressions, because of the diversity of the philosophers' temperaments and the consequent inequality in the distribution of emphasis among the several parts, or because of the drawing of dissimilar conclusions from partially identical premises. To the common logical or pseudo-logical or affective ingredients behind the surface-dissimilarities the historian of individual ideas will seek to penetrate.

These elements will not always, or usually, correspond to the terms which we are accustomed to use in naming the great historic conceptions of mankind. There are those who have attempted to write histories of the idea of God, and it is well that such histories should be written. But the idea of God is not a unit-idea. By this I do not mean merely the truism that different men have employed the one name to signify superhuman beings of utterly diverse and incongruous kinds; I mean also that beneath any *one* of these beliefs you may usually discover something, or several things, more elemental and more explanatory, if not more significant, than itself. It is true that the God of Aristotle had almost nothing in common with the God of the Sermon on the Mount — though, by one of the strangest and most momentous paradoxes in Western history, the philosophical theology of Christendom identified them, and defined the chief end of man as the imitation of both. But it is also true that Aristotle's conception of the being to whom he gave the most honorific name he knew was merely one consequence of a certain more general way of thinking, a species of dialectic (of which I shall later speak) not peculiar to him but highly characteristic of the Greek and almost wholly foreign to the ancient Jewish mind — which has historically manifested its influence in ethics and aesthetics, and sometimes even in astronomy, as well as in theology. And it would, in such a case, be to the prior idea, at once more fundamental and more variously operative, that the historian of ideas would apply his method of inquiry. It is in the persistent dynamic factors, the ideas that produce effects in the history of thought, that he is especially interested. Now a formulated doctrine is sometimes a relatively inert thing. The conclusion reached by a process of thought is also not infrequently the conclusion of the process of thought. The more significant factor in the matter may be, not the dogma which certain persons proclaim — be that single or manifold in its meaning — but the motives or reasons which have led them to it. And motives and reasons partly identical may contribute to the production of very diverse conclusions, and the same substantive conclusions may, at different periods, or in different minds, be generated by entirely distinct logical or other motives.

It is not, perhaps, superfluous to remark also that the doctrines or tendencies that are designated by familiar names ending in *-ism* or *-ity*, though they occasionally may be, usually are not, units of the sort which the historian of ideas seeks to discriminate. They commonly constitute, rather, compounds to which his method of analysis needs to be applied. Idealism, romanticism, rationalism, transcendentalism, pragmatism — all these trouble-breeding and usually thought-obscuring terms, which one sometimes wishes to see expunged from the vocabulary of the philosopher and the historian altogether, are names of complexes, not of simples — and of complexes in two senses. They stand, as a rule, not for one doctrine, but for several distinct and often conflicting doctrines held by different individuals or groups to whose way of thinking these appellations have been applied, either by themselves or in the traditional terminology of historians; and each of these doctrines, in turn, is likely to be resolvable into simpler elements, often very strangely combined and derivative from a variety of dissimilar motives and historic influences. The term 'Christianity', for example, is not the name for any single unit of the type for which the historian of specific ideas looks. I mean by this not merely the notorious fact that persons who have equally professed and called themselves Christians have, in the course of history, held all manner of distinct and conflicting beliefs under the one name, but also that any one of these persons and sects has, as a rule, held under that name a very mixed collection of ideas, the combination of which into a conglomerate bearing a single name and supposed to constitute a real unity was usually the result of historic processes of a highly complicated and curious sort. It is, of course, proper and necessary that ecclesiastical historians should write books on the history of Christianity; but in doing so they are writing of a series of facts which, taken as a whole, have almost nothing in common except the name; the part of the world in which they occurred; the reverence for a certain person, whose nature and teaching, however, have been most variously conceived, so that the unity here too is largely a unity of name; and the identity of a part of their historic antecedents, of certain causes or influences which, diversely combined with other causes, have made each of these systems of belief what it is. In the whole series of creeds and movements going under the one name, and in each of them separately, it is needful to go behind the superficial appearance of singleness and identity, to crack the shell which holds the mass together, if we are to see the real units, the effective working ideas, which, in any given case, are present.

These large movements and tendencies, then, these conventionally labelled *-isms*, are not as a rule the ultimate objects of the interest of the historian of ideas; they are merely the initial materials. Of what sort, then, are the elements, the primary and persistent or recurrent dynamic units, of the history of thought, of which he is in quest? They are rather heterogeneous; I shall not attempt a formal definition, but merely mention some of the principal types.

(1) There are, first, implicit or incompletely explicit *assumptions*, or more or less *unconscious mental habits*, operating in the thought of an individual or a generation. It is the beliefs which are so much a matter of course that they are rather tacitly presupposed than formally expressed and argued for the ways of thinking which seem so natural and inevitable that they are not scrutinized with the eye of logical self-consciousness, that often are most decisive of the character of a philosopher's doctrine, and still oftener of the dominant intellectual tendencies of an age. These implicit factors may be of various sorts. One sort is a disposition to think in terms of certain categories or of particular types of imagery. There is, for example, a practically very important difference between (we have no English term for them) *esprits simplistes* — minds which habitually tend to assume that simple solutions can be found for the problems they deal with — and those habitually sensible of the general complexity of things, or, in the extreme case, the Hamlet-like natures who are oppressed and terrified by the multiplicity of considerations probably pertinent to any situation with which they are confronted, and the probable intricacy of their interrelations. The representatives of the Enlightenment of the seventeenth

and eighteenth centuries, for example, were manifestly characterized to a peculiar degree by the presumption of simplicity. Though there were numerous exceptions, though there were powerful ideas in vogue which worked in the contrary direction, it was nevertheless largely an age of *esprits simplistes*; and the fact had the most momentous practical consequences. The assumption of simplicity was, it is true, combined in some minds with a certain sense of the complexity of the universe and a consequent disparagement of the powers of man's understanding, which might at first seem entirely incongruous with it, but which in reality was not so. The typical early-eighteenth-century writer was well enough aware that the universe as a whole is physically an extremely large and complicated thing. One of the favourite pieces of edifying rhetoric of the period was Pope's warning against intellectual presumptuousness:

> He who through vast immensity can pierce,
> See worlds on worlds compose one universe,
> Observe how system into system runs,
> What other planets circle other suns,
> What vary'd being peoples every star,
> May tell why Heaven has made us as we are.
> But of this frame, the bearing and the ties,
> The strong connections, nice dependencies,
> Gradations just, has thy pervading soul
> Look'd thro? Or can a part contain the whole?

You may find this sort of thing in abundance in the popular philosophy of that time. This pose of intellectual modesty was, in fact, an almost universally prevalent characteristic of the period, which Locke, perhaps, more than anyone else had brought into fashion. Man must become habitually mindful of the limitations of his mental powers, must be content with that 'relative and practical understanding' which is the only organ of knowledge that he possesses. 'Men', as Locke puts it in a familiar passage:

> Men may find matter sufficient to busy their heads, and employ their minds with variety, delight and satisfaction, if they will not boldly quarrel with their own constitution, and throw away the blessings their hands are filled with, because they are not big enough to grasp everything.

We must not

> . . . loose our thoughts into the vast ocean of being, as if all that
> boundless extent were the natural and undoubted possession of our
> understandings, wherein is nothing exempt from its decisions or that
> escapes its comprehension. But we shall not have much reason to
> complain of the narrowness of our minds, if we will but employ
> them about what may be of use to us, for of that they are very cap-
> able . . . It will be no excuse to an idle and untoward servant, who
> would not attend his business by candle-light, to plead that he had
> not broad sunshine. The candle that is set up in us shines bright
> enough for all our purposes. The discoveries we can make with this
> ought to satisfy us, and we shall then use our understandings right,
> when we entertain all objects in that way and proportion that they
> are suited to our faculties.

But though this tone of becoming diffidence, this ostentatious
modesty in the recognition of the disproportion between man's
intellect and the universe, was one of the most prevalent intellectual
fashions of a great part of the eighteenth century, it was frequently
accompanied by an extreme presumption of the simplicity of the truths
that *are* needful for man and within his reach, by a confidence in the
possibility of 'short and easy methods', not only with the deists, but
with pretty much all matters of legitimate human concern. 'Simplicity,
noblest ornament of truth', wrote John Toland, characteristically; and
one can see that to him, and to many of his time and temper, simplicity
was in fact, not merely an extrinsic ornament, but almost a necessary
attribute of any conception or doctrine which they were willing to
accept as true, or even fairly to examine. When Pope, in his most
familiar lines, exhorted his contemporaries:

> Know then thyself! Presume not God to scan!
> The proper study of mankind is man,

he implied that the problems of theology and speculative metaphysics
are too vast for human thought; but he also implied, to the contemporary ear, that man is a tolerably simple kind of entity, to plumb whose
nature was well within the scope of the decidedly limited and simple
intellectual powers with which he was endowed. Assuming human
nature to be a simple thing, the Enlightenment also, as a rule, assumed
political and social problems to be simple, and therefore easy of solu-

tion. Rid man's mind of a few ancient errors, purge his beliefs of the artificial complications of metaphysical 'systems' and theological dogmas, restore to his social relations something like the simplicity of the state of nature, and his natural excellence would, it was assumed, be realized, and mankind would live happily ever after. The two tendencies I have been mentioning, in short, may probably be traced to a common root. The limitation of the scope of activity of man's interest and even of the ranging of his imagination was itself a manifestation of a preference for simple schemes of ideas; the temper of intellectual modesty was partly the expression of an aversion for the incomprehensible, the involved, the mysterious. When, on the other hand, you pass on to the Romantic Period, you find the simple becoming an object of suspicion and even detestation, and what Friedrich Schlegel characteristically called *eine romantische Verwirrung* the quality most valued in temperaments, in poems, and in universes.

(2) These endemic assumptions, these intellectual habits, are often of so general and so vague a sort that it is possible for them to influence the course of man's reflections on almost any subject. A class of ideas which is of a kindred type may be termed dialectical motives. You may, namely, find much of the thinking of an individual, a school, or even a generation, dominated and determined by one or another turn of reasoning, trick of logic, methodological assumption, which if explicit would amount to a large and important and perhaps highly debatable proposition in logic or metaphyics. A thing which constantly reappears, for example, is the nominalistic motive – the tendency, almost instinctive with some men, to reduce the meaning of all general notions to an enumeration of the concrete and sensible particulars which fall under those notions. This shows itself in fields quite remote from technical philosophy, and in philosophy it appears as a determinant in many other doctrines besides those customarily labelled nominalism. Much of William James's pragmatism bears witness to the influence upon him of this way of thinking; while in Dewey's pragmatism it plays, I think, a much smaller part. Again, there is the organismic or flower-in-the-crannied-wall motive, the habit of assuming that, where you have a complex of one or another kind, no element in that complex can be understood, or can, indeed, be what it is apart from its relations to all the other components of the system to which it belongs. This, too, you may find operative in some men's characteristic modes of thinking even upon non-philosophical matters; while it, also, shows itself in systems of philosophy other than those which make a formal dogma of the principle of the essentiality of relations.

(3) Another type of factor in the history of ideas may be described as susceptibilities to diverse kinds of metaphysical pathos. This influential cause in the determination of philosophical fashions and speculative tendencies has been so little considered that I find no recognized name for it, and have been compelled to invent one which is not, perhaps, wholly self-explanatory. 'Metaphysical pathos' is exemplified in any description of the nature of things, any characterization of the world to which one belongs, in terms which, like the words of a poem, awaken through their associations, and through a sort of empathy which they engender, a congenial mood or tone of feeling on the part of the philosopher or his readers. For many people — for most of the laity, I suspect — the reading of a philosophical book is usually nothing but a form of aesthetic experience, even in the case of writings which seem destitute of all outward aesthetic charms; voluminous emotional reverberations, of one or another sort, are aroused in the reader without the intervention of any definite imagery. Now of metaphysical pathos there are a good many kinds; and people differ in their degree of susceptibility to any one kind. There is, in the first place, the pathos of sheer obscurity, the loveliness of the incomprehensible, which has, I fear, stood many a philosopher in good stead with his public, even though he was innocent of intending any such effect. The phrase *omne ignotum pro mirifico* concisely explains a considerable part of the vogue of a number of philosophies, including some which have enjoyed great popular reputation in our own time. The reader doesn't know exactly what they mean, but they have all the more on that account an air of sublimity; an agreeable feeling at once of awe and of exaltation comes over him as he contemplates thoughts of so immeasurable a profundity —their profundity being convincingly evidenced to him by the fact that he can see no bottom to them. Akin to this is the pathos of the esoteric. How exciting and how welcome is the sense of initiation into hidden mysteries! And how effectively have certain philosophers — notably Schelling and Hegel a century ago, and Bergson in our own generation — satisfied the human craving for this experience, by representing the central insight of their philosophy as a thing to be reached, not through a consecutive progress of thought guided by the ordinary logic available to every man, but through a sudden leap whereby one rises to a plane of insight wholly different in its principles from the level of the mere understanding. There are expressions of certain disciples of M. Bergson which admirably illustrate the place which the pathos of the esoteric has in this philosophy, or at least in the response to it. M. Rageot, for example, declares that unless one is in some sense born again one can-

not acquire that *intuition philosophique* which is the secret of the new teaching; and M. Le Roy writes:

> A veil interposed between the real and ourselves, which falls of a sudden as if an enchantment were dissipated, and leaves open before the mind depths of light hitherto unimagined, wherein is revealed before our very eyes, for the first time, reality itself: such is the feeling which is experienced at every page, with singular intensity, by the reader of M. Bergson.

These two types of pathos, however, inhere not so much in the attributes which a given philosophy ascribes to the universe as in the attributes which it ascribes to itself — or which its votaries ascribe to it. Some examples of metaphysical pathos in the stricter sense ought therefore to be given. A potent variety is the eternalistic pathos — the aesthetic pleasure which the bare abstract idea of immutability gives us. The greater philosophical poets know well how to evoke it. In English poetry it is illustrated by those familiar lines in Shelley's *Adonais* of which we have all at some time felt the magic:

> The One remains, the many change and pass,
> Heaven's light forever shines, earth's shadows fly . . .

It is not self-evident that remaining forever unchanged should be regarded as an excellence; yet through the associations and the half-formed images which the mere conception of changelessness arouses — for one thing, the feeling of rest which its *innere Nachahmung* induces in us in our tired moods — a philosophy which tells us that at the heart of things there is a reality wherein is no variableness nor shadow that is cast by turning, is sure to find its response in our emotional natures, at all events in certain phases of individual or group experience. Shelley's lines exemplify also another sort of metaphysical pathos, often conjoined with the last — the monistic or pantheistic pathos. That it should afford so may people a peculiar satisfaction to say that All is One is, as William James once remarked, a rather puzzling thing. What is there more beautiful or more venerable about the numeral *one* than about any other number? But psychologically the force of the monistic pathos is in some degree intelligible when one considers the nature of the implicit responses which talk about oneness produces. It affords, for example, a welcome sense of freedom, arising from a triumph over, or an absolution from, the troublesome cleavages and disjunctions of things. To recognize that things which we have hitherto kept apart in our minds are somehow the same thing — that, of itself, is normally an agreeable experience for human beings. (You will remember James's essay 'On Some Hegelisms' and on Mr B.P. Blood's book called *The Anaesthetic Revelation.*) So, again, when a monistic philosophy declares, or suggests, that one is oneself a part of the universal Oneness, a whole complex of obscure emotional responses is released. The deliquescence of the sense — the often so fatiguing sense — of separate personality, for example, which comes in various ways (as in the so-called mob-spirit), is also capable of excitation, and of really powerful excitation, too, by a mere metaphysical theorem. Mr Santayana's sonnet beginning 'I would I might forget that I am I' almost perfectly expresses the mood in which conscious individuality, as such, becomes a burden. Just such escape for our imaginations from the sense of being a limited, particular self the monistic philosophies sometimes give us. Distinct from the monistic pathos is the voluntaristic — though Fichte and others have contrived to unite them. Here it is the response of our active and volitional nature, perhaps even, as the phrase goes, of our fighting blood, which is aroused by the character which is ascribed to the total universe with which we feel ourselves consubstantial. Now all this has nothing to do with philosophy as a science; but it has a great deal to do with philosophy as a factor in history, for the reason that it is not chiefly as a science that philosophy has been a factor in history. The susceptibility to different sorts of metaphysical pathos plays, I am convinced, a great part, both in the formation of philosophical systems by subtly guiding many a philosopher's logic, and in partially causing the vogue and influence of different philosophies among groups or generations which they have affected. And the delicate task of discovering these varying susceptibilities and showing how they help to shape a system or to give an idea plausibility and currency is a part of the work of the historian of ideas.

(4) Another part of his business, if he means to take cognizance of the genuinely operative factors in the larger movements of thought, is an inquiry which may be called philosophical semantics — a study of the sacred words and phrases of a period or a movement, with a view to a clearing up of their ambiguities, a listing of their various shades of meaning, and an examination of the way in which confused associations of ideas arising from these ambiguities have influenced the development of doctrines, or accelerated the insensible transformation of one fashion of thought into another, perhaps its very opposite. It is largely because of their ambiguities that mere words are capable of this inde-

pendent action as forces in history. A term, a phrase, a formula, which gains currency or acceptance because one of its meanings, or of the thoughts which it suggests, is congenial to the prevalent beliefs, the standards of value, the tastes of a certain age, may help to alter beliefs, standards of value, and tastes, because other meanings or suggested implications, not clearly distinguished by those who employ it, gradually become the dominant elements of its signification. The word 'nature', it need hardly be said, is the most extraordinary example of this, and the most pregnant subject for the investigations of philosophical semantics.

(5) The type of 'idea' with which we shall be concerned is, however, more definite and explicit, and therefore easier to isolate and identify with confidence, than those of which I have been hitherto speaking. It consists in a single specific proposition or 'principle' expressly enunciated by the most influential of early European philosophers, together with some further propositions which are, or have been supposed to be, its corollaries. This proposition was, as we shall see, an attempted answer to a philosophical question which it was natural for man to ask — which reflective thought could hardly have failed to ask, sooner or later. It proved to have a natural logical affinity for certain other principles, originally advanced in the course of reflection upon certain quite different questions, which consequently became agglutinated with it. The character of this type of ideas, and of the processes which constitute their history, need not be further described in general terms, since all that follows will illustrate it.

Second: any unit-idea which the historian thus isolates he next seeks to trace through more than one — ultimately, indeed, through all — of the provinces of history in which it figures in any important degree, whether those provinces are called philosophy, science, literature, art, religion, or politics. The postulate of such a study is that the working of a given conception, of an explicit or tacit presupposition, of a type of mental habit, or of a specific thesis or argument, needs, if its nature and its historic role are to be fully understood, to be traced connectedly through all the phases of men's reflective life in which those workings manifest themselves, or through as many of them as the historian's resources permit. It is inspired by the belief that there is a great deal more that is common to more than one of these provinces than is usually recognized, that the same idea often appears, sometimes considerably disguised, in the most diverse regions of the intellectual world. Landscape-gardening, for example, seems a topic fairly remote from philosophy; yet at one point, at least, the history of land-scape-gardening becomes a part of any truly philosophical history of modern thought. The vogue of the so-called 'English garden', which spread so rapidly in France and Germany after 1730, was, as M. Mornet and others have shown, the thin end of the wedge of Romanticism, or of one kind of Romanticism. That vogue itself — partly, no doubt, the expression of a natural revulsion of taste from an overdose of the formal gardening of the seventeenth century — was partly also an incident of the general craze for English fashions of all kinds, which Voltaire, Prévost, Diderot, and the Huguenot *journalistes* in Holland had introduced. But this change of taste in gardening was to be the beginning and — I do not, assuredly, say, *the* cause, but the fore-shadowing, and one of the joint causes — of a change of taste in all the arts and, indeed, of a change of taste in universes. In one of its aspects that many-sided thing called Romanticism may not inaccurately be described as a conviction that the world is an *englischer Garten* on a grand scale. The God of the seventeenth century, like its gardeners, always geometrized; the God of Romanticism was one in whose universe things grew wild and without trimming and in all the rich diversity of their natural shapes. The preference for irregularity, the aversion from that which is wholly intellectualized, the yearning for *échappées* into misty distances — these, which were eventually to invade the intellectual life of Europe at all points, made their first modern appearance on a grand scale early in the eighteenth century in the form of the new fashion in pleasure-gardens; and it is not impossible to trace the successive phases of their growth and diffusion.[1]

While the history of ideas — in so far as it may be spoken of in the present tense and the indicative mood — is thus an attempt at historical synthesis, this does not mean that it is a mere conglomerate, still less that it aspires to be a comprehensive unification, of other historical disciplines. It is concerned only with a certain group of factors in history, and with these only in so far as they can be seen at work in what are commonly considered separate divisions of the intellectual world; and it is especially interested in the processes by which influ-ences pass over from one province to another. Even the partial realization of such a programme would do much, I cannot but think, to give a needed unifying background to many now unconnected and, consequently, poorly understood facts. It would help to put gates through the fences which, in the course of a praiseworthy effort after specialization and division of labour, have come to be set up in most of our universities between departments whose work ought to be constantly correlated. I have in mind especially the departments of philosophy and of the modern literatures. Most teachers of literature would perhaps readily enough admit that it is to be *studied* — I by no means say, can solely be enjoyed — chiefly for its thought-content, and that the interest of the history of literature is largely as a record of the movement of ideas — of the ideas which have affected men's imaginations and emotions and behaviour. And the ideas in serious reflective literature are, of course, in great part philosophical ideas in dilution — to change the figure, growths from seed scattered by great philosophic systems which themselves, perhaps, have ceased to be. But, through a lack of adequate training in philosophy, students and even learned historians of literature often, I think, have not recognized such an idea when they met it — have not, at least, known its historic lineage, its logical import and implications, its other appearances in human thought. Happily, this condition is fast altering for the better. On the other hand, those who investigate or teach the history of philosophy sometimes take very little interest in an idea when it does not wear philosophical full dress —or war-paint — and are prone to disregard its ulterior workings in the minds of the non-philosophic world. But the historian of ideas, while he oftenest will seek for the initial emergence of a conception or presupposition in some philosophic or religious system or scientific theory, will seek for its most significant manifestations in art, and above all in literature. For, as Mr Whitehead has said, 'it is in literature that the concrete outlook of humanity receives its expression. Accordingly, it is to literature that we must look, particularly in its more concrete forms, if we hope to discover the inward thoughts of a generation.'[2] And, as I think — though there is not time to defend the opinion — it is by first distinguishing and analysing the major ideas which appear again and again, and by observing each of them as a recurrent unit in many contexts, that the philosophic background of literature can best be illuminated.

Third: in common with what is called the study of comparative literature, the history of ideas expresses a protest against the consequences which have often resulted from the conventional division of literary and some other historical studies by nationalities or languages. There are some good, and obvious, reasons why the history of political institutions and movements, since it must in some way be broken up into smaller units, should be divided upon national lines; yet even these branches of historical inquiry have in recent times gained greatly in accuracy and fruitfulness through an increasing realization of the necessity of investigating events or tendencies or policies in one country in order to understand the real causes of many events, tendencies, or policies in another. And it is far from self-evident that in the study of the history of literature, not to speak of that of philosophy, in which this practice has been generally abandoned, departmentalization by languages is the best way of recognizing the necessity for specialization. The existing scheme of division is partly a historical accident, a survival of the time when most professors of foreign literatures were primarily language-masters. As soon as the historical study of literature is conceived as a thorough investigation of any causal process — even the comparatively trivial one of the migration of stories — it must inevitably disregard national and linguistic boundary lines; for nothing is more certain than that a great proportion of the processes to be investigated disregard those lines. And if the function of teachers or the training of advanced students is to be determined by the affinity of certain minds for certain subjects, or certain types of thought, it is at least dubious whether, instead of professors of English or French or German literature, we ought not to have professors of the Renaissance, of the later Middle Ages, of the Enlightenment, of the Romantic Period, and the like. For there was doubtless, on the whole, more in common, in fundamental ideas and tastes and moral temper, between a typical educated Englishman and a Frenchman or Italian of the later sixteenth century than between an Englishman of that period and an Englishman of the 1730s or the 1830s or the 1930s — just as there is manifestly more in common between an average New Englander and an Englishman of 1930 than between a New Englander of 1630 and his present posterity. If, then, a special capacity for sympathetic understanding of that with which he deals is desirable in the historical specialist, a division of these studies by periods, or groups within periods, would, it might plausibly be argued, be more appropriate than a division by countries, races, or languages. I do not seriously urge such a reorganization of the humanistic departments of universities; there are obvious practical difficulties in the way. But these difficulties have little to do with any real cleavages among the facts studied — least of all when the facts have to do with the history of ruling categories, of beliefs, of tastes, of intellectual fashions. As Friedrich Schlegel long ago said: 'Wenn die regionellen Theile der modernen Poesie, aus ihrem Zusammenhang gerissen, und als einzelne für sich bestehende Ganze betrachtet werden, so sind sie unerklärlich. Sie bekommen erst durch einander Haltung und Bedeutung.'[3]

Fourth: Another characteristic of the study of the history of ideas, as I should wish to define it, is that it is especially concerned with the manifestations of specific unit-ideas in the collective thought of large groups of persons, not merely in the doctrines or opinions of a small number of profound thinkers or eminent writers. It seeks to investigate the effects of the sort of factors which it has — in the bacteriologist's sense — isolated, in the beliefs, prejudices, pieties, tastes, aspirations, current among the educated classes through, it may be, a whole generation, or many generations. It is, in short, most interested in ideas which attain a wide diffusion, which become a part of the stock of many minds. It is this characteristic of the study of the history of ideas in literature which often puzzles students — even advanced students — in the present-day literature departments in our universities. Some of them, at least, my colleagues in those departments often tell me, are repelled when called upon to study some writer whose work, *as* literature, is now dead — or at best, of extremely slight value, according to our present aesthetic and intellectual standards. Why not stick to the masterpieces, such students exclaim — or at least to these *plus* the minor classics — the things that can be still read with pleasure, or with a feeling of the significance for men of the present age of the ideas or the moods of feeling which they express? This is a natural enough state of mind, if you don't regard the study of literary history as including within its province the study of the ideas and feelings which other men in past times have been moved by, and of the processes by which what may be called literary and philosophical public opinion is formed. But if you *do* think the historian of literature ought to concern himself with these matters, your minor writer may be as important as — he may often, from this point of view, be more important than — the authors of what are now regarded as the masterpieces. Professor Palmer has said, with equal truth and felicity:

> The tendencies of an age appear more distinctly in its writers of inferior rank than in those of commanding genius. These latter tell of past and future as well as of the age in which they live. They are for all time. But on the sensitive responsive souls, of less creative power, current ideals record themselves with clearness.[4]

And it is, of course, in any case true that a historical understanding even of the few great writers of an age is impossible without an acquaintance with their general background in the intellectual life and common moral and aesthetic valuations of that age; and that the character of this background has to be ascertained by actual historical inquiry into the nature and interrelations of the ideas then generally prevalent.

Finally, it is a part of the eventual task of the history of ideas to apply its own distinctive analytic method in the attempt to understand how *new* beliefs and intellectual fashions are introduced and diffused, to help to elucidate the psychological character of the processes by which changes in the vogue and influence of ideas have come about; to make clear, if possible, how conceptions dominant, or extensively prevalent, in one generation lose their hold upon men's minds and give place to others. To this large and difficult and important branch of historical interpretation the method of study of which I am speaking can make only one contribution among many; but it is, I can't but think, a necessary contribution. For the process can hardly be made intelligible until the natures of the separate ideas which enter as factors in it are discriminated and separately observed in their general historic working.

These lectures, then, are intended to exemplify in some small measure the sort of philosophical-historical inquiry of which I have been merely sketching the general aims and method. We shall first discriminate, not, indeed, a single and simple idea, but three ideas which have, throughout the greater part of the history of the West, been so closely and constantly associated that they have often operated as a unit, and have, when thus taken together, produced a conception – one of the major conceptions in Occidental thought – which came to be expressed by a single term: 'the Great Chain of Being'; and we shall observe the workings of these both separately and in conjunction. The example will necessarily be inadequate, even as a treatment of the special topic chosen, being restricted not only by limitations of time but by the insufficiency of the lecturer's knowledge. Nevertheless, so far as these limitations permit, we shall try to trace these ideas to their historic sources in the minds of certain philosophers; to observe their fusion; to note some of the most important of their widely ramifying influences in many periods and in diverse fields – metaphysics, religion, certain phases of the history of modern science, the theory of the purpose of art and the criteria of excellence therein, moral valuations, and even, though to a relatively slight extent, in political tendencies; to see how later generations derived from them conclusions undesired and undreamed-of by their originators; to mark some of their effects upon men's emotions and upon the poetic imagination; and in the end, perhaps, to draw a philosophic moral from the tale.

But I ought, I think, to close this preamble with three notes of warning. The first relates to the very programme which I have outlined. The study of the history of ideas is full of dangers and pitfalls; it has its characteristic excess. Precisely because it aims at interpretation and unification and seeks to correlate things which often are not on the surface connected, it may easily degenerate into a species of merely imaginative historical generalization; and because the historian of an idea is compelled by the nature of his enterprise to gather material from several fields of knowledge, he is inevitably, in at least some parts of his synthesis, liable to the errors which lie in wait for the non-specialist. I can only say that I am not unmindful of these dangers and have done what I could to avoid them; it would be too sanguine to suppose that I have in all cases succeeded in doing so. In spite of the probability, or perhaps the certainty, of partial failure, the enterprise seems worth attempting.

The other warnings are addressed to my hearers. Our plan of procedure requires that we deal only with a part of the thought of any one philosopher or any one age. The part, therefore, must never be mistaken for the whole. We shall not, indeed, confine our view solely to the three connected ideas which are the theme of the course. For their philosophical significance and historic operation can be understood only by contrast. The story to be told is in great part a story of conflict, at first latent, eventually overt, between these ideas and a series of antagonistic conceptions, some of the antagonists being their own offspring. We must, then, observe them throughout in the light of their antitheses. But nothing that is to be said is to be construed as a comprehensive exposition either of any system of doctrine or of the tendencies of any period. Finally, it is evident that, when one tries to relate in this fashion the biography of even one idea, a heavy demand is made upon the catholicity of the intellectual interests of one's auditors. In tracing the influence of the conceptions which form the subject of this course we shall be obliged, as has been intimated, to take account of episodes in the history of a number of disciplines usually supposed to have little to do with one another, and usually studied in comparative isolation. The history of ideas is therefore no subject for highly departmentalized minds; and it is pursued with some difficulty in an age of departmentalized minds. It presupposes, also, an interest in the workings of human thought in the past even when these are, or seem to many of our generation to be, misguided, confused, or even absurd. The history of philosophy and of all phases of man's reflection *is*, in great part, a history of confusions of ideas; and the chapter of it with which we shall be occupied is no exception to this rule. To some of us it is not less interesting, and little less instructive, on that account. Since man, for better or worse, is by nature, and by the most distinctive impulse of his nature, a reflective and interpretative animal, always seeking *rerum cognoscere causas*, to find in the bare data of experience more than meets the eye, the record of the reactions of his intellect upon the brute facts of his sensible existence constitutes, at the least, an essential part of the natural history of the species, or subspecies, which has somewhat too flatteringly named itself *homo sapiens*; and I have never been able to see why what is distinctive in the natural history of that species should appear — especially to a member of it — a less respectable subject of study than the natural history of the *paramecium* or the white rat. No doubt man's quest of intelligibility in nature and in himself, and of the kinds of emotional satisfaction which are conditioned by a sense of intelligibility, often, like the caged rat's quest of food, has found no end, in wandering mazes lost. But though the history of ideas is a history of trial-and-error, even the errors illuminate the peculiar nature, the cravings, the endowments, and the limitations of the creature that falls into them, as well as the logic of the problems in reflection upon which they have arisen; and they may further serve to remind us that the ruling modes of thought of our own age, which some among us are prone to regard as clear and coherent and firmly grounded and final, are unlikely to appear in the eyes of posterity to have any of those attributes. The adequate record of even the confusions of our forebears may help, not only to clarify those confusions, but to engender a salutary doubt whether we are wholly immune from different but equally great confusions. For though we have more empirical information at our disposal, we have not different or better minds; and it is, after all, the action of the mind upon facts that makes both philosophy and science — and, indeed, largely makes the 'facts'. Nevertheless, those who do not care for the natural history of man in his most characteristic activity, who have neither curiosity nor patience to follow the workings of other minds proceeding from premises which they do not share, or entangled in what seem to them, and often are, strange confusions, or engaged in speculative enterprises which they may regard as hopeless, ought in fairness to be warned that much of the story which I am to try to tell will be for them without interest. On the other hand, I think it only fair to warn those who, for such reasons, are indifferent to the story here to be told, that without an acquaintance with it no understanding of the movement of thought in the Occident, in most of its major provinces, is possible.

Notes

1. Cf. the writer's papers on 'The Chinese Origin of a Romanticism', *Journal of English and Germanic Philology* (1933), pp. 1-20, and 'The First Gothic Revival and the Return to Nature', *Modern Language Notes* (1932), pp. 419-46.

2. *Science and the Modern World* (1926), p. 106.

3. *Ueber das Studium der griechischen Poesie* (Minor, Fr. *Schlegel, 1792-1804*, I, 95).

4. Preface to *The English Works of George Herbert* (1905), p. xii.

Source

A.O. Lovejoy, 'The Study of the History of Ideas' in *The Great Chain of Being: The Study of the History of an Idea*, (Cambridge, Mass., Harvard University Press, 1936), pp. 3-23.

8 ON LOVEJOY'S HISTORIOGRAPHY

Maurice Mandelbaum

1

Those who are at present interested in the methodological problems of the historian of philosophy cannot fail to take note of the existence of what has come to be called 'the history of ideas'. The latter term has been used in a variety of senses, sometimes being equated with intellectual history generally.[1] However, it is not in that wider sense that I wish to consider it. Instead, I shall in the first instance confine my attention to problems which arise out of two important parallel movements, each of which may be regarded as an attempt to promote the study of 'the history of ideas' in a narrower and more technical sense: the movement in the United States of which A.O. Lovejoy was the originator and the dominant spokesman, and the movement inspired in Germany by Dilthey's work, and now represented by Erich Rothacker's *Archiv für Begriffsgeschichte*. Because Lovejoy and his close collaborators have written at greater length concerning their methodological presuppositions than have those connected with the *Archiv*, and also because these presuppositions seem to raise a greater variety of issues in a somewhat more acute form, it is with the former group, rather than the latter, that I shall here be concerned.[2]

It is probably fair to say that there were two dominant and quite distinct motifs in A.O. Lovejoy's conception of the history of ideas, and that both received emphasis in almost all of his methodological writings. One of these *motifs* concerned the need for inter-disciplinary studies. Connected with it was the conviction that intellectual history should be free to cross national and linguistic boundaries in spite of the conventional departmentalizations of academic learning; also connected with it was a recognition of the need for co-operative inquiries in the development of the history of ideas.[3] These aspects of Lovejoy's programme have had an undoubted influence, but they raise few, if any, special methodological issues: therefore, it is not with them that I shall here be concerned. Instead, I wish to deal at some length with the second *motif* in Lovejoy's conception of the history of ideas, for it is this aspect of his views which is at once the more original and the more problematic. This second *motif* is to be found in his concern with what he termed 'unit-ideas'.

It was Lovejoy's belief that the history of ideas — in his special, technical sense of that term — should not deal directly with *'systems'* or *'-isms'* but with what he regarded as their elemental components, namely the unit-ideas which are to be found within them. As he said on the opening page of *The Great Chain of Being*:

> By the history of ideas I mean something at once more specific and less restricted than the history of philosophy. It is differentiated primarily by the character of the units with which it concerns itself. Though it deals in great part with the same material as the other branches of the history of thought and depends greatly upon their prior labors, it divides that material in a special way, brings the parts into new groupings and relations, views it from the standpoint of a distinctive purpose. Its initial procedure may be said — though the parallel has its dangers — to be somewhat analogous to that of analytic chemistry. In dealing with the history of philosophical doctrines, for example, it cuts into the hard-and-fast individual systems and, for its own purposes, breaks them up into their unit-ideas.[4]

The unit-ideas with which Lovejoy's programme was concerned were of many varieties. In one listing he mentioned

> types of categories, thoughts concerning particular aspects of common experience, implicit or explicit presuppositions, sacred formulas and catchwords, specific philosophic theorems, or the larger hypotheses, generalizations or methodological assumptions of various sciences.[5]

Now, it was Lovejoy's contention that in any system of thought, or any *'-ism'*, unit-ideas of these various types might be found; as he said, 'the total body of doctrine of any philosopher or school is almost always a complex and heterogeneous aggregate',[6] and he believed that 'most philosophic systems are original or distinctive rather in their patterns than in their components'.[7] In fact, in the same passage he went on to suggest that the number of basic unit-ideas may be rather limited, and that 'the seeming novelty of many a system is due solely to the novelty of the application or arrangement of the old elements which enter into it.'[8]

One might well subscribe to these statements without drawing from them the conclusion that in intellectual history generally, or in the history of philosophy specifically, the proper way to grasp the nature of any '*-ism*', or any individual system of thought, is — in Lovejoy's phrase — to break it up into elemental components, that is, into those unit-ideas which are discriminable within it.[9] However, if one examines much of Lovejoy's own historiographical practice, as well as some of his most explicit methodological statements, it seems that it was in these elemental components that he found 'the real units, the effective working ideas' in major creeds and movements, that he took these unit-ideas to be 'the dynamic units of the history of thought'.[10]

As a contrast to Lovejoy's position in this matter we might cite Ernst Cassirer's statement concerning his own methodological convictions. Speaking of his studies of the Renaissance and the Enlightenment, Cassirer said that the aim of his approach was 'to elucidate the inner formative forces' in the historical epochs with which he was dealing, and he then proceeded to say:

> Such a presentation of philosophical doctrines and systems endeavors as it were to give a 'phenomenology of the philosophic spirit'; it is an attempt to show how this spirit, struggling with purely objective problems, achieves clarity and depth in its understanding of its own nature and destiny, and of its own fundamental character and mission.[11]

One need not, of course, accept Cassirer's conception of inner, formative forces as constituting the only alternative to Lovejoy's methodological beliefs. I have cited it only because it illustrates how another eminent intellectual historian has stressed a point which Lovejoy's programme of inquiry into specific unit-ideas left out of account the role which is often played in the thought of a person or of a period by a dominant philosophic issue which serves to incite and in large measure to control that thought. The possible determinative influence of problems and issues which are larger than single unit-ideas was not denied by Lovejoy. However, a consideration of them was not included in his programme: it was with *the continuities of the elements*, and not with the formative influences that helped determine the patterns into which these elements fitted, that he was primarily concerned.[12] Now, Lovejoy's own work has clearly shown that studies of these elements very frequently illuminate important segments of a philosopher's thought, and that an understanding of precisely these segments of his thought may on occasion be crucial for an understanding of that thought as a whole. Nevertheless, a stress on the continuity of the unit-ideas which enter into a particular philosophic system usually fails to yield an interpretation of the basic aim and motivating power of that system. That this should be so may be said to follow analytically from Lovejoy's assumption that originality is more often found in the pattern of a thinker's thought than in the specific unit-ideas which are discriminable within it: the more original and creative a thinker may be, the more one who follows Lovejoy's programme will be forced to neglect the original aspects of his work through concentrating on the history of the unit-ideas which he tended to share with others.[13] From this it further follows that the method of tracing unit-ideas stands in danger of underestimating or of misconstruing the influence of a philosopher on subsequent thought, for that influence may stem directly from the pattern of his thought, no less than from the specific unit-ideas which were embedded within it.

There is a second problematic feature of Lovejoy's programme to which I should now like to call attention. It consists in the fact that the unit-ideas which are said to constitute the basic elements in the thought of particular writers at different times are assumed to have continuous life-histories of their own. As Lovejoy defines the subject-matter of the history of ideas it is . . .

> the study of the [so far as possible] total life-history of individual ideas, in which the many parts that any one of them plays upon the historic scene, the different facets which it exhibits, its interplay, conflicts and alliances with other ideas, and the diverse human reactions to it, are traced out with adequate and critical documentation.[14]

In referring to what strikes me as a problematic feature of this programme, I do not suggest that Lovejoy believed, or ever wrote as if he believed, that these unit-ideas had a life-history of their own apart from the persons who entertained them, or apart from the works in which they are to be found. What strikes me as problematic is, rather, the assumption that when one analyses idea-complexes into unit-ideas, the way to understand the occurrence of these unit-ideas in the thought of a particular person is always (or even usually) by tracing them backwards in time. I should not of course wish to deny that there are many cases in which this can fruitfully be done: the concept of 'the great chain of being' is a concept with respect to which it has been most successfully done. Also, it may well be the case that the concept of 'primitivism' stands for ideas which have had a long unitary history, and that the occurrence of these ideas at any particular time may well have been dependent upon the formative influence of one or more of their prior occurrences. Such unit-ideas may best be designated as '*continuing* ideas'. On the other hand, there may also be unit-ideas which could best be designated as '*recurrent* ideas'. Such would be those unit-ideas which human beings are apt to entertain on many different occasions, quite independently of whether or not others had previously entertained them. The difference between these two types of ideas would be analogous to the difference between those cases in which an anthropologist accounts for two similar types of artifact in terms of diffusion and those in which he holds that independent invention has taken place. Now, in the case of unit-ideas, no less than in the case of material artifacts, it is sometimes not readily discernible from examining isolated instances of similar ideas whether diffusion or independent invention is to be regarded as the more plausible hypothesis: only a comparative study of distribution over time and space, as well as evidence concerning the other elements with which these units are associated, will provide the basis for a reasonable hypothesis.

In the case of Lovejoy's own programme, the possibility that many unit-ideas might be *recurrent* ideas seems to me to have been either overlooked or too little stressed. For example, it would seem plausible to hold that the normative uses to which the concept of 'nature' has been put is an example of a recurrent idea, rather than one which has a single continuous history. That this is plausible would seem to follow from the fact that in his investigation of the meaning of the concept 'nature' in antiquity, Lovejoy discriminated 66 different senses in which that concept was connected with norms.[15] Given this variety within a short span of time, and given the fact that these 66 meanings were not all directly related to one another, it seems rash to assume that a conception of this kind should be regarded as having a unitary life-history wherever and whenever it is found.[16] Yet, in his preface to his *Essays in the History of Ideas*, when Lovejoy wished to illustrate 'the presence and influence of the same presuppositions or other operative "ideas" in very diverse provinces of thought and in different periods', he said:

the underlying idea-complex, summed up in the word 'nature' in one of its senses which is exhibited as shaping both religious heterodoxy and aesthetic orthodoxy in the eighteenth century, is also shown . . . as at work in the mind of a third century Christian apologist [Tertullian] ... The fundamental identity of the idea, and of the logic of the reasonings to which it gave rise, is not annulled by the dissimilarities of the concomitant ideas with which it was associated, nor by the differing preoccupations and temperamental biases of the writers into whose thinking it entered ... In this case we have one of the major and persistent ideas of Western thought, which, since the fourth century BC, has scarcely ever disappeared altogether, though in some periods it has been dominant and in others highly recessive.[17]

If, in this passage, 'the fundamental identity of the idea' were simply taken to mean that one can find that something believed by Tertullian was also believed by eighteenth-century writers, and if one were *not* attempting to trace a genetic connection between these different occurrences of the same philosophic conception, then Lovejoy's statement would not be open to challenge. However, his own assumption seems to have been that what the historian of ideas was concerned to do was to show 'the processes by which influences pass over from one province [of the intellectual world] to another.'[18] Furthermore, in my opinion, it is only this interpretation that is consistent with his general theory of historiography.[19] Thus, it is an *historical* connection, and not merely a logical connection, or a similarity in the use of two concepts, which the historian of ideas is purportedly interested in discovering. Yet, by what means can such a connection be established? In his fullest explanation of how to establish historical connections, Lovejoy stressed the importance of a preliminary logical analysis of unit-ideas, and a psychological analysis of their likely affinities and incompatibilities, before attempting to trace their actual historical relations to one another.[20] Such a preliminary exploration of the materials he compared to the construction of a tentative hypothesis in the natural scientist's mind: the historian of ideas is to carry out preliminary logical and psychological analyses 'before he goes on to confront their results with the historical evidence to be found in the sources'.[21] The formation of such tentative hypotheses as to what one is likely to find in the sources is often immensely valuable, and I should suppose that few intellectual historians have been so successful as Lovejoy in later documenting their hypotheses by a careful tracing of the genetic succession of these transformations in literary and philosophical texts. However, the extent of his success in *some* cases simply points up the difficulty of the problem in *other* cases — and most notably in such a case as that in which he suggested the continuity from Tertullian to the eighteenth century, or in the case in which he claimed that there probably was an historical influence of certain ideas held by philosophers and literary men in the

1780s and 1790s upon the formation of the state of mind which led to the appeal of totalitarian ideologies in the 1920s. In neither of these cases did Lovejoy attempt to cite texts which would have been sufficient to allow us to trace the genetic connections which were presupposed; and when one bears in mind the fact that at least some unit-ideas may be recurrent, rather than continuing, a *similarity* between two unit-ideas is insufficient to establish a direct historical connection between them.[22]

Yet, even in those cases in which Lovejoy's programme of analysis may have failed in its attempt to establish historical *connections*, it may none the less be immensely valuable in indicating historical *parallels*. By calling attention to possible parallels in the use to which concepts have been put by different thinkers, and in showing the ambiguities and confusions which some of these concepts may contain, Lovejoy has given the intellectual historian a powerful set of analytic tools, and has provided an example of their use from which anyone can profit. None the less, as I have attempted to indicate, if we consider Lovejoy's methodological convictions as if they embodied a self-sufficient programme for the intellectual historian to follow, such a programme would have great disadvantages: it would frequently lead us away from those features of an author's work which were most likely to be central to his motivation, and which might also be most important for his historical influence; it might also lead us to minimize the independence of an author's thought, suggesting lines of historical connection where such connections have not been established, and may not have existed. If one were to ask why Lovejoy himself may have failed to note these dangers, or having noted them failed to discuss them, the answer (I surmise) is to be found in one fundamental characteristic of his philosophic temper: his passion for drawing distinctions in order to gain analytical clarity. No one can have read much of his work, whether philosophic of historical, without being aware of how important a role the distaste for ambiguities and the demand for precision played in his thought. The strength of this motivation may perhaps be most strikingly illustrated by the fact that when he singled out three recurrent phenomena to which his various essays in the history of ideas bore witness, one of the three referred to semantic confusions and a second referred to the conflicting ideas which may be present in the thought of the same individual.[23] An interest in ferreting out such intellectual lapses was what − in some measure at least − led Lovejoy to his programme for the history of ideas. What was of primary concern to him was to bring into sharp focus the detailed intellectual content of literary and philosophic works, and to examine their meanings and implications in a spirit of critical detachment, rather than attempt to measure the scope of these works, to assess their value, or to trace the full range of their individual influences.

2

If the foregoing sketch of Lovejoy's programme for the history of ideas was an accurate one, there is much that would seem to belong to intellectual and cultural history that it is bound to leave out of account. And if we are to discuss the tasks of historians of philosophy, assessing their relations to historians of ideas, it may be well to raise these more general problems of intellectual and cultural history.

In this connection we must first note a rather strange fact: those who have concerned themselves with the general problems of historiographical method have rarely discussed the question of how the methods of 'special histories', such as histories of philosophy, or of art, or of technology, or of law, are related to what they regard as paradigmatic cases of historiographical practice. For example, in handbooks such as those of Bernheim, or of Langlois and Seignobos, or of Bauer, the models for what are taken to be standard practices with respect to internal and external criticism, and with respect to historiographical synthesis, are not drawn from the fields of what I shall call 'special histories'.[24] To be sure, some treatises on historiography pay a good deal of attention to what the general historian may learn by means of special historical accounts;[25] furthermore, neither methodologists nor present-day historians minimize the importance of investigations in intellectual, cultural, and social history as aids to understanding what has occurred in the past. What one misses, however, is any substantial body of writing which concerns itself directly with the problem of whether particular forms of specialized history differ in aim and in practice among themselves, or which attempts to examine how these various special histories relate to what (for our present purposes) we may designate as 'general' history.[26]

One may of course find more or less explicit methodological statements in almost every specialized history, and among the more theoretically-minded of the special historians one frequently finds illuminating discussions of what is entailed by their own practice, and by the practice of those with whom they disagree. In addition, in recent years there has been a growing body of literature concerned with the nature and aims of 'intellectual history',[27] and of social history, as well as of the relations between them; there has also been at least one lengthy essay of a systematic sort which has sought to distinguish and define the various co-ordinates by means of which we can operate in an historical analysis of ideas.[28] However, each of these discussions has tended to involve the advocacy of a particular position, rather than attempting to analyse the various alternative types of position which special historians have taken, or might be expected to take. Until such an analysis is made it is likely that we shall be handicapped in seeking to discuss the methodological problems which can be raised concerning the history of philosophy, or concerning other special histories. It is for this reason that I shall now attempt to classify various types of approach which may be adopted, and which have indeed been adopted, with respect to special histories, even though I recognize that within the scope of the present paper I can only make the most tentative of conjectures in this difficult and neglected area of historiographical methodology.

Notes

1. For example, in an article entitled 'Historiography of Philosophy', Sterling P. Lamprecht says: 'The history of philosophy is the history of the philosopher thinking; the history of ideas is the history of man thinking', *Journal of Philosophy*, XXXVI (1939), p. 457. A similarly extended use of the term 'history of ideas', making it synonymous with 'intellectual historiography', may seem to be sanctioned by the usage of A.O. Lovejoy in the prefatory article to Volume I of *The Journal of the History of Ideas* (1940), pp. 3-23. However, that article must be read in the light of Lovejoy's other, earlier, methodological statements, and it must also be remembered that the *Journal* was not founded merely to promote 'the history of ideas' in its narrowest sense; from the first it took as its province a wide variety of interdisciplinary studies in the general area of intellectual history. Cf. P.P. Wiener in *Studies in Intellectual History*, see below, note 2, item *11*, p. 169f.

2. For Rothacker's statement of his intention, cf. 'Das "Begriffsgeschichtliche Wörterbuch der Philosophie' in *Zeitschrift für Philosophische Forschung*, VI (1951), pp. 133-6, as well as in *Archiv für Begriffsgeschichte*, I (1955), pp. 5-9. The chief methodological discussions of the Lovejoy group may be listed as follows:

   (*1*) A.O. Lovejoy and G. Boas, *A Documentary History of Primitivism and Related Ideas* (Baltimore, 1935), pp. ix-xiii and pp. 1-22.

   (2) A.O. Lovejoy, *The Great Chain of Being* (Cambridge, Mass., 1936), pp. 3-23.

   (*3*) A.O. Lovejoy, 'The Historiography of Ideas', *Proceedings of the American Philosophical Society*, LXXVIII (1938), pp. 529-43. Reprinted in A.O. Lovejoy, *Essays in the History of Ideas* (Baltimore, 1948), pp. 1-13.

(4)   Marjorie H. Nicolson, 'The History of Literature and the History of
      Thought', *English Institute Annual, 1939* (New York, 1940).

(5)   A.O. Lovejoy, 'Reflections on the History of Ideas', *Journal of the
      History of Ideas*, I (1940), pp. 3-23. Reprinted in P.P. Wiener and
      A. Noland (eds.), *Ideas in Cultural Perspective* (New York, 1962),
      pp. 3-23.

(6)   A.O. Lovejoy, 'The Meaning of Romanticism for the Historian of
      Ideas', *Journal of the History of Ideas*, II (1941) pp. 237-78.

(7)   A.O. Lovejoy, 'Reply to Professor Spitzer', *Journal of the History of
      Ideas*, V (1944), pp. 204-19.

(8)   A.O. Lovejoy, *Essays in the History of Ideas* (1948), pp. xiii-xvii.

(9)   George Boas, 'A.O. Lovejoy as Historian of Philosophy', *Journal of the
      History of Ideas*, IX (1948), pp. 404-11.

(10) Marjorie H. Nicolson, 'A.O. Lovejoy as Teacher', *Journal of the
      History of Ideas*, IX (1948), pp. 428-38.

(11) G. Boas, H. Cherniss, *et al., Studies in Intellectual History* (Baltimore,
      1953). In particular, the essays of Boas, Stimson, and Wiener relate to
      the methodological questions under present consideration.

(12) P.P. Wiener, 'Some Problems and Methods in the History of Ideas',
      Journal of the History of Ideas, XXII (1961), pp. 531-48. Reprinted in
      Wiener and Noland, pp. 24-41.

[In what follows I shall use the above italicized numbers in designating the book or
article to which reference is being made.]

The European and American movements which have, by and large, been distinct
may perhaps now be drawing together. The publisher's announcements of the
newly founded *Archives internationales d'histoire des idées* contains a definition of
what is meant by the history of ideas which closely resembles Lovejoy's definition
of that term. At the same time it defines its province as 'the intellectual conditions of intellectual life' (as distinct from the material conditions) and it says of
these conditions that they 'give to each period its own character and in a large
measure mould even the most independent geniuses.' The latter mode of speaking
would surely be more reminiscent of the thought of Dilthey than of that of
Lovejoy. To be sure, Ludwig Edelstein and Roy H. Pearce have both mentioned
to the present writer that relatively late in his life A.O. Lovejoy expressed the
view that his method and that of Dilthey were not far apart, but such a *rapprochement* does not seem to be concretely evidenced in any of Lovejoy's published
writings.

3. A similar plea for co-operative inquiries is to be found in Lovejoy's presi-
dential address to the American Philosophical Association, 'On Some Conditions
of Progress in Philosophical Inquiry', *Philosophical Review*, XXVI (1917), pp.
123-63.

4. *2*, p. 3. Cf. the following earlier statement: 'In the historiography of ideas,
it is the fortunes of distinct "unit-ideas", and their interrelations of congruity or
opposition, that are to be exhibited, not the "systems" of philosophers or schools
. . . ' (*I*, p. xii).

5. *3*, p. 533. This listing of the generic classes of unit-ideas may be compared
with the not dissimilar one given in *4*, 4. However, in the earlier and fuller treatment of the issue in *The Great Chain of Being* (pp. 7-15), a different classification
of these genera had been proposed. There unit-ideas were identified as belonging
to the following types: (1) implicit or incompletely explicit assumptions, or
more or less unconscious mental habits; (2) dialectical motives; (3) types of metaphysical pathos; (4) sacred words or phrases; (5) specific propositions or principles
(among which was 'the great chain of being' itself).

6. *2*, p. 3.

7. *2*, p. 3.

8. *2*, 4.

9. In fact, those who recall that Lovejoy was one of the staunchest defenders of the doctrine of emergence in his generation may well be surprised that he regarded the complex whole which is a philosophic system as analysable into certain elemental component ideas. They may in particular be surprised that he would in this connection use the analogy between the history of ideas and analytic chemistry, since chemical combinations had been used as a paradigmatic case in defence of the doctrine of emergence from the time of Mill to the discussions of Lovejoy and Broad. For Lovejoy's treatments of the problem of emergence, cf. 'The Discontinuities of Evolution', *University of California Publications in Philosophy*, V (1924), pp. 173-220, and 'The Meanings of "Emergence" and its Modes', *Journal of Philosophical Studies*, II (1927), pp. 167-81. Substantially the same article appeared under the same title in the *Proceedings of the Sixth International Congress of Philosophy* (New York, 1927), pp. 20-33.

10. *2*, pp. 6, 7. Also, cf. *8*, p. 253. — It was in this connection that Lovejoy's colleague, Leo Spitzer, launched an attack on Lovejoy's method, and forced him to consider the relevance of the doctrine of emergence. Cf. Spitzer: 'Geistesgeschichte vs. History of Ideas as Applied to Hitlerism', *Journal of the History of Ideas*, V, 1944), pp. 191-203, and Lovejoy's 'Reply to Professor Spitzer', ibid., especially pp. 204-11. However, in his reply, Lovejoy was content to criticize a variety of points in Spitzer's argument, and he did not give a clear answer with respect to that issue. He insisted, rightly enough: 'The thought of an individual writer or of a school, or the dominant fashion of thought of a period, may, and usually does, contain a number of . . . distinct conceptual and affective components. To understand such a complex as a whole, it is necessary to discriminate these components and observe their relations and interplay' (ibid., p. 204). Such a statement is, of course, compatible with holding that there may *also* be emergent properties which result from such combinations of components. Lovejoy explicitly recognized this possibility, and also recognized that it might have a bearing upon the history of thought (p. 209). However, he did not discuss that more general methodological question, but shifted his attention to one of the other aspects of Spitzer's attack. Thus, in the end, the general question of whether unit-ideas are indeed 'the dynamic units of the history of thought' was not really discussed by Lovejoy in this unhappy interchange.

11. *The Philosophy of the Enlightenment* (Princeton, 1951), p. vi.

12. Cf. *2*, p. 4. To a certain extent, although less noticeably, this stress on the continuity of specific characteristics of a doctrine, rather than on what was novel in it as a whole, was a characteristic of Lovejoy's earlier essays on the history of philosophy, as well as of his later studies in the history of ideas. For example, cf. 'On Kant's Reply to Hume', *Archiv für Geschichte der Philosophie*, XIX (1906), pp. 380-407. However, such was definitely not the case in his appreciative essay 'William James as Philosopher', *International Journal of Ethics*, XXI (1911), pp. 125-53, reprinted in *The Thirteen Pragmatisms and Other Essays* (Baltimore, 1963).

13. A similar point may be made with respect to literary works. Lovejoy himself noted (e.g., 2, pp. 19-20) that the history of ideas, as he conceived it, was especially concerned with the appearance of the unit-ideas in large groups of persons, and not merely in eminent writers. Thus, by its own intent, it leaves to one side questions of comparative literary value, and will thereby be forced to leave to one side questions concerning the effective influences of some works. To this extent it is of limited value — though certainly not without value — for the history of literature.

14. Section 3, p. 532.

15. Cf. Appendix to *1*.

16. It is startling that Lovejoy should not himself have been led to challenge the assumption of continuity, since in P.-E. Dumont's essay on 'Primitivism in Indian Literature', it is pointed out that in this independent body of literature there is a parallel to Western primitivism (cf. *I*, p. 446). Furthermore, among the unit-ideas which Lovejoy mentions are 'dialectical motives', such as the nominalistic motive, which he describes as a tendency, 'almost instinctive with some men, to reduce the meaning of all general notions to an enumeration of the concrete and sensible particulars which fall under those notions' (*2*, p. 10). This manner of phrasing such a dialectical motive suggests that it is what I have termed a recurrent idea, rather than one which has a specific life-history.

17. *7*, p. xiv.

18. *2*, p. 16. Cf. the following statement: 'Ideas are the most migratory things in the world. A preconception, category, postulate, dialectical motive, pregnant metaphor or analogy, 'sacred word', mood of thought, or explicit doctrine, which makes its first apperance upon the scene in one of the conventionally distinguished provinces of history (most often, perhaps, in philosophy) may, and frequently does, cross over into a dozen others" (*4*, p. 4). Also, cf. the statement of purpose of The History of Ideas Club at The Johns Hopkins University (*10*, p. 178).

19. Cf. my article 'Arthur O. Lovejoy and the Theory of Historiography', *Journal of the History of Ideas*, IX (1948), pp. 412-23.

20. *5*, pp. 261-70.

21. *5*, p. 264. It was this doctrine that Spitzer attacked – quite unfairly – as 'the apriori approach advocated by Lovejoy' (*op. cit.*, p. 193 f.).

22. With respect to the connection between Tertullian and the eighteenth century, my point may best be illustrated by the fact that Lovejoy himself says of the conception of 'nature': 'Its very ambiguity was, and in the history of Christian thought was destined to be, a positive factor in influencing the movement of ideas. Once adopt "nature" or "the natural" as the norm in general, or in certain of its senses, and it was easy to slip over unconsciously to other senses" (*7*, p. 336). This, however, merely suggests that at various times the ambiguity in a particular term may be exploited in similar ways, not that a particular meaning assigned to that term in the first instance was causally connected to a similar use of it in a later instance. With respect to the continuity of the ideas of the 1780s in nineteenth and twentieth-century German philosophy, and their efficacy as a preparation for the ideology of Nazism, Lovejoy's reply to Spitzer admittedly failed to bring forward the necessary textual evidence (*6*, pp. 217-19); and the original article had itself assuredly failed to supply such evidence (cf. *5*, pp. 272-8).

23. Cf. *7*, pp. xiv-xvi. The three phenomena which he singles out for the reader's attention are: *First*, 'The presence and influence of the same presuppositions or other operative "ideas" in very diverse provinces of thought and in different epochs'; *Second*, 'The role of semantic confusions, of shifts and ambiguities in the meanings of terms, in the history of thought and of taste'; *Third*, 'The internal tensions or waverings in the mind of almost every individual writer – sometimes discernible even in a single writing or on a single page – arising from conflicting ideas or incongruous propensities of feeling or taste, to which, so to say, he is susceptible.'

24. In fact, among these three only Bernheim's work takes cognizance of special histories; see *Lehrbuch der historischen Methode*, 6th Edn (Leipzig, 1908), pp. 54-5 and pp. 69-70. While he does recognize a difference between the concerns of a general historian and those which are characteristic of persons

writing special histories (cf. note 26, below), Bernheim does not seem to recognize that a new sort of methodological problem may accompany the attempt to write the latter. — The general neglect of problems concerning special histories is all the more striking since one of the most characteristic aspects of nineteenth-century historiography was the proliferation of separate historical treatments of the various facets of culture, in other words the proliferation of special histories. As Huizinga remarked: 'Klio hatte eine ganze Schar von Enkeln in ihrem Haus aufwachsen sehen. Ich meine hier die speziellen Studienfächer, deren Wesen historisch ist, ohne mit Geschichte als solcher zusammenzufallen', and in this connection he lists the history of art and of literature, etc.; see J. Huizinga, *Im Bann der Geschichte* (Zurich and Bruxelles, 1942), p. 16.

25. This is especially characteristic of Gustav Wolf, *Einführung in das Studium der neueren Geschichte* (Berlin, 1910).

26. The sole instance of anything like such a discussion which I have found in the usual treatises on historiographical method is a very brief passage in Louis Gottschalk, *Understanding History* (New York, 1958), pp. 34-6. Among philosophers, the problem of special histories has been somewhat more frequently mentioned, but has not been satisfactorily discussed. Mention of it may be found in the introduction to Hegel's *Lectures on the Philosophy of History*, transl. J. Sibree (New York, 1899), pp. 7-8, where he classes such special histories as the history of art as the fourth sub-class of reflective histories, standing at the threshold of philosophical history. Heinrich Rickert also noted that there might be special problems with reference to the writing of specialized histories; cf. *Die Grenzen der Naturwissenschaftlichen Begriffsbildung* (5th edn), pp. 556-7, but he did not undertake to discuss these problems. R.G. Collingwood also referred to various specialized histories, and discussed them at considerable length, *The Idea of History* (Oxford, 1946), pp. 309-15, but he did so only in so far as it was necessary to justify his own characterization of the task of the historian as a re-enactment of past *thought*.

27. An article by John C. Greene entitled 'Objectives and Methods in Intellectual History', *Mississippi Valley Historical Review*, XLIV (1957-58), pp. 58-74, is particularly helpful for the bibliographical references to be extracted from it; it is also one of the most careful and thoughtful essays in the field.

28. Abraham Edel, 'Context and Content in the Theory of Ideas', in *Philosophy for the Future*, ed. R.W. Sellars, V.J. McGill, and Marvin Farber (New York, 1949), pp. 419-52. At a later point I shall also mention a methodological essay which takes its point of departure from Lovejoy's programme for the history of ideas, viz., Roy Harvey Pearce, 'A Note on Method in the History of Ideas', *Journal of the History of Ideas*, IX (1948), pp. 372-9.

Source

Maurice Mandelbaum, 'On Lovejoy's Historiography', taken from 'The History of Ideas, Intellectual History and the History of Philosophy', *History and Theory* vol. 4, no. 3, (1965), Beiheft 5, pp. 33-43.

PART FIVE

STRAUSS

9 POLITICAL PHILOSOPHY AND HISTORY

Leo Strauss

Political philosophy is not a historical discipline. The philosophic questions of the nature of political things and of the best, or just, political order are fundamentally different from historical questions, which always concern individuals: individual groups, individual human beings, individual achievements, individual 'civilizations', the one individual 'process' of human civilization from its beginning to the present, and so on. In particular, political philosophy is fundamentally different from the history of political philosophy itself. The question of the nature of political things and the answer to it cannot possibly be mistaken for the question of how this or that philosopher or all philosophers have approached, discussed or answered the philosophic question mentioned. This does not mean that political philosophy is absolutely independent of history. Without the experience of the variety of political institutions and convictions in different countries and at different times, the questions of the nature of political things and of the best, or the just, political order could never have been raised. And after they have been raised, only historical knowledge can prevent one from mistaking the specific features of the political life of one's time and one's country for the nature of political things. Similar considerations apply to the history of political thought and the history of political philosophy. But however important historical knowledge may be for political philosophy, it is only preliminary and auxiliary to political philosophy; it does not form an integral part of it.

This view of the relation of political philosophy to history was unquestionably predominant at least up to the end of the eighteenth century. In our time it is frequently rejected in favour of 'historicism', that is, of the assertion that the fundamental distinction between philosophic and historical questions cannot in the last analysis be maintained. Historicism may therefore be said to question the possibility of political philosophy. At any rate it challenges a premiss that was common to the whole tradition of political philosophy and apparently never doubted by it. It thus seems to go deeper to the roots, or to be more philosophic, than the political philosophy of the past. In any case,

213

it casts a doubt on the very questions of the nature of political things and of the best, or the just, political order. Thus it creates an entirely new situation for political philosophy. The question that it raises is to-day the most urgent question for political philosophy.

It may well be doubted whether the fusion of philosophy and history, as advocated by historicism, has ever been achieved, or even whether it can be achieved. Nevertheless that fusion appears to be, as it were, the natural goal toward which the victorious trends of nineteenth- and early-twentieth-century thought converge. At any rate, historicism is not just one philosophic school among many, but a most powerful agent that affects more or less all present-day thought. As far as we can speak at all of the spirit of a time, we can assert with confidence that the spirit of our time is historicism.

Never before has man devoted such an intensive and such a comprehensive interest to his whole past, and to all aspects of his past, as he does to-day. The number of historical disciplines, the range of each, and the interdependence of them all are increasing almost constantly. Nor are these historical studies carried on by thousands of ever more specialized students considered merely instrumental, and without value in themselves: we take it for granted that historical knowledge forms an integral part of the highest kind of learning. To see this fact in the proper perspective, we need only look back to the past. When Plato sketched in his *Republic* a plan of studies he mentioned arithmetic, geometry, astronomy, and so on: he did not even allude to history. We cannot recall too often the saying of Aristotle (who was responsible for much of the most outstanding historical research done in classical antiquity) that poetry is more philosophic than history. This attitude was characteristic of all the classical philosophers and of all the philosophers of the Middle Ages. History was praised most highly not by the philosophers but by the rhetoricians. The history of philosophy in particular was not considered a philosophic discipline: it was left to antiquarians rather than to philosophers.

A fundamental change began to make itself felt only in the sixteenth century. The opposition then offered to all earlier philosophy, and especially to all earlier political philosophy, was marked from the outset by a novel emphasis on history. That early turn toward history was literally absorbed by the 'unhistorical' teachings of the Age of Reason. The 'rationalism' of the seventeenth and eighteenth centuries was fundamentally much more 'historical' than the 'rationalism' of premodern times. From the seventeenth century onward, the *rapprochement* of philosophy and history increased almost from generation to generation at an ever accelerated pace. Towards the end of the seventeenth century it became customary to speak of 'the spirit of a time'. In the middle of the eighteenth century the term 'philosophy of history' was coined. In the nineteenth century, the history of philosophy came to be generally considered a philosophical discipline. The teaching of the outstanding philosopher of the nineteenth century, Hegel, was meant to be a 'synthesis' of philosophy and history. The 'historical school' of the nineteenth century brought about the substitution of historical jurisprudence, historical political science, historical economic science for a jurisprudence, a political science, an economic science that were evidently 'unhistorical' or at least a-historical.

The specific historicism of the first half of the nineteenth century was violently attacked because it seemed to lose itself in the contemplation of the past. Its victorious opponents did not, however, replace it by a non-historical philosophy, but by a more 'advanced', and in some cases a more 'sophisticated' form of historicism. The typical historicism of the twentieth century demands that each generation reinterpret the past on the basis of its own experience and with a view to its own future. It is no longer contemplative, but activistic; and it attaches to that study of the past which is guided by the anticipated future, or which starts from and returns to the analysis of the present, a crucial philosophic significance: it expects from it the ultimate guidance for political life. The result is visible in practically every curriculum and textbook of our time. One has the impression that the question of the nature of political things has been superseded by the question of the characteristic 'trends' of the social life of the present and of their historical origins, and that the question of the best, or the just, political order has been superseded by the question of the probable or desirable future. The questions of the modern state, of modern government, of the ideals of Western civilisation, and so forth, occupy a place that was formerly occupied by the questions of *the* state and of *the* right way of life. Philosophic questions have been transformed into historical questions – or more precisely into historical questions of a 'futuristic' character.

This orientation characteristic of our time can be rendered legitimate only by historicism. Historicism appears in the most varied guises and on the most different levels. Tenets and arguments that are the boast of one type of historicism, provoke the smile of the adherents of others. The most common form of historicism expresses itself in the demand that the questions of the nature of political things, of *the* state, of the nature of man, and so forth, be replaced by the questions of the modern state, of modern government, of the present political situation, of modern man, of our society, our culture, our civilzation, and so forth. Since it is hard to see, however, how one can speak adequately of the modern state, of our civilization, of modern man, etc., without knowing first what a state is, what a civilization is, what man's nature is, the more thoughtful forms of historicism admit that the universal questions of traditional philosophy cannot be abandoned. Yet they assert that any answer to these questions, any attempt at clarifying or discussing them, and indeed any precise formulation of them, is bound to be 'historically conditioned', that is, to remain dependent on the specific situation in which they are suggested. No answer to, no treatment or precise formulation of, the universal questions can claim to be of universal validity, of validity for all times. Other historicists go to the end of the road by declaring that while the universal questions of traditional philosophy cannot be abandoned without abandoning philosophy itself, philosophy itself and its universal questions themselves are 'historically conditioned', i.e., essentially related to a specific 'historic' type, for example, to Western man or to the Greeks and their intellectual heirs.

To indicate the range of historicism, we may refer to two assumptions characteristic of historicism and to-day generally accepted. 'History' designated originally a particular kind of knowledge or inquiry. Historicism assumes that the object of historical knowledge, which it calls 'History', is a 'field', a 'world' of its own fundamentally different from, although of course related to, that other 'field', 'Nature'. This assumption distinguishes historicism most clearly from the pre-historicist view, for which 'History' as an object of knowledge did not exist, and which therefore did not even dream of a 'philosophy of history' as an analysis of, or a speculation about, a specific 'dimension of reality'. The gravity of the assumption in question appears only after one has started wondering what the Bible or Plato, for example, would have called that X which we are in the habit of calling 'History'. Equally characteristic of historicism is the assumption that restorations of earlier teachings are impossible, or that every intended restoration necessarily leads to an essential modification of the restored teaching. This assumption can most easily be understood as a necessary consequence of the view that every teaching is essentially related to an unrepeatable 'historical' situation.

An adequate discussion of historicism would be identical with a critical analysis of modern philosophy in general. We cannot dare try more than indicate some considerations which should prevent one from taking historicism for granted.

To begin with, we must dispose of a popular misunderstanding which is apt to blur the issue. It goes back to the attacks of early historicism on the political philosophy which had paved the way for the French Revolution. The representatives of the 'historical school' assumed that certain influential philosophers of the eighteenth century had conceived of the right political order, or of the rational political order, as an order which should or could be established at any time and in any place, without any regard to the particular conditions of time and place. Over against this opinion they asserted that the only legitimate approach to political matters is the 'historical' approach, that is, the understanding of the institutions of a given country as a product of its past. Legitimate political action must be based on such historical understanding, as distinguished from, and opposed to, the 'abstract principles' of 1789 or any other 'abstract principles'. Whatever the deficiencies of eighteenth-century political philosophy may be, they certainly do not justify the suggestion that the non-historical philosophic approach must be replaced by a historical approach. Most political philosophers of the past, in spite or rather because of the non-historical character of their thought, distinguished as a matter of course between the philosophic question of the best political order, and the practical question as to whether that order could or should be established in a given country at a given time. They naturally knew that all political action, as distinguished from political philosophy, is concerned with individual situations, and must therefore be based on a clear grasp of the situation concerned, and therefore normally on an understanding of the causes or antecedents of that situation. They took it for granted that political action guided by the belief that what is most desirable in itself must be put into practice in all circumstances, regardless of the circumstances, befits harmless doves, ignorant of the wisdom of the serpent, but not sensible and good men. In short, the truism that all political action is concerned with, and therefore presupposes appropriate knowledge of, individual situations, individual commonwealths, individual institutions, and so on, is wholly irrelevant to the question raised by historicism.

For a large number, that question is decided by the fact that historicism comes later in time than the non-historical political philosophy: 'history' itself seems to have decided in favour of historicism. If, however, we do not worship 'success' as such, we cannot maintain that the victorious cause is necessarily the cause of truth. For even if we grant that truth will prevail in the end, we cannot be certain that the end has already come. Those who prefer historicism to non-historical political philosophy because of the temporal relation of the two, interpret then that relation in a specific manner: they believe that the position which historically comes later can be presumed, other things being equal, to be more mature than the positions preceding it. Historicism, they would say, is based on an experience which required many centuries to mature – on the experience of many centuries which teaches us that non-historical political philosophy is a failure or a delusion. The political philosophers of the past attempted to answer the question of the best political order once and for all. But the result of all their efforts has been that there are almost as many answers, as many political philosophies as there have been political philosophers. The mere spectacle of 'the anarchy of systems', of 'the disgraceful variety' of philosophies seems to refute the claim of each philosophy. The history of political philosophy, it is asserted, refutes non-historical political philosophy as such, since the many irreconcilable political philosophies refute each other.

Actually, however, that history does not teach us that the political philosophies of the past refute each other. It teaches us merely that they contradict each other. It confronts us then with the philosophic question as to which of two given contradictory theses concerning political fundamentals is true. In studying the history of political philosophy we observe, for example, that some political philosophers distinguish between State and Society, whereas others explicitly or implicitly reject that distinction. This observation compels us to raise the philosophic question whether and how far the distinction is adequate. Even if history could teach us that the political philosophy of the past has failed, it would not teach us more than that non-historical political philosophy has hitherto failed. But what else would this mean except that we do not truly know the nature of political things and the best, or just, political order? This is so far from being a new insight due to historicism that it is implied in the very name 'philosophy'. If the 'anarchy of systems' exhibited by the history of philosophy proves anything, it proves our ignorance concerning the most important subjects (of which ignorance we can be aware without historicism), and therewith it proves the necessity of philosophy. It may be added that the 'anarchy' of the historical political philosophies of our time, or of present-day interpretations of the past, is not conspicuously smaller than that of the non-historical political philosophies of the past.

Yet it is not the mere variety of political philosophies which allegedly shows the futility of non-historical political philosophy. Most historicists consider decisive the fact, which can be established by historical studies, that a close relation exists between each political philosophy and the historical situation in which it emerged. The variety of political philosophies, they hold, is above all a function of the variety of historical situations. The history of political philosophy does not teach merely that the political philosophy of Plato, for example, is irreconcilable with the political philosophy, say, of Locke. It also teaches that Plato's political philosophy is essentially related to the Greek city of the fourth century BC, just as Locke's political philosophy is essentially related to the English revolution of 1688. It thus shows that no political philosophy can reasonably claim to be valid beyond the historical situation to which it is essentially related.

Yet, not to repeat what has been indicated in the paragraph before the last, the historical evidence invoked in favour of historicism has a much more limited bearing than seems to be assumed. In the first place, historicists do not make sufficient allowance for the deliberate adaptation, on the part of the political philosophers of the past, of their views to the prejudices of their contemporaries. Superficial readers are apt to think that a political philosopher was under the spell of the historical situation in which he thought, when he was merely adapting the expression of his thought to that situation in order to be listened to at all. Many political philosophers of the past presented their teachings, not in scientific treatises proper, but in what we may call treatise-pamphlets. They did not limit themselves to expounding what they considered *the* political truth. They combined with that exposition an exposition of what they considered desirable or feasible in the circumstances, or intelligible on the basis of the generally received opinions, they communicated their views in a manner which was not purely 'philosophical,' but at the same time 'civil.'[1] Accordingly, by proving that their political teaching as a whole is 'historically conditioned,' we do not at all prove that their political philosophy proper is 'historically conditioned.'

Above all, it is gratuitously assumed that the relation between doctrines and their 'times' is wholly unambiguous. The obvious possibility is overlooked that the situation to which one particular doctrine is related, is particularly favourable to the discovery of *the* truth, whereas all other situations may be more or less unfavourable. More generally expressed, in understanding the genesis of a doctrine we are not necessarily driven to the conclusion that the doctrine in question cannot simply be true. By proving, for example, that certain propositions of modern natural law 'go back' to positive Roman law, we have not yet proven that the propositions in questions are not *de jure naturali* but merely *de jure positivo*. For it is perfectly possible that the Roman jurists mistook certain principles of natural law for those of positive law, or that they merely 'divined' and did not truly know, important elements of natural law. We cannot then stop at ascertaining the relations between a doctrine and its historical origins. We have to interpret these relations; and such interpretation presupposes the philosophic study of the doctrine in itself with a view to its truth or falsehood. At any rate, the fact (if it is a fact) that each doctrine is 'related' to a particular historical setting does not prove at all that no doctrine can simply be true.

The old fashioned, not familiar with the ravages wrought by historicism, may ridicule us for drawing a conclusion which amounts to the truism that we cannot reasonably reject a serious doctrine before we have examined it adequately. In the circumstances we are compelled to state explicitly that prior to careful investigation we cannot exclude the possibility that a political philosophy which emerged many centuries ago is *the* true political philosophy, as true to-day as it was when it was first expounded. In other words, a political philosophy does not become obsolete merely because the historical situation , and in particular the political situation to which it was related has ceased to exist. For every political situation contains elements which are essential to all political situations: how else could one intelligibly call all these different political situations 'political situations'?

Let us consider very briefly, and in a most preliminary fashion, the most important example. Classical political philosophy is not refuted, as some seem to believe, by the mere fact that the city, apparently the central subject of classical political philosophy, has been superseded by the modern state. Most classical philosophers considered the city the most perfect form of political organization, not because they were ignorant of any other form, nor because they followed blindly the lead given by their ancestors or contemporaries, but because they realized, at least as clearly as we realize it today, that the city is essentially superior to the other forms of political association known to classical antiquity, the tribe and the Eastern monarchy. The tribe, we may say tentatively, is characterized by freedom (public spirit) and lack of civilization (high development of the arts and sciences), and the Eastern monarchy is characterized by civilization and lack of freedom. Classical political philosophers consciously and reasonably preferred the city to other forms of political association, in the light of the standards of freedom and civilization. And this preference was not a peculiarity bound up with their particular historical situation. Up to and including the eighteenth century, some of the most outstanding political philosophers quite justifiably preferred the city to the modern state which had emerged since the sixteenth century, precisely because they measured the modern state of their time by the standards of freedom and civilization. Only in the nineteenth century did classical political philosophy in a sense become obsolete. The reason was that the state of the nineteenth century, as distinguished from the Macedonian and Roman empires, the feudal monarchy, and the absolute monarchy of the modern period, could plausibly claim to be at least as much in accordance with the standards of freedom and civilization as the Greek city had been. Even then classical political philosophy did not become completely obsolete, since it was classical political philosophy which had expounded in a 'classic' manner the standards of freedom and civilization. This is not to deny that the emergence of modern democracy in particular has elicited, if it has not been the outcome of, such a reinterpretation of both 'freedom' and 'civilization' as could not have been foreseen by classical political philosophy. Yet that reinterpretation is of fundamental significance, not because modern democracy has superseded earlier forms of political association, or because it has been victorious — it has not always been victorious, and not everywhere — but because there are definite reasons for considering that reinterpretation intrinsically superior to the original version. Naturally, there are some who doubt the standards mentioned. But that doubt is as little restricted to specific historical situations as the standards themselves. There were classical political philosophers who decided in favour of the Eastern monarchy.

Before we can make an intelligent use of the historically ascertained relations between philosophic teachings and their 'times', we must have subjected the doctrines concerned to a philosophic critique concerned exclusively with their truth or falsehood. A philosophic critique in its turn presupposes an adequate understanding of the doctrine subjected to the critique. An adequate interpretation is such an interpretation as understands the thought of a philosopher exactly as he understood it himself. All historical evidence adduced in support of historicism presupposes as a matter of course that adequate understanding of the philosophy of the past is possible on the basis of historicism. This presupposition is open to grave doubts. To see this we must consider historicism in the light of the standards of historical exactness which, according to common belief, historicism was the first to perceive, to elaborate, or at least to divine.

Historicism discovered these standards while fighting the doctrine which preceded it and paved the way for it. That doctrine was the belief in progress: the conviction of the superiority, say, of the late eighteenth century to all earlier ages, and the expectation of still further progress in the future. The belief in progress stands midway between the non-historical view of the philosophic tradition and historicism. It agrees with the philosophic tradition in so far as both admit that .there are universally valid standards which do not require, or which are not susceptible of, historical proof. It deviates from the philosophic tradition in so far as it is essentially a view concerning 'the historical process'; it asserts that there is such a thing as 'the historical process' and that that process is, generally speaking, a 'progress': a progress of thought and institutions toward an order which fully agrees with certain presupposed universal standards of human excellence.

In consequence, the belief in progress, as distinguished from the views of the philosophic tradition, can be legitimately criticized on purely historical grounds. This was done by early historicism, which showed in a number of cases — the most famous example is the interpretation of the Middle Ages — that the 'progressivist' view of the past was based on an utterly insufficient understanding of the past. It is evident that our understanding of the past will tend to be the more adequate, the more we are interested in the past. But we cannot be passionately interested, seriously interested in the past if we know beforehand that the present is in the most important respect superior to the past. Historians who started from this assumption felt no necessity to understand the past in itself; they understood it only as a preparation for the present. In studying a doctrine of the past, they did not ask primarily, what was the concious and deliberate intention of its originator? They preferred to ask, what is the contribution of the doctrine to our beliefs? What is the meaning, unknown to the originator, of the doctrine from the point of view of the present? What is its meaning in the light of later discoveries or inventions? They took it for granted then that it is possible and even necessary to understand the thinkers of the past better than those thinkers understood themselves.

Against this approach, the 'historical consciousness' rightly protested in the interest of historical truth, of historical exactness. The task of the historian of thought is to understand the thinkers of the past exactly as they understood themselves, or to revitalize their thought according to their own interpretation. If we abandon this goal, we abandon the only practicable criterion of 'objectivity' in the history of thought. For, as is well-known, the same historical phenomenon appears in different lights in different historical situations; new experience seems to shed new light on old texts. Observations of this kind seem to suggest that the claim of any one interpretation to be *the* true interpretation is untenable. Yet the observations in question do not justify this suggestion. For the seemingly infinite variety of ways in which a given teaching can be understood does not do away with the fact that the originator of the doctrine understood it in one way only, provided he was not confused. The indefinitely large variety of equally legitimate interpretations of a doctrine of the past is due to conscious or unconscious attempts to understand its author better than he understood himself. But there is only one way of understanding him as he understood himself.

Now, historicism is constitutionally unable to live up to the very standards of historical exactness which it might be said to have discovered. For historicism is the belief that the historicist approach is superior to the non-historical approach, but practically the whole thought of the past was radically 'unhistorical'. Historicism is therefore compelled, by its principle, to attempt to understand the philosophy of the past better than it understood itself. The philosophy of the past understood itself in a non-historical manner, but historicism must understand it 'historically.' The philosophers of the past claimed to have found *the* truth, and not merely the truth for their times. The historicist, on the other hand, believes that they were mistaken in making that claim, and he cannot help making that belief the basis of his interpretation. Historicism then merely repeats, if sometimes in a more subtle form, the sin for which it upbraided so severely the 'progressivist' historiography. For, to repeat, our understanding of the thought of the past is liable to be the more adequate, the less the historian is convinced of the superiority of his own point of view, or the more he is prepared to admit the possibility that he may have to learn something, not merely about the thinkers of the past, but from them. To understand a serious teaching, we must be seriously interested in it, we must take it seriously, *i.e.*, we must be willing to consider the possibility that it is simply true. The historicist as such denies that possibility as regards any philosophy of the past. Historicism naturally attaches a much greater importance to the history of philosophy than any earlier philosophy has done. But unlike most earlier philosophies, it endangers by its principle, if contrary to its original intention, any adequate understanding of the philosophies of the past.

It would be a mistake to think that historicism could be the outcome of an unbiased study of the history of philosophy, and in particular of the history of political philosophy. The historian may have ascertained that all political philosophies are related to specific historical settings, or that only such men as live in a specific historical situation have a natural aptitude for accepting a given political philosophy. He cannot thus rule out the possibility that the historical setting of one particular political philosophy is the ideal condition for the discovery of *the* political truth. Historicism cannot then be established by historical evidence. Its basis is a philosophic analysis of thought, knowledge, truth, philosophy, political things, political ideals; and so on, a philosophic analysis allegedly leading to the result that thought, knowledge, truth, philosophy, political things, political ideals, and so on, are essentially and radically 'historical.' The philosophic analysis in question presents itself as the authentic interpretation of the experience of many centuries with political philosophy. The political philosophers of the past attempted to answer the question of the best political order once and for all. Each of them held explicitly or implicitly that all others had failed. It is only after a long period of trial and error that political philosophers started questioning the possibility of answering the fundamental questions once and for all. The ultimate result of that reflection is historicism.

Let us consider how far that result would affect political philosophy. Historicism cannot reasonably claim that the fundamental questions of political philosophy must be replaced by questions of a historical character. The question of the best political order, for example, cannot be replaced by a discussion 'of the operative ideals which maintain a particular type of state,' modern democracy, *e.g.*; for 'any thorough discussion' of those ideals 'is bound to give some consideration to the absolute worth of such ideals.'[2] Nor can the question of the best political order be replaced by the question of the future order. For even if we could know with certainty that the future order is to be, say, a communist world society, we should not know more than that the communist world society is the only alternative to the destruction of modern civilization, and we should still have to wonder which alternative is preferable. Under no circumstances can we avoid the question as to whether the probable future order is desirable, indifferent or abominable. In fact, our answer to that question may influence the prospects of the probable future order becoming actually the order of the future. What we consider desirable in the circumstances depends ultimately on universal principles of preference, on principles whose political implications, if duly elaborated, would present our answer to the question of the best political order.

What historicism could reasonably say, if the philosophic analysis on which it is based is correct, is that all answers to the universal philosophic questions are necessarily 'historically conditioned', or that no answer to the universal questions will in fact be universally valid. Now, every answer to a universal question necessarily intends to be universally valid. The historicist thesis amounts then to this, that there is an inevitable contradiction between the intention of philosophy and its fate, between the non-historical intention of the philosophic answers and their fate always to remain 'historically conditioned'. The contradiction is inevitable because, on the one hand, evident reasons compel us to raise the universal questions and to attempt to arrive at adequate answers, that is, universal answers; and, on the other hand, all human thought is enthralled by opinions and convictions which differ from historical situation to historical situation. The historical limitation of a given answer necessarily escapes him who gives the answer. The historical conditions which prevent any answer from being universally valid have the character of invisible walls. For if a man knew that his answer would be determined, not by his free insight into the truth, but by his historical situation, he could no longer identify himself with or wholeheartedly believe in, his answer. We should then know with certainty that no answer which suggests itself to us can be simply true, but we could not know the precise reason why this is the case. The precise reason would be the problematic validity of the deepest prejudice, necessarily hidden from us, of our time. If this view is correct, political philosophy would still have to raise the fundamental and universal questions which no thinking man can help raising once he has become aware of them, and to try to answer them. But the philosopher would have to accompany his philosophic effort by a coherent reflection on his historical situation in order to emancipate himself as far as possible from the prejudices of his age. That historical reflection would be in the service of the philosophic effort proper, but would by no means be identical with it.

On the basis of historicism, philosophic efforts would then be enlightened from the outset as to the fact that the answers to which they may lead will necessarily be 'historically conditioned'. They would be accompanied by coherent reflections on the historical situation in which they were undertaken. We might think that such philosophic efforts could justly claim to have risen to a higher level of reflection, or to be more philosophic, than the 'naïve' non-historical philosophy of the past. We might think for a moment that historical political philosophy is less apt to degenerate into dogmatism than was its predecessor.

But a moment's reflection suffices to dispel that delusion. Whereas for the genuine philosopher of the past all the answers of which he could possibly think were, prior to his examination of them, open possibilities, the historicist philosopher excludes, prior to his examining them, all the answers suggested in former ages. He is no less dogmatic, he is much more dogmatic, than the average philosopher of the past. In particular, the coherent reflection of the philosopher on his historical situation is not necessarily a sign that, other things being equal, his philosophic reflection is on a higher level than that of philosophers who were not greatly concerned with their historical situation. For it is quite possible that the modern philosopher is in much greater need of reflection on his situation because, having abandoned the resolve to look at things *sub specie aeternitatis*, he is much more exposed to, and enthralled by, the convictions and 'trends' dominating his age. Reflection on one's historical situation may very well be no more than a remedy for a deficiency which has been caused by historicism, or rather by the deeper motives which express themselves in historicism, and which did not hamper the philosophic efforts of former ages.

It seems as if historicism were animated by the certainty that the future will bring about the realization of possibilities of which no one has ever dreamt, or can ever dream, whereas non-historical political philosophy lived not in such an open horizon, but in a horizon closed by the possibilities known at the time. Yet the possibilities of the future are not unlimited as long as the differences between men and angels and between men and brutes have not been abolished, or as long as there are political things. The possibilities of the future are not wholly unknown, since their limits are known. It is true that no one can possibily foresee what sensible or mad possibilities, whose realization is within the limits of human nature, will be discovered in the future. But it is also true that it is hard to say anything at present about possibilities which are at present not even imagined. Therefore, we cannot help following the precedent set by the attitude of earlier political philosophy toward the possibilities which have been discovered, or even realized since. We must leave it to the political philosophers of the future to discuss the possibilities which will be known only in the future. Even the absolute certainty that the future will witness such fundamental and at the same time sensible changes of outlook as can not even be imagined now, could not possibly influence the questions and the procedure of political philosophy.

It would likewise be wrong to say that whereas non-historical political philosophy believed in the possibility of answering fundamental questions once and for all, historicism implies the insight that final answers to fundamental questions are impossible. Every philosophic position implies such answers to fundamental questions as claim to be final, to be true once and for all. Those who believe in 'the primary significance of the unique and morally ultimate character of the concrete situation', and therefore reject the quest for 'general answers supposed to have a universal meaning that covers and dominates all particulars', do not hesitate to offer what claim to be final and universal answers to the questions as to what 'a moral situation' is and as to what '*the* distinctively moral traits', or '*the* virtues' are.[3] Those who believe in progress toward a goal which itself is essentially progressive, and therefore reject the question of the best political order as 'too static', are convinced that their insight into the actuality of such a progress 'has come to stay'. Similarly, historicism merely replaced one kind of finality by another kind of finality, by the final conviction that all human answers are essentially and radically 'historical'. Only under one condition could historicism claim to have done away with all pretence to finality, if it presented the historicist thesis not as simply true, but as true for the time being only. In fact, if the historicist thesis is correct, we cannot escape the consequence that that thesis itself is 'historical' or valid, because meaningful, for a specific historical situation only. Historicism is not a cab which one can stop at his convenience: historicism must be applied to itself. It will thus reveal itself as relative to modern man; and this will imply that it will be replaced, in due time, by a position which is no longer historicist. Some historicists would consider such a development a manifest decline. But in so doing they would ascribe to the historical situation favourable to historicism an absoluteness which, as a matter of principle, they refuse to ascribe to any historical situation.

Precisely the historicist approach would compel us then to raise the question of the essential relation of historicism to modern man, or, more exactly, the question as to what specific need, characteristic of modern man, as distinguished from pre-modern man, underlies his passionate turn to history. To elucidate this question, as far as possible in the present context, we shall consider the argument in favour of the fusion of philosophic and historical studies which appears to be most convincing.

Political philosophy is the attempt to replace our opinions about political fundamentals by knowledge about them. Its first task consists therefore in making fully explicit our political ideas, so that they can be subjected to critical analysis. 'Our ideas' are only partly our ideas.

Most of our ideas are abbreviations or residues of the thought of other people, of our teachers (in the broadest sense of the term) and of our teachers' teachers; they are abbreviations and residues of the thought of the past. These thoughts were once explicit and in the centre of consideration and discussion. It may even be presumed that they were once perfectly lucid. By being transmitted to later generations they have possibly been transformed, and there is no certainty that the transformation was effected consciously and with full clarity. At any rate, what were once certainly explicit ideas passionately discussed, although not necessarily lucid ideas have now degenerated into mere implications and tacit presuppositions. Therefore, if we want to clarify the political ideas we have inherited, we must actualize their implications, which were explicit in the past, and this can be done only by means of the history of political ideas. This means that the clarification of our political ideas insensibly changes into and becomes indistinguishable from the history of political ideas. To this extent the philosophic effort and the historical effort have become completely fused.

Now, the more we are impressed by the necessity of engaging in historical studies in order to clarify our political ideas, the more we must be struck by the observation that the political philosophers of former ages did not feel such a necessity at all. A glance at Aristotle's *Politics*, for example, suffices to convince us that Aristotle succeeded perfectly in clarifying the political ideas obtaining in his age, although he never bothered about the history of those ideas. The most natural, and the most cautious, explanation of this paradoxical fact would be, that perhaps our political ideas have a character fundamentally different from that of the political ideas of former ages. Our political ideas have the particular character that they cannot be clarified fully except by means of historical studies, whereas the political ideas of the past could be clarified perfectly without any recourse to their history.

To express this suggestion somewhat differently, we shall make a somewhat free use of the convenient terminology of Hume. According to Hume, our ideas are derived from 'impressions' — from what we may call first-hand experience. To clarify our ideas and to distinguish between their genuine and their spurious elements (or between those elements which are in accordance with first-hand experience and those which are not), we must trace each of our ideas to the impressions from which it is derived. Now it is doubtful whether all ideas are related to impressions in fundamentally the same way. The idea of the city, for example, can be said to be derived from the impressions of cities in fundamentally the same way as the idea of the dog is derived from the impressions of dogs. The idea of the state, on the other hand, is not derived simply from the impression of states. It emerged partly owing to the transformation, or reinterpretation, of more elementary ideas, of the idea of the city in particular. Ideas which are derived directly from impressions can be clarified without any recourse to history; but ideas which have emerged owing to a specific transformation of more elementary ideas cannot be clarified but by means of the history of ideas.

We have illustrated the difference between our political ideas and earlier political ideas by the examples of the ideas of the state and of the city. The choice of these examples was not accidental; for the difference with which we are concerned is the specific difference between the character of modern philosophy on the one hand, and that of pre-modern philosophy on the other. This fundamental difference was described by Hegel in the following terms:

> The manner of study in ancient times is distinct from that of modern times, in that the former consisted in the veritable training and perfecting of the natural consciousness. Trying its powers at each part of its life severally, and philosophizing about everything it came across, the natural consciousness transformed itself into a universality of abstract understanding which was active in every matter and in every respect. In modern times, however, the individual finds the abstract form ready made.[4]

Classical philosophy originally acquired the fundamental concepts of political philosophy by starting from political phenomena as they present themselves to 'the natural consciousness', which is a prephilosophic consciousness. These concepts can therefore be understood, and their validity can be checked, by direct reference to phenomena as they are accessible to 'the natural consciousness'. The fundamental concepts which were the final result of the philosophic efforts of the Middle Ages, were the starting-point of the philosophic efforts of classical antiquity, and which remained the basis of the philosophic efforts of the modern period. They were partly taken for granted and partly modified by the founders of modern political philosophy. In a still more modified form they underlie the political philosophy or political science of our time. In so far as modern political philosophy emerges, not simply from 'the natural consciousness', but by way of a modification of, and even in opposition to, an earlier political philosophy, a tradition of political philosophy, its fundamental concepts cannot be fully understood until we have understood the earlier political philosophy from which, and in opposition to which, they were acquired, and the specific modification by virtue of which they were acquired.

It is not the mere 'dependence' of modern philosophy on classical philosophy, but the specific character of that 'dependence', which accounts for the fact that the former needs to be supplemented by an intrinsically philosophic history of philosophy. For medieval philosophy too was 'dependent' on classical philosophy, and yet it was not in need of the history of philosophy as an integral part of its philosophic efforts. When a medieval philosopher studied Aristotle's *Politics*, for example, he did not engage in a historical study. The *Politics* was for him an authoritative text. Aristotle was *the* philosopher, and hence the teaching of the *Politics* was, in principle, *the* true philosophic teaching. However he might deviate from Aristotle in details, or as regards the application of the true teaching to circumstances which Aristotle could not have foreseen, the basis of the medieval philosopher's thought remained the Aristotelian teaching. That basis was always present to him, it was contemporaneous with him. His philosophic study was identical with the adequate understanding of the Aristotelian teaching. It was for this reason that he did not need historical studies in order to understand the basis of his own thought. It is precisely that contemporaneous philosophic thought with its basis which no longer exists in modern philosophy, and whose absence explains the eventual transformation of modern philosophy into an intrinsically historical philosophy. Modern thought is in all its forms, directly or indirectly, determined by the idea of progress. This idea implies that the most elementary questions can be settled once and for all so that future generations can dispense with their further discussion, but can erect on the foundations once laid an ever-growing structure. In this way, the foundations are covered up. The only proof necessary to guarantee their solidity seems to be that the structure stands and grows. Since philosophy demands, however, not merely solidity so understood, but lucidity and truth, a special kind of inquiry becomes necessary whose purpose it is to keep alive the recollection, and the problem, of the foundations hidden by progress. This philosophic enquiry is the history of philosophy or of science.

We must distinguish between inherited knowledge and independently acquired knowledge. By inherited knowledge we understand the philosophic or scientific knowledge a man takes over from former generations, or, more generally expressed, from others; by independently acquired knowledge we understand the philosophic or scientific knowledge a mature scholar acquires in his unbiased intercourse, as fully enlightened as possible as to its horizon and its presuppositions, with his subject matter. On the basis of the belief in progress, this difference tends to lose its crucial significance. When speaking of a 'body of knowledge' or of 'the results of research', for example, we tacitly assign the same cognitive status to inherited knowledge and to independently acquired knowledge. To counteract this tendency a special effort is required to transform inherited knowledge into genuine knowledge by re-vitalizing its original discovery, and to discriminate between the genuine and the spurious elements of what claims to be inherited knowledge. This truly philosophic function is fulfilled by the history of philosophy or of science.

If, as we must, we apply historicism to itself, we must explain historicism in terms of the specific character of modern thought, or, more precisely, of modern philosophy. In doing so, we observe that modern political philosophy or science, as distinguished from pre-modern political philosophy or science, is in need of the history of political philosophy or science as an integral part of its own efforts, since, as modern political philosophy or science itself admits or even emphasizes, it consists to a considerable extent of inherited knowledge whose basis is no longer contemporaneous or immediately accessible. The recognition of this necessity cannot be mistaken for historicism. For historicism asserts that the fusion of philosophic and historical questions marks in itself a progress beyond 'naive' non-historical philosophy, whereas we limit ourselves to asserting that that fusion is, within the limits indicated, inevitable on the basis of modern philosophy, as distinguished from pre-modern philosophy or 'the philosopy of the future'.

Notes

1. Compare Locke, *Of Civil Government*, I, Sect. 109, and II, Sect. 52, with his *Essay Concerning Human Understanding*, III, ch. 9, Sects. 3 and 22.

2. A.D. Lindsay, *The Modern Democratic State* (Oxford, 1943), I, p. 45.

3. John Dewey, *Reconstruction in Philosophy* (New York, 1920), pp. 189, 163 f.

4. *The Phenomenology of the Mind*, trans. J.B. Baillie, 2nd edn (London, New York, 1931), p. 94. I have changed Baillie's translation a little in order to bring out somewhat more clearly the intention of Hegel's remark. For a more precise analysis, see Jacob Klein, 'Die griechische Logistik und die Entstehung der modernen Algebra', *Quellen und Studien zur Geschichte der Mathematik, Astronomie und Physik*, vol. 3, Heft 1 (Berlin, 1934), pp. 64-6, and Heft 2 (Berlin, 1936), pp. 122 ff.

Source

Leo Strauss, 'Political Philosophy and History', *Journal of the History of Ideas*, vol. 10, no. 1 (1949) pp. 30-50, reprinted in Strauss, *What Is Political Philosophy: and Other Studies* (New York, Free Press, 1959), pp. 56-77.

10 THE MYTH OF THE TRADITION

John G. Gunnell

Some of the most influential accounts of the history of political philosophy as well as interpretations of particular texts have been informed
by a concern with developing a critique of contemporary politics and
political thought. This attempt to explain and evaluate the present in
terms of its intellectual antecedents has contributed to the entrench-
ment of the belief that the conventional chronology of classic texts
(including at least the works of Plato, Aristotle, St Augustine, St
Thomas Aquinas, Machiavelli, Hobbes, Locke, Rousseau, Hegel, and
Marx) constitutes an actual historical tradition or inherited pattern of
thought. It is assumed that these works belong to a distinct genre, that
they are the product of a discrete activity with a recognisable temporal
career, and that they represent the evolution of Western political ideas.
This reconstructed tradition has become the principal context for
understanding the meaning of past texts, and the significance attributed to a work has become largely a matter of its role in this historical
narrative. The argument of Leo Strauss presents a paradigm case of the
myth of the tradition.

There is no doubt that Leo Strauss significantly influenced teaching
and research in the history of political philosophy, yet although he has
been summarized, criticized, eulogized and elegized, the character of
the Straussian enterprise has still remained elusive. This is in part
because discussions of his work have been caught between polemics
and apologetics and have often focused on such narrow but controversial issues as his attack on modern social science, his iconoclastic
interpretations of figures such as Machiavelli and Locke, his defence of
natural law, his concern with esoteric writing, and his animadversions
on contemporary politics. But it is also in part because it is not easy to
characterize the activity in which Strauss is engaged and the criteria
appropriate for understanding and judging his arguments. The history
of political philosophy is not a well-defined discipline with accepted
research programmes, and to locate Strauss within this field is of
limited value. To understand Strauss requires a comprehensive view of
his enterprise and a careful examination of what he has to say about it,
but a clarification of Strauss's work may yield some insight into certain

other literature usually subsumed under the category of the 'history of political philosophy'.

Although some of Strauss's critics denigrate the study of the history of political philosophy in general, many of the disputes generated by his work have been interspecific, and, consequently, some of the family resemblances between his arguments and other literature in the field have received little attention. In many respects Strauss's concept of a tradition of political philosophy exemplifies a regulative paradigm discernible in textbooks and other general treatments of the history of political philosophy as well as studies of individual works. My purpose is to present a systematic exposition and analysis of Strauss's argument about, and approach to, the history of political philosophy. However, I also wish to identify and illuminate the structural attributes and governing intentions characteristic of this type of literature.

In recent years, there has been an increasing concern with the 'methodology' of the history of ideas and the exegesis of historical texts which carries important implications for research in the history of political philosophy.[1] But relevant criticism in this field should also entail an understanding of the premises underlying this activity. Strauss's work is distinctive in many ways, yet it belongs to a genre which has dominated teaching and research in this area for some time. I do not suggest that Strauss speaks for the field; however, his work is more representative than either his defenders or his critics acknowledge.

1

Strauss maintains that his attempt to understand the works of past political philosophers and the development of political ideas does not derive from a *'pain-loving antiquarianism'* or 'intoxicating romanticism' but from a confrontation with what he diagnoses as the crisis of modernity: 'We are impelled to do so by the crisis of our time, the crisis of the West.'[2] The purpose of the enterprise is essentially therapeutic.

The crisis which Strauss alleges is both intellectual and political and pervades every aspect of contemporary culture. Although the crisis, its symptoms, and its causes tend to blur somewhat in his analysis, this is because he sees the crisis as the product of historical evolution. An understanding of the character of this modern predicament, its sources, and the key to its solution is accessible only through exploration of its origins. Strauss views the crisis as a result of the degeneration of the Western tradition, and, in particular, the tradition of political philosophy. The history of political philosophy must examine the process which led to this decline and regain what has been lost. The task is one of recapitulation and restoration.

Politically, the crisis involves the threat of 'communism' and an 'Eastern despotism', and Strauss argues that already 'some decline of the West has taken place before our eyes', and that the 'West's very survival is endangered by the East' in a manner unparalleled since ancient times.[3] But, according to Strauss, the external threat is complemented by an even more serious internal problem: the West has 'become uncertain of its purpose'.[4] The 'decline of liberal democracy into permissive egalitariansm' has endangered its very existence, since 'a permissive society which permits its members every sort of non-permissiveness will soon cease to be permissive. It will vanish from the face of the earth.'[5] In our time, he argues, 'liberalism has abandoned its absolutist basis and is trying to become entirely relativistic'.[6] Modern liberalism, which is characterized by a 'passionate rejection of all "absolutes" ' including those on which its own legitimacy is based, is actually a 'seminary of intolerance' in disguise.[7]

Strauss maintains that the thesis 'that we are in the grip of a crisis is hardly in need of proof' and that it is equally evident that the cause of this crisis is 'the modern project' and its search for the conquest of nature.[8] He argues that the 'inadequacy of the modern project, which has now become a matter of general knowledge and of general concern, compels us to entertain the thought that this new kind of society, our kind of society, must be animated by a spirit other than that which animated it from the beginning'.[9] Apart from his roster of 'isms' (communism, historicism, relativism, liberalism, positivism, nihilism, etc.), Strauss is not very specific about the agents of the threat to the West, but he insists that the conditions of the age are such that

> we are are now brought face to face with a tyranny which holds out the threat of becoming, thanks to 'the conquest of nature' and in particular human nature, what no earlier tyranny ever became: perpetual and universal . . . The manifest and deliberate collectivization or coordination of thought is being prepared in a hidden and frequently quite unconscious way by the spread of the teaching that all human thought is collective independently of any human effort to this end, because all thought is historical.[10]

The political crisis, then, is the consequence of a fundamental intellectual crisis. This, he contends, may in turn be attributed to the decline of political philosophy. In the modern age, 'what was originally a political philosophy has turned into an ideology', and this is 'the core of the contemporary crisis of the West'.[11]

In a functional sense, Strauss defines political philosophy as an activity which seeks knowledge for the purpose of changing the present, as far as practicable. Just as philosophy in general is concerned with replacing opinions with knowledge, political philosophy is 'the attempt to replace opinion about the nature of political things by knowledge of the nature of political things' which is primarily knowledge about the right or good political order.[12] But Strauss also wishes to locate political philosophy historically and to distinguish it from the wider category of political thought. While the latter, he suggests, is 'as old as the human race and political life itself', the former 'appeared at a knowable time in the recorded past' and 'has been cultivated since its beginnings almost without any interruption until a relatively short time ago. Today, political philosophy is in a state of decay and perhaps of putrefaction, if it has not vanished altogether.'[13] As a specific historical phenomenon, political philosophy was 'originated by Socrates',[14] elaborated by Plato and Aristotle, and continued, at least in an attenuated form, until contemporary times.

Although Strauss insists that 'Science and History, those two great powers of the modern world, have finally succeeded in destroying the very possibility of political philosophy',[15] they are as much the product of the tradition of political philosophy, and in particular modern political philosophy which emerged in the sixteenth and seventeenth centuries, as the cause of its demise. Thus we must study the history of political philosophy to understand what has been lost and how it has been lost. Positivism and historicism together create a climate of 'unqualified relativism' which has come to characterize 'Western thought in general' and which, in its rejection of the possibility of 'knowledge of natural right' transcending particular social and historical contexts, 'leads to nihilism' or the reluctance and 'the inability to take a stand for civilization against cannibalism'.[16] Just as political philosophy in its most classic form embodied the purpose of discovering the nature of political things including the nature of the good society, positivism and historicism, which constitute a denial of the validity and possibility of that undertaking, are most characteristically expressed in contemporary social science.

Strauss argues that positivism has been the basic intellectual stance of socal science since the nineteenth century. With its identification of science and knowledge with empiricism and its equation of values with 'blind preferences', positivism undercuts political philosophy.[17] But 'positivism necessarily transforms itself into historicism' which in its various forms constitutes 'the spirit of our time' and is by far the most 'serious antagonist of political philosophy'.[18] Historicism goes beyond positivism by regarding *all* claims to knowledge as relative to particular modes of culturally and historically conditioned experience and incapable of ultimate justification.[19] Historicism spawned a paralysis of thought and action which not only weakened the moral nerve of Europe in 1933 but continues to pervade Western culture and encourages the assumption that all value judgements are equally worthy.

Strauss declines to attribute base motives to contemporary social science, but he views it as a repository of modern ideas which reinforces while it reflects these ideas. Social science, with its positivist and historicist assumptions, is unprepared for either a defence or constructive criticism of liberal democracy, let alone the required 'relentless critique of communism'.[20] Thus it contributes to the political crisis, and although it directly 'fosters not so much nihilism as conformism and philistinism', it is closely tied to both the intellectual and political dimensions of modern nihilism.[21]

For Strauss, political science, which is the direct heir to the tradition of political philosophy, is the existential manifestation of the decline of political philosophy. What Strauss terms the 'new science of politics', typified by American political science, may not have caused the 'crisis of the modern Western world', but 'it is surely contemporary with that crisis'.[22] Since Strauss views modern political science as rejecting traditional political philosophy and adopting the ideas of postivism and historicism, he selects it as a major object of attack. He perceives the 'new political science' not merely as an academic discipline based on false premises but as an educational institution which 'wields very great authority'.[23]

Strauss's indictment of modern political science includes the charges that it 'rests on a dogmatic atheism', and involves the 'consistent denial of a common good'. He charges also that it denies that 'man has natural ends' or that 'there is any essential difference between men and brutes', and accepts a thoroughgoing relativism which 'unwittingly contributes to the victory of the gutter'. Furthermore, since it is 'permissive or liberal' in its implications, it reflects the most dangerous proclivities of democracy by teaching 'the equality of literally all desires'.[24] He holds that there is not only a 'harmony between the new political science and a particular vision of liberal democracy', but its extreme 'democratism' tends to depreciate differences 'between liberal democracy and communism'.[25] It not only blurs the doctrinal distinctions but treats them as simply two incommensurable historical ideologies and consequently 'has nothing to say against those who unhesitatingly prefer surrender, that is, the abandonment of liberal democracy, to war'.[26] Thus it contributes to the external threat to the West by weakening the internal foundations of democracy and by refusing to make value judgements and recognize 'tyranny' for 'what it really is'.[27] But Strauss insists that modern political science, despite its perverse tendencies and influence, is more naïve than 'diabolic' in a Neronic sense. 'It is excused by two factors: it does not know that it fiddles, and it does not know that Rome burns.'[28]

Since, for Strauss, the explanation of the modern crisis is the decline of political philosophy, any solution to the crisis presupposes an understanding of this decline and knowledge of the original character of political philosophy. He argues that 'we are therefore in need of historical studies in order to familiarize ourselves with the whole complexity of the issues'.[29] Yet he insists on differentiating his undertaking from histories of political philosophy informed by historicist premisses. Strauss contends that 'the decay of political philosophy into ideology reveals itself most obviously in the fact that in both research and teaching, political philosophy has been replaced by the history of political philosophy'.[30]

Strauss argues that the purpose of research in the history of political philosophy is not to gain knowledge about the past, or the present, as an end in itself. It is an exercise necessary for the diagnosis of modern ills and the restoration of political philosophy in its original form. Although historical knowledge may in some sense be useful to political philosophy in gaining knowledge of political phenomena, 'political philosophy is not a historical discipline' and 'is fundamentally different from the history of political philosophy itself'.[31] Strauss maintains that while most modern historians accept the premisses of nineteenth-century historicism and assume that all political thought has an equal claim on truth, his own history aims, in part, at exposing the error of what amounts to a denial of 'the fundamental distinction between philosophic and historical questions'.[32] The assumption that all works are merely expressions of their historical period constitutes a rejection of the original conception of political philosophy as a means of discovering universal truths about politics.

The historicist approach to the past is instrumental in the sense that its purpose is 'activist' rather than 'contemplative' and involves the demand 'that each generation reinterpret the past on the basis of its own experience and with a view to its own future' and 'ultimate guidance for political life'.[33] Although he maintains that the study of the past cannot provide 'recipes' for the present, he does allow that

> an adequate understanding of the principles as elaborated by the classics may be the indispensable starting point for an adequate analysis, to be achieved by us, of present-day society in its peculiar character, and for the wise application, to be achieved by us, of these principles to our tasks.[34]

Strauss's instrumentalism is actually more radical, since he implies that once the task of the history of political philosophy is completed, such histories could in principle be eliminated and replaced by political philosophy itself or the knowledge achieved by a particular philosophy.

Strauss realizes the paradox in his insistence, on the one hand, that political philosophy is a non-historical activity and his contention, on the other hand, that historical studies are required to recover political philosophy. He admits that this inevitable tension makes it difficult to maintain the necessary separation between philosophy and history. However, he insists that to engage in the history of political philosophy simply to prevent 'the burial of a great tradition' is something which 'is not merely a half-measure but an absurdity: to replace political philosophy by the history of political philosophy means to replace a doctrine which claims to be true by a survey of more or less brilliant errors'.[35]

It is not only that the modern crisis demands the history of political philosophy but also that, in a fundamental sense, it makes it feasible by facilitating a break with traditional patterns of thought. The task of achieving adequate knowledge of the past has 'been rendered possible by the shaking of all traditions; the crisis of our time may have the accidental advantage of enabling us to understand in an untraditional or fresh manner what was hitherto only understood in a traditional or derivative manner'.[36] The tradition becomes accessible at the point of its crisis. Only at such a propitious moment is it possible to detach oneself from the tradition sufficiently to maintain the requisite objectivity to gain 'solid knowledge' of the past and 'to study the political philosophies as they were understood by their originators'.[37]

There are, in Strauss's view, 'two opposed ways in which one can study the thought of the past'. The variety of historicist interpretations have in common the implicit or explicit denial that it is possible to achieve objective historical knowledge and 'understand the thinkers of the past exactly as they understood themselves'.[38] They insist on understanding these thinkers in light of their significance for the present and engage in a creative attempt 'to understand the thinkers of the past better than those thinkers understood themselves' which always involves 'a questionable mixture of interpretation and critique'.[39] But Strauss maintains that the goal must be 'to understand the thought of the past "as it really has been", that is, to understand it as exactly as possible as it was actually understood by its authors'.[40]

Once the ideas of the past have been objectively understood, they can then be submitted to a 'philosophic critique concerned exclusively with their truth or falsehood', and it becomes apparent that 'what at first sight is merely the result of the demands of historical exactness is actually the result of the demand for a philosophic re-examination of our basic assumptions'.[41] By understanding the thinkers of the past exactly, we come to a more clear and self-conscious understanding of ourselves. Modern political philosophy requires the aid of the history of political philosophy, since 'it consists to a considerable extent of inherited knowledge whose basis is no longer contemporaneous or immediately accessible'. Thus 'a special effort is required to transform inherited knowledge into genuine knowledge by revitalizing its original discovery, and to discriminate between the genuine and spurious elements'.[42] The goal of the history of political philosophy is 'the restoration of political philosophy',[43] but this restoration must be accompanied by a critical or destructive effort which strips away the distortions of a tradition that has separated the modern age from a true understanding of politics.

According to Strauss, the 'great tradition' of political philosophy may be broken down into the classical and modern periods. In his view, this is not an arbitrary division but a distinction grounded in a deliberate transformation of the classical teaching by modern philosophers. 'Modern political philosophy came into being through the conscious break with the principles established by Socrates', and it can only be understood as at once a derivation from and a rejection of those principles.[44] To comprehend the spirit of the modern age, one must understand that it rests on the suppositions of modern political philosophy, but the latter has in turn evolved from classical political philosophy, despite its divergence from it. Classical political philosophy becomes the essential starting point for understanding the entire tradition.

A crucial element in Strauss's argument is his thesis that 'classical political philosophy is the true science of political things', and he maintains that the 'essential character of all political situations was grasped by the old political science'.[45] Strauss maintains that when starting from a historicist perspective 'the obvious possibility is overlooked that the situation to which one particular doctrine is related, is particularly favorable to the discovery of *the* truth' or that 'a political philosophy which emerged many centuries ago is *the* true political philosophy'.[46] The aim of the history of political philosophy must be to penetrate the tradition, to peel away the accretions, and to reach a point where classical political philosophy can be viewed directly, just as it viewed political things directly, rather than 'through the lenses of modern political philosophy and its various successors'.[47] The modern break with classical political philosophy marks the beginning of the decline of political philosophy, and thus

> we have to go back to the point where the destruction of political philosophy began, to the beginnings of modern political philosophy, when modern philosophy still had to fight against the older political philosophy, classical political philosophy, the political philosophy originated by Socrates and elaborated above all by Aristotle. At the same time, the quarrel of the ancients and moderns took place . . . It was fundamentally a quarrel between modern philosophy, or science, and the older philosophy, or science . . . Our task is to re-awaken that quarrel, now that the modern answer has been given the opportunity to reveal its virtues and to do its worst to the old answer for more than three centuries.[48]

Strauss wishes to illuminate and reopen this old quarrel between the ancients and the moderns for a very practical purpose. Since the modern 'project' was originated by modern political philosophy, to uncover the hidden meaning of modern political philosophy and destroy its creditability is to undercut foundations of modern liberalism, communism, and allied doctrines which are, in his view, at the centre of the crisis of the West.[49] By demonstrating the defective and derivative character of modern political philosophy and comparing it with the indefectible and primary character of classical political philosophy, he attempts to call into question the claims of modernity regarding both its understanding and practice of politics.

Strauss maintains that 'our political ideas have the particular character that they cannot be clarified fully except by means of historical studies, whereas the political ideas of the past could be clarified perfectly without any recourse to their history'.[50]

> Classical political philosophy is non-traditional, because it belongs to the fertile moment when all political traditions were shaken, and there was not yet in existence a tradition of political philosophy. In all later epochs, the philosophers' study of political things was mediated by a tradition of political philosophy which acted like a screen between the philosopher and political things, regardless of whether the individual philosopher cherished or rejected that tradition. From this it follows that the classical political philosophers see the political things with a freshness and directness which never have been equalled.[51]

All subsequent political thought is distinguished by an increasing tendency towards the 'abstract' and away from the 'concrete' and 'simple and primary issues'.[52] This is particularly manifest in modern social science which, standing at the end of the tradition, 'abstracts from essential elements of social reality' and is removed from the terms of 'common-sense thinking' or the point of view and language of the citizen.[53]

Classical political philosophy achieved an unmediated grasp of political phenomena, since it 'acquired the fundamental concepts of political philosophy by starting from political phenomena as they present themselves to "the natural consciousness", which is pre-philosophic consciousness'.[54] The meaning of these seminal concepts was subsequently modified in the course of the tradition until there was no longer a correspondence between the concepts and political reality. But the phenomena themselves were in a sense also transformed, because after classical Greece, philosophy became part of political life. Only at that one crucial moment in history did a non-traditional mode of thought confront a philosophically uncontaminated political life. And only now, when the tradition has run dry and Western culture falls into crisis, does the opportunity present itself to commence an intellectual journey, through the medium of the history of political philosophy, for the purpose of regaining that original understanding of political phenomena.

Strauss seems to suggest, however, that the essential nature of political things has remained constant despite transformations in historical form, because the nature of man and human relations are unchanging. Yet original political concepts have become so modified and tradition-laden that their original meaning can only be regained by radical re-thinking. 'These concepts can . . . be understood, and their validity can be checked, by direct reference to phenomena as they are accessible to "natural consciousness",'[55] but the modern consciousness is not natural but traditional. Strauss does not elaborate on this 'phenomenological' epistemology, but he insists that the means of achieving a 'natural consciousness' of 'political things' cannot be created by a mere act of will in the present. It can be won only by a historical penetration of the tradition which brings us back to Aristotle's *Politics* and classical political science's virginal encounter with political phenomena.[56]

Most of Strauss's particular studies of the writings of political philosophers, as well as those of many of his students and epigones, are devoted to an explication of, or are approached in terms of, his general vision of the structure and meaning of the tradition of political philosophy. Overall, the vision is one of progressive deterioration, but the fundamental division is between the ancient and modern periods, since all modern political philosophies 'have a fundamental principle in common' which is the 'rejection of the classical scheme as unrealistic'.[57] Strauss contends that this rejection and transformation marked the beginning of cumulative error in the tradition. Just as Socrates was the founder of the classical portion of the tradition, Strauss maintains that 'the founder of modern political philosophy is Machiavelli'.[58]

Strauss insists that modern political science, which is blind to the difference between tyranny and other regimes, has its origin in Machiavelli's work which is characterized by the same indifference, and to understand the assumptions of modern political science, it is necessary to understand the character of the change in the tradition that was consciously brought about by Machiavelli.[59] Machiavelli

> tried to effect, and he did effect, a break with the whole tradition of political philosophy. He compared his achievement to that of men like Columbus. He claimed to have discovered a new moral continent. His claim is well founded; his political teaching is "wholly new." The only question is whether the new continent is fit for human habitation.[60]

Strauss maintains that Machiavelli, in attempting to set out his 'new route', deliberately truncated political philosophy by excluding from its scope questions which had previously guided inquiry such as those relating to how human beings ought to live and the character of the best political order. While the classics had little idea that such an order could be actualized except by chance, given the limitations of human nature and usual circumstances, it served as a standard for the old political science which aimed at realizing it in so far as possible. What constituted the tradition-shaking contribution of Machiavelli, which provided the orientation for all modern political philosophy, was his teaching 'that one should take one's bearings, not by how men ought to live but by how they actually live'. This led to a 'lowering of the standards of political life' and an emphasis on overcoming *fortuna* and realizing pragmatic goals. Strauss suggests that this concern with the attainment of 'ideals' in the process of human affairs eventually contributed 'to the emergence of "philosophy of history"' and the historicism of the modern age.[61]

Strauss's attack on Machiavelli is passionate. Strauss characterizes him as 'a great master of blasphemy', 'a devil', and a 'teacher of evil' who engaged in 'a critique of religion and a critique of morality' in his 'diabolical' tract and who rejected virtue as a standard and substituted, at best, the 'objectives which are actually pursued by all societies' and, at worst, a set of immoral goals'.[62] Strauss observes that it is easy, 'after a few centuries of Machiavellianization of Western thought, to give Machiavelli's teaching an air of perfect respectability', and therefore he resolves to demonstrate what a fundamental inversion of the tradition he produced.[63] Modern interpreters of Machiavelli fail to see the immoral character of his teaching and label him a patriot or scientist, but in Strauss's view this is because they are 'pupils of Machiavelli' and their work is based on a 'dogmatic acceptance of his principles. They do not see the evil character of his thought because they are the heirs of the Machiavellian tradition; because they, or the forgotten teachers of their teachers have been corrupted by Machiavelli.'[64] For Strauss, Machiavelli was a conspirator and revolutionary who taught conspiracy and revolution not only against political institutions but against the very tradition itself.

Strauss suggests that already by the time of Machiavelli 'the classical tradition had undergone profound changes', but that neither these changes nor the changes effected by Machiavelli and his successors brought increased knowledge. Machiavelli's work involved merely a 'contraction of the horizon', presented as if it were a discovery, and was 'the first example of a spectacle which has renewed itself in almost every generation since'.[65] Strauss argues, however, that Machiavelli initiated an intellectual movement which, in both substance and approach, continued through the modern tradition right up to the *Federalist Papers* and beyond, and his success in dominating the tradition was so profound that Strauss apparently finds no difficulty in speaking of 'that Machiavellian, Karl Marx'.[66]

Machiavelli's success was outstripped by the subsequent 'transformation of his scheme', but this transformation was nevertheless 'inspired by his own principle',[67] At times, Strauss seems to elevate Hobbes as the founder of modern political philosophy because of his fundamental break with traditional natural law and other principles of classical political philosophy. In Strauss's rendition of the tradition, Hobbes also receives the title of 'originator of modernity'. Strauss insists that we must realize that today 'our perspective is identical with Hobbes's perspective' and that Hobbes was 'the founder of liberalism'.[68] But Hobbes's great (or infamous) accomplishment was that he softened the 'revolting character' of Machiavelli's teaching in order to make it more palatable and capable of realization.[69] However, even 'Hobbes's teaching was still much too bold to be acceptable. It too was in need of mitigation. The mitigation was the work of Locke.'[70] Strauss contends that Locke largely propagated Hobbesian principles and that through Locke the doctrines originating with Machiavelli found their way into the thought and action of modern liberal democracy.

This segment of the tradition, or what Strauss designates as the 'first wave of modernity', was complemented by the attack on natural law which evolved out of the French Enlightenment and received its most important expression in the work of Rousseau. 'With Rousseau there begins what we may call the second wave of modernity: the wave which bore both German idealistic philosophy and the romanticism of all ranks in all countries.'[71] Strauss argues that Rousseau, by his acceptance of the general will as the criterion of political judgement, his denial of any essential nature of man, and his rejection of natural and transcendent standards of justice, fostered a relativism which in effect allows that 'cannibalism is as just as its opposite'.[72]

The philosophy of history of the nineteenth century, typified by Hegel and Marx, attempted to locate all values in the inner logic and direction of the historical process itself and to demonstrate that right order was an immanent product of that process, independent of purposive human action. But the failure of this vision, the denial of meaning in history, left nothing but the record of the historical process itself and a series of incomparable cultural perspectives. This prepared the way for the emergence of 'the third wave of modernity — of the wave that bears us today. This last epoch was inaugurated by Nietzsche,' who is '*the* philosopher of relativism', and who in his revolt against a 'decayed Hegelianism', laid the foundation for the present situation of radical historicism or the belief, characteristic of existentialism and philosophers such as Heidegger, that the human being is 'essentially historical'.[73] Strauss concludes that, together, these three waves of modernity have culminated in the crisis of our time.

2

Since the scope of this essay does not allow a detailed comparison of Strauss's argument with other secondary literature in the history of political philosophy, my claim regarding a significant generic similarity must remain a hypothesis. But this similarity will be evident to those familiar with the work of Eric Voegelin, Hannah Arendt, and, in varying degrees, numerous other commentators, historians, and textbook authors who have adopted the tradition of political philosophy as a vehicle for their arguments. My principal concern in discussing Strauss is to indicate a characteristic thematic motive of this kind of literature.

Strauss's enterprise is thoroughly instrumental or practical. It is instrumental not only in that he seeks to explain and evaluate the present rather than merely illuminate the past but in that he utilizes the history of political philosophy to mount an attack on what he believes to be the philosophical foundations of contemporary politics. It is perfectly reasonable to make a distinction between what one is doing and the purpose for which one does it, and an understanding of the former is not necessarily dependent on an understanding of the latter. But in Strauss's case they are not separable. His particular reconstruction of the tradition of political philosophy is intelligible only in view of his strategic reasons for undertaking it; that his interpretation of figures such as Locke is designed to impugn the commonly accepted foundation of modern liberalism is too obvious to be ignored. Within the limits of this discussion I cannot demonstrate fully the extent to which Strauss's choice and interpretation of particular works are intended to serve his critique of modernity, but I can indicate the instrumental purpose which informs both his use of the idea of the tradition and his account of the tradition.

Although Strauss puts great emphasis on understanding authors as they understood themselves, this prescription remains, for the most part, at the level of a maxim or the enunciation of an attitude. Apart from his well-known thesis about the relationship between persecution and political theory and the need to look beyond exoteric arguments and apparent inconsistency for arcane meaning, Strauss has little to say about criteria of interpretation. But even this thesis would seem to be more a plausible hypothesis in some instances than a generally applicable principle. He maintains that the fact that all societies rest on prejudice and opinion places limitations on 'the philosophers' public speech or writing' and 'gives rise to a specific art of writing' which conceals the 'beauty of those hidden treasures'.[74] Thus 'the understanding of this danger and the various forms it has taken, and which it may take, is the foremost task, and indeed the sole task, of the sociology of philosophy'.[75] Why Strauss believes that this is the only, and yet imperative, contextual consideration is not revealed. This claim seems principally to place his interpretations based on this premise outside the realm of falsification and debate. This is quite necessary, since his vision of the tradition is an organic one in which the role assigned each figure is essential to the integrity of the entire structure.

Nowhere does Strauss set forth anything approaching a general theory of textual interpretation or principles of hermeneutical historiography that would give substance to his demand for objectivity. But to approach Strauss's work on the assumption that he is simply engaged in the history of ideas is, despite the great ambiguity regarding the criteria of explanation in this field and notwithstanding the historical form of his argument, to miss the point of what he is doing. Strauss's explication of the tradition of political philosophy is not a research conclusion but a dramaturgical account of the corruption of modernity designed to lend authority to his assertions about the crisis of our time. It is an epic history, complete with epic formulae. Strauss does not demonstrate the existence of the tradition but he assumes it or at least expects his audience to assume it. His description already presupposes the tradition as a datum. He neither discusses what a tradition is nor defends the assumption that the diverse works from Plato to Nietzsche which provide the subject matter of his analysis constitute an inherited pattern of thought with causal implications for contemporary politics and political ideas. He offers neither an account of actual historical connections between the ideas of the figures who comprise this putative tradition nor an explanation of their impact on politics.

Strauss articulates a distinctive tradition myth; but the myth of the tradition, in one form or another, has been a pervasive feature of most of the scholarship in the history of political philosophy. Academic convention selects a basic repertoire of classic works, extending at least from Plato to Marx, arranges them chronologically, infuses them with evolutionary significance, and treats them as a preconstituted tradition which, for better or worse, culminates in modern political theory and practice. Arguments about the history of political philosophy have become arguments about the meaning of this tradition and about the significance of particular works for an understanding of the tradition. Although certain classic texts are always considered essential elements of the tradition, the criteria for inclusion and emphasis usually depend, as does the interpretation of the specific works selected, on a vision of the tradition's total structure.

Despite obvious disparities between the intentions and purposes of particular classic authors, the types of literary composition, and the circumstances of production, these works are approached at a level of abstraction suggesting that they may be understood as belonging to a common genre and concerned with a common set of problems or ideas (representation, freedom, authority, power, justice, obligation, etc.). The presumption is created that significant transitions can be charted by moving from paradigmatic figure to paradigmatic figure. It is suggested that these works may be fruitfully understood, quite literally, as the basic components of a continuing dialogue regarding the great perennial issues of politics and that the differences between these works may be conceived as innovations in the tradition and the similarities construed as continuities.[76]

Historians of political philosophy differ regarding the precise content, meaning, direction, and impact of the tradition. While individuals such as Dunning and Sabine saw a generally progressive development toward scientific knowledge and democracy, despite some aberrations, others, such as Strauss, Arendt, and Voegelin, agree that modernity, and its conception of science and politics, is the product of a tradition that has brought the West to a situation of social and intellectual crisis.[77] While the earlier writers explored a movement toward enlightenment, the latter are engaged in a study of the pathology of the tradition and in a historical subliming operation that seeks to locate the point of derailment in the tradition and to recapture a moment of truth in the past which provides the basis for a critical assessment of modernity and, possibly, an awareness that holds the promise of redemption. The specific intellectual grounds of these synoptic visions of the tradition may differ considerably, but, despite a common rejection of the philosophy of history characteristic of the nineteenth century as the apotheosis of the ideas that have precipitated the modern crisis, they all seem to reflect the structure of the historicist pattern of thought.

But whatever the genealogy of these visions may be, the myth of the tradition has contributed to the development of a dominant syndrome in the study of the history of political philosophy.

The 'tradition' is a retrospective analytical construction which produces a rationalized version of the past. It is a virtual tradition calculated to evoke a particular image of our collective public psyche and the political condition of our age, if not the human condition itself. It professes to tell us who we are and how we have arrived at our present situation. As in the case of Strauss's interpretation of Machiavelli, particular works are inevitably approached and understood largely in terms of their assigned role in this tradition and in terms of prior assumptions about the nature of political philosophy. In Strauss's scheme, and in most of the other analyses of this sort, political philosophy, as both action and product is an ideal typification based on an extrapolation from Greek political thought and general characteristics of the other classic works associated with the tradition. This model is reified and treated as if it were a historically delimited activity in which the individuals selected self-consciously engaged. Thus it becomes possible for 'historians' such as Strauss to speak of a beginning, inversion, end or 'death', and even a revival of the tradition and to advance what seem to be empirical, rather than merely analytical or categorical, claims about its structure and qualitative features. What emerges is a historical drama, but the import of any substantive version depends initially on the audience's predisposition to accept the tradition as a reality. Strauss consciously plays upon this predisposition, and much of what he has to say involves little more than subtle emendations to received opinion about Socrates and the origin of political philosophy in Greece, Machiavelli as the precursor of modern political science, and the division between ancient and modern thought.

I do not argue that this kind of exercise is illegitimate; however, sometimes those who engage in it may become captives of their own myth while others accept it without realizing its implications or the intentions of its creators. Those educated within the myth of the tradition and who assume that the primary purpose of interpreting a classical text in political philosophy is to illuminate a segment of the tradition, may be unaware of some of the more obvious methodological problems implicit in this approach.

To speak of political philosophy as a tradition begun by Socrates, transformed by Machiavelli, and atrophying in the modern age, or to postulate and characterize a modern political crisis in terms of a catalogue of 'isms' explained by the evolution of other 'isms', is to make reasonable critical discussion impossible. Strauss's description of both the current crisis and the intellectual forces which have produced it lacks contact with concrete events and involves a kind of abstraction which conflicts with his own insistence on confronting ideas on their own terms. He persistently conflates politics and political ideas, and sometimes treats political philosophers as if they were legislators for an age or the tradition and sometimes as if they were representatives of stages in the tradition. Strauss never specifies how individuals such as Machiavelli have effected the great impact on society that he attributes to them, and does not even suggest the evidence substantiating the causal connections between ideas and action to which he continuously alludes.

Similar difficulties are apparent in Strauss's approach to the interpretation of particular works. Although he repeatedly emphasizes the need to understand authors as they understood themselves and rejects those approaches that merely relate their thought to historical situations, he does not systematically confront the manifold problems of textual interpretation involving the relationship between text and context. Strauss approaches authors as having set out to write political philosophy as Strauss defines it and already counts them as participants in the alleged tradition. The substantive 'intention' (such as Machiavelli's intention to transform classical political philosophy or Hobbes's intention to ameliorate Machiavelli's teaching) which Strauss attributes to authors is often largely a function of the place Strauss assigns them in the reconstructed tradition rather than something clearly elicited from their work. Although Strauss enjoins interpreters to avoid, and claims that he avoids, 'extraneous information', 'modern hypotheses', and 'conventions' of scholarship and instead move entirely within the 'circle of ideas' of authors themselves,[78] it is difficult to see how Strauss carries out this programme, or given his preconception about the existence and character of the tradition and his instrumental concerns, could, even in principle, carry it out. The figures he selects to construct the tradition are simply already meaningful within the vision of the tradition he wishes to impart before he sets out interpreting their work.

Such difficulties characterize much of the literature on the history of political philosophy, but there may be limited relevance in emphasizing these problems. They are relevant only if we assume that the intentions defining the activity of individuals such as Strauss are what would commonly be termed 'historical' and 'exegetical'. What constitutes 'historicity' is a complex issue, but this issue may not be the proper context for a critical discussion of much of the secondary literature in this field.

It is indeed strange that Strauss's account of the tradition, with such features as his 'wave' metaphor describing the development of modern thought, seems to reflect the very historicism which he so vehemently repudiates. Once pieced together, it is apparent that his story of the decline of the West embodies an extravagant symbolism which plays, in part, upon various eschatological and prophetic motifs. Despite his stress on separating philosophy and history and distinguishing between interpretation and critique, in his approach, philosophical understanding of politics entirely depends on historical analysis, and interpretations of past thinkers are absolutely inseparable from his critique of the present. His condemnation of modernity involves an invocation of its origins and the revelation of a truth that lies buried in the past beneath the dross of the tradition. His assertion that historical investigation is merely a preliminary undertaking to the recovery of the true character of political philosophy and an unadulterated perception of political phenomena and political ends is difficult to accept when most of Strauss's scholarship consists of this type of investigation.

Perhaps he is simply unable to extricate himself from the very intellectual tendencies that he abhors, but it may be more reasonable to suggest that he consciously employs a 'historical' argument because he believes he must do so in an age in which only historical arguments carry meaning and authority. It requires very little effort to expose the 'methodological' difficulties that may arise from approaching the history of political philosophy from within the framework of the myth of the tradition, and it is more important to indicate how this virtual tradition provides a field of action for the therapeutically inclined historian and serves as a vehicle for his venture in the discovery of error and the recovery of truth.

Since the modern crisis is in large measure the result of historical thinking, Strauss suggests that there is 'no more appropriate way of combating this teaching than the study of history' and the employment of a 'historical form' of critique.[79] In one place, Strauss argues that 'only because public speech demands a mixture of seriousness and playfulness, can a true Platonist present the serious teaching, the philosophical teaching, in a historical and hence, playful garb'.[80] My concern is not to conjecture about Strauss's true teaching, but to note the rhetorical function of the myth of the tradition and the instrumental tasks served by this kind of argument. In Strauss's case, the account of the tradition may be employed as a correlate to a philosophical argument, or as a surrogate when discursive argument is inadequate, much as Plato employs mythohistorical tales in his dialogues. From another perspective, what Strauss is about may be likened to what Aristophanes is doing in the *Frogs* when lamenting the passing of tragedy and its role as the educator of society. Just as Aristophanes brings Aeschylus from the underworld to do battle with Euripides, a dramatic confrontation between the old and new teachers of the *polis*, Strauss descends into history to resurrect the ancients and confront the moderns. In both cases, the moderns, in the existential world, have won the *agon*, but, in the realm of the drama, the old teachings are vindicated.

Nothing has more obscured the meaning of many of the classic texts in political philosophy, and deflected attention away from the criteria for judging claims about such meaning, than the literature propagating the myth of the tradition and its historical etiology. I do not intend to imply that there are no historical connections between these texts or that there are no traditions of political thought, or even that there is no reasonable sense in which these works could be construed as comprising a tradition. But what has been taken to be *the* tradition is a piece of academic folklore. Even the term 'political philosophy' is problematic, since there is no greater interpretive prejudice than approaching these works as if they were philosophical exercises undertaken within the conventions of some particular ongoing activity. There are similarities between these works and similarities between the circumstances and concerns of their authors which justify comparison and generalization and an attempt to isolate them analytically and consider them as a type of literature which can be related to contemporary thought. But it is one thing to engage in a conversation with the past and quite another thing to stage a conversation with the past.

Notes

1. See Quentin Skinner, 'Meaning and Understanding in the History of Ideas', *History and Theory*, 8 (1969), pp. 3-53; and 'Some Problems in the Analysis of Political Thought and Action', *Political Theory*, 2 (August 1974), pp. 277-303. For critical discussions of Skinner's arguments and further analysis of these problems, see Richard Ashcraft, 'On the Problem of Methodology and the Nature of Political Theory', *Political Theory*, 3 (February 1975), pp. 5-25; Bhiku Parekh and R.N. Berki, 'The History of Political Ideas: a Critique of Q. Skinner's Methodology', *Journal of History of Ideas*, 34 (1973), pp. 163-84; Margaret Leslie, 'In Defense of Anachronism', *Political Studies*, 4 (1970), pp. 433-47; J.G.A. Pocock, *Politics, Language, and Time* (New York: Atheneum, 1971); Gordon Schochet, 'Quentin Skinner's Method', *Political Theory*, 2 (August

1974), pp. 261-76; Charles Tarlton, 'Historicity, Meaning and Revisionism in the Study of Political Thought', *History and Theory*, 12 (1973), pp. 307-28.

Despite the importance of the issues raised, these studies, for the most part, do not explore the intentions of the historian of political theory, and they assume that his endeavour can be comprehended and evaluated as a species of intellectual history. For a discussion of these problems as well as an analysis of other secondary literature on the history of poltical theory, see John G. Gunnell, *Political Theory: Tradition and Interpretation* (Cambridge: Winthrop, 1978).

2. Leo Strauss, *The City and Man* (Chicago:Rand McNally, 1964), p. 1.

3. Leo Strauss, *The City and Man*, pp. 2-3.

4. Ibid., p. 3.

5. Leo Strauss, 'Political Philosophy and the Crisis of our Time', in *The Post-Behavioral Era*, eds. George J. Graham, Jr and George W. Carey (New York: David McKay, 1972),p. 242.

6. Leo Strauss, 'Relativism', in *Relativism and the Study of Man*, eds., Helmut Shoeck and James W. Wiggins (Princeton: D.Van Nostrand, 1961), p. 140.

7. Leo Strauss, *Natural Right and History* (Chicago: University of Chicago Press, 1953), pp. 5-6.

8. 'Political Philosophy and the Crisis of Our Time', pp. 217-18.

9. 'Political Philosophy and the Crisis of Our Time', p. 217.

10. Leo Strauss, *On Tyranny* (Glencoe: Free Press, 1963), pp. 26-7.

11. 'Political Philosophy and the Crisis of Our Time', p. 218; *The City and Man*, p. 2.

12. Leo Strauss, *What is Political Philosophy?* (Glencoe: Free Press, 1959), pp. 11-12.

13. Ibid., pp. 12-13, 17.

14. Leo Strauss, 'Introduction', in *History of Poltical Philosophy*, eds., Leo Strauss and Joseph Cropsey (Chicago: Rand McNally, 1963), p. 2; Leo Strauss, *Socrates and Aristophanes* (New York: Basic Books, 1960), p. 3.

15. *What is Political Philosophy?*, p. 18.

16. *Natural Right and History*, pp. 2-3, 5; Leo Strauss, 'Social Science and Humanism', in *The State of the Social Sciences*, ed., Leonard D. White (Chicago: University of Chicago Press, 1956), p. 422.

17. *Natural Right and History*, p. 4.

18. *What is Political Philosophy?*, pp. 25-26, 57.

19. *Natural Right and History*, pp. 18-19.

20. 'Social Science and Humanism', p. 418.

21. *What is Political Philosophy?*, p. 20.

22. Leo Strauss, 'Epilogue', in *Essays on the Scientific Study of Politics*, ed., Herbert J. Storing (New York: Holt, Rinehart and Winston, 1962), p. 307.

23. Ibid., p. 307.

24. Ibid., pp. 322-26.

25. Leo Strauss, 'Epilogue', pp. 319, 326.

26. Ibid., p. 327.

27. *On Tyranny*, p. 22.

28. 'Epilogue', p. 327.

29. *Natural Right and History*, p. 7.

30. *The City and Man*, pp. 7-8.

31. *What is Political Philosophy?*, p. 56.

32. *What is Political Philosophy?*, p. 57.

33. Ibid., p. 59.

34. *The City and Man*, p. 11.

35. Ibid., p. 8.

36. *The City and Man*, p. 9.

37. Ibid., p. 9.

254   *The Myth of the Tradition*

38. *On Tyranny*, p. 24; *What is Political Philosophy?*, p. 67.
39. *On Tyranny*, p. 24.
40. Ibid., p. 24.
41. *What is Political Philosophy?*, p. 66; Leo Strauss, 'On a New Interpretation of Plato's Political Philosophy', *Social Research*, 13 (1946), pp. 332.
42. *What is Political Philosophy?*, p. 77.
43. 'Political Philosophy and the Crisis of Our Time', p. 218.
44. 'Introduction', p. 2.
45. *The City and Man*, p. 10; 'Epilogue', p. 313.
46. *What is Political Philosophy?*, pp. 68, 69.
47. *The City and Man*, p. 9.
48. 'Political Philosophy and the Crisis of Our Time', pp. 217-18.
49. *What is Political Philosophy?*, p. 172.
50. Ibid., p. 74.
51. *What is Political Philosophy?*, p. 27.
52. Ibid., p. 28.
53. 'Social Science and Humanism', p. 417.
54. *What is Political Philosophy?*, p. 75.
55. *What is Political Philosophy?*, p. 75.
56. *The City and Man*, p. 12.
57. *What is Political Philosophy?*, p. 40.
58. Ibid., p. 40.
59. *On Tyranny*, p. 23.
60. *What is Political Philosophy?*, p. 40.
61. *On Tyranny*, pp. 110-11.
62. *What is Political Philosophy?*, p. 41; Leo Strauss, *Thoughts on Machiavelli* (Glencoe: Free Press, 1958), pp. 9, 13.
63. *What is Political Philosophy?*, p. 43.
64. *Thoughts on Machiavelli*, p. 12.
65. *What is Political Philosophy?*, p. 43.
66. Ibid., p. 41.
67. Ibid., p. 47.
68. Ibid., p. 172; Leo Strauss, *Spinoza's Critique of Religion* (New York: Schocken Books, 1965), p. 338.
69. *What is Political Philosophy?*, pp. 47-8.
70. Ibid., p. 49.
71. *What is Political Philosophy?*, p. 50.
72. Ibid., p. 51.
73. 'Relativism', p. 515; *What is Political Philosophy?*, pp. 54-5; *Spinoza's Critique of Religion*, p. 12.
74. Leo Strauss, *Liberalism, Ancient and Modern* (New York: Basic Books, 1968), p. viii; Leo Strauss, *Persecution and the Art of Writing* (Glencoe: Free Press, 1952), p. 37.
75. *Persecution and the Art of Writing*, p. 21.
76. Cf. Pocock, *Politics, Language, and Time*, pp. 4-5.
77. See, for example, Eric Voegelin, *The New Science of Politics* (Chicago: University of Chicago Press, 1952) and *Science, Politics, and Gnosticism* (Chicago: Regnery, 1968); Hannah Arendt, *The Human Condition* (Chicago: University of Chicago Press, 1958), and *Between Past and Future* (New York: Viking, 1968).
78. *On Tyranny*, p. 25.
79. *On Tyranny*, p. 27.
80. Leo Strauss, 'Farabi's Plato', in *Louis Ginsberg Jubilee Volume* (New York: The American Academy for Jewish Research, 1945), pp. 376-7.

Source

John G. Gunnell, 'The Myth of the Tradition', *American Political Science Review* vol. 72, no. 1 (1978), pp. 122-34.

PART SIX

SKINNER

11 CONVENTIONS AND THE UNDERSTANDING OF SPEECH ACTS

Quentin Skinner

The following argument[1] provides an instance, for the case of J.L. Austin's work in *How to do things with Words*,[2] of what Austin himself called the law of diminishing fleas. This represents, however, an unintended although unavoidable consequence of the argument rather that its intended effect. The actual intention is first to focus on the doubts Austin himself expressed about his central theory concerning the illocutionary force of utterances; next to consider the attempts which have subsequently been made to resolve these doubts by more extended analysis; next to suggest certain tentative doubts about these resolutions of Austin's doubts; and finally, even more tentatively, to suggest a different form of resolution.

1

Austin's original suggestion (p.98) that every serious utterance has some particular illocutionary force co-ordinate with its ordinary meaning as a locution provided the centre-point of the classificatory scheme developed in *How to do things with Words*. Yet the theory, by Austin's own admission, remains incomplete in two crucial respects. First, Austin treated it as essential (p. 116) to the achievement of any given illocutionary act that the intended force of the speaker's (S's) utterance should secure 'uptake' from A, his audience. But Austin himself provided no analysis of the conditions necessary for such an act of communication to be performed, and so no account of what is involved in A's successful uptake and understanding of S's utterance and its intended illocutionary force. Secondly, Austin was particularly concerned to distinguish what he designated (p. 101) the 'perlocutionary' act a speaker might intend to perform (the act, that is, of achieving a certain effect or response from his audience *by* speaking) from the illocutionary act performed *in* speaking with a certain force. But this suggested distinction in terms of 'in' and 'by' (p. 121) retains a rather intuitive and preliminary air, and remains inadequate, as Austin acknow-

259

ledged, in two essential respects. It does not invariably provide a test for distinguishing illocutionary from perlocutionary acts. And it does not provide a test at all for distinguishing acts which are genuinely illocutionary from what Austin perceived (p. 121) to be 'another whole range' of things ('expressive' and 'non-literal' as well as 'non-serious' things) which we might be doing in using words.

It seems important to devote some further attention to these lacunae: not only because they are there, but also because Austin's failure to clarify these issues has already given rise to considerable confusion in the literature derived from his analysis. The attempt by Professor Forguson, for example, to vindicate Austin's 'consideration of the force of utterances' turns on the claim (following up one of Austin's own examples) that 'I can express anger, surprise, terror; I can warn you, accuse you of laxity, inform you, and any number of other things, all in saying merely "There's a bull in the field".[3] Now this is doubtless true, but as an exposition of Austin's theory the claim merely seems to rest on and perpetuate the failure to distinguish genuine illocutions from the range of other linguistic acts. Even if the test of applying an explicit performative prefix can be regarded (as Forguson here assumes) as reliable in itself (which there is good reason to doubt), there seems to be a further difficulty about applying it in several of these cases. For while some of the acts cited here are clearly illocutionary, in other cases (such as the expression of anger, surprise or terror) there seems to be no sense at all in which the addition of the prefatory 'I am angry that . . . ' and so on makes *explicit* what I was *doing in* saying 'there's a bull in the field' in the way that Austin's theory requires. A similar confusion appears to mark Professor Alston's suggestion that a 'crucial test' for 'deciding in a particular case what linguistic act has been performed' should consist of seeing what 'retorts, cavils, criticisms, complaints' would be accepted as relevant by the speaker.[4] Quite apart from the fact (which I hope to demonstrate) that the chosen paradigm of a communication situation has certain helpfully oversimplified features, it has not been made clear how this test can be applied to reveal specifically *illocutionary* acts. The retort offered by A to S might for example merely be 'Are you trying to make a fool of me?' (which points to a non-serious non-illocutionary act – perhaps joking); or 'What are you driving at?' (which points to a non-literal non-illocutionary act – perhaps insinuation); or 'Are you really telling me or just showing off?' (which points to an expressive non-illocutionary act). Whatever the merits of the 'retort' test, therefore (and it was originally suggested by Austin himself, p. 28), it still appears to rest on and to perpetuate the same lack of proper distinction between genuine illocutions and the other whole range (still to be analysed) of things one might be doing in using words.

One very important attempt has, however, been made, by Professor Strawson, to overcome these confusions and in effect to fill in both the lacunae left in Austin's account.[5] Strawson's procedure is to set out the conditions sufficient or at least necessary for the uptake of specifically illocutionary acts, and thus to establish the means of distinguishing them both from perlocutionary acts and from the range of other things one may do with words. This procedure itself is in turn established by adapting and extending H. P. Grice's doctrine concerning the 'non-natural' meaning of utterances[6] into a set of conditions for the performance and understanding of an act of communication, and so for the attainment of uptake by A of what S *meant* by his utterance.

Before considering this most original and important attempt to criticize and extend Austin's general theory it is worth pausing to neutralize one possible source of doubt about the status of Strawson's model itself. For it has recently been insisted by Professor Ziff that Grice's original dicussion of meaning was mistaken in failing to distinguish between 'what S meant by his utterance' and 'what S meant by uttering his utterance'.[7] It seems well worth adopting this distinction. But this is not because it seems to cast any doubt on Strawson's model for the understanding of utterances. For there seems no reason why the model should not be adapted to deal with the utterance of utterances, rather than merely their alleged non-natural meaning, if such a refinement seems desirable. (I shall therefore adopt this alteration in what follows.) The reason for stressing the distinction is rather that it can be used to cast doubt on the value of the scepticism which has recently been expressed by Mr Cohen about the 'existence' of any forces of utterances separable from their meanings.[8] The only sense, Cohen insists, which can be given to the concept of illocutions is that they represent a special form or aspect of the meanings of utterances: they cannot have the sense – which it was Austin's whole point. to give them – of a special type of force co-ordinate with meaning. If Ziff's suggested distinction is valid, however, we can imagine a limiting case in which S could mean something by uttering his utterance (it could have illocutionary force) even though the utterance (although uttered to gain a seriously-intended effect or response) had no meaning in itself at all. Children and Members of Parliament, for example, conventionally register their objections to unduly evasive or sententious utterances by means of a range of locutions the utterance of which is accepted as having a quite clear significance or non-natural meaning, even though the utterances themselves, while they thereby have a particular force, have no meaning as locutions at all. Here then is at least one type of case in which it cannot be true that the force of an utterance is merely an aspect or part of its meaning. Cohen's somewhat sensational scepticism, therefore, is perhaps not entirely well-founded. In any case, I think we may legitimately proceed.

It is clear that Strawson's model of an act of communication is of the greatest value in removing both the remaining sources of confusion in Austin's theory. Strawson's suggestion is that A's uptake of the force of S's utterance is necessarily a matter of A's understanding a complex and 'essentially avowable' intention on S's part. He thus provides the required defining characteristic of all illocutionary acts. At the same time he provides a test for excluding from the status of genuine illocutionary acts the range of other things (which had puzzled Austin) which we can do with words. For no act can be illocutionary which is not a 'wholly overt' and 'essentially avowable' act of communication. These conclusions, however, are left subject by Strawson himself to at least two reservations. The first is only a detail, though important: the question of whether it is a strictly necessary condition of a verb's being the name of a genuine illocutionary act that the necessary 'avowal' should be capable of being performed by means of what Austin called the verb's explicit performative form. Austin cannot be held to have pronounced decisively on this point. At one moment (p. 103) the condition seems to be thought necessary; but elsewhere it is merely said to be highly characteristic, and 'pretty close' (p. 130) to a necessary condition. Stawson deliberately leaves the issue open, saying only that it seems 'a sufficient, though not, I think, a necessary condition' (p. 441), even though there is undoubtedly a 'general possibility and utility' (p. 452) of avowal by this means. Strawson's second reservation is more general. He applies his model of understanding only to what he regards as the two standard cases of illocutionary acts: the case of convention or rule-governed utterances of the type to which Austin devoted his exclusive attention; and the case of more ordinary and non-conventional utterances which Austin ignored and which it is Strawson's whole point to emphasize. At the end, however, he then insists that 'there is something misleading about the sharpness of this contrast' (p. 460), and that further studies of linguistic communication should expect to uncover qualifications and intermediate cases. As my present argument is intended as one such further study, it will be most convenient to proceed by focusing first on these two points of uncertainty which

Strawson has indicated but left unresolved.

2

First I take up the suggestion that there may be types of illocutionary act different from the two standard cases with which Strawson is concerned and in some way intermediate between them. There seems to be some evidence in favour of such a belief. For there is no doubt that there may be cases (at least in the usages of polite society) in which S performs an illocutionary act in uttering some utterance to A and yet performs the necessary act of communication in some oblique way. There may thus be cases (to state them in Strawson's terms) in which there may be a possibility and yet *no* utility attached to making explicit the intended force of the communication by means of the performative formula. The most obvious occasions for these (actually very familiar) usages are those in which some advice, or warning, or direction, has to be issued by S to A, but in which there is a premium on achieving this 'exercitive' communication (in Austinian parlance) with as much finesse as possible.

Consider the following examples, all of which appear to fall under such a description (they could obviously and easily be indefinitely extended):

   (i)   'I wonder if you would mind accompanying me to the police station, sir?'
  (ii)   'It would be appreciated if this account could now be settled as soon as convenient.'
 (iii)   'The manager feels you may wish to know you are now overdrawn on your current account.'
 (iv)   'Do come upstairs and let me show you my etchings.'

There seems no doubt that example (i) has the evident form and illocutionary force of enquiring; (ii) of assuring; (iii) of telling; and (iv) of inviting. And yet it is surely accepted (by some process which it becomes our business to explain) that despite such appearances the real force of (i) is at the very least that of a request, and probably an order; (ii) is at least a directive and probably a threat; (iii) is a warning or at least a caution; and (iv) is (or at least once was) notoriously not just an invitation but a proposition or enquiry with a special (not merely aesthetic but also sexual) point. All these examples thus appear to be cases of illocutionary acts in which the primary intention, although fully intended to be understood and not merely suspected, is nevertheless not explicitly avowed. This does not mean, of course, that it is actually impossible to avow the real force of such utterances. There is certainly no difficulty about adding what Strawson has called a 'subjoined quasi-comment' to clarify the precise nature of the intended act of communication. Example (i) could thus be made explicit, for instance, as 'I wonder if you would mind accompanying me to the police-station, sir — I'm afraid I really must request you to do so.' The peculiarity here, however, is that the motive which S has in all standard cases for making his intentions as clear as possible seems in this type of case at least to some extent to be dissipated. Something seems to be lost rather than gained in these forms of communication if the speaker elects to make his intentions absolutely explicit by some performative formula.

Next I take up the more specific question left unresolved by Strawson's (and Austin's) account, the question of whether it is a necessary condition of a verb's being the name of a genuine illocutionary act that it should have an explicit performative form. Here I advance an argument complementary to, but stronger than, the one above. I have suggested that there may be illocutionary acts in which, while there is a possibility, there is *no* utility attached to the use of the performative. I now wish to suggest that there are indeed verbs for which, while they name genuine illocutionary acts, there is no *possibility* of avowal by means of an explicit performative at all.

Consider the following lists of verbs, all of which appear to fall under this description (the groupings are clearly intuitive, but I think intuitively clear):

(A)	(i)	patronize	(ii)	sneer	(iii)	court
		flatter		scoff		flirt
		propitiate		gloat		entice
		conciliate		flaunt		lure
		coax		abuse		beguile
		cajole		snub/rebuff		
		bully/browbeat		taunt/tease		
				mock/scorn		
(B)	(i)	allude	(ii)	ignore		
		indicate		gloss over		
		adumbrate		cut dead		

Various strategies owed to Austin himself might now be used to cast

doubt on the status claimed for these lists, or at least to whittle down
their numbers. It might be objected that several of these acts are not, in
their standard form, performed verbally at all. This might at least cause
'ignoring' and 'cutting dead' to be crossed off. It is true that Austin
himself does not seem to have regarded this as a real objection. He
points out (p. 118) that certain illocutionary acts can be performed by
non-verbal means, and even seems to believe that certain forms of
invariably non-verbal communication can nevertheless be the names of
genuine illocutionary acts. Austin's own example (p. 118) is 'cocking a
snook' by way of protest (though the experts assure us this act is no
longer performed). But if this is allowable there seem no grounds at
least for excluding 'cutting dead', which indeed looks very similar (and
is undoubtedly still performed). There still seems to be a good case,
however, for allowing this (not very important) objection to stand, not
only in order to restrict the discussion to locutions, but also because
Austin's own failure to do so at this point suggests a certain confusion.
He may only have intended to point out that a non-verbal warning, for
example, is still the name of an illocutionary act, in the sense that there
is a standard case in which to warn is to speak with a certain illocutionary force. If he intended the further claim, however, that there can be
genuine illocutionary acts which *never* involve the use of words, it is
not clear how this squares with the stated intention (pp. 91 and 94) of
concentrating on the relations between *saying* something' and the illocutionary force of such *utterances*.

A second and more fruitful objection might be that several of the
acts mentioned in these lists have got tangled up in the confusion which
Austin (p. 109) mainly anticipated in the use of his scheme — the confusion between illocutionary and perlocutionary acts. And such a suspicion might well seem to be verified by a consideration of at least
the following pairs of verbs: the cases of conciliating and coaxing, and
of luring and beguiling. We should normally say that S conciliated or
beguiled A *by* saying something, and we should perhaps treat these
two cases as examples of bringing it about *by* saying something that
something else (an effect or response) happened — that A was in fact
conciliated or beguiled. Nevertheless, there still seems to be some
sense, if not so surely with conciliating or beguiling, at least with
coaxing and luring, in which we may decide whether S was in fact performing these acts without touching on the question of any perlocutionary effect. (It may still be true, for example, that I am coaxing you
in what I say, and that this is the intended force of my utterance, even
if you are not in fact coaxed by what I say.) And this would seem to

rescue even these doubtful cases for the status of genuine illocutionary acts. Even if it still seems plausible, however, to reserve some doubt in these cases, this hardly seems necessary with any of the other verbs listed. A convenient and important means of corroborating this claim is provided by contrasting these verbs with the case of 'insulting', an act over whose direction Austin frequently (pp. 31, 65, 68) expressed some doubt. The act of S insulting A looks very close, in particular, to several of the acts named in list (A) (ii) above. The point of the contrast, however, is that it seems to place the case of insulting in an almost wholly perlocutionary light, whilst this scarcely seems to happen at all with any of these verbs, such as the cases of S abusing or snubbing or rebuffing A. The question, in the first place, of whether I am snubbing or rebuffing you in saying what I say is obviously a question essentially for the speaker to answer, in a way that hardly seems to hold with the more perlocutionary question of whether I am causing you to feel insulted. (I may seek to insult you, in short, and *only* succeed in amusing you: but if I snub you I do snub you, whatever else happens.) And in the second place, as Austin insisted (p. 109), we must always 'distinguish consequences'. An insult seems to be a consequence, in the sense that it is an effect of what I say. But a snub or a rebuff and so on are quite clearly not effects of anything said, but things which I do *in* saying things. Nor do these cases seem to be assimilable to that of 'implying to be a clever effect', which is how Austin at one point (p. 105) rather oddly classifies the case of 'insinuating'.[9] For we must distinguish effects of speaking from speaking for effect: the former is obviously a perlocutionary matter, but the latter (even if not illocutionary) is not.

The most important means of objecting, however, to the status claimed for these verbs would be to question whether they do in fact name acts of full and intended communication in the manner required by Strawson's model for the uptake of specifically illocutionary acts. And if we try to locate lists (A) and (B) on the map proposed by Austin (p. 150) for classifying types of illocutionary act, the suspicion may well appear valid. For while the verbs in list (A) look quite like 'behabitives' and those in list (B) quite like 'expositives', both the lists look much closer respectively to the dimensions of 'expressive' and 'non-literal' usage which were intuitively marked off from illocutions by Austin, and which Strawson's model can be used to distinguish from illocutionary acts.

It is my central contention, however, that if we now feed any of these verbs through Strawson's intentionalist model they do all emerge with the required status of fully-intended acts of communication, and of genuine illocutionary acts. None of them seems to fail in any of the ways that 'expressive' usages (here the example Austin gave, and to which Strawson applies his model, is 'showing off') or 'non-literal' usages (here the example which has been considered is 'insinuating') have been shown to fail as genuine illocutionary acts.

Consider first some examples from list (A), the near-expressive candidates for the status of illocutionary acts. To be very draconic, one might insist for a start on excluding cases such as S cajoling A, on the grounds (as with showing off) that S's success will depend on A *not* seeing that this is S's intention in uttering his utterance. But even here it seems doubtful if this is necessary, while in other cases — for example S flattering or patronizing A — there seems no difficulty at all about accommodating these acts to Strawson's model. If S utters some utterance to A with the intended force of flattery or patronage, it is clear in the first place that S must have a primary intention to gain a particular effect or (as Strawson marginally prefers to put it) to evoke a particular response by means of speaking in this way. Such a response will normally be cognitive as well as affective — S might be said to intend (say, in the case of patronizing) that A should feel insulted, or merely insignificant, or both. It is clear, in any case, that S (to follow Strawson's notation) fulfils the first requirement of the model, by having the primary intention (i_1) of intending to evoke a particular response. But it also seems clear that S fulfils the second condition by having the further intention that this intention should be recognized. For if A is to gain uptake in the manner sought by S there must be an intention (i_2) on S's part that A should recognize his primary intention as being the intention to offer, say, an insult. It follows from this, moreover, that S must have the further required intention (i_3) that A's recognition of his primary intention (i_1) should certainly function as part at least of the reason for A's response. It may happen, of course, that A fails to grasp S's primary intention, in which case this further intention (i_3) will necessarily be frustrated. But this is only to say that A has failed to gain uptake, a shock to which all illocutionary acts are obviously and equally heir. Finally, there seems no doubt with any of these examples that S has the further required intention (i_4) that all his intentions should be recognized. There is no intention (as with showing off) that the means to evoke the intended response should not be recognized: such partial communication would positively destroy any primary intention, say, to flatter or patronize A. And there is no intention (as with insinuating) that the intention to evoke the intended response should only be suspected: such equivocation would entail that A could only suspect S's intention, say, to patronize or flatter — a different response, though one which it is of course perfectly possible to intend to evoke. The verbs in list (A), in short, appear to apply to situations in which the speaker intends both that it should be firmly understood that he feels himself to be in a particular relation to his audience and that this intention itself should also be firmly understood. It might be objected, of course, that S could intend, say, to patronize A without caring whether the intended effect is understood by A at all. But this seems sufficiently met by the stipulation that uptake is required — that the acts in question should be intended acts of communication. And there is no doubt that there is at least a standard case in which S intends his act of patronage to be fully understood. In this type of case, moreover, S will want to find means (to put the point colloquially) by which he can make A grasp that he intends to evoke a particular response. He has indeed the standard motive for doing so. There is thus an overall intention to be understood of exactly the character required by Strawson's model for a full act of communication.

Consider next some examples from list (B), the near-non-literal candidates for the status of illocutionary acts. Again, to be draconic one might insist for a start at least on excluding the case of S adumbrating something to A, on the grounds (as with insinuating) that S's success will depend on A merely suspecting the intention to evoke a particular response. Such cases at least seem to come very close to a whole group of verbs which (as Austin noted) are concerned basically with innuendo, and so with conveying something 'essentially different' from at least the standard types of illocutionary act. (At one point (p. 75) Austin gives a list of them: evincing, intimating, insinuating, giving to understand, enabling to infer, conveying, expressing — to which one might add giving an inkling of, hinting at, and so on.) It may be that the whole of list (B) ought after all to be assimilated to this non-literal dimension of things we can be doing in using words. There is, moreover, another possible objection to list (B) — which does not seem to infect list (A) at all — the objection that for S to avow what he is doing in such cases is not to make explicit but merely to describe what he is doing. There is undoubtedly a real difficulty in handling Austin's theory at this point (as he admitted himself, pp. 69-70), and it might be held in particular to infect such examples as the case of S alluding in uttering an utterance to A.

The verbs on list (B), then, do present special difficulties. Nevertheless, they do still seem to be the names of acts of communication. There is no doubt, for example, that S in uttering a given utterance to A might intend it to be understood that he intends an allusion to be understood. And if this is so it would seem to make sense to say that S in such a case has both the required primary intention (i_1) to evoke a particular (cognitive) response and the further intention (i_2) that this intention should be recognized. Again, it would then follow that S must also intend (i_3) that A's recognition of this primary intention (i_1) to evoke a given response should at least contribute to the reason for A's response. And here it does seem possible to insist that such cases are separable from cases such as insinuating. It is not S's intention that A should merely suspect, say, his intention to make an allusion, for unless A firmly grasps that this is in fact S's complex intention, his primary intention will remain unfulfilled. Finally, it again seems clear that S in such cases does have the further required intention (i_4) that all his intentions should be fully understood. In this type of case, in fact, S will typically try (to put the point colloquially again) to make A see that he is trying to make A see that he is trying to gain some response from A by his intention, say, to allude to something (or to ignore, gloss over, and so on). There is again an overall intention on S's part to be understood in all the ways set out in Strawson's model for the performance of a full act of communication.

Even if each of the preliminary doubts and objections I have raised should prove well-founded, we are still left with a score or more verbs from the lists above which appear to be the names of genuine illocutionary acts. (And this is to provide, in an Austinian phrase, no more than a preliminary flounder around the relevant area.) But in none of these cases— and this is their significance — do the apparently genuine acts of communication performed with these verbs seem capable of any explicit avowal by the standard means of reduction to the performative formula. A final doubt might of course be expressed about this claim. For there seems no difficulty at least about avowing that 'I scoff at that' or 'I'm only teasing you'. Yet even in these cases there does seem to be something paradoxical about adding such avowals: their addition seems to serve not merely to make explicit the basic utterance, but also — or rather — to suggest that there must already be some hitch in the intended act of communication for such an added avowal to become necessary. And with most of the verbs listed this paradox comes out even more decisively. This is not to say, of course, that with such verbs it becomes literally impossible to avow what one is doing. For it is *possible*, after all, even to avow that one is making a joke. (Mr

Pooter is the immortal example.) And it is not just that the performative formula in such cases would normally be very awkward and incapable of reduction to the standard form 'I x that . . . ', where x is a performative verb. For this difficulty in fact arises (although Cohen in particular seems to ignore its implications) with nearly half the performative verbs set out by Austin himself in his final lists. The difficulty and the paradox lie rather in the fact that the process of making the intention explicit, in the case of the verbs in lists (A) and (B), actually seems to defeat the intention itself. List (B), if allowable, brings this out particularly well. To avow that in uttering utterance x one is alluding to or glossing over something certainly appears to make explicit the intended force of uttering utterance x. But to avow of one's utterance that it *is* an allusion must strictly speaking be a paradox in much the same way that it is paradoxical to avow of one's utterance that it is a lie.[10] And to 'subjoin' the comment that in uttering one's previous utterance one *was* alluding is no longer to allude but to mention or refer, just as to avow that one was glossing over is no longer to gloss over but to notice or point out. List (A) brings out much the same paradox. For there simply is something irreducibly odd about avowing that 'I hereby flatter you, patronize you', and so on. It seems indispensable to the nature of the intended act of communication in all such cases that it should be achieved without having in this way to be avowed. To avow, in fact, that I do intend in what I say to flatter, patronize and so on, may well be to make explicit what I am doing, but it equally suggests that I have already in some way failed to do it. This even seems to be so in the doubtful case of S teasing A. If A fails to grasp that this is S's primary intention in uttering his utterance, any response he makes is likely to be quite inappropriate. If S feels the need, however, to guard against such failure of uptake by making an explicit avowal of his primary intention, the point of uttering his utterance would seem *thereby* to be more or less negated. The act of avowal, in all these cases, seems not (as in the standard case) to underpin, but actually to undermine, the intended act of communication.

3

I have now attempted to analyse two non-standard types of linguistic acts of communication: the case of the oblique and the case of the non-avowable illocutionary act. As already hinted, these examples can now be used to help decide on the two questions left unresolved in Strawson's account. The cases of oblique acts of communication indicate the existence of at least one 'intermediate' type of illocutionary act. And the lists of verbs naming non-avowable acts of communication indicate that it cannot be a necessary condition of a verb's being the name of an illocutionary act that it should have an explicit performative form. The next and more important question must be to ask whether these points carry implications of any more general significance for Strawson's analysis of uptake and Austin's general theory of illocutionary force. I shall argue that two such implications can in fact be pursued.

First, the existence of these non-standard illocutionary forms provides a special — and I think decisive — means of combatting the scepticism Cohen has expressed about the distinction between illocutionary force and meaning. On the one hand Cohen would seem to be committed to insisting (to take his own example) that it must still be as part of the meaning of the utterance 'Your haystack is on fire' that it can be used, say, not to warn but merely (by means of the oblique form of communication I have discussed) to taunt you, or gloat over you, and so on. But while the force of warning, which has an obvious performative form, looks quite plausibly part of the meaning of the basic utterance, it seems very odd to suggest that it is in virtue of its meaning that it can equally have the oblique but no less intended (and intended to be understood) force of taunting or gloating over your misfortune. And on the other hand Cohen would seem to be committed to insisting that it must equally be as part of the meaning of, say, the request 'Do come upstairs and let me show you my etchings' that it has its notoriously specific force. But this same invitation can also be uttered with complete innocence, or even as a joke about the fact that it is not usually uttered with complete innocence. The first of these cases yields a quite different illocutionary act; the second does not seem to yield an illoctuionary act at all. (The joking man, that is, may be speaking with a given illocutionary force: but joking in itself is not, I think, an illocutionary act.) If Cohen were right, it would have to be as part of the meaning of the basic utterance that it can be both an innocent and a less innocent invitation as well as a parody of either. Again, it is hard to see how the concept of meaning can be made to bear so much weight.

The other and much more important implication is that Strawson, in setting out his model of the conditions necessary for the understanding of an act of verbal communication, has committed himself to two general conclusions, both of which now appear to be wrong. The first is

Strawson's conclusion (p. 454) that 'an essential feature of the intentions which make up the illocutionary complex is their overtness. They have, one might say, essential avowability'. Strawson's most general claim, in fact, is (p. 456) that 'the notion of wholly overt or essentially avowable intention plays an essential part' in any illocutionary act of communication. Now Strawson shows that the type of intention at least necessary for the performance of such acts is of the complex kind set out in the adaptation of Grice's model. It would seem to follow, then, that for S to have such an intention is for S both to be performing an illocutionary act and to have an intention which is essentially avowable by some means, and standardly by the use of an explicit performative. Yet this does not seem to be the case. For in both the types of example I have considered, S's intention appears to pass all the tests for being intended to be understood and yet remains in all cases essentially non-avowable.

The second doubt arises over the whole question (central to Strawson's critique) of whether Austin was correct in speaking of illocutionary acts as being acts 'done as conforming to a convention' (p. 105). Against this assumption Strawson makes two points. First, he claims, 'the doctrine of the conventional nature of the illocutionary act does not hold generally' (p. 445). For 'surely there may be cases in which to utter the words "The ice over there is very thin" to a skater is to issue a warning (is to say something with the *force* of a warning) without its being the case that there is any statable convention at all (other than those which bear on the nature of the *locutionary* act) such that the speaker's act can be said to be an act done as conforming to that convention' (p. 444). This leads on to Strawson's second point, that to treat illocutionary acts as conventional is in effect to concentrate only on one type, in which 'the act is identified as the act it is just because it is performed by the utterance of a form of words conventional for the performance of that act' (p. 458). Strawson is thus essentially concerned to insist on a distinction between these fully conventional types of illocutionary act 'belonging to convention-constituted procedures' (p. 459), and other *non*-conventional types of illocutionary act 'in which it is not as conforming to an accepted *convention* of any kind (other than those linguistic conventions which help to fix the meaning of the utterance) that an illocutionary act is performed' (p. 443).

It is at this point that the two non-standard illocutionary forms with which I have been concerned appear to present a difficulty. Neither appears to be assimilable at all to those rule-governed situations (such as games) which Strawson treats as the standard form of 'conventional' illocutionary acts. And yet both seem to presuppose the presence of some element of convention much stronger than Strawson allows for in his discussion of 'non-conventional' illocutionary acts. If there can be situations, for example, in which S can make an enquiry and yet validly intend to communicate — and successfully be understood to have intended to communicate — an order, or in which S can similarly make a statement and successfully communicate a threat, it would seem that the success of such acts of communication must to a considerable extent be dependent on the conventions governing what counts as ordering, threatening, and so on, in such a (polite) society. Similarly, if it is possible to understand that S intends, and intends you to understand, that he is patronizing or flattering you in what he says, and yet it is possible (even essential) to grasp this intention without there being any explicit avowal of it on S's part, it would seem again that the success of such acts of communication must at least to a similar extent depend on the existence of conventions governing what counts in that particular situation as a case of flattery, patronage, and so on. In both cases in short, some fairly extensive awareness of social as well as linguistic conventions seems indispensably necessary for the successful uptake of such illocutionary acts.

Some caution, however, must be exercised in trying to determine what, if anything, should be made of this point. For there seems no doubt that Strawson has established a genuine and important distinction between conventional and non-conventional illocutionary acts, which Austin (and his followers) can be shown to have missed. The distinction, that is, not only seems valid but has considerable critical purchase. It can be used in particular to dismiss the recent suggestion (by Professor Sesonske) that the defining characteristic of a performative utterance must be that it is 'an utterance whose point is to alter formal relations', where these are defined as situations in which the range of possible responses is convention-determined, in contrast to 'psychological' relations (concerned with bringing about a change in attitude) and 'generative' relations (in which the speech act is intended to bring about an action).[11] It has been alleged (by Sesonske himself) that this typology succeeds where Austin himself failed in isolating the special feature of all performative utterances. And these distinctions have since been hailed as 'a major development in our appreciation of performatives'.[12] It is evident, however, that this 'new definition' of performatives merely restates the mistake which Austin made and which Strawson's distinction serves to point out. If I warn you by issuing the explicit performative utterance 'I warn you that the ice over there is very thin', it need never be the case either that this is a warning done as conforming to a convention in Austin's sense, or that there is any formal relation concerned with or altered by the utterance. Indeed, in so far as the suggested new definition and typology apply in this case at all, the warning would appear to be an instance of an utterance designed to affect a 'generative' relationship: part of S's primary intention in issuing the warning is to get A to perform an (avoiding) action.

If Strawson's distinction, then, between intentions and conventions in speech acts is both valid and effective in this way, we are still left with the question of what, if anything, to make of the fact that my two non-standard types of illocutionary act seem to be non-conventional in Strawson's sense, and yet presuppose some conventional knowledge of a more than purely linguistic kind in order to be understood. Two answers suggest themselves. It might simply be claimed that the peculiarity fits very well with Strawson's expectation that between the two standard cases he distinguished we may expect to find a variety of intermediate types. An alternative answer, however (which I propose finally to suggest and defend), is that these non-standard types cast some doubt on Strawson's whole discussion of non-conventional illocutionary acts. For if it can be said, for example, that an apparent enquiry may in appropriate circumstances and by social convention be correctly taken as an order, it might equally be said that it must be in virtue of *some* convention that an intended act of warning (as in the case of the skater) can be understood *as* the communication of a warning, and not as some other (perhaps oblique) illocutionary act. If there is a question of convention involved here, moreover, it will obviously involve more than the trivial point, mentioned and dismissed by Strawson, that to warn is by (linguistic) convention to warn. The point is rather that even when the locution (always a factor limiting the possible range of illocutionary force) and the circumstances (always relevant to the determination of illocutionary force)[13] are both appropriate (as they obviously are in the case of the skater) for the act performed to be assessable as one of warning, a further question still remains, as to whether there exists any mutually-recognized convention such that to speak in the way S speaks in warning A will be *acceptable* as a form of warning, and so capable of being taken by A *as* a warning. And this seems to be a question essentially about the nature and the extent of the social conventions which S may expect A to regard as appropriate for the regulation of their social (and so verbal) relationships.

The suggestion that at least this element of social convention is omnipresent in illocutionary acts, and so a further necessary condition for their understanding, may perhaps be brought out more clearly if we continue with the non-conventional case (the skater) first mentioned by Strawson, and adopt the device of enquiring into the possible motives S might have in this situation for deciding *not* to carry out his intention to warn A, the skater, that 'the ice over there is very thin'. I shall consider three possible reasons, and try to assess the status of Strawson's model in terms of them.

First possible reason for inaction: some doubt on S's part as to whether his warning would gain an appropriate effect or response, even if A were to gain uptake of the intended force of his utterance. If S believed that in uttering utterance x to warn A he was also likely to succeed in alarming or irritating him, this might constitute a sufficient reason for deciding against issuing the warning. But this is easily accommodated to Strawson's model. The doubt here is merely that an intended illocutionary act might have an unintended perlocutionary effect. Second possible reason: some doubt on S's part as to whether A would gain uptake of the *exact* intended force of his utterance. If S intended in uttering utterance x merely to warn A, he might well be inhibited by the consideration that he might be taken rather to be pleading or entreating with A. (For example, Jane Austen's heroines frequently explain their silences at crucial moments in precisely these terms.) Now this type of case (as Strawson concedes) seems much less easy to accommodate to his intentionalist model for the understanding of illocutionary acts. The question, in fact, of how to find means to make clear *how exactly* (or how forcibly) one intends one's intentions to be taken is one which seems to bring us very close to the need to invoke the availability of certain social as well as linguistic conventions. Third possible reason: some doubt on S's part as to whether his intention in uttering utterance x to warn A might not be taken as being some wholly different type of intention. This form of doubt must be (though it never has been) absolutely distinguished from the first possible reason suggested for inaction on S's part. In the first case the doubt was whether A would 'take' the warning even if he understood it as such; in the present case the doubt centres on *what* intention A might take him to be intending to be understood. And this does not seem capable of being accommodated to Strawson's intentionalist model at all, unless some element of convention and the mutual understanding of it is added to the scheme. For we can imagine a situation in which it might be impossible for A to gain uptake of the act as an act of warning simply because there was no convention at all that S in uttering such an utterance could be understood as intending to perform that illocutionary act. (If there is simply *no* convention such that to inform the Emperor that he is wearing no clothes will be acceptable *as* a case of intending to inform (rather than intending to challenge or ridicule) him, then the Emperor will go naked.) We are dealing, in short, with a situation in which S's inhibition appears to be due to some doubt as to whether his utterance would be regarded as falling within the conventions applied to the issuing of warnings, and so would be capable in principle of being assessed and understood as having been intended as an act of warning, rather than as some other intended act.

The point of these distinctions is thus to suggest that although it need not, yet it may always, be the case that S's decision not to warn A could be motivated by some doubt as to the nature or strength of the conventions in force. The fact, conversely, that S can be understood in saying 'the ice over there is very thin' to be warning A must be due at least in part to the prior existence and mutual acceptance of certain (social) conventions governing the behaviour regarded as appropriate in dealing with skaters in possible danger. But it is only because such social conventions happen to be moderately clear and strong that it is possible for A to be at all sure that S must have been intending to warn him, rather than to perform the wholly different but intended illocutionary act, say, of directing or admonishing A, perhaps even of criticizing or deprecating his behaviour. And this is not an issue merely about the possible (perlocutionary) effects of S's utterance, or even about its exact intended tone. It is firmly an issue about the part played by social convention in the performance of any successful communication between S and A. The point is that any intention capable of being correctly understood by A as the intention intended by S to be understood by A must always be a socially conventional intention – must fall, that is, within a given and established range of acts which can be conventionally grasped as being cases of that intention. It must follow that one of the necessary conditions for understanding in any situation what it is that S in uttering utterance x must be doing to A must be some understanding of what it is that people in general, when behaving in a conventional manner, are usually doing in that society and in that situation in uttering such utterances.

4

It might finally be asked what general significance and range of application can be claimed for the argument I have now sought to present about the essential conventionality of speech-acts. For it might seem that if any attempt were now made to apply the theory generally, it might be found to consist of little more than an elaborate endorsement of the position (mocked by Strawson) of supposing 'that there could be no love affairs which did not proceed on lines laid down in the *Roman de la Rose*'.

A case can instead be made, however, for saying that the dialogue situation which has hitherto been treated as paradigmatic in all these discussions about the understanding of statements — the straightforward and synchronic situation, that is, in which S speaks directly to A and A directly replies — is in itself a special case which misleadingly oversimplifies the role of conventions. So far I have sought to insist that even in this type of situation the achievement of understanding necessarily depends on at least a mutual intuiting of a whole complex of social as well as linguistic conventions. I now turn to consider some more complicated types of communication situation which can equally well arise. I focus on these partly because they have been generally ignored, but also because they raise further intrinsically important and relevant issues: they can be shown, that is, to raise special problems about the whole question of the conditions for understanding utterances, and they can be used to cast decisive doubts on the results which have hitherto been gained from considering only the more straightforward synchronic situations.

One complication which can arise in a wholly synchronic communication situation has already been mentioned: the case in which S duly utters his utterance to A, but intends to communicate less with A than with N, a number of perhaps more sophisticated or more sympathetic bystanders. This refinement arises perhaps most obviously in the case where S's primary intention is in fact to communicate an intention to patronize, to condescend, and so on. The point here, as with all such non-avowable illocutionary acts, is that the capacity of N to grasp what S is really doing will very particularly turn on the capacity to intuit a set of conventions. The same point can be made about another complication which can arise even in a synchronic communication situation: the case in which S's communication with A is overheard by N. S may of course intend his communication to be overheard, or else may communicate unintentionally with N as well as intentionally with A in this way. In either case a new question arises about S's utterance and the understanding of S's utterance of it: the question of how N should 'take' the force of the utterance. Now the answer to this question will at least in part depend on knowing whether or not S *was* aware of N, and whether it should be expected that such an awareness would in itself affect S's behaviour. But it is simply another way of putting this point to say that an understanding of the intended force of the utterance will thus depend on some prior knowledge of the nature and strength of the conventions governing the distinctions, regarded as appropriate in the given situation and society, between more public and more private utterances.

Further complications arise if we turn to the type of situation in which A might be concerned to understand the utterance of some utterance by S, or S might be concerned to communicate with A, but in which S and A stand in a non-synchronic relation to each other. Such situations are doubtless only encountered with any frequency by historians, but they do bring out important refinements analogous to those which can arise with synchronic but oblique communications. Analogous to the case of overhearing is the situation in which S intends not to communicate with A, an immediate audience or society, but to appeal over its head to some indeterminate future audience, perhaps to posterity itself. (The history of innovation in the arts has been characteristically punctuated by such avowals.) Analogous to the case of oblique communication is the situation in which S both intends to communicate with A and yet to modulate his tone so that it may appeal at the same time to a future or more remote audience. (Such a mixed tone has perhaps been most consciously adopted by the writers of certain sorts of diary or Will, and in the ancient world by the writers of certain sorts of public inscriptions. It has always been a tone characteristic of the more self-conscious statesmen and historians.) The problem with these types of situation is, of course, that of grasping the criteria by which they may be recognized and discriminated. And the point here is that an answer to this question can only begin with a consideration of the conventions governing ordinary synchronic communication in the given society, and the extent to which such conventions themselves may appear to have been modulated rather than followed in the situation under consideration.

The most difficult — but also the most familiar —complications of non-synchronic communication arise, however, in the type of situation in which A may wish to understand the meaning and force of a given utterance uttered by S, but in which S did not in fact intend to communicate with A. This is, of course, merely to state abstractly the position, and the dilemma, in which any historian or social anthropologist characteristically finds himself when attempting to understand the verbal behaviour of an alien culture or some utterance uttered in the past. The relation of the speaker to the audience concerned to understand him is wholly non-synchronic in both such cases, in the sense that although A may hope to understand what S meant, he may typically be confronted, in trying to understand the utterance of S's utterance, not merely with an alien set of social as well as linguistic conventions, but even with an apparently alien conception of what constitutes rationality itself.

It is this type of situation which seems most decisively to support the contention that an understanding of conventions, however implicit, must remain a necessary condition for an understanding of all types of speech act. Consider for example the case of S at t_1 (where this represents either an alien culture or an alien historical period) intending in uttering a given utterance to perform some act of communication. It must be a necessary condition of such communication that the form of S's utterance should fall within the conventions and limits acceptable at t_1 as applying to those particular forms of communication. For even if S can in principle conceive, he cannot in practice communicate an intention which is not already conventional in the sense of being capable of being understood, executed in the way S intends, as being a case of that intention.[14] Nor does this claim seem to be vitiated by the (none the less very intractable) issues which must arise in connection with any attempt to account for innovation in such a situation. If S's speech act is also an act of social and linguistic innovation which S nevertheless intends or at least hopes will be understood, the act must necessarily, and for that reason, take the form of an extension or criticism of some existing attitude or project which is already convention-governed and understood. It seems a necessary truth that unless the innovation either takes such a form, or can be reduced to it, it will stand no chance of being understood, and so can hardly count even as an intended act of communication. And it must follow from this that if A at t_2 wishes to understand what it was that S at t_1 intended at t_1 to communicate, it must be a necessary condition of such understanding that A should first grasp the (possibly very complex and wholly alien) conventions governing the methods regarded as acceptable at t_1 for communicating intentions of the class within which S's may appear to fall.

The need for this prior understanding by A at t_2 of the whole range of conventions at t_1 within which S's utterance must be located in order to be understood — and the dangers of misunderstanding which must correspond to the extent to which this need is ignored — can perhaps be most vividly illustrated from the literature on social anthropology. The same problems seem no less to arise, however, and seem even less easy to identify, when we attempt to understand the history of the changing concepts and conventions which have characterized our own culture. A primitive culture, after all, is likely to strike the observer as more obviously alien than the culture, say, of pre-industrial Western Europe. It is the very impression of familiarity, however, which constitutes the added barrier to understanding. The historians of our own past still tend, perhaps in consequence, to be much less self-aware than the social anthropologists have become about the danger that an application of familiar concepts and conventions may actually be self-defeating if the project is the understanding of the past. The danger in both types of study is in any case much the same — which is also why this type of evidence seems of particular importance for the whole discussion of speech acts: the danger that A at t_2 will 'understand' S at t_1 to have intended to communicate something which S at t_1 might not or even could not have been in a position at t_1 to have had as his intention.

It is worth developing this dilemma, since it is neither philosophically trivial in itself, nor in the practice of these disciplines can it be readily overcome. The eventual aim, as I have now stated it, is an understanding by A at t_2 of what S at t_1 intended at t_1 to communicate. The problem then is this. On the one hand such understanding clearly presupposes that A should be so imbued with the concepts and conventions available to S at t_1 that he can elucidate not simply the question of how far (or whether) S's utterance makes any sense at t_2 but can also explain what exact meaning and force S's utterance of his utterance at t_1 must have registered. On the other hand, if it is to be said that S has been understood by A it also seems indispensable that A should be capable of performing some act of translation of the concepts and conventions employed by S at t_1 into terms which are familiar at t_2 to A himself, not to mention others to whom A at t_2 may wish to communicate his understanding. It will not be enough for A to show that S's utterance is convention-governed according to the criteria acceptable at t_1, for this is precisely to beg the question of how to render these criteria intelligible to those at t_2 who may not share or appreciate them.[15] It will be necessary, in short, if it is to be said that A has *understood* S at all, that he should be capable of rendering into terms that make sense at t_2 the meaning and force at t_1 of S's utterance and his utterance of it. And that this may sometimes be flatly impossible to achieve should perhaps be treated more as something to be expected and less as something to be deplored: for it is the limit of our imaginative grasp as well as our lack of information that makes the past a foreign country, just as it is imaginative grasp as well as control of information that makes the historian.

The grasp of meaning and illocutionary force in this type of situation, therefore, appears as a dilemma in the sense that it requires two equally essential but almost contradictory acts of understanding. The overwhelming tendency in practice for these two components to become conflated can of course be readily illustrated.[16] The relevant point here, however, is that this type of conflation can now be seen as the result of a failure to grasp precisely the conventional nature of speech acts on which I have sought to insist. The consequence is that A at t_2 may be betrayed by the familiarity of the conventions governing his own utterances into 'understanding' S's given utterance at t_1 as having the force (say) of a revelation, whereas it amounted at t_1 to nothing more than a platitude. (A would thus be failing to see that the illocutionary force of the given utterance at t_1 could only have been somewhere on the spectrum of endorsing, emphasizing, siding with, adhering to, insisting on an accepted attitude or belief.) *Or* the converse and even more likely misunderstanding might arise. (A would then be failing to see that whereas the utterance of S's utterance at t_2 would be a platitude, it could only have been intended at t_1 with the illocutionary force of criticizing, rejecting, refuting, repudiating or denouncing an accepted attitude or belief.) *Or*, most likely of all, a large number of intermediate misunderstandings might arise at t_2 over the question of what exact meaning and illocutionary force S intended his utterance at t_1 to bear.

The point, then, of singling out and emphasizing all these possible complications of the basic communication situation — the oblique, the overheard, and the various non-synchronic types — is that they all make specially clear the point which seems to be so easily elided when we focus only on the more straightforward situations which have usually been treated as paradigmatic of speech acts: the point that the success of any act of communication necessarily depends on at least a mutual intuiting by S and A of a whole complex of conventions, social as well as linguistic, about what can and cannot be stated, what sorts of meanings and allusions can be expected to be understood without having to be explicitly stated at all, and in general what criteria for the application of any given concept (for example, that of warning) are conventionally accepted as applying in that given situation and society. I have sought to argue that this is no less true, but only less evident, in the standard synchronic situation. I have focussed on these more complex situations partly because they are clearly of intrinsic interest and yet have been ignored, but mainly because they seem particularly well-adapted to corroborating this central point.

5

The special types of situation, then, which historians and social anthropologists typically try to understand can be said to carry their own philosophical point. It is tempting to end by pointing the moral, tangential as well as obvious though it may be, which this seems to suggest for students of these disciplines. It would amount to suggesting that they might do well to give rather more self-conscious attention to the special philosophical issues raised by their claims to understand both alien conceptual schemes and utterances uttered in the past. One of the most important of these issues is the question of what conditions must sufficiently or at least necessarily be fulfilled for any such claims to count as genuine cases of understanding given utterances – understanding the uttering of them, their meanings and their illocutionary force. Such questions have of course begun to attract considerable attention in social anthropology and even in sociology. But the historians, with so much the greater tradition of practising their subject behind them, still appear overwhelmingly to take the view that it is best not to think about their subject but merely to do it, as if these were self-evidently separate activities.

Perhaps there is also a converse moral to be drawn here, however, both less obvious and less tangential, towards which the trend of my argument in the previous section might be said to point. This would amount to suggesting that if the social studies in general, and the history of ideas in particular, do raise special issues about the conditions for understanding speech acts, then philosophers interested in these issues might do well to give some attention at least to the sheer amount of relevant information, and of attempts to make sense of it, which these disciplines can at least supply. Again, an important start has, of course, been made in the philosophy of the social sciences. But again this has scarcely happened in the philosophy of history, which is still obsessively enough marked by a single preoccupation – the nature of explanation – and even by a single preoccupation within that preoccupation – the question of whether historical explanations must conform to a deductive model. Hardly any attention has recently been paid to the place of understanding statements made in the past, or to the special problems this might raise and the special insights it might

yield. This amounts, then, to the somewhat Hegelian plea that philosophers might again take seriously the special status and importance of
such historical knowledge. In the name, one might think, at the very
least of more Austinian 'field-work' on the subject of statements and
their understanding, this might well seem a genuinely fruitful direction
in which to step out — though the ice over there is undoubtedly very
thin.

Notes

1. I am greatly indebted to Professor B.A.O. Williams for reading and commenting on successive drafts of this paper, and for suggesting a number of
important additions (which I have incorporated) as well as for correcting a
number of mistakes.

2. In all subsequent discussion of Austin's work I am referring by page to this
book, ed., J.O. Urmson (Oxford, 1962).

3. L.W. Forguson, 'In Pursuit of Performatives', *Philosophy* 41 (1966), pp.
341-7.

4. William P. Alston, 'Linguistic Acts', *American Philosophical Quarterly* 1
(1964), pp. 138-46. It may be, of course, that Professor Alston would treat this as
beside the point, since his concern is with linguistic acts in general and since he
insists, despite the fact that his analysis is 'very similar' to Austin's, that 'there are
important differences' (p. 138 n.). His own account, however, does focus on
'something which one can do only when one utters a sentence or sentence-surro-
gate, but which is not simply the uttering of that sentence, and which does not
consist in, or require, the production of any particular effect of the utterance'
(p. 138). This does look exactly the same as Austin's distinction between
locutions, illocutions and perlocutions. But all I am concerned here to claim is
(1) that if Alston's scheme does not seek to mark off illocutions from other things
I may do in saying things, this seems an important lacuna, and that (2) if it does
seek to, it does not manage.

5. P.F. Strawson, 'Intention and Convention in Speech Acts', *The
Philosophical Review* 73 (1964), pp. 439-60.

6. H.P. Grice, 'Meaning', *The Philosophical Review* 66 (1957), pp. 377-88.
I assume familiarity in what follows, of course with the rather complex details
of both Grice's and Strawson's theories.

7. Paul Ziff, 'On H.P. Grice's Account of Meaning', *Analysis* 28 (1967),
pp. 1-8.

8. L. Jonathan Cohen, 'Do Illocutionary Forces Exist?', *The Philosophical
Quarterly* 14 (1964), pp. 118-37.

9. Austin's text in any case seems garbled at this point, or perhaps was never
clear. Cf. Urmson's Appendix, p. 165, noting this fact.

10. I owe this way of putting the point to Dr J.W. Burrow.

11. Alexander Sesonsko, 'Performatives', *The Journal of Philosophy* 62
(1965), pp. 459-68, esp. p. 467.

12. Herbert Fingarotto, 'Performatives', *American Philosophical Quarterly* 4
(1967), p. 45.

13. A knowledge of circumstance is, of course, crucially but I think obviously
relevant. Say that A is not a skater but someone employed to break up the ice. If
S now says 'The ice over there is very thin' the illocutionary force of this utterance

can hardly be on the warning-pleading-entreating spectrum; it must be on something more like a spectrum of recommending-instructing-directing.

14. The point has, of course, been made familiar since Wittgenstein's *Philosophical Investigations*. For an important application of such a claim specifically to historical and social-scientific issues, see Alasdair MacIntyre, 'A Mistake about Causality in Social Science', *Philosophy, Politics and Society* II, eds., Peter Laslett and W.G. Runciman (Oxford, 1962), pp. 48-70.

15. It is this question which, it seems to me, would necessarily be begged if one were to adopt the approach recommended in Peter Winch, 'Understanding a Primitive Society', *American Philosophical Quarterly* 1 (1964), pp. 307-24.

16. This I have tried to do in my article 'Meaning and Understanding in the History of Ideas', *History and Theory* 8 (1969), pp. 3-53. Cf. also John Dunn, 'The Identity of the History of Ideas', *Philosophy* 43 (1968), pp. 85-104.

Source

Quentin Skinner, 'Conventions and the Understanding of Speech Acts', *Philosophical Quarterly*, vol. 20, no. 78 (1970), pp. 118-38.

THE THEORY OF CONTEXT AND THE CASE OF
HOBBES

Preston King

1: Austin and Skinner

Quentin Skinner, like many contemporaries of similar views, may be said
to have fallen under the spell of J.L. Austin. This dependence upon
Austin is in part acknowledged, but is also transparent to a degree
which obviates any need for acknowledgement. Some of the crucial
difficulties found in Skinner are in fact traceable to Austin. It is important, accordingly, to preface any review of the former with some at
least fleeting, and perhaps more than fleeting, reference to the latter.

One might say that a chief concern of Austin's (1961) was to eliminate altogether the notion of 'universals' — were it not for his disarming
claim that 'I do not know what they are.' As so often with philosophers, Austin quickly reverses himself — thus: 'Universal *means* . . .
that x which is present, one and identical, in the different sensa which
we call the same name'. For Austin, 'universal', taken as a word, has a
meaning, but no 'universal', taken as an entity, exists. Thus he maintains that an argument, such as that, 'there are universals', is 'wrong',
on the view that universals will likely be mistakenly projected as
'objects of thought' or of 'contemplation', so inducing us to 'embark
on mythologies' and the invention of 'myths'.

Basically, the moral of the tale, for Austin, is to keep one's distance
from universals: 'there is remarkably little', he confides, 'to be said in
favour of "universals", even as an admitted logical construction'. Austin
is impressed by the particularity of existence, and would impress upon
us the fact, and the legitimacy of the fact, that identical words signify
different things. As he puts it: ' "grey" and "grey" are *not* the same'. By
implication, one's experience, for Austin, is particular: one's experience of 'grey' involves sensing a specific greyness; one has no sense or
experience of 'grey' in the abstract or universally (pp. 1-9).

What is of immediate importance, in the context of the present
discussion, is not whether 'there *are* universals', but whether saying this
may not be (or have been) mistaken for saying, even by Austin himself,
that 'universal *statements*' are somehow systematically misleading.

285

Austin seems to take this position in a peculiar, but significant, way. In his aversion to universals, Austin at points seeks to reduce them to mere generalizations, to past experience, to what is already known. Let us see how he does this. According to Austin (1962, 1965), if one claims that 'All swans are white', one can still be right, despite the presence of black swans in Australia. How is this possible? Because one may have made this claim prior to the discovery of Australia — more relevantly prior to one's knowledge of the existence of black swans in Australia. So that when confronted with the Australian counter-example, one is entitled to claim, according to Austin, that one was not really talking about *all* swans, about swans *everywhere*, and especially not about swans *in Australia*, or 'on Mars', etc. Such an approach may, for good reason, be considered perverse. But Austin could only resort to it because of his implicit aversion to universal statements.

'Reference', Austin insists, 'depends on knowledge at the time of utterance'. This is itself a universal statement which is simply false. We refer all the time to things of which, 'at the time of utterance', we simply do not have knowledge, 'knowledge' in the sense of 'enjoying direct sense experience of' whatever it is we are said to know. If one says 'All swans', one is entitled to be taken to mean '*All* swans'. Of course, one may always interpose qualifications, as when one says, 'All swans [but only in America and Europe and only in 1776] are white'. Without such qualifications, however, the discovery of a non-white swan simply refutes one's otherwise unqualified universal. Even quite vague generalizations, in the realm of practical experience, will justifiably be read as universals. The prospective traveller who is told that Sydney's hottest or Nairobi's fairest or London's bleakest months are December/January, will justifiably read any such assertion as a stipulation regarding the sort of weather to expect in these places in future at the time of year indicated (perhaps 'until further notice'). It may well be that we say what we say as far as we can on the basis of what we know — i.e., have experienced or learned. What is certainly true is that whatever we do say is commonly anticipatory or future-oriented or universal in character and is directed as a claim upon experiences which we cannot in fact have had. It is obvious that we cannot enjoy direct sense experience of future events or circumstances, given that they have not yet occurred. But this in no way prohibits us from making *reference* to them. Such is the work of universals. And a future conceived as total novelty would simply terrify us; it would be a future upon which we could make *no* anticipatory claims.

We do not necessarily require any such formula as: 'universals *exist*'. The relevant point is that we do and must utilize universal statements all the same; that these are in various ways future-oriented and infinitely extensive; and did we anticipate the immediate future to differ so radically from the present, if we expected that *all* our present anticipations must fail to lead us in any way through future time, then the only thing we should perhaps be left to anticipate would be some form of large-scale psychological disintegration. Austin's claim about reference depending on knowledge at 'the time of utterance' is really quite remarkable. For in saying this, he implicitly rules out universals as viable types of statement. Worse, he implies that such universals as one does formulate batten upon and depend on or derive only from past experience (reflecting a primitive inductivism). But worst of all, he implies that we are always allowed, in regard to the universals we do formulate, to ensure ourselves against error in formulating them; by abandoning logical responsibility for all statements made about what we have not yet experienced (which, from one perspective, of course is all of future time). Austin's contention, then, that 'the reference' in effect of all universal 'statements . . . is limited to the known' (1962, 1965, p. 143) is untenable.

Austin was not only concerned to play down 'universals'. He was also committed generally to drawing away some of the attention customarily accorded to questions of truth and falsity in philosophical discourse. 'It was for too long', claimed Austin (1962, 1965), 'the assumption of philosophers that the business of a "statement" can only be to "describe" some state of affairs, or to "state some fact", which it must do either truly or falsely' (p. 1). Still earlier, in his 1950 essay on 'Truth', Austin (1961) had written: 'The principle of Logic, that "Every proposition must be true or false", has too long operated as the simplest, most persuasive and most pervasive form of the descriptive fallacy' (p. 99). One of the considerations which obviously troubled Austin was the fact that descriptions, which we assess as true or false, are selective, and are often enough uttered to serve some purpose other than the attainment of truth (p. 144). When, for example, we speak of descriptions as being 'balanced' or 'unbalanced', as 'germane' or 'relevant', and so on, it is clear that we are not just eliciting their truth-value. And to concentrate only upon the truth-value of what is said may distort the actual thrust or 'force' of the utterance. Austin was concerned to urge 'that what we have to study is *not* the sentence but the issuing of an utterance in a speech situation' (p. 138). Austin regarded it as unsafe merely to inspect 'statements', only to focus upon the question of their truth or falsity. Hence his concern to broaden interest in speech as an 'act' and as a whole. 'The total speech act', he wrote, 'in the total situation is the *only actual* phenomenon which, in the last resort, we are engaged in elucidating' (p. 147).

Austin's strategy was to detail the variety of things that one can do 'in' and 'by' speech, and to shift the focus away from any exclusive concern with making true and false statements. 'Utterances' are of course of different kinds and legitimately serve different purposes. A question ('Who goes there?') or exclamation ('Whew!') or order ('Take over!') may be 'good'/'bad', 'apt'/'inept', etc. — but it will not relevantly be assessed as 'true' or 'false' ('relevantly' in the sense of taking account of its primary thrust). Austin was 'right' in claiming that we cannot pigeonhole *all* utterances as simply 'true' or 'false': much that we say and declare will not be assessed most 'happily' with respect to a putative truth-value. This broad conclusion, of course, is not new: historically, philosophers at least have been as much committed to the pursuit of 'good' and 'evil' as to that of the 'true' and the 'false'. But this need not matter unduly. If to distinguish between the true and the false has not exclusively absorbed philosophical attention, it has certainly taken up a good deal of philosophical time. And there is no particular reason why Austin (or anyone else) should not inspect some other question, in as far as there *is* some other question, and assuming it to be worthy of inspection.

Austin's assumption was that to focus merely upon the truth or falsity of a proposition was to narrow, and thus to distort, the object of the concern. He declared an interest instead in the 'total speech act', in the 'total speech situation', as 'the *only actual* phenomenon' to be explained. Austin betrays an attitude indeed almost scornful: 'I admit to an inclination', he tells us, 'to play old Harry with ... (1) the true/false fetish, (2) the value/fact fetish' (p. 150). But Austin appears to regard the true/false distinction as a fetish, a dichotomy irrationally reverenced, for the reason that focus upon it cannot elucidate the 'total speech act'. But the question one is entitled to ask is whether the 'total speech act', *qua* totality, can ever be elucidated anyway.

If the 'total' speech act, or 'total' speech situation, actually exists, it is difficult to suppose that we shall ever know it as such. Basically, what we shall have are descriptions of it. But, as we know, these descriptions can never be exhaustive. This means that they are selective. Any given utterance will and can only cover a limited part of all that might be uttered. It is not only descriptions said to be true or false that are selective and that are uttered for a purpose: all propositions or statements or utterances, broadly conceived, just by being the particulars they are, reveal themselves to be selective, and hence serve a purpose. If every judgement, every assessment, every 'speech act' *is* selective, then equally so is every judgement of a judgement, every assessment of an assessment, and every speech act about a speech act. Every speech act that we know is known as a selective perception — attended by an infinite range of assumption, implication, entailment, application, atmosphere, motive, intention, consequence (intended and unintended). If we must speak about a 'total speech act' and 'a total speech situation' then we must take all of these things together. To do this is to speak about everything — the entire world, the whole of reality — at once. And this we cannot do.

This is not to say that Austin is without interest or relevance. His analysis of 'performatives' is acute and helpful and is widely recognized to be such. Austin correctly observed that statements serve other purposes than that of asserting truth and falsity — as where they are employed to express commands, wishes, exclamations, and questions. In the case of 'performatives', the utterance, Austin argues, serves less as the description of behaviour than as the performance of an act. Austin provides the example of an individual who declares: 'I take this woman to be my lawfully wedded wife.' The statement is less to be read as a formula to be adjudged true or false, than as a significant part of an engagement — i.e. marriage — upon which one embarks.

While it may be useful to draw attention to this category of 'performatives', it would be seriously misleading to suppose that the analysis of a philosophical text in terms of its performative effect could itself serve as a serious piece of philosophical investigation. If one sought, for example, to decipher Hobbes's *Leviathan* in terms of its author, Hobbes, promising or allowing or commanding something, we should have overlooked in this a more immediate concern with the logic of the book's argument. And it is principally this logic, particularly in relation to the question of political obligation, that has attracted the attention and often admiration of later readers (for example of Warrender, Watkins, Gauthier, McNally and others).

It would be most surprising to discover that philosophers were ever relevantly and importantly concerned with issuing verdicts, orders, permission, and a variety of social signals as opposed to their 'traditional' and 'fetishistic' concern with 'expounding' or 'exposing' or 'expositing' both the true and false and the good and bad. The ethical and political and metaphysical philosophers who are customarily accorded greatness have, as with their less highly touted predecessors and successors and associates, never been spared the local trials, troubles, indeed turmoil elsewhere and elsewhen. But the fact of their local entrapment is not normally regarded as a respectable reason for ceasing to study them *philosophically*. There is a limit on the extent to which a detailed philosophical understanding of Hobbes will provide an equally detailed historical understanding of seventeenth-century England. Inversely, as we shall see, a detailed historical appreciation of Hobbes's period will not, in fact, make it much easier for the student to grasp the logical structure of Hobbes's argument. No more than a firm and detailed purchase on Newton's *context* will significantly facilitate the non-mathematically endowed student's grasp of Newtonian principles — as much as one may value for the novice this grasp of circumstantial data.

2: Text and Context

Skinner (1969a) proposes to attack two views. The first is that 'it is the *context* "of religious, political, and economic factors" which determines the meaning of any given text, and so must provide "the ultimate framework" for any attempt to understand it'. The second view attacked is claimed to be one which 'insists on the autonomy of the *text* itself as the sole necessary key to its own meaning, and so dismisses any attempt to reconstitute the "total context" as "gratuitous, and worse" ' (p. 3). Skinner's conclusion is that 'neither approach seems a sufficient or even appropriate means of achieving a proper understanding of any given literary or philosophical work' (p. 4). But let us take the first of these views.

No one of note, as far as I am aware, has ever maintained that the context alone 'determines the meaning of any given text'. The author, F.W. Bateson (1953), from whom Skinner quotes in formulating this 'orthodoxy', is simply misinterpreted. Bateson nowhere says, and plainly does not intend, that it is the *context*, whether alone or for the most part, which determines the meaning of any given text. What Bateson actually urges upon his readers, in his words, is 'a philosophy of critical balance' (p. 26), an 'equilibrium between literary meaning in the ordinary sense and the social context in which meaning alone acquires value' (p. 25).

We are not required to insist that Bateson's distinction between 'literary meaning in the ordinary sense', on the one hand, and 'the social context', on the other, is entirely clear. It is not. And it is here that Bateson may have muddled Skinner. It remains that the distinction *is* made. When Bateson complains about critics like William Empson, his grievance is that parts of poems, or parts of novels, are wrenched out of context, and so misread — but only out of the literary context *of the poem or novel as a whole* (i.e. of the text). Similarly, when Bateson complains about critics like Lionel Trilling, his objection is that such exegetes, burdened by too exclusively sociological an orientation, 'in such a hurry to get to the implicit ideas and social attitudes', end up *skimming* 'the literature instead of reading it' (p. 25). So far then from Bateson maintaining that the religious, political and social context *determines* the meaning of any given context, he is really negating such a position. He does this by distinguishing between 'a literary context', which is the poem or novel taken as a whole, and 'a literary background' such as the 'author's biography, the social history of his age', earlier criticism etc., all of which Bateson regards as 'background topics' which have only 'extrinsic' interest and are of 'limited critical relevance' (p. 14).

For Bateson, then, the text constitutes its own context, at least at what he calls 'the *verbal* and *literary* levels'. The 'social context' is regarded by him less as a final determinant of meaning, than as a fourth level of explanation (after the 'intellectual') 'of which the critical reader of literature', he suggests, 'must retain an *awareness*' (p. 16, my italics). So Bateson's is an argument for balance, not at all for the exclusive virtues of 'the *context* of religious, political and economic factors', as Skinner puts it.

A part of the difficulty with Bateson is that he does not emphatically distinguish (as Skinner does) between text and context. In his advocacy, a part of what he means by 'context' is in fact the *text* of a work of literature taken as a whole — not some isolated line or phrase 'taken out of context'. He also, however, makes a case, as we have seen, for an *awareness* of the intellectual and social contexts, as distinct from the immediate context (or simply text) of the work of literature itself.

It will clearly be difficult to find anyone of weight who maintains that the socio-economic context somehow itself alone determines the meaning of any given text. To argue that the social context provides an 'ultimate framework' for understanding, is not the same as maintaining that this framework 'determines the meaning'. If a framework 'determined' the meaning of a text, it could by implication serve as a substitute for it. If the framework cannot substitute for the text, then neither can it fully or exclusively determine its meaning.

If the argument for understanding the social context merely presupposes that it may facilitate our understanding of a text, then the position is not a contentious one. The position may be elaborated as follows. Any writer, in fashioning his text, makes assumptions which reach beyond it. One must be familiar with at least some of these to make sense of what is written. Another way of putting this is, that not everything which a writer means will be directly formulated in his text, so that to pay attention only to the text (where it represents a fairly alien experience) may lead the reader astray, or (more precisely) leave him astray. The way in which a writer writes may be governed by rules of grammar, without the writer enunciating those rules. A writer may be governed by social assumptions, an etiquette, an outlook, without actually articulating these things. A writer may be prompted by a paradigm, without ever pinpointing that model which alone makes sense of his words. (The nineteenth-century historian who wrote of a declining house that it was 'running out of steam' said something which, to a medieval monk, would presumably have been wholly unintelligible: the paradigm assumed by the writer, but not explained, could not have formed any part of the furniture of that more distant reader's mind, and may well become alien in a future time far less remote.) There is then a case, as Bateson contends, for the awareness of social context. The question is: how much of a case?

The second view which Skinner attacks is said to insist 'on the autonomy of the *text* itself as the sole necessary key to its own meaning'. Skinner appears to attribute such a view to F.R. Leavis. But this attribution, like his attribution to Bateson, is not altogether reliable. (It does not quite matter that Leavis, nettled as he was by the man, should himself have failed to get right Bateson's position.) Although Leavis (1953) did dismiss 'any attempt to reconstitute the "total context" as "gratuitous, and worse",' he did not argue for the *text* as 'the sole necessary key to its own meaning'. At the very outset, Leavis concedes (it is 'freely granted' and 'will not be disputed'), in regard to 'the observations from which Mr Bateson starts', that 'some scholarly knowledge may be necessary' in order to be able 'to judge' a text – in this case, 'a poem' (p. 162). Leavis regards it as a 'commonplace observation that a poem is in some way related to the world in which it is written' – to repeat *commonplace*, but not false (p. 173). Leavis goes on to deny that he would like 'to insulate literature for study, in some pure realm of "literary values"', affirming that 'I do indeed (as I have explained in detail elsewhere) think that the study of literature should be associated with extra-literary studies' (p. 174).

Leavis is not enamoured of 'the way in which scholarship is set over against criticism' and clearly believes that the former must be associated with the latter. What he would have us aim for is 'accuracy', and is pleased to accept 'scholarship' in so far as it does not distract us from the 'matter of relevance'. The 'insistence on an immense apparatus of scholarship before one can read intelligently is characteristic', he writes, of 'the academic overemphasis on scholarly' — meaning extra-textual — 'knowledge'. The problem, for Leavis, is to avoid misdirection, overemphasis, irrelevance. He assumes it a mistake, for a start, to begin with the assumption that 'the necessary scholarly knowledge' is only to be found outside the texts which one proposes to explore. He contends that 'some' — not all — 'of the most essential [scholarly knowledge] can be got only through much intelligent reading' or 'practical criticism' of the texts themselves. He believes that these, so often, if 'duly pondered', cannot fail to leave the reader (as for example of seventeenth-century poetry) 'aware of period peculiarities of idiom, linguistic usage, convention, and so on' (p. 163). Leavis then contends that much of the social context can be inferred from a careful reading of a piece of literature, and that the critic's primary, but not necessarily exclusive, emphasis should be upon the text itself. To have it the other way round, Leavis insists, must 'stultify' literary criticism, for the reason that the 'context', or the prior commitment to understanding it, by contrast with the 'text', is infinitely regressive, 'expands indeterminately' (p. 174), and cannot ultimately be wrestled to the ground.

If the argument for understanding a text is that one must, to do this, concentrate first and foremost upon that text itself, then all undue insistence upon the contrary may appear odd. A text is what it is and no other. Assuming identical initial conditions, which is to say a given historical time-frame, and the emplacement of many different writers at work within it, we normally regard it as impossible, before the fact, to project that some specific work of genius, say *Leviathan*, shall emerge. Such an *oeuvre*, we only celebrate after, not before, the event. Thus at any point that we call a text 'original', which is what we may presume a work of genius to be (among other things), we also imply that it, specifically, cannot have been inferred merely from the broad social context out of which it emerged. If we cannot infer a specific text from its context, in advance of its emergence, then neither presumably can any subsequent exploration of the context on its own provide a distinctive and authoritative account of the character of that text. The conclusion is, that where the aim is to understand a text, there can be no substitute for textual analysis, whether we say 'in the first place' or per contra 'in the end', as long as the focus is specifically upon that which we seek to know. And this is consistent, of course, with Leavis's position, to the effect that, if we do not control the study of 'social context' with regard to relevance, immersion in it can take us an illimitably long way from our textual beginning, with no certain hope of ever being led back to it at all.

In sum, both Bateson and Leavis are misread by Skinner. (Perhaps one should observe that the heat between the first two was sufficiently intense to explain the mutual unintelligibility which attended their clash.) It is not the case that Bateson argues for exclusive resort to context and Leavis for the text as 'the sole necessary key to its own meaning'. Both men argue for a certain emphasis. With Bateson, the emphasis is upon a balance between the 'verbal', 'literary', 'intellectual' and 'social' texts and contexts, with a call for greater stress upon these last contexts than previously. With Leavis, some concession is made to context, accompanied by the objection that too great an obsession therewith may lead one away from *accurate* criticism focused directly upon the literature itself. These contrasting positions are not to be seen as either clear and/or absolutely firm oppositions. The commonsensical position would seem to be the right one: to understand a text, one may require some knowledge, independently gleaned, of social and other contexts; at the same time, one cannot expect to grow familiar with a text by spending the bulk of one's time ignoring *it* and attending instead to its context. The question is whether one may expect to be able to say much more than this.

It is a part of Skinner's contention that to 'focus simply on the texts themselves . . . must necessarily remain a wholly inadequate methodology for the conduct of the history of ideas' (1969a: 31). This is both true and false. It is true in the sense that any text, as suggested earlier, presupposes conventions of various kinds which cannot be made explicit in the text. It is false in the sense that one does not *necessarily* have 'to adopt an interpretation on the strength of evidence quite outside the texts themselves' (p. 35). (For example, a moderately well-educated Briton cannot be thought to require any special education to grasp the import of G. Lowes Dickenson's *A Modern Symposium*, 1905.)

A part of the difficulty stems from the fundamental consideration that no text, if in any way intelligible at all, can ever possibly be regarded as completely detached from its environment anyway. Just as assumptions and outlooks characteristic of the social setting may prepare the ground for the interpretation of a text, so will the text, by its assumptions, implications and applications, lead one back into the social environment. Anyone therefore who argues for the text alone (although such a proponent is really a straw man) contradicts what he must assume – since the text, in the basic sense suggested, never *is* alone. But, also, anyone who argues that there can be no adequate interpretation of texts without reference to 'evidence quite outside the texts themselves' equally contradicts himself. If the evidence in question really is 'quite outside the texts themselves', then such evidence cannot literally be necessary to the understanding of these texts. Suppose, for example, 'outside evidence' for the reading of a text is taken to be the views of the writer's contemporaries regarding what that writer was up to. It is essential to keep it in mind that contemporaries are, alas, often enough mistaken: imagine Richard Nixon providing a reliable account of Herbert Marcuse's *intentions*. (We shall later see that Skinner himself was mistaken in embracing seventeenth-century views about Hobbes on ethics.)

3: From Text to Context

It seems fair to say that Skinner has expended a great proportion of his energies attacking the difficulties associated, mostly, with textual analysis (as in the work of Lovejoy, Strauss and others of like views). He has tried to work out his own variety of contextual analysis while blunting its implications (i.e. by refusing to *reduce* any author's meaning to an understanding of his context).

Skinner holds to be mistaken 'the fundamental assumption of the contextual methodology [namely] that the ideas of a given text should be understood *in terms of* its social context' (1969a, p. 43). Skinner apparently intends that one understands a text 'in terms of' its context where one seeks to clear up 'puzzles about actions . . . simply by stating the conditions of their occurrence' (p. 44). The idea here seems to be that a philosophical work might be regarded as 'caused' by certain antecedent conditions; for example, a chaotic civil war might be regarded as somehow having 'caused' or induced Hobbes to write *Leviathan*; or corrupt, aristocratic rule might be held to have somehow 'caused' Rousseau to write the *Origin of Inequality* and *Emile*. It might be implied in this that a complete reconstruction of the context would necessarily yield up the text – treating the latter as the textual effect of the contextual cause. Contexts then cannot be said, not in any tight sense, to 'produce' or 'cause' the writing of texts, although they may, resorting to a looser terminology, 'occasion' them. Skinner is right to seek to lay the ghost of so clumsy a contention. How to do it is another matter.

Skinner sets about the task in a complicated way. He conceives of texts as statements, which are governed less by causes than by intentions, and intentions of two quite distinct sorts — in the first case 'an intention to have' stated whatever one stated, 'but also an intention in doing it, which cannot be a cause, but which must be grasped if the action itself is to be correctly. . . understood, (1969a, p. 45). Skinner distinguishes in short between 'an intention to do x' and 'an intention in doing x', where the former refers to those reasons entertained by a writer and which effectively prompt his statement, while the latter refers to 'the *point* of the action for the agent who performed it' (p. 44).

In the course of his argument, Skinner takes it that 'meaning' and 'understanding' are not 'strictly correlative terms' and cites J.L. Austin's *How to Do Things with Words* (Oxford, 1962) to support the conclusion. The effect of this would be that 'even if the study of the social context of texts could serve to *explain* them, this would not amount to the same as providing the means to *understand* them' (1969a p. 46). Skinner's contention here, following Austin, is that every 'given utterance' has both a meaning and 'an intended illocutionary force'.

For Skinner (1969a) the object of the history of ideas is to enable us to recover 'the actual intention of the given writer' as writers to whom we direct attention (p. 49). Skinner excludes the possibility of 'the *text* itself' being the 'sole necessary key to its own meaning' (p. 3). He equally excludes the possibility of the context *determining* this meaning. If we exclude, as with Skinner, examination of both the text and the context as a means of establishing meaning — unless we intend that text and context should somehow be taken together — it is difficult to know which way to turn. If we look at Skinner's practice, what we note is either an evasion or a turning away from textual analysis. We also notice, despite formal protestations, a reliance upon contextual reconstruction. For while Skinner does not perceive the context as determining an author's meaning, he does see it as providing 'an ultimate framework for helping to decide what conventionally recognizable meanings . . . it might in principle have been possible for someone to have intended to communicate' (p. 49).

It is not so much that Skinner is opposed to 'contextualist argument', as that he does not wish such argument to become fully reductionist. The ideological context of any thinker is plainly of great importance to Skinner. The difference is that he thinks to employ this contextual material merely negatively, not itself directly to establish the meaning of any text. The borderline between negative and positive readings may not prove so easy to establish. If we fall back, for example, upon Hobbes's 'ideological context' to rule out contemporary deontological views as apposite, we are simultaneously, as it happens, merely confirming views consistent with those held by many of Hobbes's contemporaries, and our own, which conceive Hobbes's morality to be dictated at best by prudential concerns.

If we take together the, in effect, very limited objection which Skinner opposes to contextualist argument, with the marked displeasure directed by him to textual criticism, then the nature of Skinner's penchant appears somewhat clearer. Cautiously, but briskly, he directs us back through time to Collingwood, at the height of the latter's historicist phase. Skinner − 'to revive Collingwood's way of putting it' − skeletally indicates that 'there simply are no perennial problems in philosophy', 'no universal truths', and that to believe otherwise is 'foolishly and needlessly naive'. For Skinner, 'the classic texts cannot be concerned with our questions and answers, but only with their own'. For him, 'any statement . . . is inescapably the embodiment of a particular intention, on a particular occasion, addressed to the solution of a particular problem'. For Skinner, accordingly, the classic texts 'help to reveal . . . not the essential sameness, but rather the essential variety of viable moral assumptions and political commitments' (p. 52). It is Skinner's assumption that we may 'discover from the history of thought' that there are no such timeless concepts, that universal truths do not exist, and it appears that this discovery itself constitutes for him a timeless or universal or transhistorical truth (an inconsistency which Strauss insisted it was impossible for the historicist to avoid). In short, to discover that there are 'no timeless concepts' nor any 'universal truths' is, for Skinner, 'to discover a general truth not merely about the past but about ourselves as well' (p. 53).

Obviously enough, to advise that there are no perennially valid answers and no universal truths, while simultaneously holding out for at least one such perennially valid answer and at least one such universal truth, is at least infelicitous. It is a difficulty often enough pointed out: we may none the less allow that 'Skinner has implicitly disavowed at least some forms of relativism' (Schochet 1974, n. 17). But we must also note that the disavowal (Skinner 1972c: p. 152) is exiguous, indirect and several years late. Besides, any thinker taken for a relativist must also be assumed to regard his relativism, at least, as non-relative. This form of non-relativism seems to be quite as much as one can honestly elicit from what Skinner actually writes.

Skinner (1966b) disarmingly allows that 'to insist upon the uniqueness' or particularity of every idea or event *could* make it impossible to explain everything (p. 200). But the problem is far more serious: to accede to such a view must imply that explantion *is* impossible. Given this particularist commitment, Skinner appears virtually compelled to exclude the possibility of a later writer being influenced by any predecessor. If, Skinner maintains, the historian asserts such a connection, he may be mistaken. If the historian bases his assertion directly on the claim of the later writer, the latter may be mistaken — perhaps even 'lying about his intellectual connections' (p. 206). Even if a later writer genuinely thinks he *has* been influenced by an antecedent, we only have valid evidence that he *thinks* this, not evidence that he is *correct* in thinking this. The later writer, most importantly, may simply be reading his own thoughts back into the writings of the earlier figure. And even if an earlier and a later writer actually seem to be saying substantively the same thing, it remains that these 'correlations' may be random, and not based upon a 'necessary inner connection' of influence at all (p. 208). For Skinner, accordingly, 'the attempt to trace influences must be irreducibly arbitrary'. Hence valid evidence for even a single case of influence is 'impossible to recover' (p. 210). Three years later, Skinner (1969a) waters down his position, regarding the tracing of intellectual influences, less now as 'impossible' than as 'extremely elusive' (25). But he does not tell us why, that is for what *reasons*, he shifts in this way. The effect is to leave his argument standing. And what it stands on and draws its strength from is the rich harvest of detail, and the contextual reconstruction upon which this tightly and unendingly depends.

As Skinner (1966b) puts it, the 'appropriate strategy must then be not to begin by abstracting leading ideas or events, but rather by describing as fully as possible the . . . matrix within which the idea or event to be explained can be most meaningfully located' (p. 213). For Skinner, in a manner similar to Oakeshott's, 'the only approach to an understanding "of historical influence" must be to construct a complete account of the historical situation'; not 'to explain, but only in the fullest detail to describe'; to lay out 'a total historical context'; to examine and describe 'the context itself in the greatest detail' (p. 214).

To describe 'the context . . . in the greatest detail' can of course prove a highly absorbing endeavour. It is also in principle unending. It is as important, in understanding a writer, to seize his 'problem' as much as his 'solution'. But these are normally to be expected to be revealed by the text itself — if at least it is perspicuous enough. The 'intention' of the writer, and the 'occasion' of the writing, how-

ever, are different matters. We must normally go beyond the text
to appreciate what is involved. And the trouble is, that we can go
so much further, that the question of deciding what to pay prior attention to — text or context — should not be looked upon as a subject which it is in any way profitable for the bystander to advise upon.

In this connection, let us cite a statement cited by Skinner, from
Machiavelli, to the effect that, 'a prince must learn not to be virtuous'
(call it APriM). But we shall use it to make a divergent point. The
meaning of APriM (i.e. its sense and reference) is clear enough, even
if it is not clear whether in its time, it was a mere commonplace, or
by contrast strikingly new. It is useful to decide between these possibilities, since to do so enables us to determine whether Machiavelli
intended to introduce a novelty or to lend his weight to an item of traditional morality. What we must first accept, however, is that Machiavelli's formula is either new or not; that no direct answer is easily to be
found in Machiavelli; and thus that we must seek for an answer elsewhere. The problem is: where? The more obvious answer would be: in
the social or intellectual context.

Now any such statement as APriM, assuming that its meaning is
plain, will qualify for assessment as true/false or correct/incorrect or
good/bad etc. Whatever the actual assessment, it remains that the
statement itself reposes on a bed of bottomless assumption. One of
these assumptions, as held by the propounder of the statement, may be
that APriM is either novel or traditional. If we wish to know *fully*
what M, the propounder of APriM, meant, we must elicit what he *said*
and what he *implied*, and also what he *assumed*. Such concerns, including the last, are not external to 'APriM'; they are in fact a part of it;
thus what was assumed by M (if we can ever recover it) in stating
APriM, will directly relate to the meaning of this statement. If we are
primarily concerned to establish what M said, or what he implied, we
shall inspect, first and foremost, his text. If we are primarily concerned with what M *assumed*, then we shall have to look beyond his
text. The first and least difficulty lies in deciphering what a text says;
second and more awkwardly, there is the problem of deciphering its
logic; if we are dealing with a descriptive statement, then the question
of its factual accuracy may prove equally troublesome, but finally and
most vexing, there is the problem of unearthing assumptions.

The trouble with assumptions is that they are not necessarily
entailed by or implied in statements. The 1964 Warren Commission
Report, for example, concluded that President Kennedy was assassin-
ated by Lee Harvey Oswald acting alone. This conclusion *implies* that

there was no conspiracy, an implication 'contained', as it must be, in the initial statement. What the conclusion *assumes* cannot be so clear. It may have been assumed that there really was no second gunman in an upper-storey window of the Texas Book Depository; it may have been assumed that it was simply inconvenient, publicly disquieting, to think there was a conspiracy; it may have been assumed, taken on faith, that the investigation actually was exhaustive. The assumptions that may have been made can have no limit. Nor can we clarify what was assumed merely by inspecting the text of the *Report*, unless we simply reduce 'assumption' to 'implication'. The authors may have made any one of these assumptions, and indeed assumptions of a quite different sort from any of those enumerated, and any one of these could affect the way in which we understand the conclusion to which they came about Oswald having acted alone.

Similarly with the statement by M that APriM. The logic of what is said is clear enough. But the actual skein of assumptions underlying it is not at all transparent. The chief question cannot be whether the statement APriM was somehow in wide circulation at the time M made it. The question rather would have to be: did M *think* it current then? M might have conceived APriM to be widely current among rulers but not scribes; or among scribes but not rulers; or to be the unconscious practice of rulers, formulated by no one; or formulated by everyone, but not openly admitted by anyone; or to be recognized and opposed by most, and secretly avowed by only a few; etc. If we address what M was doing, by reference to what he assumed, then no evidence will directly tell us what this was – not what *he* said, but not what his contemporaries said either. To determine, if we can, what M's contemporaries thought about APriM, or simply whether, before M's sally, they even conceived it, would not directly tell us what M himself assumed, and what *he* therefore fully intended. It is of course impossible that we should ever elicit fully what any writer fully intended, however much evidence we have on hand, since such evidence is never complete. And to attempt forlornly to elicit it is unlikely ever to prove highly rewarding. But no matter. To fully unearth M's assumptions, we must not only move beyond what he said, but equally beyond what was said by others of his age, and the trouble in all this is that we should have less and less evidence for drawing any firm conclusions about what he meant in some 'larger' sense. It is in this way that the search for assumptions, which are not clearly and logically tied to texts, takes us far afield – in fact into a bit of a swamp. The logic of a text, no doubt, is never all there is to it. But the question is, how much more is there, of a worthwhile and reasonably perspicuous sort, to which one can reliably turn one's mind. To investigate assumptions is doubtless an exciting sort of thing to do, but far from being *more* accurate, it is likely to give rise to the most extraordinary historical fantasy.

4: Conventions *qua* Context

If a writer hopes to be comprehended, then he must express himself in a manner which is comprehensible. Given that he expresses himself at a given time, given too that he hopes to be comprehended at that time, then he must express himself in the idiom, or according to the conventions, which then obtain. Of course, a writer need not hope to be understood at the time at which he writes — as we are told frequently happens with architects, musicians, and artists of every kind. But it remains that, if one seeks to be understood, one must at least express oneself in a manner that is somehow comprehensible. The problem presumably is to determine how to do this. If it is thought that one may be understood by conforming to the conventions of one's day, this in turn must suppose not only that these conventions exist, but that they are coherent. If they are incoherent, then of course one may happily proceed to do just what one likes, without 'violating' them in the least. If then we are told that, prior to understanding a philosophical or other text, written at an earlier point in time (as is true by the way of any text whatever), we must grasp 'the conventions and limits acceptable' at that time, the problem is to determine how we would grasp these 'conventions and limits'.

Conventions must presumably be coherent if one is reliably to grasp them. Presumably, too, they are never fully coherent. One may reasonably suppose that a writer like Hobbes or Rousseau or Kant attempted to create a greater coherence than that which he observed about him. If this is so, it is difficult to see how, in focusing upon a circumstantial incoherence, a contextual confusion, one will be made better able to apprehend the quest for a higher understanding characteristic of major philosophical figures. In any event, conventions not being altogether coherent, it cannot really be possible to recover *them*. One recovers divergent views, outlooks, insights, commitments, but none of this adds up to '*the*' context, or '*the*' conventions of the time. A philosopher who tries to understand a major philosophical argument by reference to 'the' context is perhaps like a record company seeking to capture the best of Charles Mingus in concert by scattering its microphones at the feet of a thumpingly appreciative audience. The 'context', the 'conventions', constitute in this sense background noise. But it remains what it is. To make a record of this background does not turn noise into music — nor context into philosophy. To recover the context is often to recoup nothing so much as gibberish — *'the'* context, which is always incoherent, does not exist.

Since the context, confused as it must be, at no point of itself implies Hobbes's (or anybody else's) solution or even formulation of a given problem, it is no use thinking to start with that context to reach and (in this central sense) to throw light on this or any other proposed solution. It cannot be 'a necessary condition' for communication at any given time 'that the form of S's utterance should fall within the conventions and limits acceptable' at that time, if it is the case that the conventions actually accepted do not cohere. Who can say, for example, what the 'conventions' are governing scientific discovery at the present time? The Popper-Kuhn (-Lakatos-Feyerabend) dispute clearly suggests that we can make no wholly confident and uniform statement on this matter. If we cannot do this for the near present, it cannot prove very much easier to do so for the more distant parts of the past. It is always major philosophical writers who take us furthest from the incoherence of ordinary discourse. Any ordinary context, taken as a whole, invariably reveals some significant incoherence, even dissonance. But it cannot be, if A at t_2 wishes to understand what it was that S at t_1 intended to communicate, that A, as a precondition, must, as Skinner (1970) requires, first grasp 'the (possibly very complex and wholly alien) conventions governing the methods regarded as acceptable at t_1' (pp. 135-6). This cannot be for the reason that one is aware of no entirely coherent convention or method that is 'acceptable' in the sense of being 'accepted' at any given time. In short, there will be no one method or convention to grasp.

If it is the contradictions and confusions in the views obtaining at the earlier time (t_1) which are to be grasped, then in so far as they are contradictory and confused, presumably they cannot be 'grasped' in the relevant sense of rendering more intelligible the distinct analysis of an author H or R or K.

It is obviously impossible to grasp any convention which is 'wholly alien'. It is only and precisely those conventions which are *not* 'wholly alien' that we have any hope of comprehending. Thus while it is perfectly possible that we may mistakenly attribute to any earlier writer views which were not his — classic anachronism this — it does not follow that one can defend against this danger by 'first' recovering 'the whole range of conventions' that were 'acceptable' at the time that the author wrote: for what is tangled, confused, and incoherent, unless we falsely construe it to be the reverse of all these things, is not readily 'grasped'. To understand the *whole* range of conventions acceptable at any given time, past or present, is obviously impossible. Perhaps such ambition may be entertained only on the basis of an unfortunate inductivism, supposing that by laying down granitic fact upon fact, one may build a high road to the heaven of truth. But as one cannot recover 'the whole range of conventions', the context as a whole, then it becomes pointless to enjoin that one should. If one retreats to the position that the 'whole' cannot be recovered, but only a part, it is automatically implied in this that the value of this part is partial — since the part recovered can never be more than a fraction of a 'whole' which we are compelled in turn to regard as infinite.

5: The Hobbesian Context

Up to this point, we have reviewed Skinner's work on a more general level. Skinner (1974) himself provides a concrete test for the viability of the more abstract general position which he adopts. And it is to this test that we now turn. Skinner's general argument is that 'the recovery of the historical meaning of any given text is a necessary condition of understanding it' (p. 285). As a concrete test of this general principle, Skinner falls back upon the case of Thomas Hobbes, principally *Leviathan*, but also including Hobbes's other main political works. 'I agree that *Leviathan* is probably the most plausible candidate [for release from the Skinnerian contextual principle] but one of the main purposes of my historical articles about Hobbes has been to establish that even in this case' no exception can be made (p. 285). The implication is that, should Skinner fail to 'elucidate the precise character of [Hobbes's] theory of political obligation', together with Hobbes's epistemology, by exploring the 'prevailing conditions' (p. 286) of Hobbes's time, the general principle collapses.

The only way in which we can judge Skinner's effort in this matter is by reviewing a series of overlapping pieces on Hobbes, some extended, others very brief, stretching from 1964 onwards. These pieces, which include book reviews, reveal their author's minor shifts of orientation and emphasis over time. Despite the variability of the pieces under inspection, there is one main thread which runs through them, and this is essentially that Hobbes's political theory of obligation, as a *philosophical* argument, can be directly explicated in

some significant way by an appreciation of his *historical* circumstances
— meaning principally the climate of opinion in Hobbes's time, the
nature and extent of his following, etc. It should be remarked that
although several of Skinner's articles are of great historical interest, the
present concern must exclusively centre upon the question of his success
in attaining the chief end which he himself has set.

What appears to be Skinner's earliest published essay is on Hobbes
and it happens for the most part to provide an exercise in textual
analysis. Skinner (1964), in a review principally of *The Divine Politics
of Thomas Hobbes* by F.C. Hood, seeks to undermine Hood's view that
political obligation, for Hobbes, is 'grounded on a recognition that the
Laws of Nature are not only the dictates of reason, but also the commands of God' (p. 321).

First, Skinner objects to Hood's concern to get at the meaning of
Leviathan by looking beyond it to other texts. To do this, Skinner
invokes Hobbes against Hood, in claiming that 'Hobbes regarded
Leviathan as the last word' (p. 324). In fact, the actual citation used
by Skinner does not bear out the latter's claim about Hobbes regarding
Leviathan 'as the last word'. This claim, moreover, is inconsistent with
Skinner's own procedure, a year later, in publishing an undated unpub-
lished fragment of four paragraphs, not in Hobbes's hand, and placed
perhaps two to three decades after *Leviathan*, and upon which Skinner
places a surprising degree of stress to bear out his own gloss on
Hobbes's views on political obligation. Skinner, in short, in later
running to ground what he implicitly took to be 'the whole doctrine' of
Hobbes, effectively followed much the same procedure as that which he
had earlier identified and attacked in Hood.

Skinner's commentary, and the four-paragraph fragment which is its
subject, are published together (Skinner, 1965b). But the length of the
commentary exceeds that of the fragment tenfold. The few paragraphs
attributed to Hobbes are qualified by Skinner himself as 'brief', 'short',
and recognized to be marred by 'notably obscure observations'. But
publication is effectively justified on the grounds of it being 'very
remarkable to find Hobbes so patiently spelling out, as he does here, a
crucial part of his political argument'. Hobbes engages in this patient
spelling out in the space of half a printed page, while Skinner claims
that the 'chief importance of the manuscript is undoubtedly for the
new information which it adds about Hobbes's political views'. What
this new information principally does, following Skinner's commentary,
is simply to give point to Skinner's 'traditional' reading of *Leviathan*.
The effect would be to undermine any reading of Hobbes as promoting

a political theory of duty — to 'contradict any attempt at a deontological interpretation' of the Hobbesian theory of obligation. A reader might be excused for thinking that Skinner makes rather a lot out of little. But no matter: he is, in this, to be seen moving beyond a principal text to secure a purchase on its meaning. But he is also to be seen engaged in an elaborate and self-conscious piece of textual exegesis.

Secondly, Skinner (1964) objects to Hood's analysis of Hobbes's meaning by reference to 'Hobbes's own claim that his intention was to assimilate politics to psychology' (p. 323). Here Skinner's quotation is more apt, where Hobbes is shown to 'ground the Civil Right of Sovereigns, and both the Duty and Liberty of subjects, upon the known natural Inclinations of Mankind'. But again, all of Skinner's substantive arguments, in seeking to counter Hood, are derived from Hobbes's text. For Skinner, Hood's account rests 'on a failure to recognize the logical structure of *Leviathan*; Hood's account is built upon 'a sequence of *textual* misunderstanding' (p. 324); or it has 'no sufficient *textual* warrant'; 'Hobbes *himself* . . . never uses the concept of artificial obligation' (p. 325); 'Hobbes did not *himself* conclude . . . ' (p. 326); 'Hobbes *himself* never makes any such division' (p. 327, all italics mine). Skinner consistently falls back upon quotation from Hobbes's text with a view to demonstrating that Hood is mistaken. And this is as it should be.

Skinner is an excellent historian of ideas. He is clearly less apt at exegesis. A part of the difficulty, in his discussion of Hobbes on political obligation, may perhaps stem from an overly generous reliance on the work of D.D. Raphael. Putting Hood's own analysis to one side — for although Hood correctly detects a genuine logical difficulty in Hobbes, he is mistaken in presenting his own as Hobbes's solution — we can see that Skinner does not really grasp the philosophical ambiguity involved in Hobbes's theory of political obligation. It is precisely this ambiguity which has given rise to so much post-war reflection on Hobbes's meaning, as most strikingly in the case of Warrender, but also in Taylor, Hood, NcNeilly, Gauthier, Watkins and several others. What Hood and some others have done is to conclude that Hobbes present us, as Skinner observes, with a political theory of duty. Skinner rejects this view, and adopts what may be called the 'traditional' position — to the effect that Hobbes's political theory of obligation, in Skinner's words, is to be 'explained as the enlightened calculation of individual self-interest' (p. 321).

Skinner justifies his rejection of the opposing gloss by reference to Hobbes's text, that for example which refers to the grounding of obligation in 'the known natural inclinations of mankind'. There are no doubt many such inclinations. But we have no difficulty in appreciating that, of these, Skinner views self-preservation as the most important or fundamental for Hobbes. This is clearly seen in a later essay by Skinner (1966a, revised in 1972d) belonging to the same period. There he is largely concerned to show how widely accepted in Hobbes's own time was that reading of *Leviathan* – the 'traditional' view regarding Hobbes's true meaning. Skinner writes that all of Hobbes's followers 'were concerned to emphasize the obligation to obey any successfully constituted political power' as well as that 'the grounds and the necessity of this obligation lay in man's pre-eminent desire for self-preservation' (1966a, p. 314). This 'traditional' reading is that which Skinner himself accepts. He quotes Wilkins with apparent approval to the effect that Hobbes 'invented' the notion that 'self-preservation as the fundamental law of nature supersedes the obligation of all others' (p. 314).

Let us take it then that Skinner regards Hobbes's position as one which argues that civil obligation is based upon man's psychology or 'natural inclinations', conjoined with the assumption that the most fundamental of these is the urge towards self-preservation. To attempt to counter the argument (whether advanced by Warrender, Hood or anyone else) that Hobbes's theory of political obligation is a theory of duty, it will be seen that to quote Hobbes and/or his followers, as we noted Skinner to do above, is in no way to clear up the issue. And this is because what Hobbes wrote, or what his followers claimed that he meant, is on this point internally unstable. It is all very well to claim that Hobbes, together with those who both opposed and supported him, insisted that 'self-preservation is the fundamental law of nature'. The trouble is that this self-preserving inclination may be regarded either as (1) an invariable physical law or (2) as an individually or collectively imposed social or behavioural rule. There is a logical ambiguity here; it lies in Hobbes's own formulation; nor can it be seen as to how one might clear it up by a mere accumulation of contextual detail. If Hobbes means (1), then it is clear that not everyone – at wild moments in life, perhaps no one – is governed by such a physical law. And if this is so, then Hobbes's initial premiss is shown to be defective. Alternatively, if Hobbes means (2), and if he only means madmen to be excepted from it, then there must presumably be some form of moral imperative involved. And if this is so, then the 'traditional' view of Hobbes (which precludes the presence of any ethic) is in turn shown to be defective. (For an extended review of this problem, see King, 1974, esp. Appendix 5.)

It is probably fair to say that one interpretation of a text can only be countered by another interpretation of that text. The two questions which always arise — we need not shrink from calling them 'perennial' — are (a) whether the text is factually correct and (b) logically sound. One may be perfectly entitled to venture outside the text — to enquire about the content of the author's letters; the demands on his purse; the source of his profits; the character of his love and of those who received it; the reception of his writing, whether with joy or pain; and so on. But at any time one does this, one must do so on the grounds, either that these matters hold out an independent interest and are not really material to the meaning of the text under review; or on the grounds that the meaning of a specific text is not necessarily to be discerned only between the covers of some nominated tome. What one cannot coherently do is to object to looking at, say, a philosopher's work 'as a whole doctrine', while simultaneously rummaging about in his private correspondence to try to get some clue as to his meaning in some singular book, essay or letter. Where we move beyond the text in this way, we inevitably attribute to the author an attempt at coherence, as expressed in the text and beyond.

At all events, Skinner provides his own textual interpretation of Hobbes. He cites Brown, Krook and Raphael as presenting the sort of interpretation he favours, together with a great deal of commentary from Hobbes's time. He pulls out the Hobbesian texts, or portions of texts, which he thinks bear a plain meaning, and holds them out to his readers for inspection. I believe it is fair to say that Skinner's interpretation is thin. His excuse or reason for this is that he seeks to say nothing 'novel', adhering as he does to the 'traditional' view. What this approach reveals, however, is that Skinner does detect the problems in the 'traditional' approach, problems which have prompted so many thinkers to attempt to pick their way round that approach.

Skinner (1964), although the bulk of the analysis is at this early stage textual, was not content to rest his case on this exercise alone. Skinner attempts to undermine Hood's analysis of Hobbes in a more roundabout fashion. Skinner's approach consists in assigning Hood to 'a particular tradition in the study of intellectual history, by which it is taken to consist (both necessarily and sufficiently) of a type of philosophical exercise'. What this means is that the student considers the work of a writer as a whole and attempts to construct from it 'the most coherent theory' he can (p. 322). 'The investigation proceeds', Skinner contends, 'exclusively by rationalizations of texts'. Skinner regards this as 'a type of study which is itself misconceived'. Skinner assimilates to this 'tradition' a variety of figures, including Hood of course, but most notably Warrender and Macpherson. All err in the same way, even if the severity of the offence is adjudged more 'acute' in some cases than in others. What is the nature of the misconception involved? Skinner explains that 'all interpretation, involving rationalizations of an author's own statements must depend in effect on textual suppressions' and that this 'allows the omission of alleged inconsistencies' (p. 323).

One difficulty for Skinner is that he admits Warrender's 'rationalizations' to be 'virtually self-justifying' and yet does not tackle the latter's work. If, in short, the strongest case of 'textual analysis' of the Hobbesian *oeuvre* available to Skinner was one which he knowingly side-stepped, he would have little basis for claiming all such approaches to be somehow 'misconceived' in principle.

A second difficulty for Skinner is that he at no point seriously attempts or demonstrably succeeds in pinning this abstract notion of a 'tradition' or method of approach upon his chief subject of review. Hood, in the preface to his book on Hobbes, welcomed 'Warrender's book on Hobbes's Theory of Obligation as opening a new era . . . in which close examination of the relevant texts should yield increasing understanding'. Perfectly plausible. It is not a universal claim. We are only entitled to infer that Hood favours textual analysis, as does everyone in some degree. Skinner's own practice in this regard, if less than stunning, can be cited in support. Hood, however, is unfairly saddled with the view, a view not expressed by him, not just that intellectual history is or ought to be, sometimes or mostly, an engagement in logical analysis – but that it is 'both necessarily and sufficiently . . . a type of philosophical exercise'. In short, Skinner attributes to Hood a more ambitious aspiration than any he ever in fact espoused.

A fourth difficulty is that Skinner puts himself in a position where any attempt to give the benefit of the doubt to an author, by allowing the strongest possible rendering of his position, must reduce 'to rationalization'. As an extension of this, any interpretation at all must violate Skinner's criteria (1964) of acceptability, since every interpretation is selective and all selection, if one wishes to put it thus, 'must depend in effect on textual suppressions'.

The important point in all this is that Skinner's only telling points against Hood are based on textual analysis. Where Skinner seeks to say more – namely that this 'type of study' *qua* type 'is itself misconceived' – he trips badly in the ways indicated. He falsely concludes of

Hood that 'exegetical coherence is gained at the expense of any historical plausibility'. What Skinner comes closest to demonstrating (here textually) is that Hood's analysis simply does not sit comfortably with what Hobbes explicitly says, that Hood's coherence renders more acute the appearance of Hobbes's incoherence. It may well be the case, in short, while being in no way demonstrated by Skinner, that 'an historical dimension' is vital to achieving some understanding of the meaning 'of a classical text' (p. 333).

The review by Skinner (1964) of Hood, unfortunately, apart from the comment on the fragment (1965b), is his first serious effort to unravel Hobbes's political theory of obligation. Skinner exhibits impressive control of historical detail. Perhaps the virtue becomes a fault. This, for the reason that so engaging a pursuit of detail may lead one to exaggerate its importance. Whatever the case, the crucial problem for Skinner must remain that of practically demonstrating a connection between deciphering the meaning of Hobbes's text and detailing as fully as may be the context out of which the text emerged.

Skinner (1965a), in his article on history and ideology in the English Revolution, does not carry this logical project any further forward. He provides a great deal of interesting detail on Hobbes's contemporaries. And he may be perfectly entitled to conclude, from the available evidence, that 'the conventional concentration of attention on Hobbes has caused his contribution to [the seventeenth-century discussion of conquest, sovereignty, and by extension political obligation to be] overestimated'. But Skinner goes on to maintain that 'Hobbes did not even provide the most original or systematic formulation of the views at issue' and that he 'may to some extent have adopted his views from earlier discussions' (p. 170). This is a remarkable claim. One difficulty stems, however, from the fact that Skinner omits to advise us as to who, specifically, was *more* original or *more* systematic than Hobbes. Skinner is ready enough to refer to the work of Ascham, Nedham and others, but is never so rash as directly to make a claim of such amplitude for them. And though it is easy for commentators to 'exaggerate' the originality of a thinker like Hobbes, who could affect not to be surprised at the discovery, in Hobbes's time, of a dozen writers expounding, as in the days of Thrasymachus, some variation of a 'might makes right' thesis — that 'Fealty and Homage [should go] to him that hath possession *de facto*'? It is often enough said, without ceasing to be true because of the currency of the view, that a philosopher's originality is less to be found in the novelty of the parts, than in the manner in which they are made to combine. One is scarcely likely to be embarrassed by the claim that Hobbes's *Leviathan* — if one cavils at the expression 'unique' — is an extraordinarily distinctive work, made so by the imaginative and sustained acuity of the analysis.

In any event, while Skinner (1965a) never expressly retracts the statements he makes about Hobbes's supposed lack of originality etc., the ensuing six years sober him to the point where he lets slip avowals whose effect is flatly to contradict the earlier position. Skinner (1972a) calls 'de facto theorists' all those who, like Hobbes, defended a title to rule as just where derived from conquest or effective control. He goes on to say that although 'all the lay defenders of "engagement" did explicitly state this new *de facto* theory of obligation none of them *argued for it in a very systematic way*' and so on (my italics, p. 93). Hobbes himself, from being a nothing, is allowed to swell a progress or two, and is suddenly elevated to the status of a 'genius' — the 'only one' now allowed to be 'at large in the discussion' (p. 94). From the position that Hobbes may have adopted his views 'from earlier discussions' (Skinner 1965a), we observe a retreat to higher ground, where Skinner (1972a) notes that the de facto theorists made claims similar to Hobbes's, not necessarily that either influenced the other, and that 'Hobbes . . . articulated their own view of political obligation in a *uniquely systematic and comprehensive way*' (my italics, p. 94). It is difficult to imagine a more complete turnabout. One is required to call it unstable simply because the author nowhere acknowledges it.

The point is not that Skinner ever entirely abandons textual analysis. In his article on Hobbes and the engagement controversy, for example, we shall find Skinner (1972a) countering those who view Hobbes as a proponent of duty with quotations from Hobbes himself, quotations designed to set the record straight. But it is no longer the textual analysis, this being all the more exiguous, which claims our attention. For in the meantime, Skinner (1966a, 1972d) sets out what he takes to be the philosophical implications of his contextual commitment. Skinner (1966a) comes to the view that to sketch in Hobbes's ideological context 'will not only produce an historically more complete picture' but will also help to resolve substantive 'questions about the proper interpretation of Hobbes's views' (p. 287). What Skinner seeks concretely to establish is that 'the historical study of Hobbes's intellectual milieu can be used to help assess the philosophers' various interpretations of Hobbes's meaning' — the meaning of his book(s). Thus Skinner maintains that the exploration of the 'ideological context . . . can be shown to carry analytical as well as historical implications' (p. 313). What a theory is, in terms of what it logically implies, cannot, claims Skinner, be divorced from the context out of which it emerges. Skinner (1972d) then purports to turn his back on the concern to determine directly — i.e. 'as a matter of textual exegesis' whether for example Warrender's kind of analytical approach 'offers the best account of Hobbes's meaning'. He takes it that 'the intellectual milieu' or the 'ideological context', where properly set out, can of itself establish or undermine the accuracy of a gloss on a text where this relates to its meaning or logical thrust. This then represents a radical twist in Skinner's argument. And this appears to be the point of his conclusion that 'the weight' of mid-seventeenth-century testimony 'is perhaps sufficient in itself' to discredit any present-day interpretation, like Warrender's, which imposes upon Hobbes a theory of duty (p. 137).

We have no difficulty in accepting Skinner's researches, on the historical level, as fruitful. But we shall be occasioned equally little difficulty in seeing that he comes to the point of exaggerating their value. Either the weight of exegetical opinion in a writer's age is itself adequate to discredit the interpretations of subsequent generations, or it is not. So we appear entitled to ignore Skinner's 'perhaps' to surmise that he thinks it is adequate. Otherwise, he would be saying nothing at all different from Pocock (1962a), for example, who maintains that history and philosophy are distinct and from which position Skinner (1964, p. 330 n. 13) consciously seeks to distance himself. Skinner then expects historical context to validate or subvert readings of philosophical texts. Accordingly, he sets out to establish how Hobbes's contemporaries understood the latter's political theory of obligation. Skinner assumes that these contemporaries, sharing the linguistic and social conventions of Hobbes himself, are authoritatively placed to elicit a fellow contemporary's meaning. Hence Skinner's conclusion that an interpretation of Hobbes in our day, which does not jell with those views of Hobbes current when he was about, is automatically subverted. What we are dealing with here, however, is only a wobbly form of probabilism. One need only consider how easily any contemporary observer may be induced to think that he has seized a position, which the author may conclude has not been properly apprehended in any one or more of its several significant aspects. If Skinner were tempted for example to think this of the present interpretation, we might discover in the thought further support for our position.

Take the case of Clarendon. Let us accept that he believed Hobbes to be expounding, not 'a theory of duty', but the view, in Clarendon's words, that 'self-preservation is the fundamental law of nature and supersedes the obligation of all others' (Clarendon in Skinner, 1972d,

p. 139). Even if *all* of Hobbes's contemporaries believed this, then that belief in no way helps to resolve the chronic logical instability, adverted to earlier, regarding the status of 'self-preservation' as a 'law of nature'. If, for example, self-preservation is ever made to imply more than just an overwhelming psychological 'drive', and instead or as well some principle to govern the behaviour of self-conscious beings, then the simple opposition between 'self-preservation' and 'a theory' or 'sense' of 'duty' cannot prove tenable. (And we know well enough that any individual who ceases to seek to preserve himself may, in other respects, prove perfectly 'normal'.) Here, we appear to get precisely nowhere, where we assume that understanding the historical context (i.e. Clarendon) explains the philosophical text (e.g. *Leviathan*). The difficulty of coming to grips with Hobbes's theory of political obligation has all the appearance of a logical problem that is internal to, and not external to, the text.

One cannot object if Skinner should seek to resolve the philosophical problem by endorsing, for example, present-day arguments for a 'prudential' Hobbesian morality. There are, as it happens, good reasons both for accepting and rejecting such an interpretation of Hobbes. But where we welcome such a gloss, we endorse an interpretation current in our own century, and one which takes us a little beyond the intellectual milieu of Hobbes's seventeenth-century contemporaries.

It is a help to us that Skinner (1966a) should pull together considerable evidence in support of the view 'that Hobbes came to be cited and accepted within his own lifetime . . . as an authority on matters of political theory' (p. 297). But if we accept Skinner's account to be accurate, all that he effectively shows is that many of Hobbes's contemporaries held views similar to his own on obligation and that virtually all of them understood Hobbes to mean that 'a man became absolutely obliged to obey *any* government that could protect him' and that 'when a subject was not adequately protected his obligation must cease' (p. 315). Let us take this to be a fair thumb-nail summary of a significant aspect of Hobbes. One consideration is that it would remain so, even had Hobbes's contemporaries taken a different view. We have already drawn attention to the intrinsic instability of the Hobbesian concept of self-preservation *qua* law of nature. But what matters is that a gloss accepted by one or even all of Hobbes's contemporaries, unless Hobbes somehow himself, directly or indirectly, sanctioned it, could not reliably or logically permit us to infer that this was Hobbes' view, as opposed to theirs. It can be instructive to piece together the way in which a writer was received. But the subject of a reception is still to be distinguished from the reception itself. It would be quite out of place to frown upon any scholar's pursuit of circumstantial detail in the attempt to enlarge our understanding of ideas. But Hobbes's historical context, researched with a view to establishing the character of contemporary opinion, remains circumstantial to Hobbes's logic, as embodied in his text. Skinner's thin textual analysis of Hobbes's theory of political obligation, conjoined with the more elaborate contextual analysis (of Hobbes's 'Intellectual Milieu'), while fascinating enough, does not appear to shed further light on that theory.

A large part of the difficulty is that Skinner simply misapprehends some of the implications of what he is doing. Skinner (1972d) may well be able to claim that Hobbes's theory of political obligation enjoyed a 'contemporary ideological relevance' (p. 130). But all that this undermines is the proposition that Hobbes's theory enjoyed no such relevance. To say however that Hobbes attracted a great deal of flak in his day (which is what Sterling Lamprecht presumably means when he maintains that there were 51 unfavourable published reactions to Hobbes during his life, and only one in favour), and that he in this sense stood alone, is not necessarily to say that Hobbes had no contemporary relevance. But even where Skinner aptly contradicts those who may mean that Hobbes was somehow obscure or unacknowledged or wholly devoid of influence, success in the matter, a success moreover to be applauded, brings one no nearer than before to affirming or controverting claims regarding the philosophical meaning of Hobbes's argument. If contemporaries were to claim that Hobbes was or was not an atheist, a materialist, a proponent of divine right, of *de facto* power or whatever, any conclusion that we might draw that he must be any of these things, on the simple grounds that these were the claims of his contemporaries, must obviously prove mistaken. Indeed, it would appear that none of Hobbes's contemporaries quite grasped the complexity of his system. We may say that Skinner himself fails to do so, if we take account of the false transparence which he projects for the Hobbesian principle of political obligation.

It is possible that no given method will yield consistently reliable results. To fall back principally upon one or a series of textual statements by the writer himself, in this case Hobbes, is an attractive proposal; and to treat such texts seriously and faithfully where we seek to elicit their meaning cannot prove an absurd rule of thumb; but it remains that an individual's claims about his own intentions are not always and necessarily either accurate or truthful. Besides, what a writer denies at one point may be admitted at another. It will not matter where one position replaces another, as long as the substitute view is itself coherent. But on occasion the contradiction is not of this simple temporal sort; it may assume the oppressive reality attributed to ghosts: the author cannot be sure that he has seen it, and may indeed be quite certain that it does not exist. The difficulty is that where contradiction is located, so too is whatever meaning or intention one chooses or is tempted to see. To fall back principally upon the reconstruction of a context to understand a text, is to many a no less attractive proposal. But this is only so where one supposes that one already understands the text. If one cannot quite make sense of what Hobbes means by grounding the science of politics upon the known natural inclinations of mankind, then further exposure to contemporaries who detail similar claims is unlikely to help.

Skinner seeks to recover Hobbes's intentions in writing his main works by investigating his seventeenth-century context. One suspects in this a confusion between the different objects of intentions. An intention may relate to a psychological motive to achieve a social or political or physical effect, such as winning a war or winning over an adversary or working a quarry. But an intention may also quite distinctly refer to a philosophical engagement to explore the logic of one or a set of propositions. The difference is that, where an intention to do something (as in the first case) exists on only one level, the intention to think through a problem (as in the second case) exists on two. The logical problem is a level to itself. But the problem solved, when resolved, may possibly be used — this places it on another level — to serve some distinct, perhaps 'secondary' purpose. Hobbes took it that he had solved a problem in logic relating to political obligation. But it is also possible to see, whatever our personal feelings about his 'secondary' object (assume this to relate to the Engagement controversy), that the logic of his solution is inadequate. Skinner's mistake appears to consist in confounding Hobbes's specific historical intention, an intention to achieve an external end (whatever this may in fact have been), with a quite distinct philosophical intention, the concern to resolve a problem in logic. In this sense, to discover what Hobbes *intended* will not necessarily tell us what he *meant*.

In his paper on Hobbes and the engagement controversy, Skinner (1972a) argues (pp. 79, 81) that 'one of Hobbes's main aims in *Leviathan* was to contribute to [a particular] debate about the rights of *de facto* powers' at the climax of the English Revolution in the opening months of 1649. Skinner later extends this conclusion to apply to 'Hobbes's main political works' as a whole, which, he writes, make a 'highly important contribution to the lay defence of "engagement" ' (p. 96). Skinner goes to considerable lengths to show that all of Hobbes's major work (which must include *De corpore politico* and *De cive*) was produced to serve one quite specific political purpose — without claiming that no other functions or purposes were served. The point would appear to be that Hobbes was not just abstractly concerned to argue 'that any political power with the capacity to protect its citizens is for that reason a justifiable political authority, and so is entitled to their obedience' — but that this argument was directed to a particular audience and was prompted by a specific set of events in 1649. Skinner works on so broad a canvas that he never allowed himself to consider a critical but obvious flaw. *De corpore politico* and *De cive*, so very like *Leviathan*, were worked out before 1642, and well before Charles was executed, and thus much in advance of the engagement controversy. An argument which was worked out in its essentials *before* the event, could not have been worked out *for* the event. Even a critic so sympathetic to Skinner as Wiener (1974) is prompted to observe that 'Hobbes's political philosophy seems to have been worked out, not at all as a response to the engagement controversy, but much earlier, in the 1630s' (p. 256). It is interesting, too, that in Skinner's reply to Wiener, this critical riposte is nowhere touched upon (Skinner, 1974). The reason for this omission may have been occasioned by Wiener's sanguine conclusion, despite the difficulty noted, that Skinner's essays on Hobbes 'demonstrate that an exclusive reliance on textual analysis leads to a faulty understanding, particularly of Hobbes's theory of obligation' (p. 258). These essays on Hobbes, which are held to prove that the discussion of the latter's contemporaries (his context), elucidates the meaning of what Hobbes wrote (his text), precisely fail to achieve this object.

Source

Specially written for this volume.

BIBLIOGRAPHY

Acton, H.B. (1952) 'Tradition and Some Other Forms of Order', *Proc Aris Soc, 53*, 1-29

Almond, G.A. (1966) 'Political Theory and Political Science', *Amer Pol Sci Rev, 60:4*, 869-79

Arnhart, L. (1979) 'On Wood's Social History of Political Theory', *Polit Theory, 7:2*, 281-2

Ashcraft, R. (1975) 'On the Problem of Methodology and the Nature of Political Theory', *Polit Theory, 3:1*, 5-26

Auspitz, J.L. (1976) 'Individuality, Civility, and Theory: The Philosophical Imagination of Michael Oakeshott', *Polit Theory, 4:3*, 261-94. (A Symposium on Michael Oakeshott) (PT)

Austin, J.L. (1961) *Philosophical Papers*, Oxford, Oxford University Press

—— (1962) *How To Do Things With Words*, Oxford, Oxford University Press.

Bateson, F.W. (1953) 'The Function of Criticism at the Present Time', *Essays in Criticism, 3:1*, 1-27

Berdyaev, N. (1936) *The Meaning of History*, trans. by G. Reavey, London

Berki, R.N. (1977) *The History of Political Thought: A Short Introduction*, London, Dent

Berlin, I. (1954) *Historical Inevitability*, Oxford, Oxford University Press

—— (1961) 'History and Theory: The Concept of Scientific History', *Hist Theor, 1:1*, 1-31

—— (1976) *Vico and Herder: Two Studies in the History of Ideas*. London, Hogarth Press

—— (1979) *Against the Current: Essays in the History of Ideas*, with bibliography by Henry Hardy (ed.), London, Hogarth Press

Bernheim, E. (1908) *Lehrbuch der Historischen Methode* 2 vols., Leipzig

Birch, A.H. (1969) 'Historical Explanation and the Study of Politics', *Govt. and Opp., 4:2*, 215-30

Black, A. (1980) 'Skinner on the Foundations of Modern Political Thought', *Pol Stud, 28:3*, 451-7

Blackburn, S. (1973) *Reason and Prediction*, Cambridge, Cambridge University Press

Bloch, M. (1955) *Reflections on the Historian's Craft*, Manchester, Manchester University Press

Boas, G. (1947) 'Review of Bertrand Russell's *History of Western Philosophy*', J Hist Ideas, 8:1, 117-23

—— (1948) 'A.O. Lovejoy as Historian of Philosophy', *J Hist Ideas, 9:4*, 404-11

—— (ed.) (1953a) *Studies in Intellectual History*, New York, Greenwood Press

—— (1953b) 'Some Problems of Intellectual History' in Boas (ed.) 1953) pp. 3-21

—— (1964) 'Bias and the History of Ideas: The Romantic Syndrome; by W.T. Jones', *J Hist Ideas, 25:3*, 451-7

—— (1969) *The History of Ideas*, New York, Scribner's

Boucher, D.E.G. (1980) 'On Shklar's and Franklin's Review of Q. Skinner, *The Foundations of Modern Political Thought, Polit Theory, 8:3*, 403-6

Braybrooke, D. (1971) A Review of Gordon Leff's, *History and Social Theory, Hist Theor, 10:1*, 122-34

Brown, K.C. (ed.) (1965) *Hobbes Studies*, Oxford

Bury, J.B. (1932) *The Idea of Progress*, New York, Dover Publishers

Calogero, G. (1963) 'On the So-Called Identity of History and Philosophy' in Kilbansky and Paton (eds.) (1963)

Carr, E.H. (1964) *What is History?* Harmondsworth, Middlesex, Penguin

Cherniss, H. (1953) 'The History of Ideas and Ancient Greek Philosophy' in Boas (ed.) (1953a), pp. 22-47

Cobban, A. (1953) 'The Decline of Political Theory', *Pol Sci Quart, 68:3*, 321-37

Cohen, L.J. (1953) 'Do Illocutionary Forces Exist?', *Essays in Criticism*, vol. 3, 119-37

Cohen, M.R. (1961)   *The Meaning of Human History*, La Salle, Ill., Open Court

Coker, R.W. (1934) *Recent Political Thought*, New York, Appleton-Century

Collingwood, R.G. (1916) *Religion and Philosophy*, London

—— (1924) *Speculum Mentis; or The Map of Knowledge*, Oxford, Clarendon Press

—— (1933) *An Essay on Philosophical Method*, Oxford, Clarendon Press

—— (1936) 'Human Nature and Human History', *Proc Brit Acad*, vol. 22. Reprinted in R.G. Collingwood, *The Idea of History*, Oxford, Clarendon Press

—— (1937) *Roman Britain and the English Settlements*, by R.G. Collingwood and J.N.L. Myres, Oxford, Clarendon Press

—— (1938a) *The Principles of Art*, Oxford, Clarendon Press

—— (1838b) 'On the So-Called Idea of Causation', *Proc Aris Soc*, vol. 38, 85-113

—— (1939) *An Autobiography*, London, Oxford University Press

—— (1940) *An Essay on Metaphysics*, Oxford, Clarendon Press

—— (1942) *The New Leviathan: or Men, Society,Civilisation and Barbarism*, Oxford, Clarendon Press

—— (1945) *The Idea of Nature* (ed.) T.M. Knox, Oxford, Clarendon Press

—— (1946) *The Idea of History* (ed.) T.M. Knox, Oxford, Clarendon Press

—— (1966) *Essays in the Philosophy of History*, with introduction by W. Debbins (ed.), New York, McGraw-Hill

—— (1970) 'Oakeshott and the Modes of Experience', review of *Experience and Its Modes* in Homberger, E. *et al.* (eds.), *The Cambridge Mind: Ninety Years of the Cambridge Review, 1879-1969*, Boston & London (CM)

Colodny, R.G. (ed.) (1962) *Frontiers of Science and Philosophy*, Pittsburgh, University of Pittsburgh Press

Condren, C. (1979) *Three Aspects of Political Theory*, Melbourne, Macmillan

Crick, B. (1967) 'Philosophy, Theory and Thought', *Pol Stud, 15:1*, 49-55

Croce, B. (1919) (1921) (1960) *History: Its Theory and Practice*, trans. by D. Ainslee, New York

Cropsey,J. (1964) *Ancients and Moderns: Essays on the Tradition of Political Philosophy in Honor of Leo Strauss*, New York, Basic Books

Danto, A. (1965) *Analytical Philosophy of History*, Cambridge, Cambridge University Press

Donagan, A. (1956) 'The Verification of Historical Theses', *Phil Quart, 6:24*, 193-208

—— (1957) 'Historical Explanation', *Mind, 66:262*, 145-64

—— (1962) *The Later Philosophy of R.G. Collingwood*, Oxford, University Press

Dray, W. (1957) *Laws and Explanation in History*, Oxford, Oxford University Press

Dray, W. (ed.) (1966) *Philosophical Analysis and History*, New York, Harper and Row

—— (1971) 'On the Nature and Role of Narrative in Historiography', *Hist Theor, 10:2*, 153-71

Dummett, M. (1964) 'Bringing about the Past', *Philosophical Review 73:3*, 338-59

Dunn, J. (1968) 'The Identity of the History of Ideas', *Philosophy, 43:164*,
    85-104. Also published in *Philosophy, Politics and Society*, Laslett, Runciman
    and Skinner (eds.), 1972
—— (1969) *The Political Thought of John Locke: An Historical Account of the
    Argument of the 'Two Treatises of Government'*, London, Cambridge
    University Press
—— (1980) *Political Obligation in its Historical Context: Essays in Political
    Theory*, Cambridge, Cambridge University Press
Easton, D. (1966) *Varieties of Political Theory*, New Jersey, Englewood Cliffs,
    Prentice Hall Inc.
Edel, A. (1946) 'Levels of Meaning and the History of Ideas', *J Hist Ideas, 7:3*,
    355-60
Elton, G.R. (1969) *The Practice of History*, London, Glasgow and Sydney,
    Fontana
—— (1970) *Political History: Principles and Practice*, London, Allen Lane,
    The Penguin Press
Ely, R.G. (1969) 'Mandelbaum on Historical Narrative', by R.G. Ely, R. Gruner
    and W. Dray, *Hist Theor, 8:2*, 275-94
Eulau, H. (1962) 'Comparative Political Analysis: A Methodological Analysis'
    Midwest J Pol Sci,6:4, 397-407
Fain, H. (1970) *Between Philosophy and History*, Princeton, NJ
Femia, J.V. (1979) 'An Historicist Critique of Revisionist Methods for Studying
    the History of Ideas', Proceedings of the International Political Science
    Association, Moscow (August)
Field, G.C. (1953) 'What is Political Theory'?, *Proc Aris Soc, 54*, 145-67
—— (1956) *Political Theory*, London, Methuen
Finberg, H.P. (ed.) (1962) *Approaches to History*, London, Routledge and
    Kegan Paul
Fischer, D.H. (1970) *Historians' Fallacies: Toward a Logic of Historical Thought*
    London, Routledge and Kegan Paul
Fling, F.M. (1920) *The Writing of History: An Introduction to Historical Method*,
    New Haven
Gallie, W.B. (1964) *Philosophy and the Historical Understanding*, New York and
    London, Chatto & Windus
—— (1972) Review of *Fact and Relevance: Essays on Historical Method*, by
    M.M. Postan and *Political History, Principles and Practice*, by G.R. Elton,
    Amer Pol Sci Rev, 66:4, 1342-3
Gardiner, P. (1952) *The Nature of Historical Explanation*, Oxford, Oxford
    University Press
Gardiner, P. (ed.) (1959) *Theories of History*, Glencoe, Ill., Free Press
Gatlung, J. (1967) *Theory and Methods of Social Research*, New York, Columbia
    University Press
Geyl, P. (1962) *Debates with Historians*, London, Fontana
Gottschalk, L.R. (1950) *Understanding History: a Primer of Historical Method*,
    New York, Knopf
—— (1964) *Generalisation in History*, Chicago, Chicago University Press
Gracia, J.J.E. (1975) 'The History of Ideas in Latin America', *J Hist Ideas, 36:1*,
    177-84
Graham, G. (1982) 'Can There Be History of Philosophy?', *Hist Theor.*, 22:1,
    37-52
Graubard, S.R. (1974) Review of Melvin Richter (ed.), *Essays in Theory and
    History: An Approach to the Social Sciences, Hist Theory, 13:3*, 335-42
Greene, J.C. (1957/8) 'Objectives and Methods in Intellectual History', *Mississippi*

Valley Historical Review, 44:1, 58-74

Greenleaf, W.H. (1964) *Order Empiricism and Politics, Two Traditions of English Political Thought*, Oxford, Oxford University Press

—— (1966) *Oakeshott's Philosophical Politics*, London, Longmans

Greenstein, F.I. (1967) 'Art and Science in the Political Life History', *Politics, 2:2*, 176-80

Gunnell, J.G. (1978) 'The Myth of the Tradition', *Amer Pol Sci Rev, 72:1*, 122-34

—— (1979) *Political Theory: Tradition and Interpretation*, Cambridge, Mass., Winthrop Publishers

—— (1982) 'Interpretation and the History of Political Theory: Apology and Epistemology', *Amer Pol Sci Rev, 76:2*, 317-27

Haddock, B.A. (1974) 'The History of Ideas and the Study of Politics', *Polit Theory, 2:4*, 420-31

Hallowell, J.H. (1954) 'Review of Leo Strauss *Natural Right and History*, *Amer Pol Sci Rev, 48:2*, 538-41

Harrison, W. (1955) 'Texts in Political Theory', *Pol Stud, 3:1*, 28-44

Hartman, R.S. (1953) *Reason in History*, New York, Bobbs-Merrill

Heinam, R. (1975) Review of J.G.A. Pocock's, *Politics, Language and Time: Essays on Political Thought and History, Amer Pol Sci Rev, 69:1*, 254-5

Hempel, C.G. (1942) 'The Function of General Laws in History', reprinted in Gardiner (1959). Also in Hempel (1965)

—— (1965) *Aspects of Scientific Explanation*, New York, Free Press

Himmelfarb, G. (1975) 'The Conservative Imagination: Michael Oakeshott', *The American Scholar, 44:3*, 405-20

Hirsh, E.D. (1967) *Validity in Interpretation*, New Haven, Yale University Press

Holmes, S.T. (1979) Review of Quentin Skinner's, *Foundations of Modern Political Thought, Amer Pol. Sci Rev, 73:4*, 1133-5

Huizinga, J. (1959) *Men and Ideas*, New York

Joynt, C.B. and N. Rescher (1961) 'The Probem of Uniqueness in History', *Hist Theory, 1:2*, 150-62

Johnson, A.H. (1946) 'Whitehead's Philosophy of History', *J Hist Ideas, 8:2*, 234-49

Jones, W.T. (1961) *The Romantic Syndrome: Towards a New Method in Cultural Anthropology and History of Ideas*, The Hague, Martinus Nijhoff

Kaplan, A. (1964) *The Conduct of Inquiry*,. San Francisco, Chandler Publishing Co.

Kaufman, W.A. (1949) 'Goethe and the History of Ideas', *J Hist Ideas, 10:4*, 503-16

Kaufman, H. (1964) 'Organization Theory and Political Theory', *Amer Pol Sci Rev, 58:1*, 5-14

Kelly, G.A. (1975) Review of Maurice Mandelbaum's, *History, Man and Reason: A Study in Nineteenth Century Thought, Amer Pol Sci Rev, 69:1*, 247-9

Kelley, D.R. (1979) Review of Skinner, *Foundations of Modern Political Thought, J Hist Ideas, 40:4*, 663-88

Kilbansky, R. and H.J. Paton (eds.) (1963) *Philosophy and History*, New York, Harper and Row

King, P. and B.C. Parekh (eds.) (1968) *Politics and Experience: Essays Presented to Michael Oakeshott*, Cambridge, Cambridge University Press

King, P. (1974) *The Ideology of Order: Comparative Analysis of Jean Bodin and Thomas Hobbes*, London, Allen & Unwin

Knox, T.M. (1946) Editor's Preface to Collingwood (1946)

Kohn, H. (1964) 'Political Theory and the History of Ideas', *J Hist Ideas, 25:2*, 303-8

Kracaver, S. (1969) *History: The Last Things Before the Last*, Oxford, New York Oxford University Press

Krammick, I. (1981) Review of Isaiah Berlin, *Against the Current: Essays in the History of Ideas, Amer Pol Sci Rev, 75:2*, 472-3

Krausz, M. (1972) *Critical Essays on the Philosophy of R.G. Collingwood*, Oxford, Clarendon Pres

Kristeller, P.O. (1946) 'The Philosophical Significance of the History of Thought, *J Hist Ideas, 7:3*, 360-6

Kuhn, T.S. (1970) *The Structure of Scientific Revolutions*, Chicago, University of Chicago Press

Kvastad, N.B. (1977) 'Semantics in the Methodology of the History of Ideas', *J Hist Ideas, 38:1*, 157-74

Laslett, P. and W.G. Runciman (eds.) (1956) *Philosophy, Politics and Society, Series II*, Oxford, Blackwell

Leavis, F.R. (1953) 'The Responsible Critic: Or the Function of Criticism at Any Time', *Scrutiny, 19:3*, 162-83

Leff, G. (1969) *History and Social Theory*, London, Merlin Press

Leslie, M. (1970) 'In Defence of Anachronism', *Political Studies, 18:4* (Dec.), 433-47

Levin, M. (1973) 'What Makes a Classic in Political Theory?' *Political Science Quarterly, 88:3* (Sept.), 462-76

Lewis, E. (1956) 'The Contribution of Medieval Thought to the American Political Tradition', *Amer Pol Sci Rev, 50:2*, 462-74

Lockyer, A. (1979) ' "Traditions" as Context in the History of Theory', *Pol Stud, 27:2*, 201-18

Lovejoy, A.O. (1920) 'Pragmatism Versus the Pragmatist' in D. Drake *et al., Essays in Critical Realism*, NewYork and London

—— (1930) *The Revolt Against Dualism: an Inquiry Concerning the Existence of Ideas*, London and New York

Lovejoy, A.O. and G.Boas (eds.) (1935) *Primitivism and Related Ideas in Antiquity*, New York

Lovejoy, A.O. (1936) *The Great Chain of Being: A Study of the History of an Idea*, Cambridge, Mass.

—— (1938) 'The Historiography of Ideas', *Proceedings of the American Philosophical Society*, reprinted in Lovejoy (1948)

—— (1939) 'Present Standpoints and Past History', reprinted in H. Mayerhoff (ed.), *The Philosophy of History in Our Time* (1959) New York

—— (1940) 'Reflections on the History of Ideas', *J Hist Ideas, 1:1* (Jan.), 3-23

—— (1948) *Essays in the History of Ideas*, Baltimore, Johns Hopkins Press

—— (1961a) *Reflections on Human Nature*, Baltimore, Johns Hopkins Press

—— (1961b) *The Reason, the Understanding, and Time*, Baltimore, Johns Hopkins Press

—— (1963) *The Thirteen Pragmatisms and Other Essays*, Baltimore, Johns Hopkins Press

Mackie, J.L. (1974) *The Cement of the Universe: A Study of Causation*, Oxford

Mandelbaum, M. (1938) *The Problem of Historical Knowledge: An Answer to Relativism* New York, Harper

—— (1948) 'Arthur O. Lovejoy and the Theory of Historiography', *J Hist Ideas, 9:4*, 412-23

—— (1955a) (1969) *The Phenomenology of Moral Experience*, Baltimore, Johns Hopkins University Press

—— (1955b) 'Concerning Recent Trends in the Theory of Historiography', *J Hist Ideas, 16:4*, 506-17

—— (1955c) (1959) 'Societal Facts' in Gardiner (1959). Originally in *British*

Journal of Sociology
—— (1961) 'Historical Explanation: the Problem of Covering Laws', *Hist Theor, 1:3*, 229-42
—— (1965) 'The History of Ideas, Intellectual History and the History of Philosophy', *Hist Theor, 4:3*, 33-66
—— (1967) 'A Note on History as Narrative', *Hist Theor, 6:3*, 413-19
—— (1971) *History, Man, and Reason: A Study in Nineteenth-Century Thought*, Baltimore, Johns Hopkins Press
—— (1977) *The Anatomy of Historical Knowledge*, Baltimore
Masu, R.G. (1952) 'William Dilthey and the History of Ideas', *J Hist Ideas, 13:1*, 94-107
Mazzeo, J.A. (1972) 'Some Interpretations of the History of Ideas', *J Hist Ideas, 33:3*, 379-94
Meyerhoff, H. (ed.) (1959) *The Philosophy of History in Our Time*, Garden City, New York
McCallum, R.B. (1943) See *Proceedings of British Academy*, vol, 29, 463-8
McIlwain, C.H. (1932) *The Growth of Political Thought in the West*, New York, Macmillan
Meehan, E. (1968) *Explanation in the Social Sciences: A System Paradigm*, Homewood, Ill.
Mink, L.O. (1966) 'The Autonomy of Historical Understanding', *Hist Theor, 5:1*, 24-47, reprinted in Dray (1966)
—— (1968) 'Collingwood's Dialectic of History', *Hist Theor, 2:1*, 3-38
—— (1971) Review of David Hackett Fischer, *Historian's Fallacies: Toward a Logic of Historical Thought, Hist. Theor, 10:1*, 107-22
—— (1978) Review of Maurice Mandelbaum, *The Anatomy of Historical Knowledge*, Hist Theor, 17:2, 211-23
Minogue, K.R. (1975) 'Oakeshott and the Idea of Freedom', *Quadrant, 19:7* 77-83 (Q)
Montefiore, A. (1975) *Neutrality and Impartiality: The University and Political Commitment*, Cambridge, Cambridge University Press
Mulligan, L. (1979) 'Intentions and Conventions: A Critique of Quentin Skinner's Method for the Study of the History of Ideas' by L. Mulligan, J. Richards and J. Graham, *Pol Stud, 27:1*, 84-98
Murphy, G.G.S. (1965) 'Sir Isaiah Berlin on "The Concept of Scientific History": A Comment', *Hist Theor, 4:2*, 234-43
Nagel, E. (1961) *The Structure of Science*, New York and London, Routledge & Kegan Paul
Newman, F.D. (1968) *Explanation by Description, An Essay on Historical Methodology*, The Hague
Nisbet, R.A. (1969) *Social Change and History*, New York, Oxford University Press
Nowell-Smith, P.H. (1957) 'Are Historical Events Unique?' *Proc Aris Soc, 56*, 107-60
Oakeshott, M. (1933) *Experience and its Modes*, Cambridge, Cambridge University Press (*Eim*)
—— (1955) 'The Activity of Being an Historian', republished in *RiP* (1962)
—— (1959) *The Voice of Poetry in the Conversation of Mankind*, London, republished in *RiP* (1962)
—— (1962) *Rationalism in Politics* and Other Essays, London & New York (*RiP*)
—— (1975) *Hobbes on Civil Association*, Oxford, Basil Blackwell
—— (1975) *On Human Conduct*, Oxford, Clarendon Press (*HC*)
Olafoon, F.A. (1969) 'Human Action and Historical Explanation' in J. Edie

(ed.), *New Essays in Phenomenology*, Chicago

Parekh, B. and Berki, R.N. (1973) 'The History of Political Ideas: A Critique of Q. Skinner's Methodology', *J Hist Ideas, 34:2*, 163-84

Passmore, J.A. (1958) 'The Objectivity of History', *Philosophy 33:125*, 97-111

—— (1965) 'The Historiography of the History of Philosophy', *Hist Theor, 4:3*, 1-32

Paton, H.J. (1936) *Philosophy and History*, New York, Harper and Row

Pocock, J.G.A. (1962a) 'The History of Political Thought: A Methodological Enquiry' in Laslett and Runciman (1962), 183-202

—— (1962b) 'The Origins of Study of the Past: a Comparative Approach', *Comp Studs Soc Hist, 4:2*, 209-46

—— (1967) ' The Dimension of Time in Systems of Political Thought', delivered in 1967 to *Amer Pol Sci Asso*. (typescript)

—— (1970) 'Working on Ideas in Time' in L.P. Curtis Jnr (ed.), *The Historian's Workshop*, New York, Alfred A. Knopf

—— (1971) *Politics, Language and Time: Essays on Political Thought and History*, New York, Atheneum

Popper, K.R. (1945) *The Open Society and Its Enemies*, London, Routledge & Kegan Paul

—— (1959) 'Prediction and Prophecy in the Social Sciences', in Gardiner (1959)

—— (1960) *The Poverty of Historicism*, London (PH)

Porter, D.H. (1975) 'History as a Process', *Hist Theor, 14:3*, 297-313

Postan, M.M. (1971) *Fact and Relevance: Essays on Historical Method*, Cambridge, Cambridge University Press

Proceedings of British Academy (1943) Obituary Notice on R.G. Collingwood, *29*, 463-85

Rees, J.C. (1957) 'Review of G.C. Fields *Political Theory*', Pol Stud, 5:1, 106-7

Richter, M. (ed.) (1970) *Essays in Theory and History: An Approach to the Social Sciences*, Cambridge, Mass., Harvard University Press

Rotenstreich, N. (1976) *Philosophy, History and Politics: Studies in Contemporary English Philosophy of History*, The Hague, Nijhoff

Rubinoff, L. (1970) *Collingwood and the Reform of Metaphysics: A Study in the Philosophy of Mind*, Toronto, University of Toronto Press

Russell, B. (1945) *History of Western Philosophy*, New York, Simon and Schuster

Sabine, G.H. (1937) *A History of of Political Theory*, New York, 3rd edn, Holt Rinehart and Winston

Schaar, J.H. (1963) 'Essays on the Scientific Study of Politics', *Amer Pol Sci Rev, 57:1*, 125-60

Schochet, G.J. (1974) 'Quentin Skinner's Method', *Polit Theory, 12:3*, 261-75

Scriven, M. (1959) 'Truisms as the Ground for Historical Explanation' in Gardiner (1959)

Sellars, R.W. *et al*. (1949) *Philosophy for the Future: The Quest of Modern Materialism*, New York, Macmillan

Shklar, J. (1979) Skinner: The Foundations of Modern Political Thought', *Polit Theory, 7:4*, 549-59

Siedentop, L.A. (1977) 'Whither Political Theory', *Pol Stud, 25:4*, 588-93

Skinner, Q. (1964) 'Hobbes's *Leviathan'*, *Hist J. 7:2*, 321-33

—— (1965a) 'History and Ideology in the English Revolution', *Hist J. 8:2*, 151-78

—— (1965b) 'Hobbes on Sovereignty: An Unknown Discussion', *Pol Stud, 13:2*, 213-18

—— (1966a) 'The Ideological Context of Hobbes's Political Thought', *Hist J, 9:3*, 286-317

—— (1966b) 'The Limits of Historical Explanations', *Philosophy, 41:157*,

199-215

—— (1966c) 'Thomas Hobbes and His Disciples in France and England', *Soc Hist, 8:2*, 153-67

—— (1966d) 'On Two Traditions of English Political Thought', *Hist J, 9:1*, 136-9

—— (1967) 'More's *Utopia', Past Pres*, no. 38, 153-68

—— (1969a) 'Meaning and Understanding in the History of Ideas', *Hist Theor, 8:1*, 3-53

—— (1969b) 'Thomas Hobbes and the Nature of the Early Royal Society', *Hist J. 12:2*, 217-39

—— (1970) 'Conventions and the Understanding of Speech Acts', *Phil Quart, 20:78*, 118-38

—— (1971) 'On Performing and Explaining Linguistic Actions', *Phil Quart, 21:82*, 1-21

—— (1972a) 'Conquest and Consent: Thomas Hobbes and the Engagement Controversy' in G.E. Aylmer (ed.), *The Interregnum*, London, Macmillan, 79-98

—— (1972b) 'Motives, Intentions and the Interpretation of Texts', *New Lit Hist, 3:2*, 393-408

—— (1972c) ' "Social Meaning" and the Explanation of Social Action' in P. Laslett, W.G. Runciman and Q. Skinner (eds.), *Philosophy Politics and Society*, Oxford, Blackwell, pp. 136-57

—— (1972d) 'The Context of Hobbes's Theory of Political Obligation', in M.W. Cranston and R.S. Peters (eds.), *Hobbes and Rousseau*, Garden City, New York, Anchor Books, 109-42. A revised version of Skinner 1966a

—— (1973) 'The Empirical Theorists of Democracy and their Critics', *Polit Theory, 1:3*, 287-305

—— (1974) 'Some Problems in the Analysis of Political Thought and Action', *Polit Theory, 2:3*, 277-303

—— (1978a) *The Foundations of Modern Political Thought: vol. 1, The Renaissance; vol. II, The Age of Reformation*, Cambridge, Cambridge University Press

—— (1978b) 'Action and Context', *The Aristotelian Society*, supplementary vol., 52, 55-69

—— (1979) 'The Idea of a Cultural Lexicon', *Essays in Criticism, 29*, 205-23

Skotheim, R.A. (1964) 'The Writing of American Histories of Ideas: Two Traditions in the Twentieth Century', *J. Hist Ideas, 25:2*, 257-78

Spencer, T. (1948) 'Lovejoy's Essays in the History of Ideas', *J Hist Ideas, 9:4*, 439-46

Spitzer, L. (1941) 'History of Ideas Versus Reading of Poetry', *South Rev, 6:3* 586-604

Staughton, L. (1969) 'Historical Past and Existential Present' in T. Roszak (ed.), *The Dissenting Academy*, London, Chatto and Windus, pp. 92-110

Stern, F. (1960) *Varieties of History*, London, Thames and Hudson (New York, 1956

Stolnitz, J. (1961) 'Beauty: Some Stages in the History of an Idea' *J Hist Ideas, 22:2*, 185-204

Storing, H.J. (1962) *Essays on the Scientific Study of Politics*, New York, Holt, Rinehart and Winston

Strauss, L. (1936) (1952c) *The Political Philosophy of Hobbes: Its Basis and Its Genesis*. Trans. E.M. Sinclair, Oxford (1st edn), Chicago (2nd edn)

—— (1945) 'On Classical Political Philosophy', *Soc Res, 12:1*, 98-117, reprinted in Strauss, 1959

—— (1948) *On Tyranny: An Interpretation of Xenophon's 'Hiero'*, New York

—— (1949) 'Political Philosophy and History', *J Hist Ideas, 10:1*, 30-50, reprinted in Strauss, 1959a

—— (1950) 'Natural Right and the Historical Approach', *Review of Politics, 12:4*, 422-42, reprinted in Strauss, 1953

—— (1952a) *Persecution and the Art of Writing*, Glencoe, Ill., Free Press

—— (1952b) 'On Collingwood's Philosophy of History', *Rev Metaph, 5:4*, 559-86

—— (1952c) See 1936

—— (1953) *Natural Right and History*, Chicago, Chicago University Press

—— (1957) 'What is Political Philosophy?' *J Polit, 19:1*, 343-68. Extended form in Strauss, 1959a

—— (1958) *Thoughts on Machiavelli*, Glencoe, Ill., Free Press

—— (1959a) *What is Political Philosophy? and Other Studies*, New York, Free Press

—— (1959b) 'The Liberalism of Classical Political Philosophy', *Rev Metaph, 12:3*, 390-439. Reprinted in Strauss, 1968

Strauss, L. and J. Cropsey (eds.) (1963) *History of Political Philosophy*, Chicago, Rand McNally

Strauss, L. (1964a) *The City and Man*. Chicago, Rand McNally

—— (1964b) 'The Crisis of Our Time' and 'The Crisis of Political Philosophy' in H.J. Spaeth (ed.) *The Predicament of Modern Politics*, Detroit

—— (1965) *Spinoza's Critique of Religion*, trans. E.M. Sinclair, New York, Schocken Books

—— (1966) *Socrates and Aristophanes,* New York, Basic Books

—— (1968) *Liberalism, Ancient and Modern*, New York, Basic Books

—— (1970) *Xenophon's Socratic Discourse: An Interpretation of the Oeconomicus*. With a new literal translation of the *Oeconomicus* by Carnes Lord, Ithaca, Cornell

—— (1975a) *The Argument and the Action of Plato's Laws*, Chicago, University of Chicago Press

—— (1975b) *Political Philosophy*, New York, Pegasus

Tarlton, C.D. (1973) 'Historicity, Meaning and Revisionism in the Study of Political Thought', *Hist Theory, 22:3*, 307-28

Teggart, F.J. (1960) *Theory and Processes of History*, Berkeley

Thomas, K. (1965)'The Social Origins of Hobbes's Political Thought' in Brown, 1965

Toynbee, A. (1945) *A Study of History*, 3rd edn, New York, Oxford University Press

Trevor-Roper, H.R. (1967) *Religion, the Reformation and Social Change*, London

Von Wright, G.H. (1971) *Explanation and Understanding*, Ithaca, New York

Walsh, W.H. (1942) 'The Intelligibility of History', *Philosophy, 17:4*, 128-43

—— (1951) *Introduction to the Philosophy of History*, London

—— (1975) 'The Causation of Ideas', *Hist Theor, 14:1*, 186-99

—— (1978) Review of Isaiah Berlin, *Two Studies in the History of Ideas, MIND, 87:2*, 284-5

Watkins, F.M. (1964) *The Age of Ideology, Political Thought, 1750 to the Present*, New Jersey, Englewood Cliffs

Watkins, J.W.N. (1955) 'Review of Perez Zagorin's *A History of Political Thought in the English Revolution*', *Pol Stud, 3:1*, 79-80

Wellmer, A. (1979) Review of Richard Bernstein, *The Restructuring of Social and Political Theory, Hist Theor, 18:1*, 84-103

White, M. (1965) *The Foundations of Historical Knowledge*, New York

Whitehead, A.N. (1925) *Science and the Modern World*, London

Whitehead, A.N. (1933) *Adventures of Ideas*, Cambridge, Cambridge University Press

Wiener, J.M. (1974) 'Quentin Skinner's Hobbes', *Polit Theory, 2:3*, 251-60

Wiener, P.P. (1946) 'Logical Significance of the History of Thought', *J Hist Ideas, 7:3*, 366-74

Weiner, P.P. (1961) 'Some Problems and Methods in the History of Ideas', *J Hist Ideas, 22:4,* 531-49

Wilkins, B.P. (1978) *Has History any Meaning?*, Hassocks, Sussex, Harvester Press

Wilson, F.G. (1949) Review of John Bowles, *Western Political Thought: An Historical Introduction from the Origins to Rousseau*, Amer Pol Sc Rev, 43:3, 606-7

Wilson, F.G. (1953) Review of Eric Voegelin, *The New Science of Politics, An Introductory Essay, Amer Pol Sci Rev, 47:2,* 542-3

Wolin, S.S. (1961) *Politics and Vision: Continuity and Innovation in Western Political Thought*, London, Allen and Unwin
——(1963) 'Essays on the Scientific Study of Politics', *Amer Pol Sci Rev, 57:1*, 125-60
—— (1969) 'Political Theory as a Vocation', *Amer Pol Sci Rev, 58:4*, 1062-82

Wood, N. (1973) Review of L. Strauss and J. Cropsey, *History of Political Philosophy, Polit Theory, 1:3*, 341-3
—— (1978) 'The Social History of Political Theory', *Polit Theory, 6:3*, 345-69

KEY TO JOURNAL ABBREVIATIONS

Amer Pol Sci Rev	American Political Science Review
Comp Studs Soc Hist	Comparative Studies in Society and History
Hist J	Historical Journal
Hist Theor	History and Theory
J Hist Ideas	Journal of the History of Ideas
J Phil	Journal of Philosophy
J Polit	Journal of Politics
Midwest J Pol Sci	Midwest Journal of Political Science
Mind	Mind
New Lit Hist	New Literary History
Past Pres	Past and Present
Philosophy	Philosophy
Phil Phenomenol Res	Philosophy and Phenomenological Research
Phil Quart	Philosophical Quarterly
Phil Rev	The Philosophical Review
Politics	Politics
Pol Stud	Political Studies
Polit Theory	Political Theory
Pop Sci Month	Popular Science Monthly
Proc Aris Soc	Proceedings of the Aristotelian Society
Rev Metaph	Review of Metaphysics
Sci Month	Scientific Monthly
Soc Res	Social Research

INDEX

NOTES ON CONTRIBUTORS

R.G. Collingwood, Late Professor of Metaphysical Philosophy, Oxford University.

John G. Gunnell, Professor of Political Science, State University of New York at Albany.

Preston King, Professor of Political Science, University of New South Wales.

A.O. Lovejoy, Late Professor of Philosophy at Johns Hopkins University.

Maurice Mandelbaum, Professor Emeritus of Philosophy and Humanities, Johns Hopkins University, and Adjunct Professor of Philosophy, Dartmouth College.

Michael Oakeshott, Professor Emeritus, London School of Economics and Political Science.

Quentin Skinner, Professor of Political Science, Cambridge University.

Leo Strauss, Late Professor of Political Science, University of Chicago.